Twin ☆ Star Exorcists
ONMYOJI

3

STORY & ART
YOSHIAKI SUKENO

Character Introduction

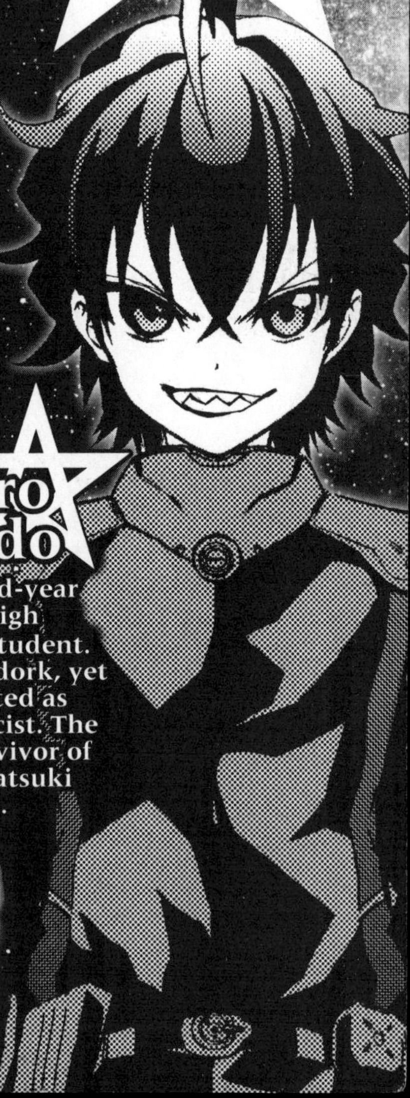

Rokuro Enmado

A second-year junior high school student. A total dork, yet very gifted as an exorcist. The sole survivor of the Hinatsuki Tragedy.

Seigen Amawaka

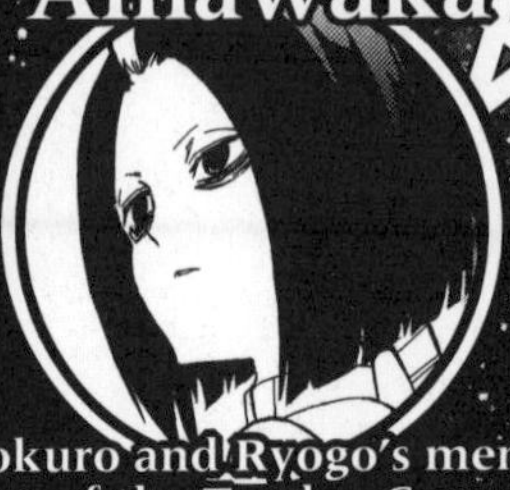

Rokuro and Ryogo's mentor. One of the Twelve Guardians, the strongest of the exorcists. He is also Mayura's father.

Mayura Otomi

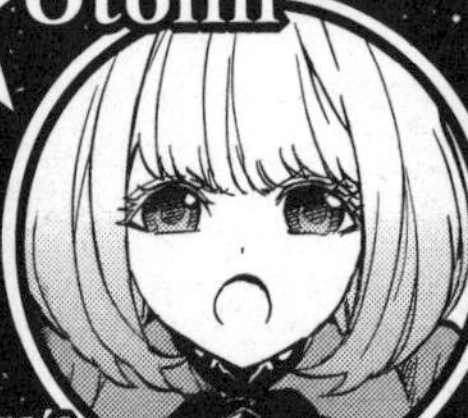

Rokuro's childhood friend, Zenkichi's granddaughter, and Seigen's daughter. Does she have feelings for Rokuro...?

Story Thus Far...

Kegare are creatures from Magano, the underworld, who come to our world to spread chaos, fear and death. It is the duty of an exorcist to hunt, exorcise and purify them. Rokuro has rejected his calling as an exorcist ever since he was involved in an attack that killed many of his friends. But one day he meets Benio, a girl who strives to destroy all the Kegare. Suffice it to say, the two don't get along...

Ryogo Nagitsuji

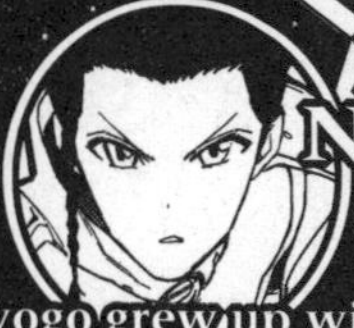

Ryogo grew up with Rokuro and is like a big brother to him. He has great faith in Rokuro's exorcism talent.

Yuto Ijika

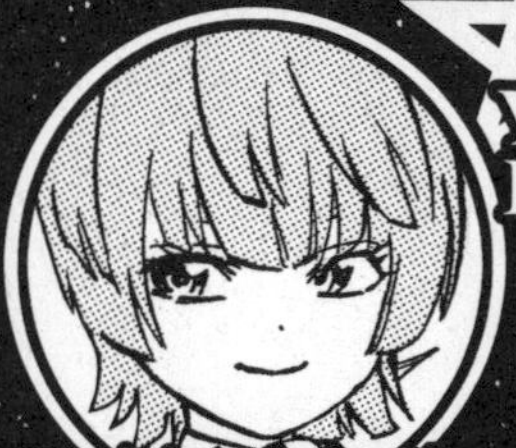

Benio's twin brother, who died in the Hinatsuki Tragedy.

Zenkichi Otomi

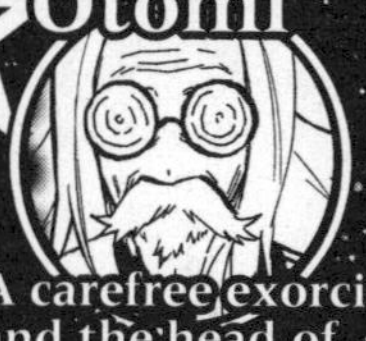

A carefree exorcist and the head of Seika Dorm.

Arima Tsuchimikado

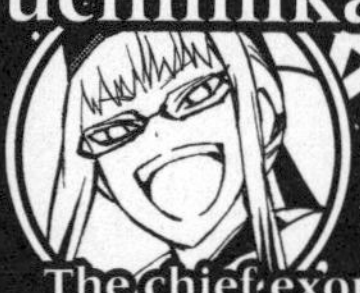

The chief exorcist of the Association of Unified Exorcists, which presides over all exorcists.

Benio Adashino

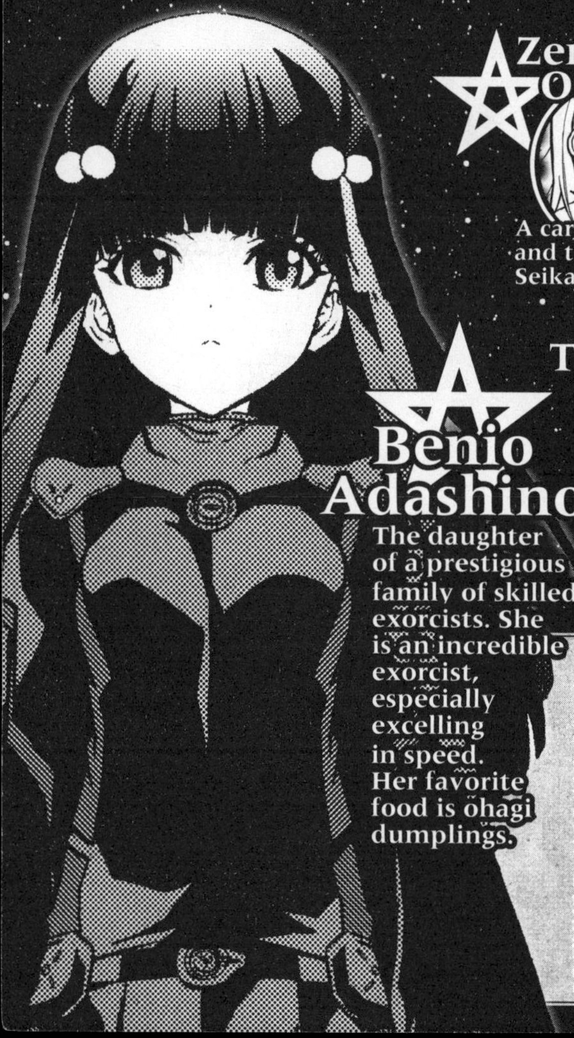

The daughter of a prestigious family of skilled exorcists. She is an incredible exorcist, especially excelling in speed. Her favorite food is ohagi dumplings.

Chief Exorcist Arima tells Rokuro and Benio that they are prophesied to become the Twin Star Exorcists, marry each other, and produce the Prophesied Child, the strongest exorcist of all. The two teenagers are not at all keen on getting together, but they grudgingly grow to respect each other's exorcism skills as they fight together against the Kegare...

Now Rokuro's former mentor, Seigen, has come to town and revealed more details about the Hinatsuki Tragedy to Benio. How will she react when she learns the disturbing truth about who murdered the exorcists in training...?!

Twin ☆ Star Exorcists

ONMYOJI

EXORCISMS

ONMYOJI have worked for the Imperial Court since the Heian era. In addition to exorcising evil spirits, as civil servants they performed a variety of roles, including advising nobles by foretelling the future, creating the calendar, observing the movements of the stars, measuring time…

#8 A Glimpse of Evil

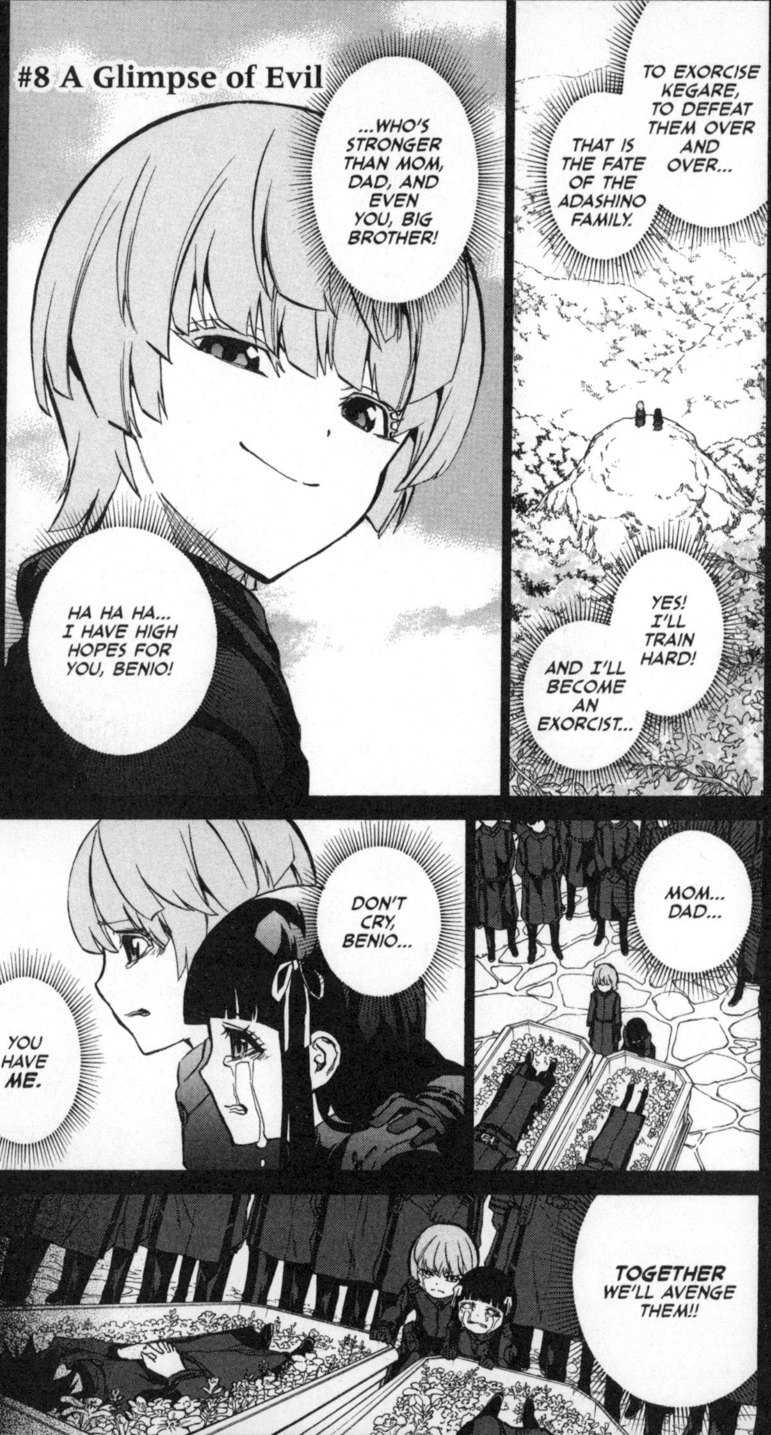
TO EXORCISE KEGARE, TO DEFEAT THEM OVER AND OVER...
THAT IS THE FATE OF THE ADASHINO FAMILY.
YES! I'LL TRAIN HARD!
AND I'LL BECOME AN EXORCIST...
...WHO'S STRONGER THAN MOM, DAD, AND EVEN YOU, BIG BROTHER!
HA HA HA... I HAVE HIGH HOPES FOR YOU, BENIO!
MOM... DAD...
DON'T CRY, BENIO...
YOU HAVE ME.
TOGETHER WE'LL AVENGE THEM!!

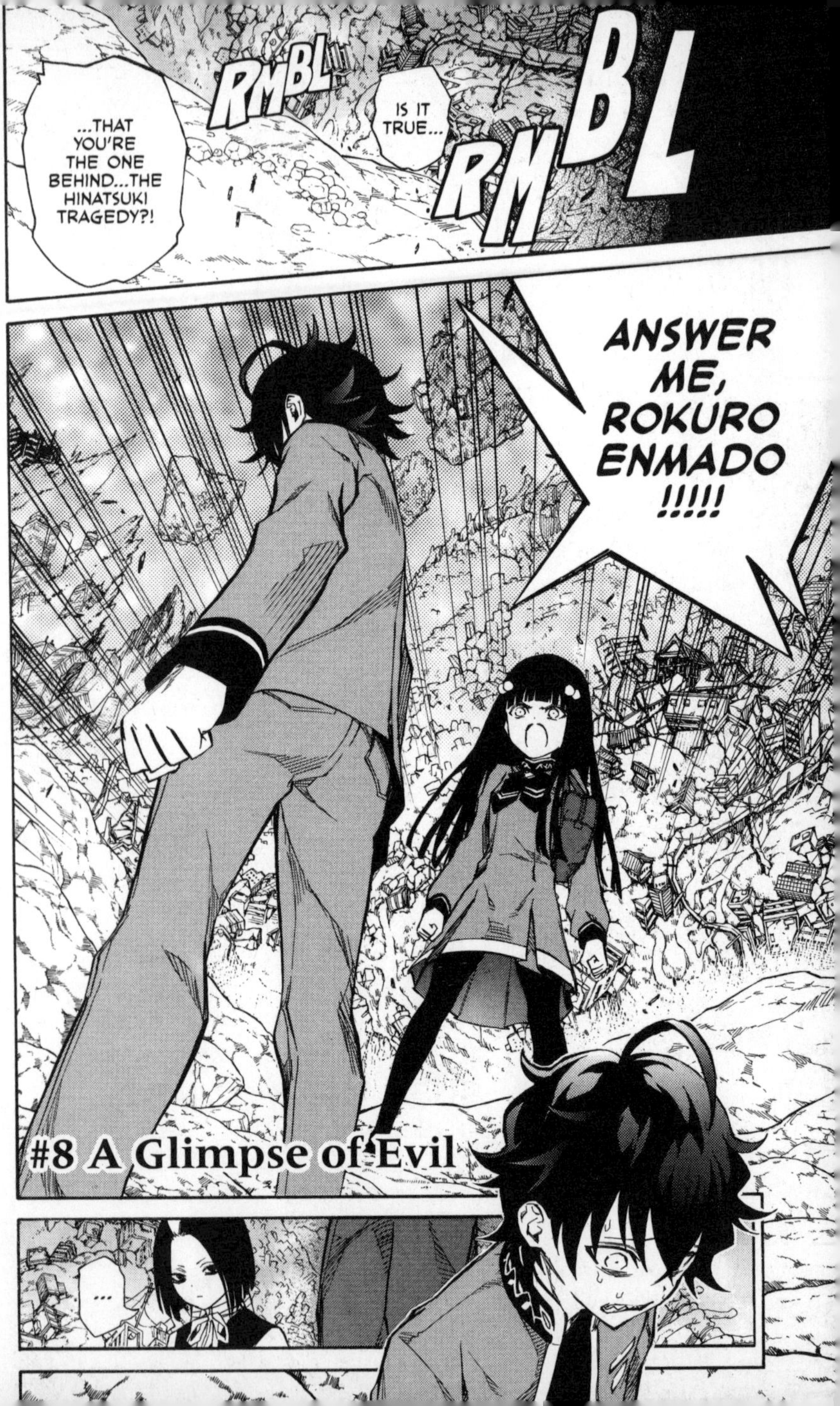
RMBL
RMBL
IS IT TRUE...
...THAT YOU'RE THE ONE BEHIND...THE HINATSUKI TRAGEDY?!
ANSWER ME, ROKURO ENMADO !!!!!
#8 A Glimpse of Evil
...

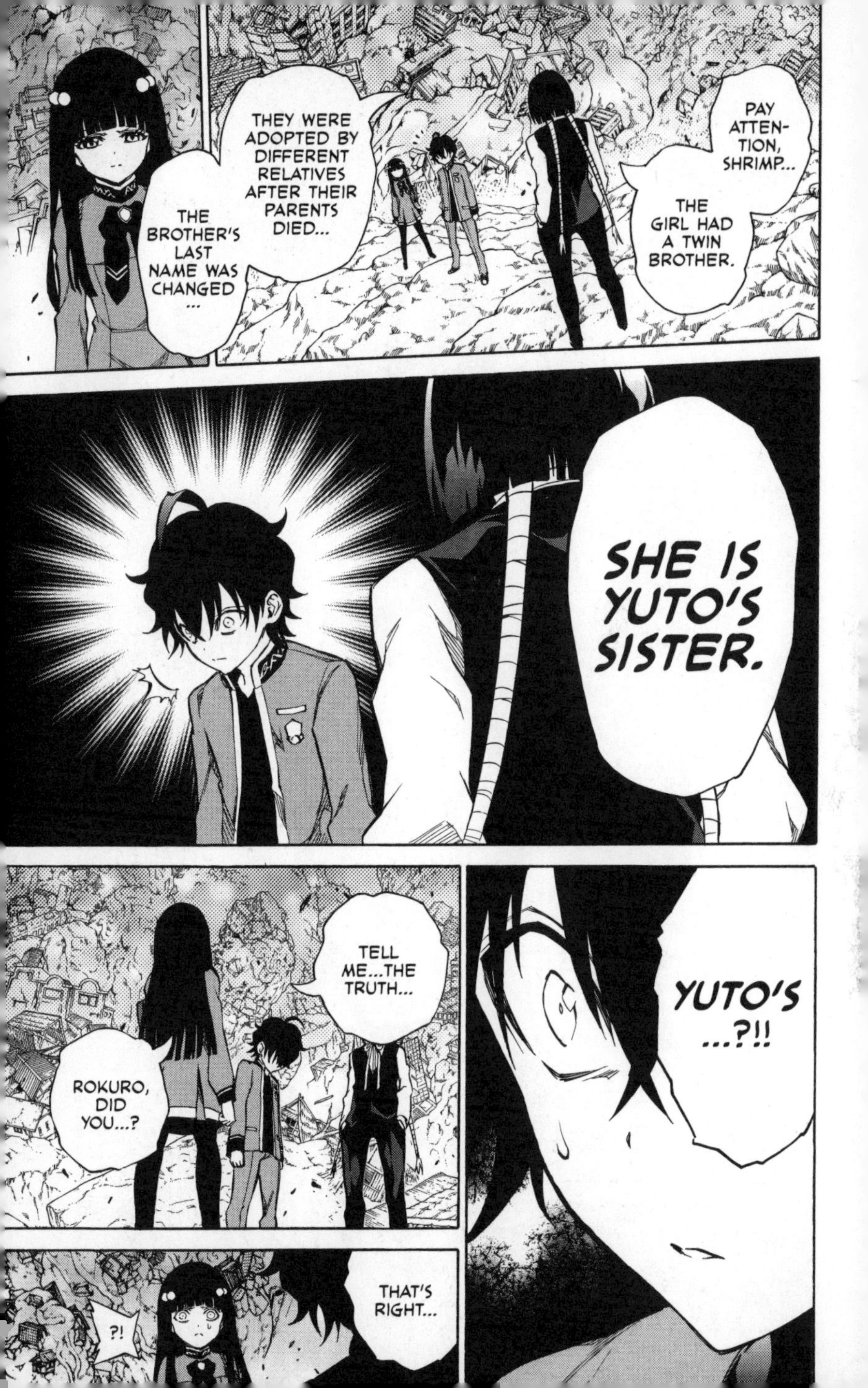

PAY ATTENTION, SHRIMP...
THE GIRL HAD A TWIN BROTHER.
THEY WERE ADOPTED BY DIFFERENT RELATIVES AFTER THEIR PARENTS DIED...
THE BROTHER'S LAST NAME WAS CHANGED ...
SHE IS YUTO'S SISTER.
YUTO'S ...?!!
TELL ME...THE TRUTH...
ROKURO, DID YOU...?
THAT'S RIGHT...
?!

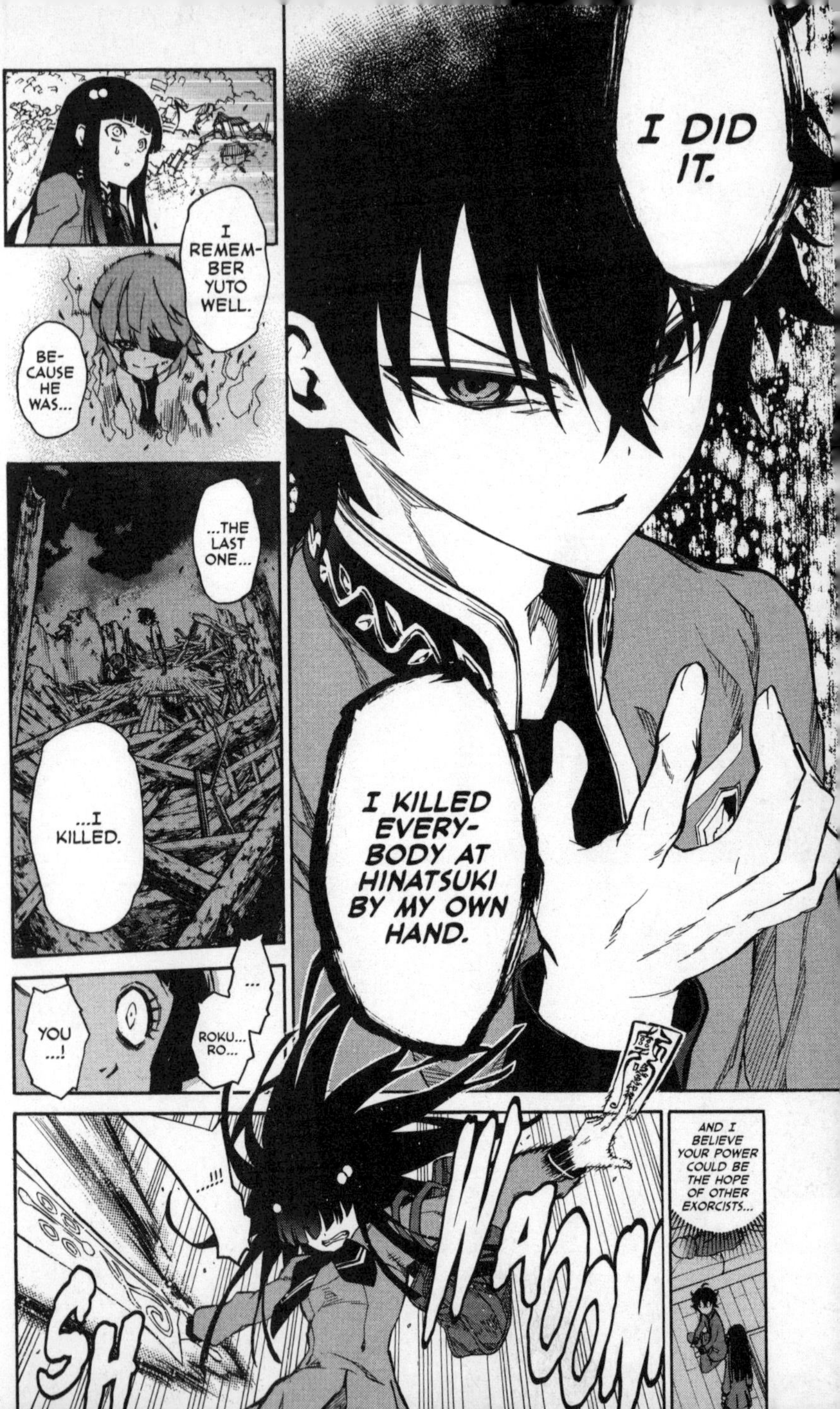
I DID IT.
I KILLED EVERYBODY AT HINATSUKI BY MY OWN HAND.
I REMEMBER YUTO WELL.
BECAUSE HE WAS...
...THE LAST ONE...
...I KILLED.
...
ROKU... RO...
YOU ...!
AND I BELIEVE YOUR POWER COULD BE THE HOPE OF OTHER EXORCISTS...
WAOOM
...!!!
SH

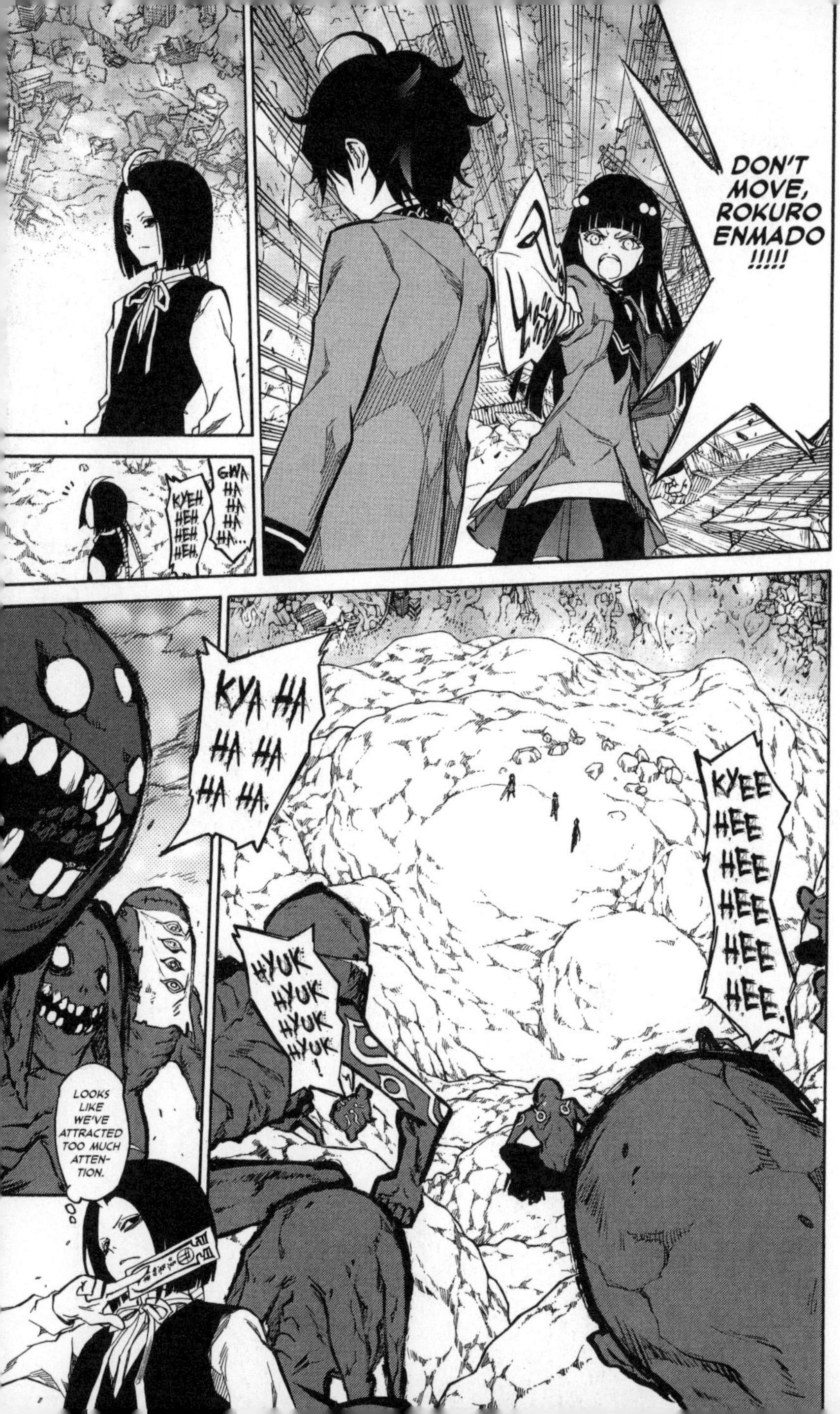
DON'T MOVE, ROKURO ENMADO !!!!!
GWA HA HA HA HA HA...
KYEH HEH HEH HEH.
KYEE HEE HEE HEE HEE HEE HEE.
KYA HA HA HA HA HA.
HYUK HYUK HYUK HYUK!
LOOKS LIKE WE'VE ATTRACTED TOO MUCH ATTENTION.

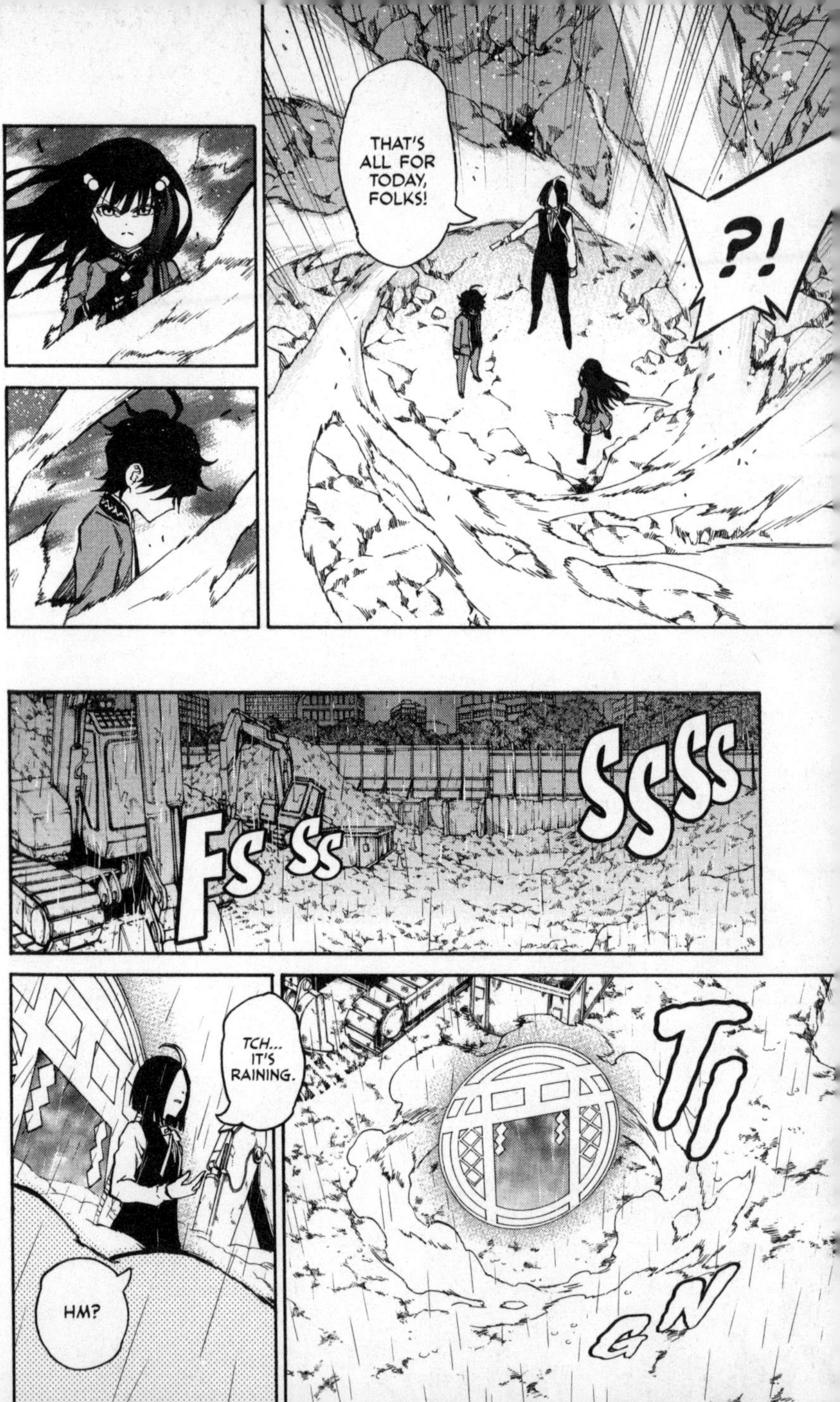
?!
THAT'S ALL FOR TODAY, FOLKS!
SSSS
Ss
Fs
TING
TCH... IT'S RAINING.
HM?

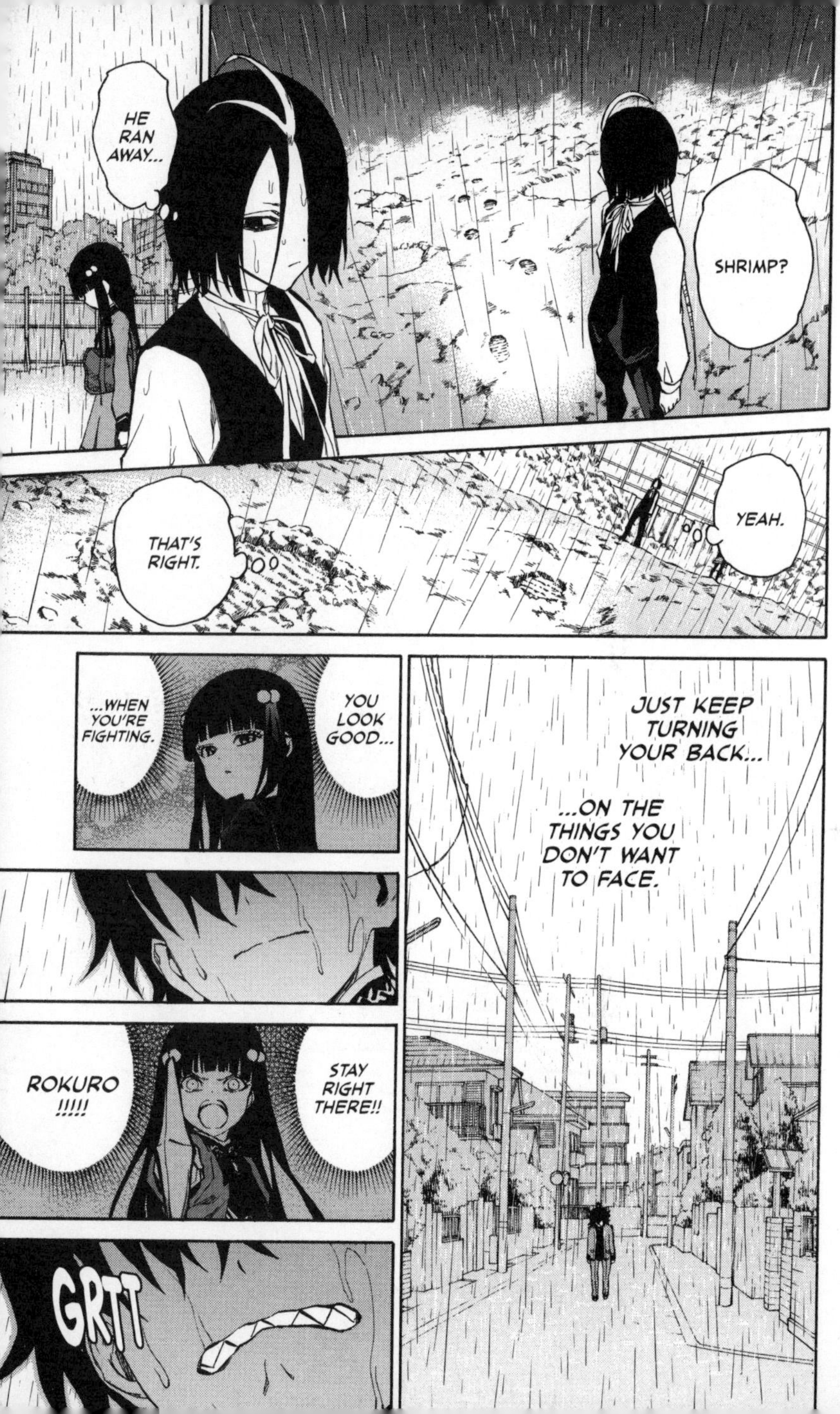
SHRIMP?
HE RAN AWAY...
YEAH.
THAT'S RIGHT.
JUST KEEP TURNING YOUR BACK...
...ON THE THINGS YOU DON'T WANT TO FACE.
YOU LOOK GOOD...
...WHEN YOU'RE FIGHTING.
STAY RIGHT THERE!!
ROKURO!!!!!
GRTT

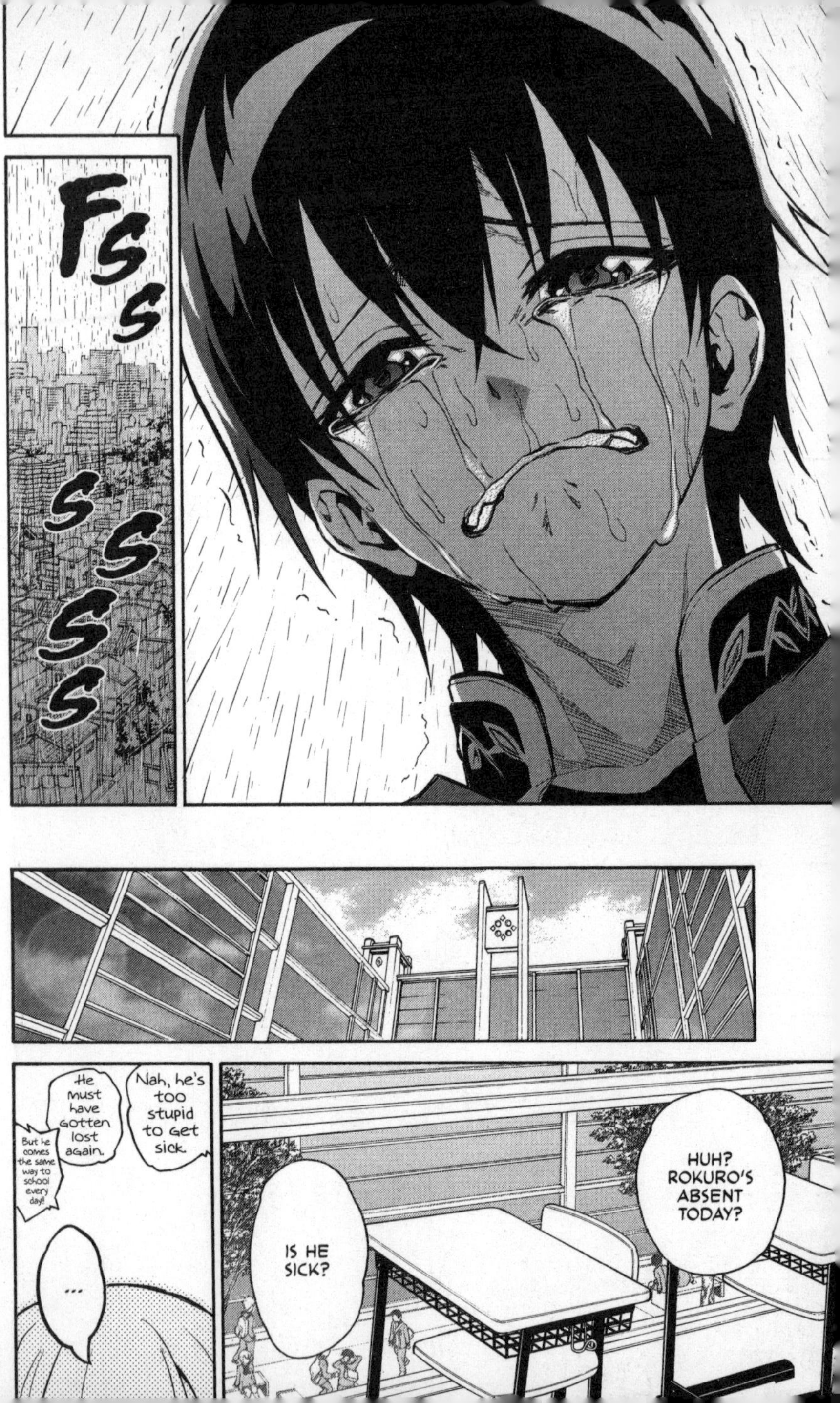
FSS
SSSS
HUH? ROKURO'S ABSENT TODAY?
IS HE SICK?
Nah, he's too stupid to get sick.
He must have gotten lost again.
But he comes the same way to school every day!!
...

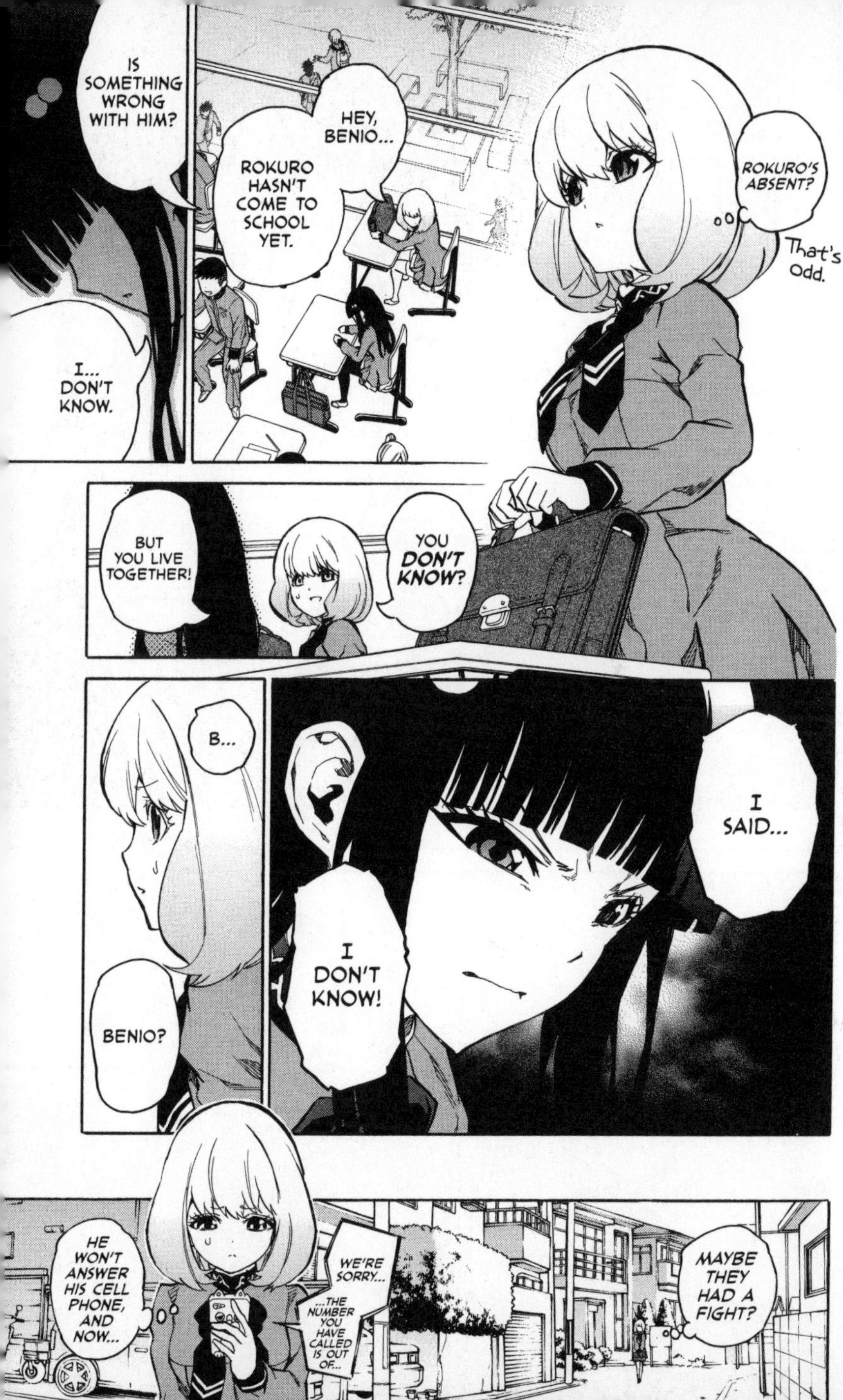
ROKURO'S ABSENT?
That's Odd.
HEY, BENIO...
ROKURO HASN'T COME TO SCHOOL YET.
IS SOMETHING WRONG WITH HIM?
I... DON'T KNOW.
YOU DON'T KNOW?
BUT YOU LIVE TOGETHER!
I SAID...
I DON'T KNOW!
B...
BENIO?
MAYBE THEY HAD A FIGHT?
WE'RE SORRY...
...THE NUMBER YOU HAVE CALLED IS OUT OF...
HE WON'T ANSWER HIS CELL PHONE, AND NOW...

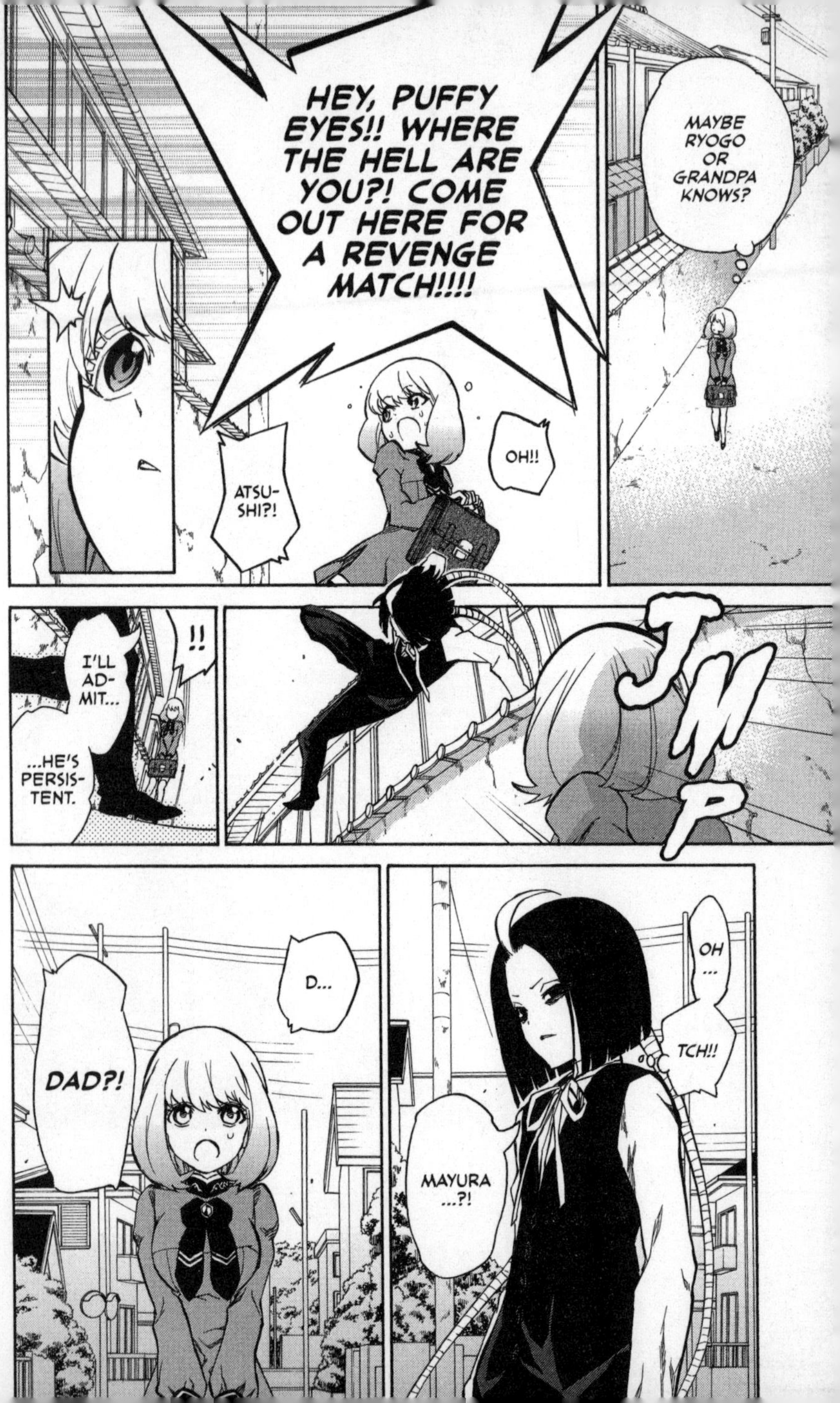
MAYBE RYOGO OR GRANDPA KNOWS?
HEY, PUFFY EYES!! WHERE THE HELL ARE YOU?! COME OUT HERE FOR A REVENGE MATCH!!!!
OH!!
ATSU-SHI?!
JMP
!!
I'LL AD-MIT...
...HE'S PERSIS-TENT.
OH...
TCH!!
MAYURA...?!
D...
DAD?!

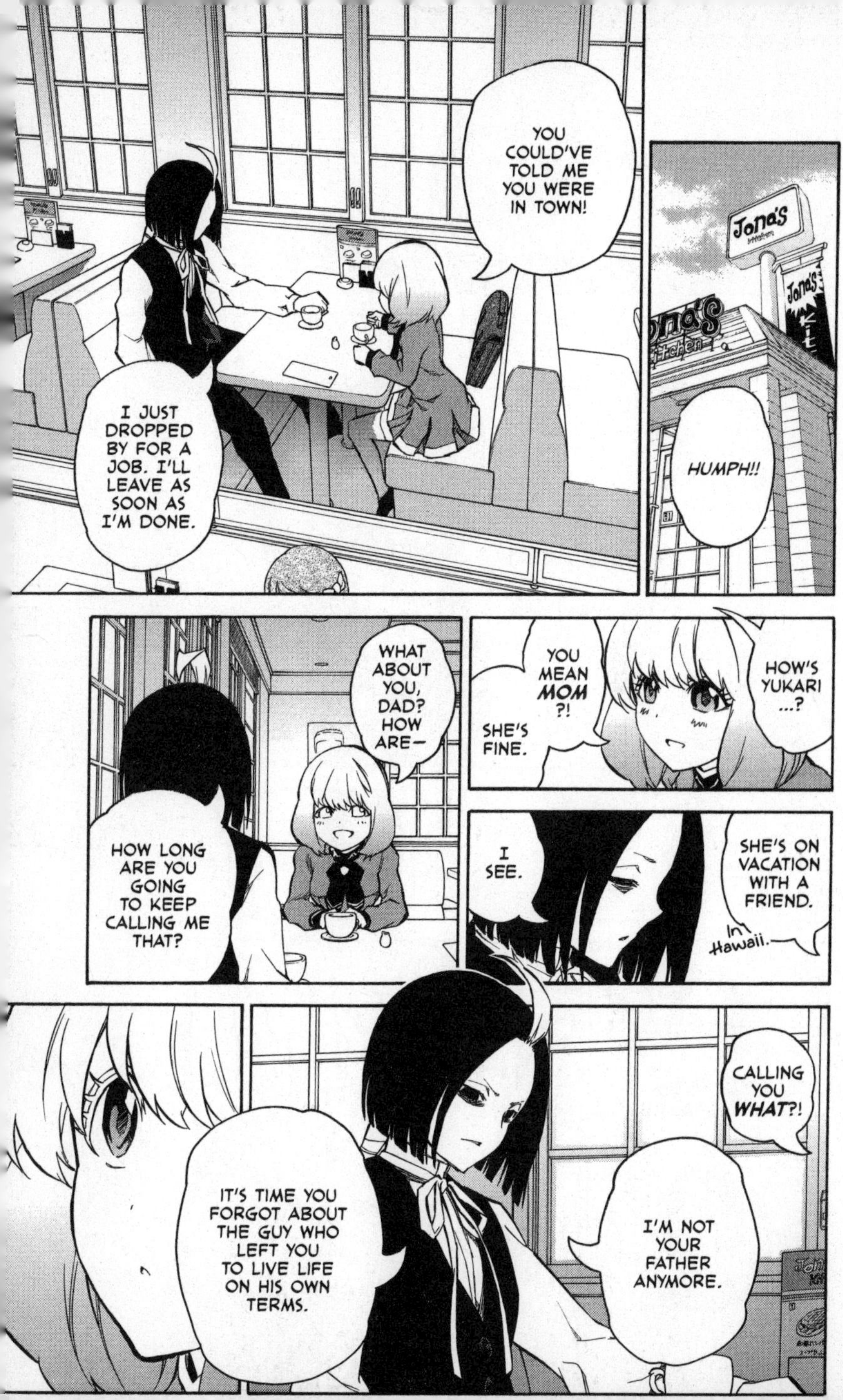
Jona's
HUMPH!!
YOU COULD'VE TOLD ME YOU WERE IN TOWN!
I JUST DROPPED BY FOR A JOB. I'LL LEAVE AS SOON AS I'M DONE.
HOW'S YUKARI ...?
YOU MEAN **MOM** ?!
SHE'S FINE.
SHE'S ON VACATION WITH A FRIEND.
In Hawaii.
I SEE.
WHAT ABOUT YOU, DAD? HOW ARE—
HOW LONG ARE YOU GOING TO KEEP CALLING ME THAT?
CALLING YOU **WHAT**?!
I'M NOT YOUR FATHER ANYMORE.
IT'S TIME YOU FORGOT ABOUT THE GUY WHO LEFT YOU TO LIVE LIFE ON HIS OWN TERMS.

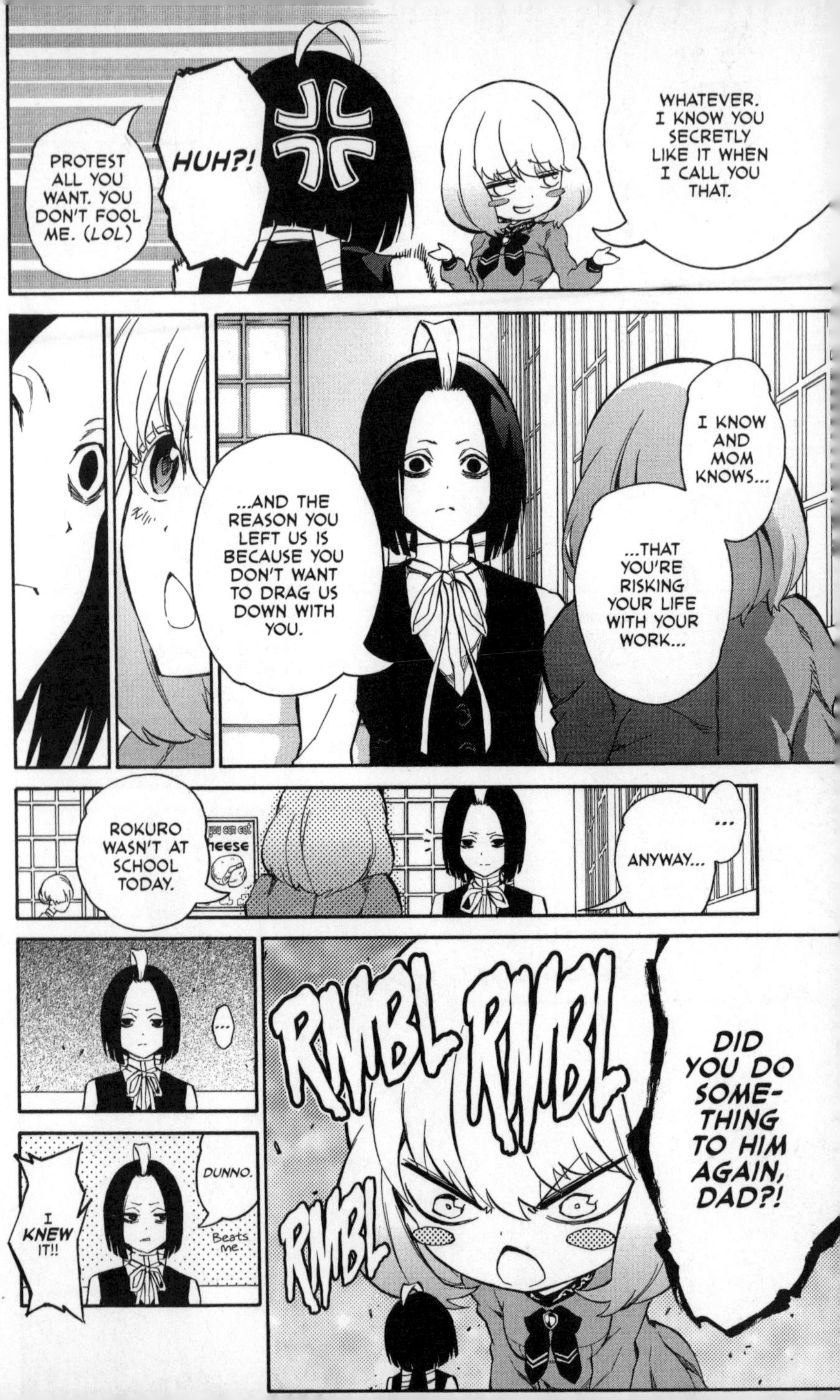
WHATEVER. I KNOW YOU SECRETLY LIKE IT WHEN I CALL YOU THAT.
HUH?!
PROTEST ALL YOU WANT. YOU DON'T FOOL ME. (LOL)
I KNOW AND MOM KNOWS...
...THAT YOU'RE RISKING YOUR LIFE WITH YOUR WORK...
...AND THE REASON YOU LEFT US IS BECAUSE YOU DON'T WANT TO DRAG US DOWN WITH YOU.
...
ANYWAY...
ROKURO WASN'T AT SCHOOL TODAY.
DID YOU DO SOMETHING TO HIM AGAIN, DAD?!
RMBL RMBL
RMBL
...
DUNNO.
Beats me.
I KNEW IT!!

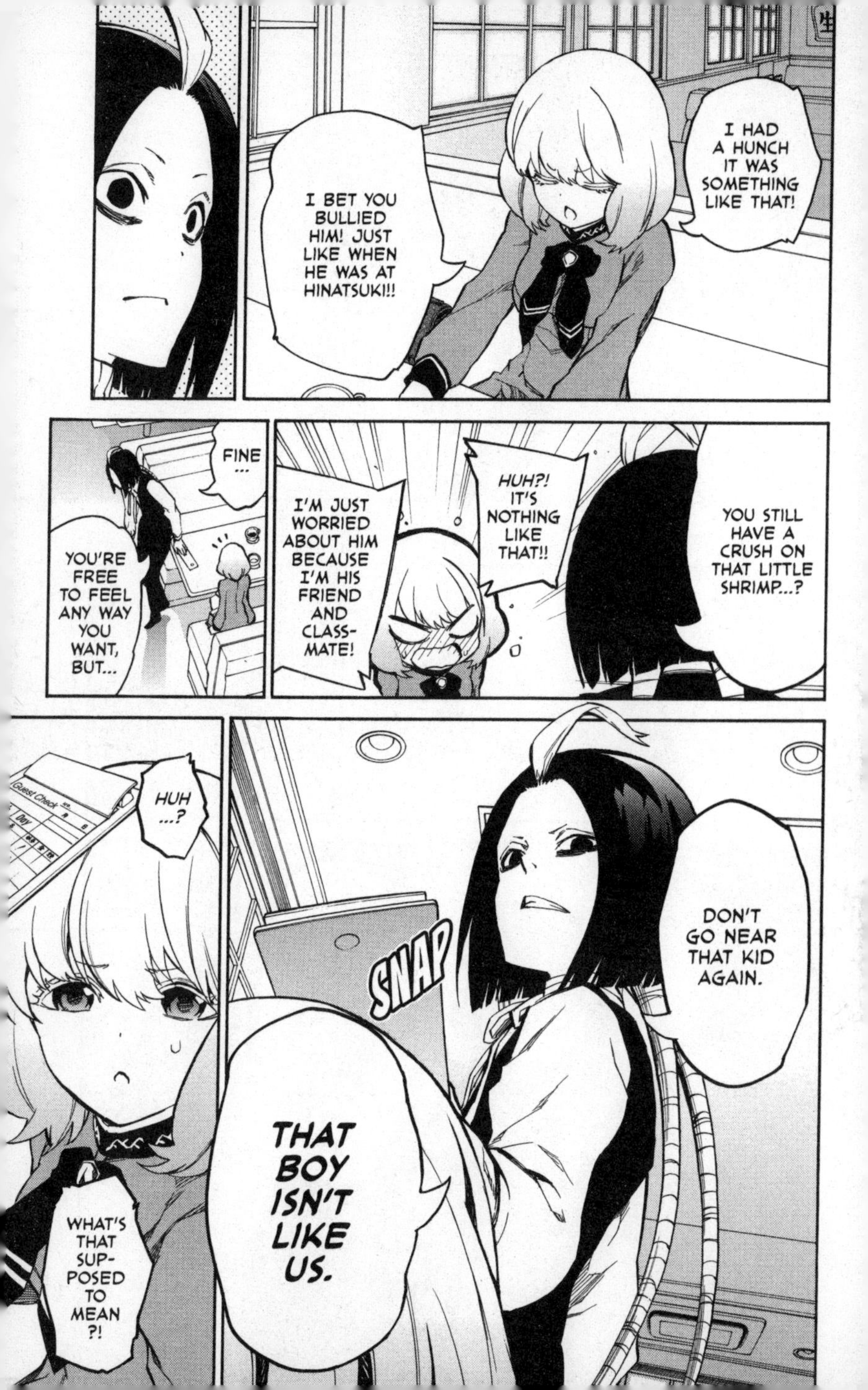
I HAD A HUNCH IT WAS SOMETHING LIKE THAT!
I BET YOU BULLIED HIM! JUST LIKE WHEN HE WAS AT HINATSUKI!!
YOU STILL HAVE A CRUSH ON THAT LITTLE SHRIMP...?
HUH?! IT'S NOTHING LIKE THAT!!
I'M JUST WORRIED ABOUT HIM BECAUSE I'M HIS FRIEND AND CLASS-MATE!
FINE ...
YOU'RE FREE TO FEEL ANY WAY YOU WANT, BUT...
DON'T GO NEAR THAT KID AGAIN.
SNAP
THAT BOY ISN'T LIKE US.
Guest Check
HUH ...?
WHAT'S THAT SUP-POSED TO MEAN ?!

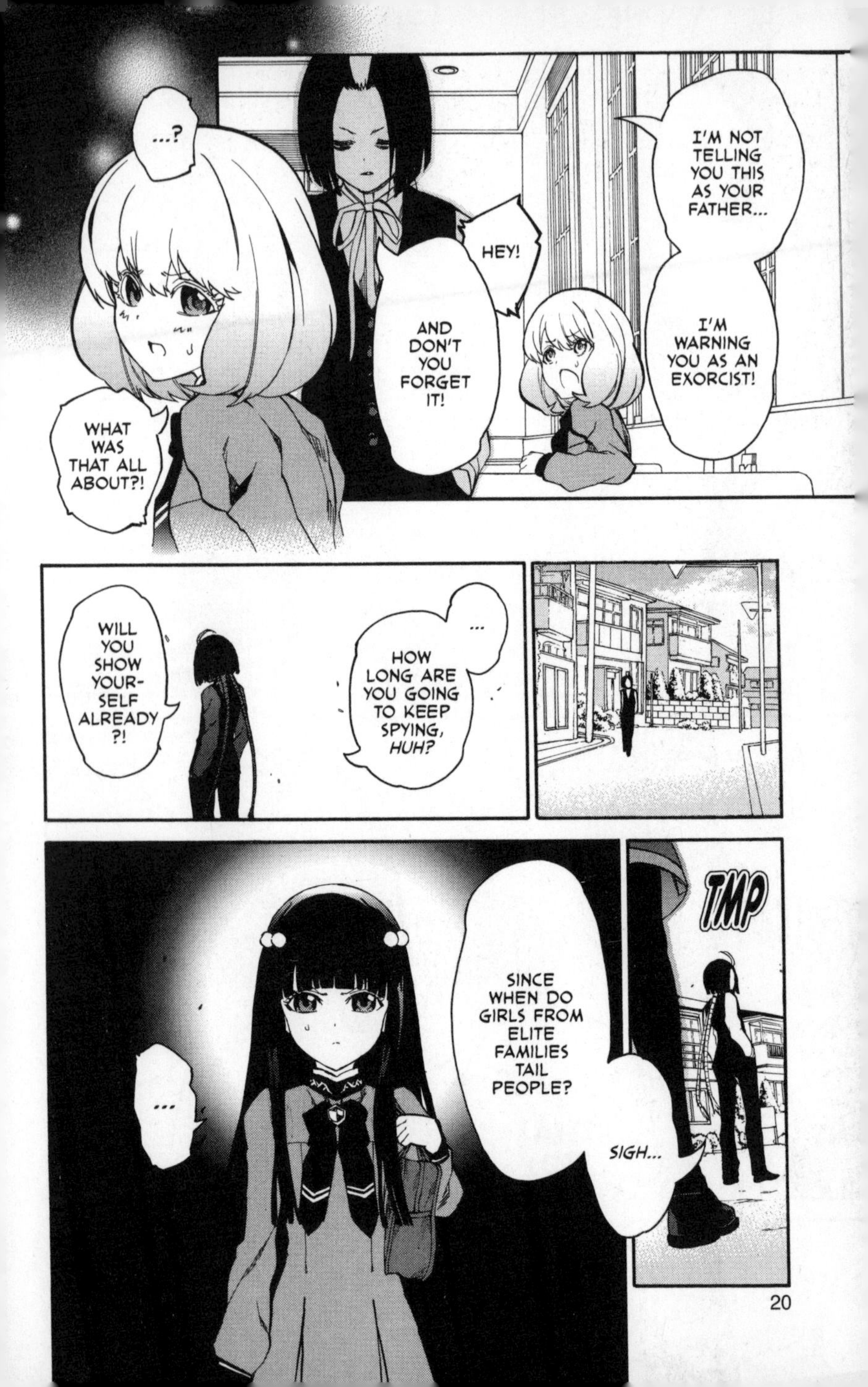
I'M NOT TELLING YOU THIS AS YOUR FATHER...
I'M WARNING YOU AS AN EXORCIST!
HEY!
AND DON'T YOU FORGET IT!
...?
WHAT WAS THAT ALL ABOUT?!
...
HOW LONG ARE YOU GOING TO KEEP SPYING, *HUH?*
WILL YOU SHOW YOURSELF ALREADY?!
TMP
SIGH...
SINCE WHEN DO GIRLS FROM ELITE FAMILIES TAIL PEOPLE?
...

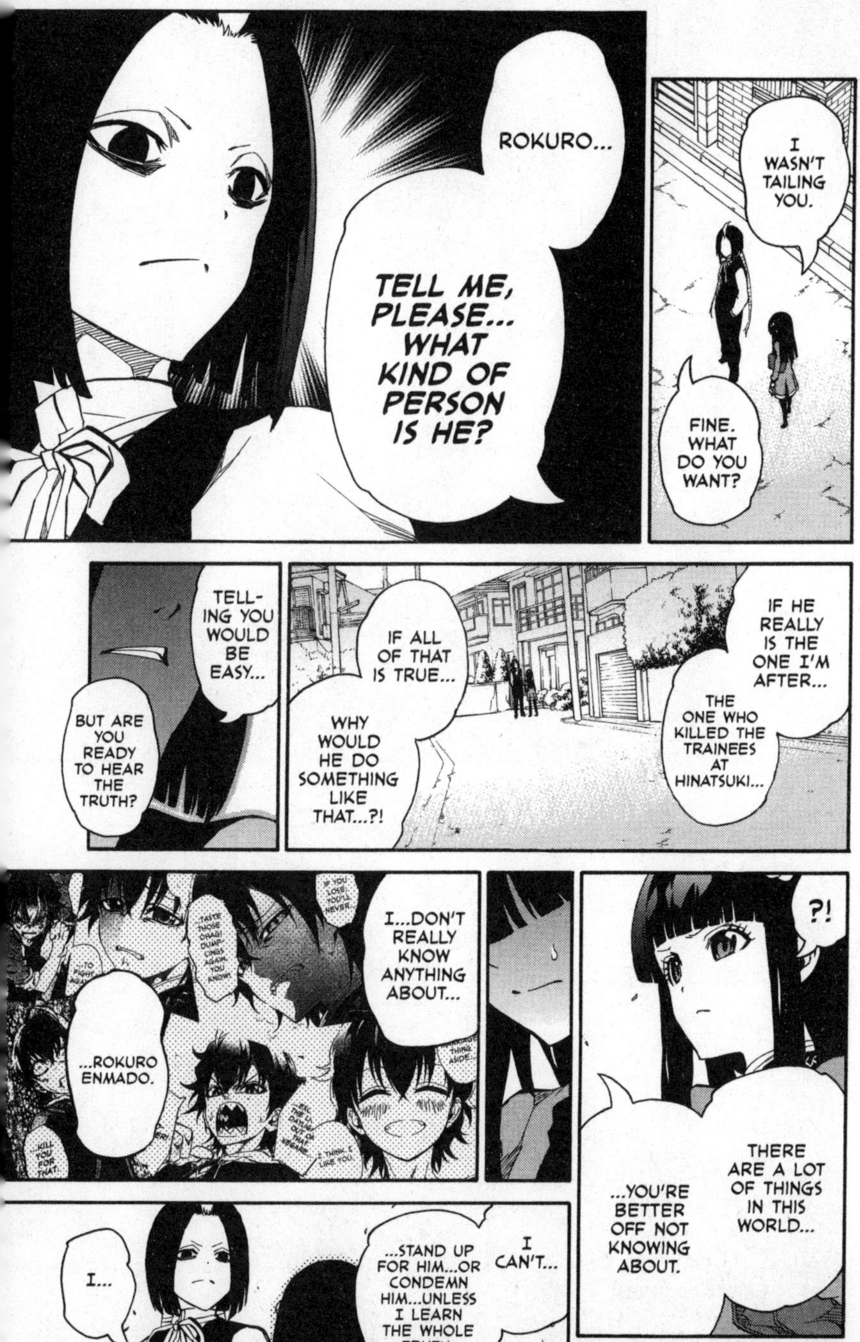
I WASN'T TAILING YOU.
FINE. WHAT DO YOU WANT?
ROKURO...
TELL ME, PLEASE... WHAT KIND OF PERSON IS HE?
IF HE REALLY IS THE ONE I'M AFTER...
THE ONE WHO KILLED THE TRAINEES AT HINATSUKI...
IF ALL OF THAT IS TRUE...
WHY WOULD HE DO SOMETHING LIKE THAT...?!
TELL-ING YOU WOULD BE EASY...
BUT ARE YOU READY TO HEAR THE TRUTH?
?!
THERE ARE A LOT OF THINGS IN THIS WORLD...
...YOU'RE BETTER OFF NOT KNOWING ABOUT.
I...DON'T REALLY KNOW ANYTHING ABOUT...
IF YOU LOSE, YOU'LL NEVER...
TASTE THOSE OHAGI DUMPLINGS AGAIN, YOU KNOW!
...ROKURO ENMADO.
I THINK I LIKE YOU.
...KILL YOU FOR THAT.
I CAN'T...
...STAND UP FOR HIM...OR CONDEMN HIM...UNLESS I LEARN THE WHOLE TRUTH.
I...

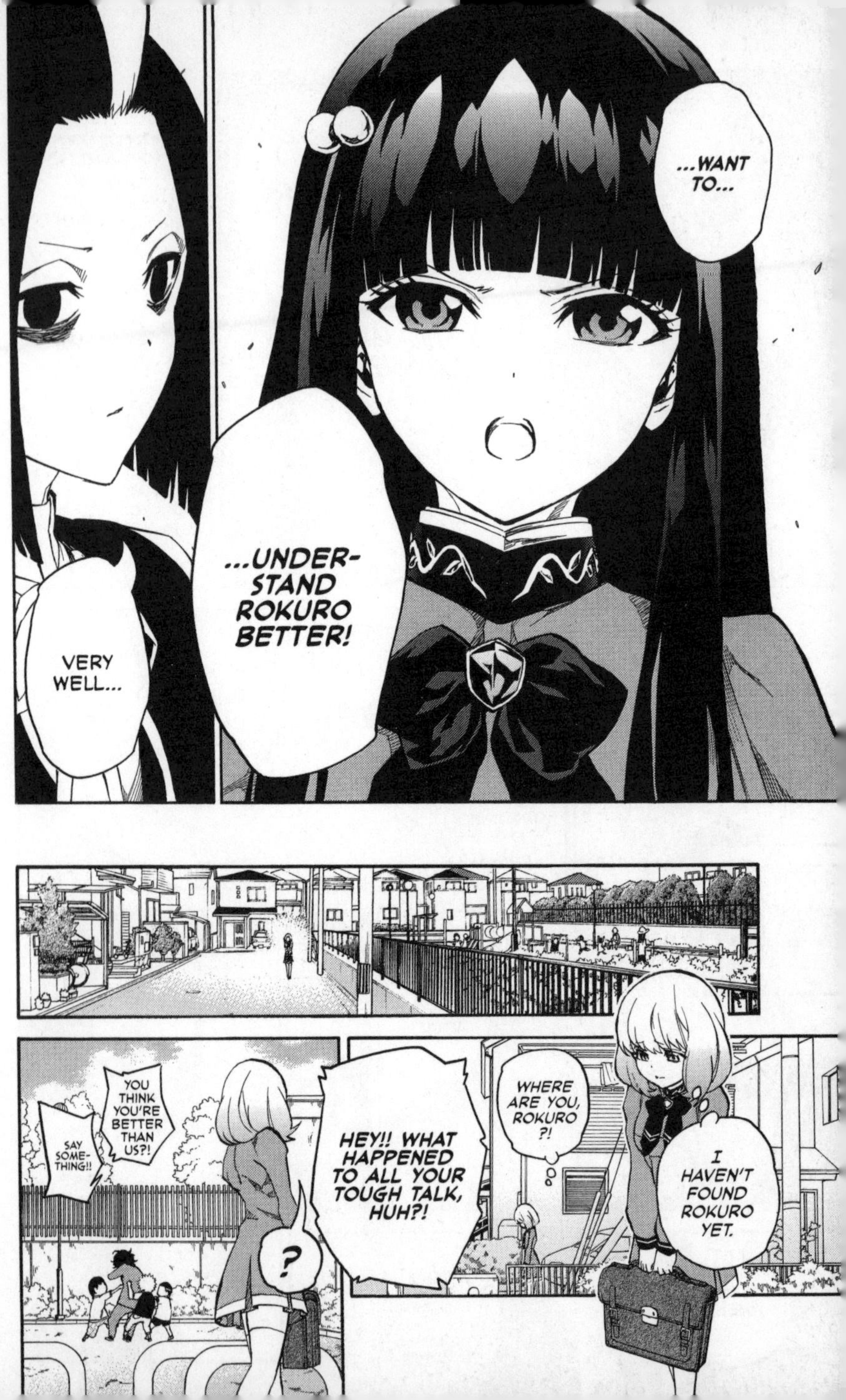

...WANT TO...
...UNDER-STAND ROKURO BETTER!
VERY WELL...
I HAVEN'T FOUND ROKURO YET.
WHERE ARE YOU, ROKURO?!
HEY!! WHAT HAPPENED TO ALL YOUR TOUGH TALK, HUH?!
?
YOU THINK YOU'RE BETTER THAN US?!
SAY SOME-THING!!

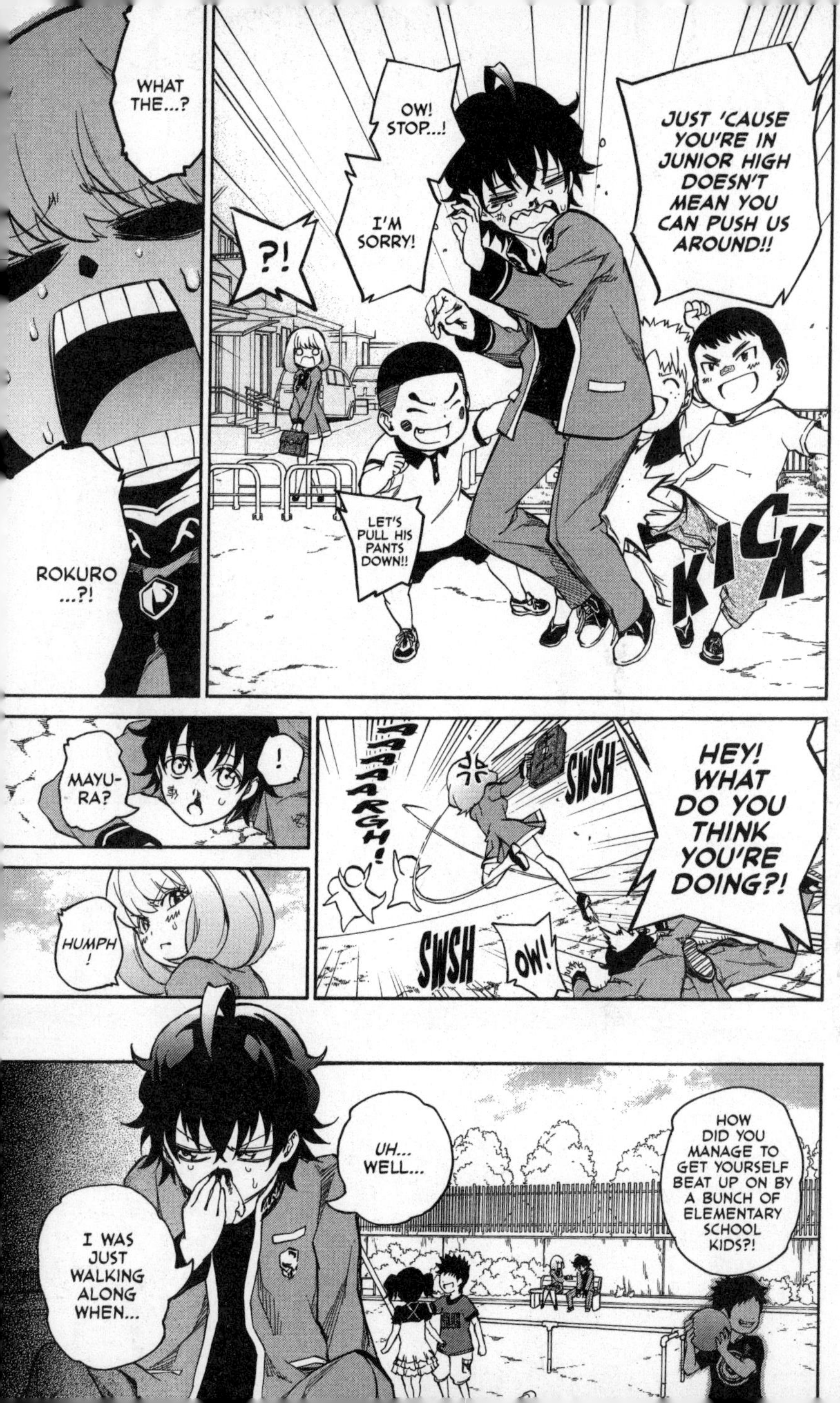
JUST 'CAUSE YOU'RE IN JUNIOR HIGH DOESN'T MEAN YOU CAN PUSH US AROUND!!
OW! STOP...!
I'M SORRY!
?!
LET'S PULL HIS PANTS DOWN!!
KICK
WHAT THE...?
ROKURO ...?!
HEY! WHAT DO YOU THINK YOU'RE DOING?!
SWSH
AAAAARGH!
SWSH
OW!
!
MAYU-RA?
HUMPH!
HOW DID YOU MANAGE TO GET YOURSELF BEAT UP ON BY A BUNCH OF ELEMENTARY SCHOOL KIDS?!
UH... WELL...
I WAS JUST WALKING ALONG WHEN...

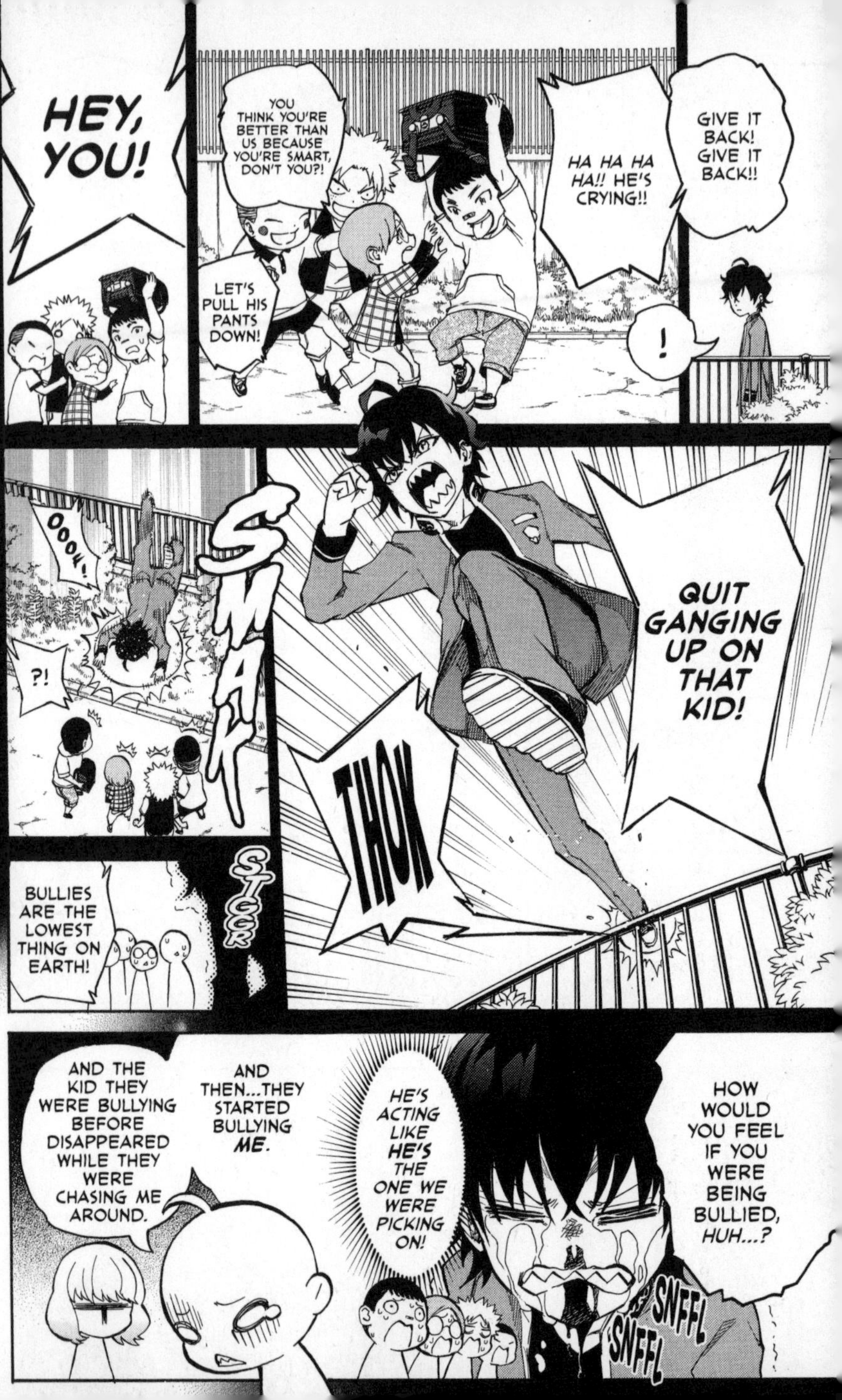
GIVE IT BACK! GIVE IT BACK!!
!
HA HA HA HA!! HE'S CRYING!!
YOU THINK YOU'RE BETTER THAN US BECAUSE YOU'RE SMART, DON'T YOU?!
LET'S PULL HIS PANTS DOWN!
HEY, YOU!
QUIT GANGING UP ON THAT KID!
SMAK
THOK
OOOOF!
?!
STIGGR
BULLIES ARE THE LOWEST THING ON EARTH!
HOW WOULD YOU FEEL IF YOU WERE BEING BULLIED, HUH...?
SNFFL
SNFFL
HE'S ACTING LIKE HE'S THE ONE WE WERE PICKING ON!
AND THEN...THEY STARTED BULLYING ME.
AND THE KID THEY WERE BULLYING BEFORE DISAPPEARED WHILE THEY WERE CHASING ME AROUND.

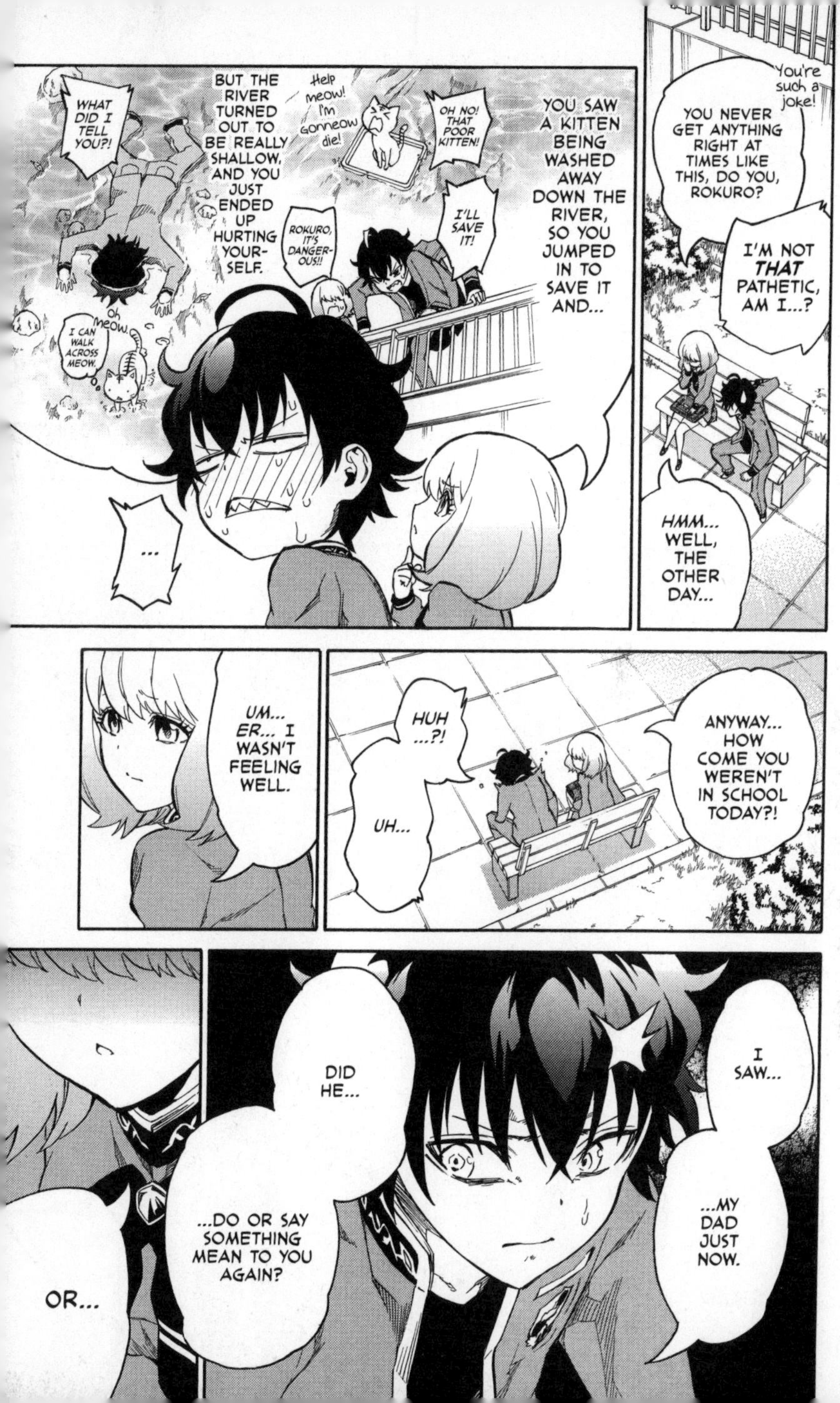
You're such a joke!
YOU NEVER GET ANYTHING RIGHT AT TIMES LIKE THIS, DO YOU, ROKURO?
I'M NOT *THAT* PATHETIC, AM I...?
HMM... WELL, THE OTHER DAY...
YOU SAW A KITTEN BEING WASHED AWAY DOWN THE RIVER, SO YOU JUMPED IN TO SAVE IT AND...
OH NO! THAT POOR KITTEN!
I'LL SAVE IT!
Help meow! I'm Gonneow die!
ROKURO, IT'S DANGER-OUS!!
BUT THE RIVER TURNED OUT TO BE REALLY SHALLOW, AND YOU JUST ENDED UP HURTING YOUR-SELF.
WHAT DID I TELL YOU?!
Oh meow.
I CAN WALK ACROSS MEOW.
...
ANYWAY... HOW COME YOU WEREN'T IN SCHOOL TODAY?!
HUH ...?!
UH...
UM... ER... I WASN'T FEELING WELL.
I SAW...
...MY DAD JUST NOW.
DID HE...
...DO OR SAY SOMETHING MEAN TO YOU AGAIN?
OR...

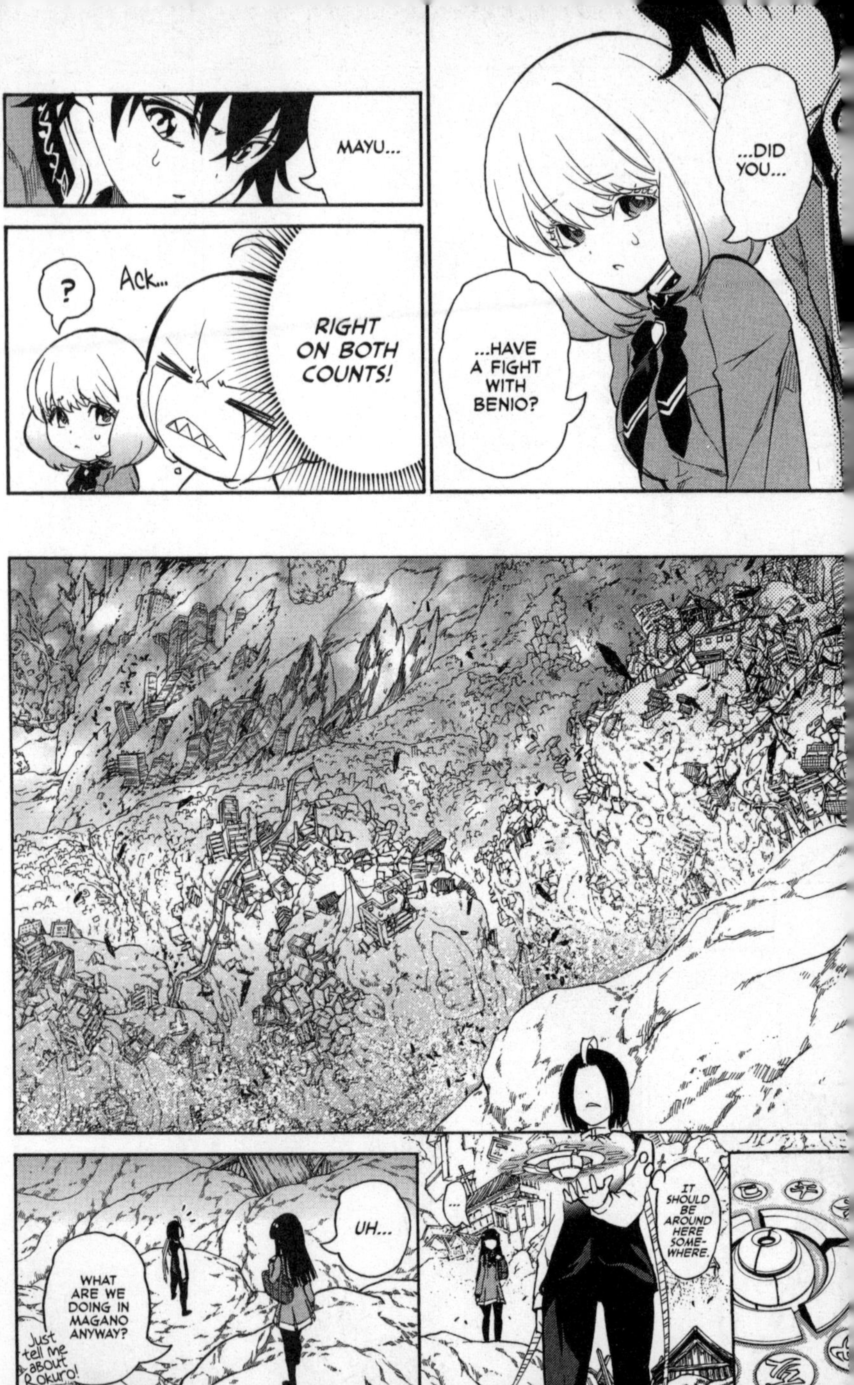
...DID YOU...
...HAVE A FIGHT WITH BENIO?
MAYU...
RIGHT ON BOTH COUNTS!
Ack...
?
IT SHOULD BE AROUND HERE SOME-WHERE.
...
UH...
WHAT ARE WE DOING IN MAGANO ANYWAY?
Just tell me about Rokuro!

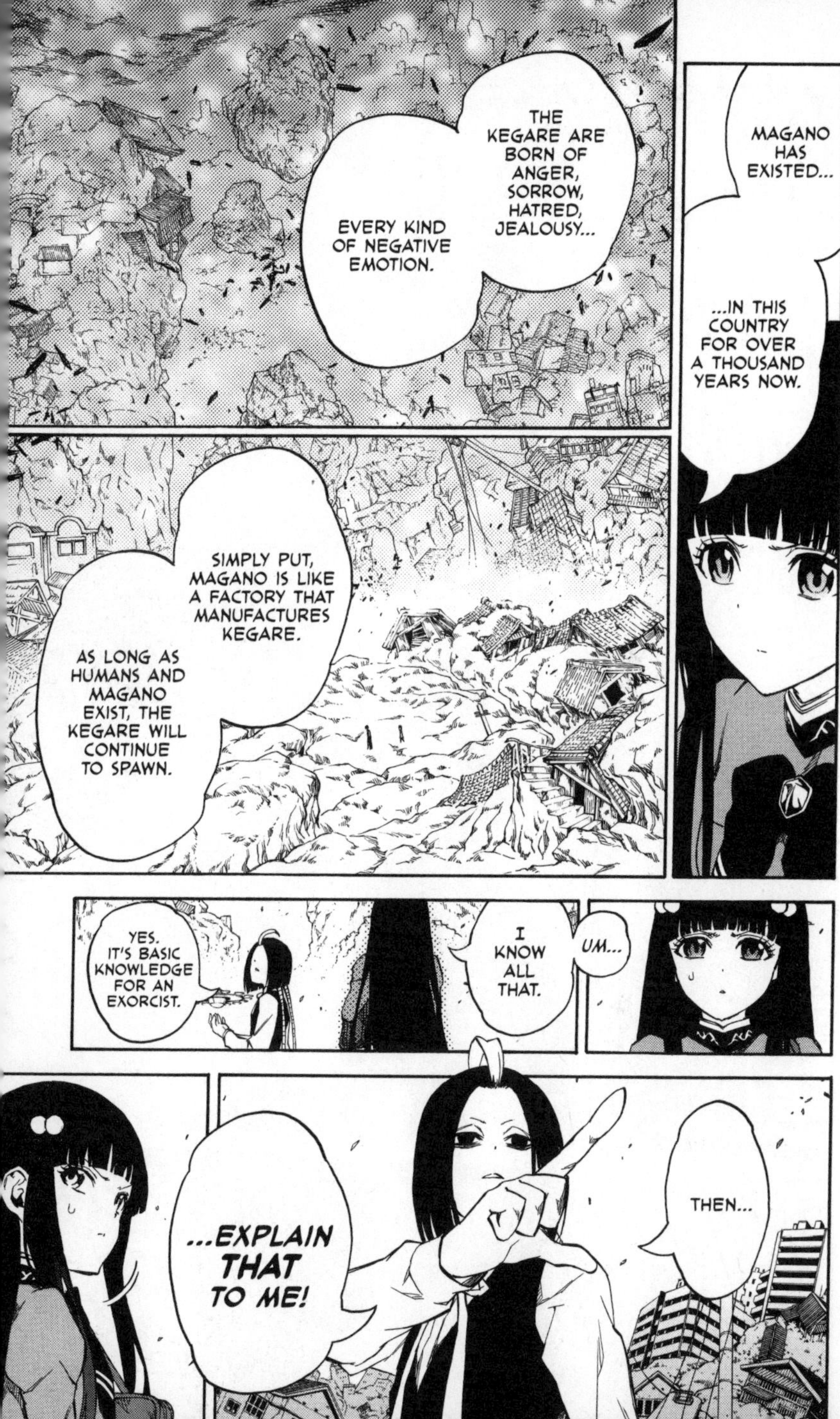
MAGANO HAS EXISTED...
...IN THIS COUNTRY FOR OVER A THOUSAND YEARS NOW.
THE KEGARE ARE BORN OF ANGER, SORROW, HATRED, JEALOUSY...
EVERY KIND OF NEGATIVE EMOTION.
SIMPLY PUT, MAGANO IS LIKE A FACTORY THAT MANUFACTURES KEGARE.
AS LONG AS HUMANS AND MAGANO EXIST, THE KEGARE WILL CONTINUE TO SPAWN.
UM...
I KNOW ALL THAT.
YES. IT'S BASIC KNOWLEDGE FOR AN EXORCIST.
THEN...
...EXPLAIN THAT TO ME!

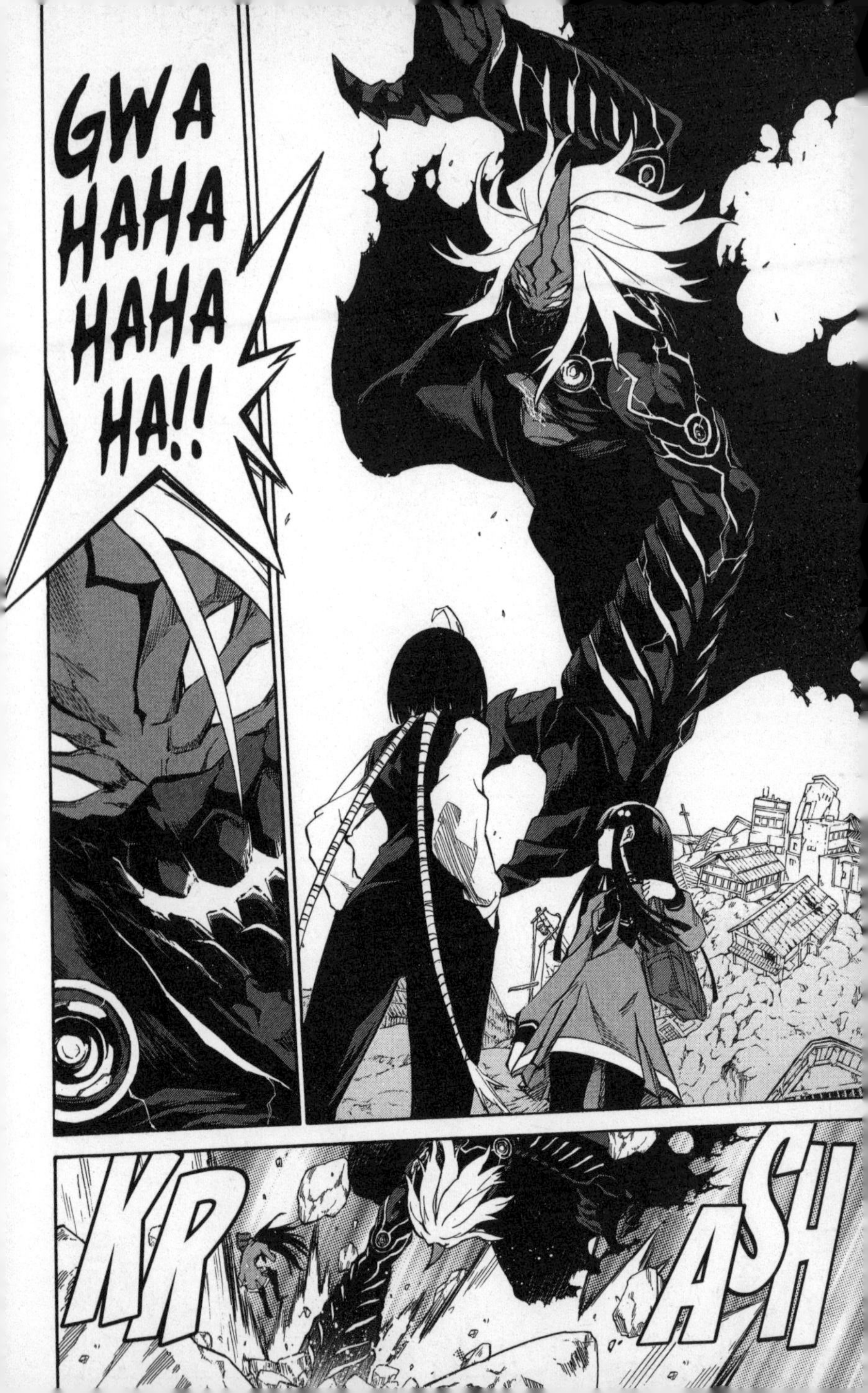
GWA HAHA HAHA HA!!
KRASH

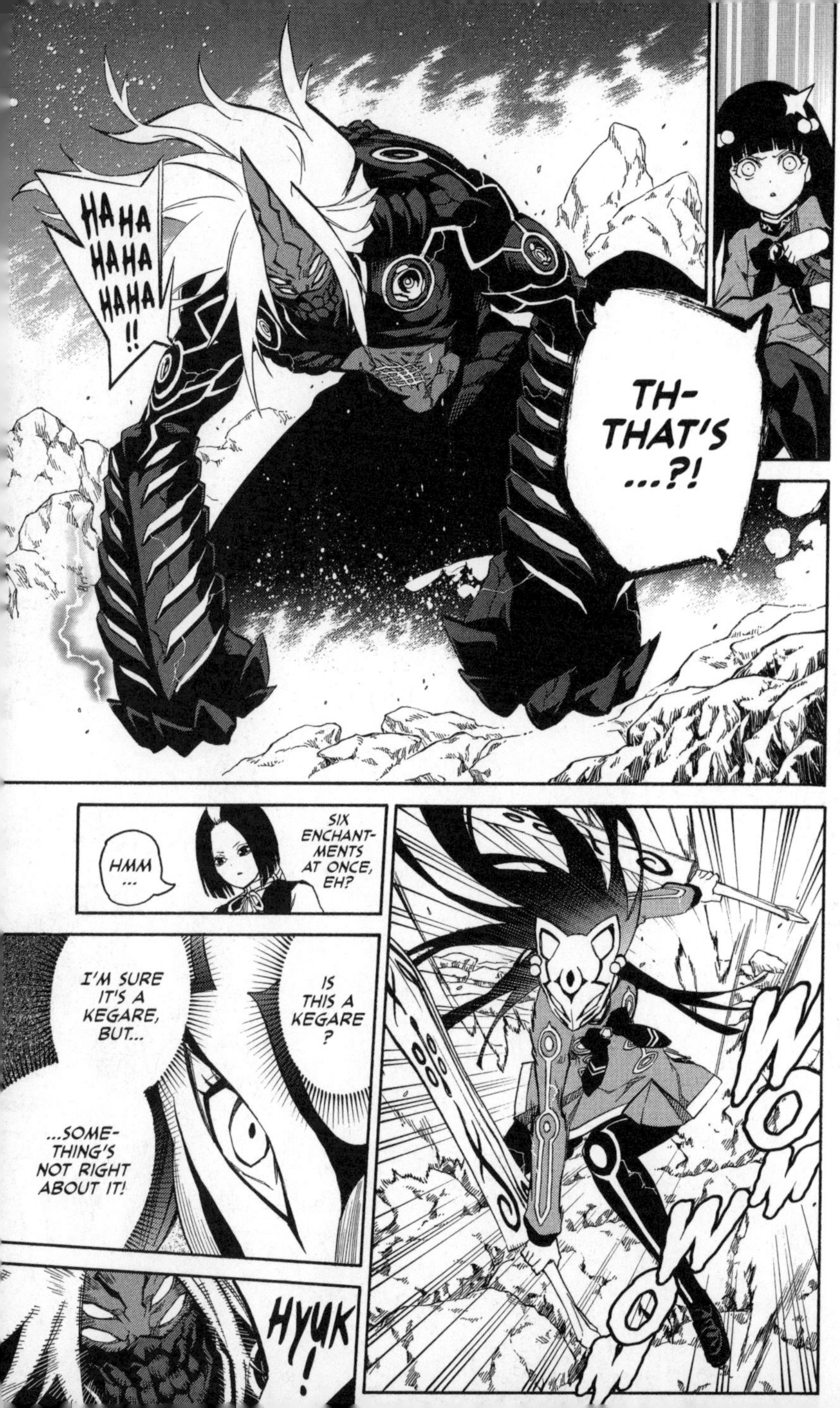
TH-THAT'S ...?!
HA HA HAHA HAHA !!
SIX ENCHANT-MENTS AT ONCE, EH?
HMM ...
IS THIS A KEGARE?
I'M SURE IT'S A KEGARE, BUT...
...SOME-THING'S NOT RIGHT ABOUT IT!
HYUK!

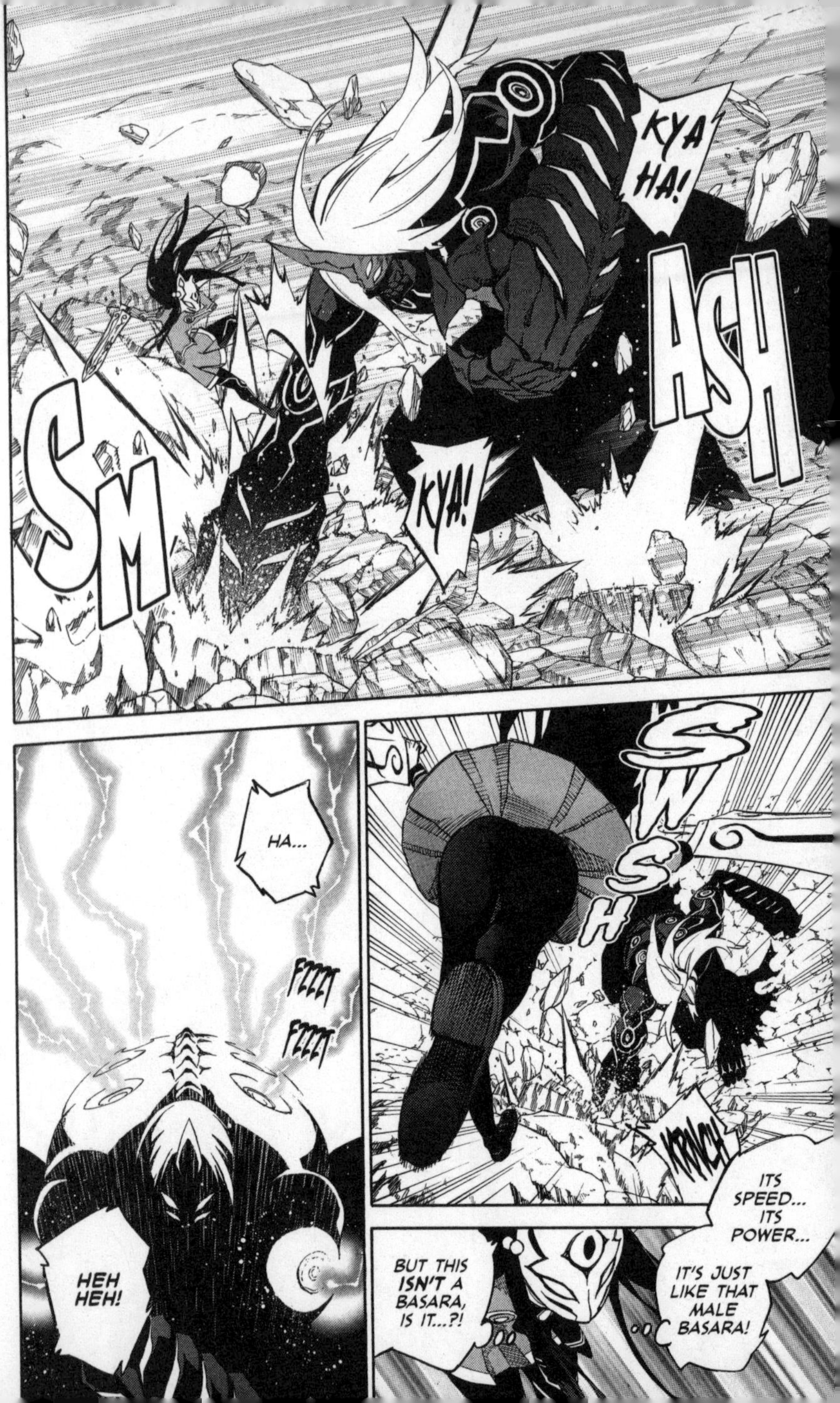
KYA HA!
ASH
KYA!
SM
SWSSH
KRNCH
HA...
FZZZT
FZZZT
ITS SPEED... ITS POWER...
IT'S JUST LIKE THAT MALE BASARA!
BUT THIS ISN'T A BASARA, IS IT...?!
HEH HEH!

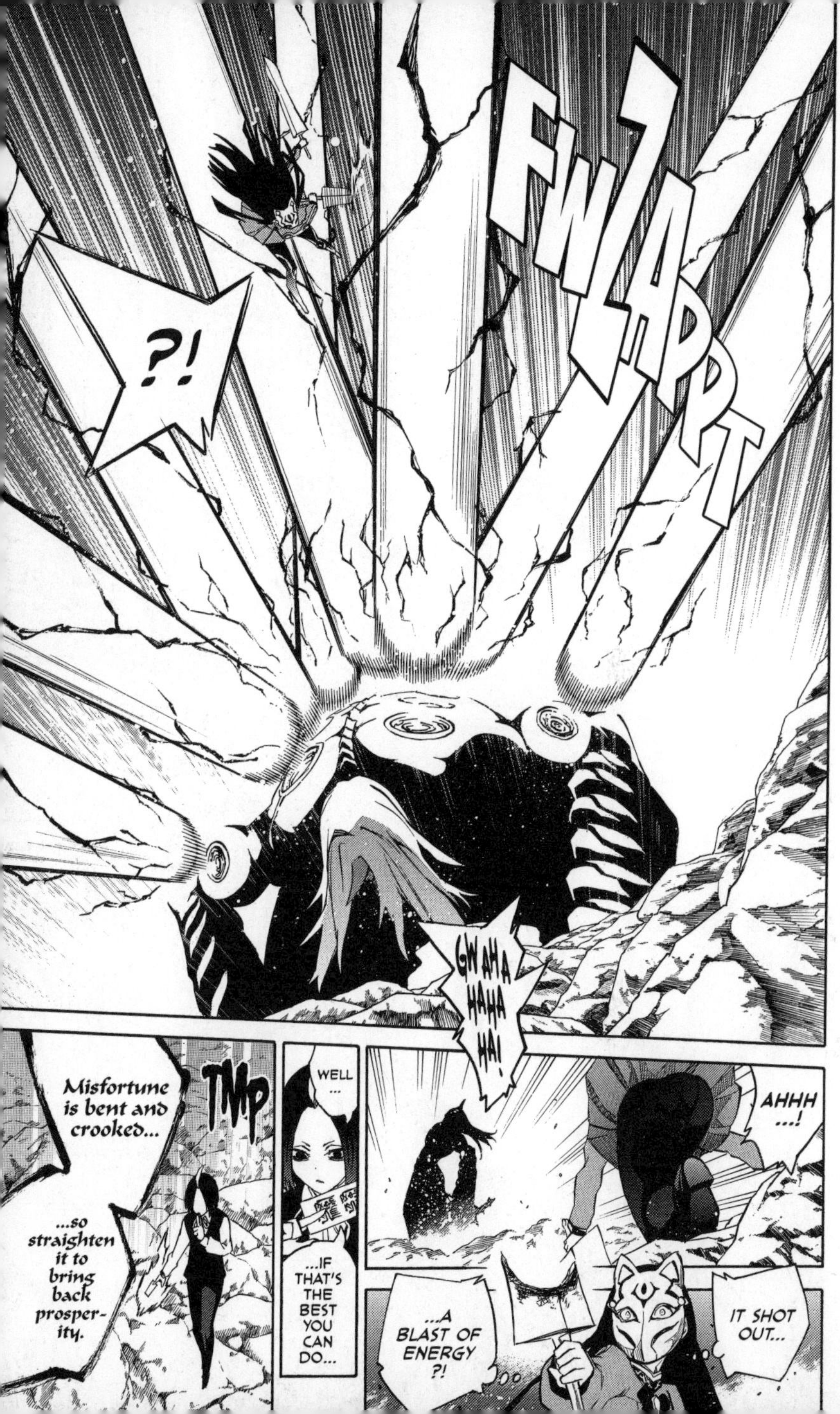
FWAPT
?!
GWAHAHAHAHA!
AHHH...!
IT SHOT OUT...
...A BLAST OF ENERGY?!
WELL...
...IF THAT'S THE BEST YOU CAN DO...
Misfortune is bent and crooked...
TMP
...so straighten it to bring back prosperity.

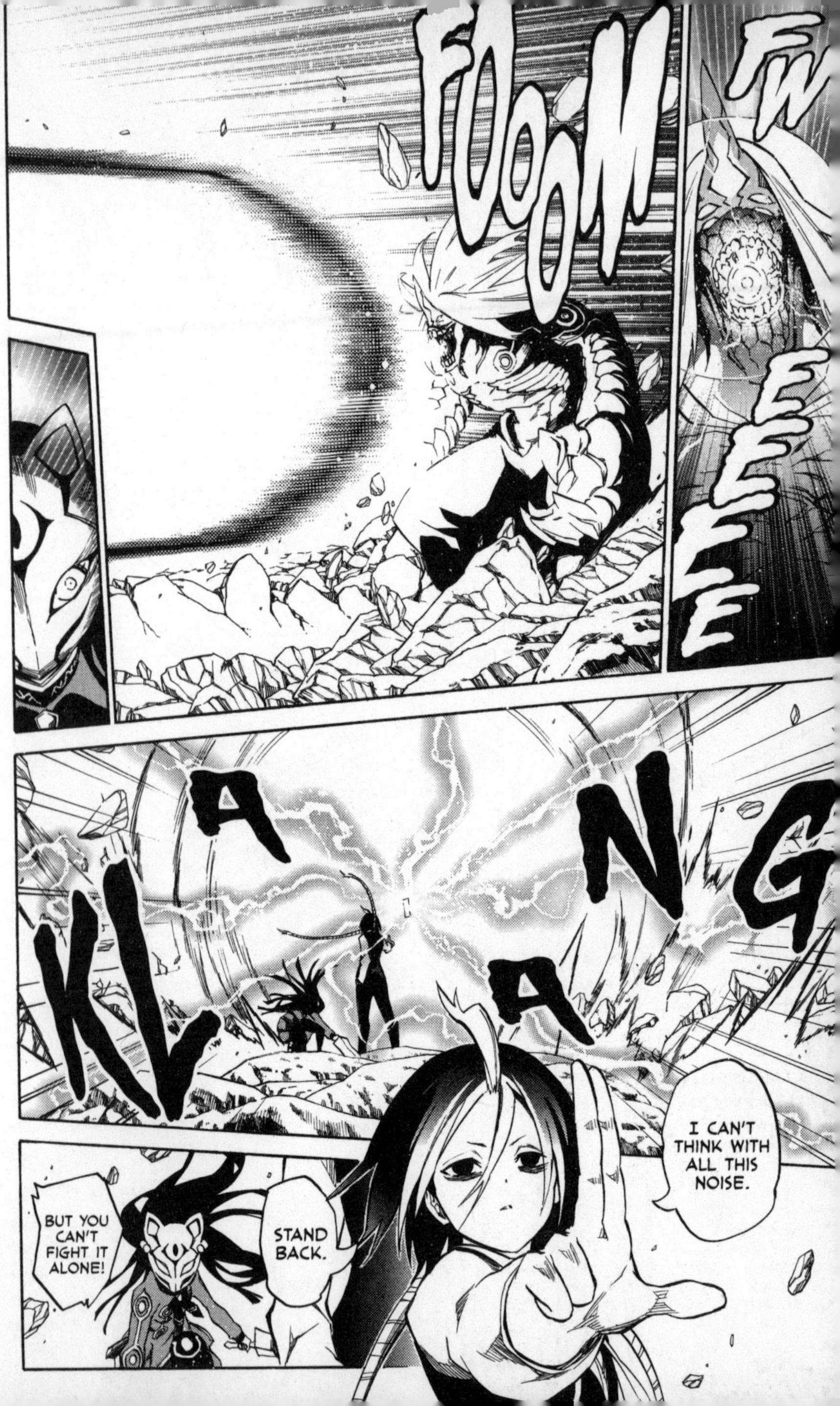
FWEEEEE
FOOOM
KLAANG
I CAN'T THINK WITH ALL THIS NOISE.
STAND BACK.
BUT YOU CAN'T FIGHT IT ALONE!

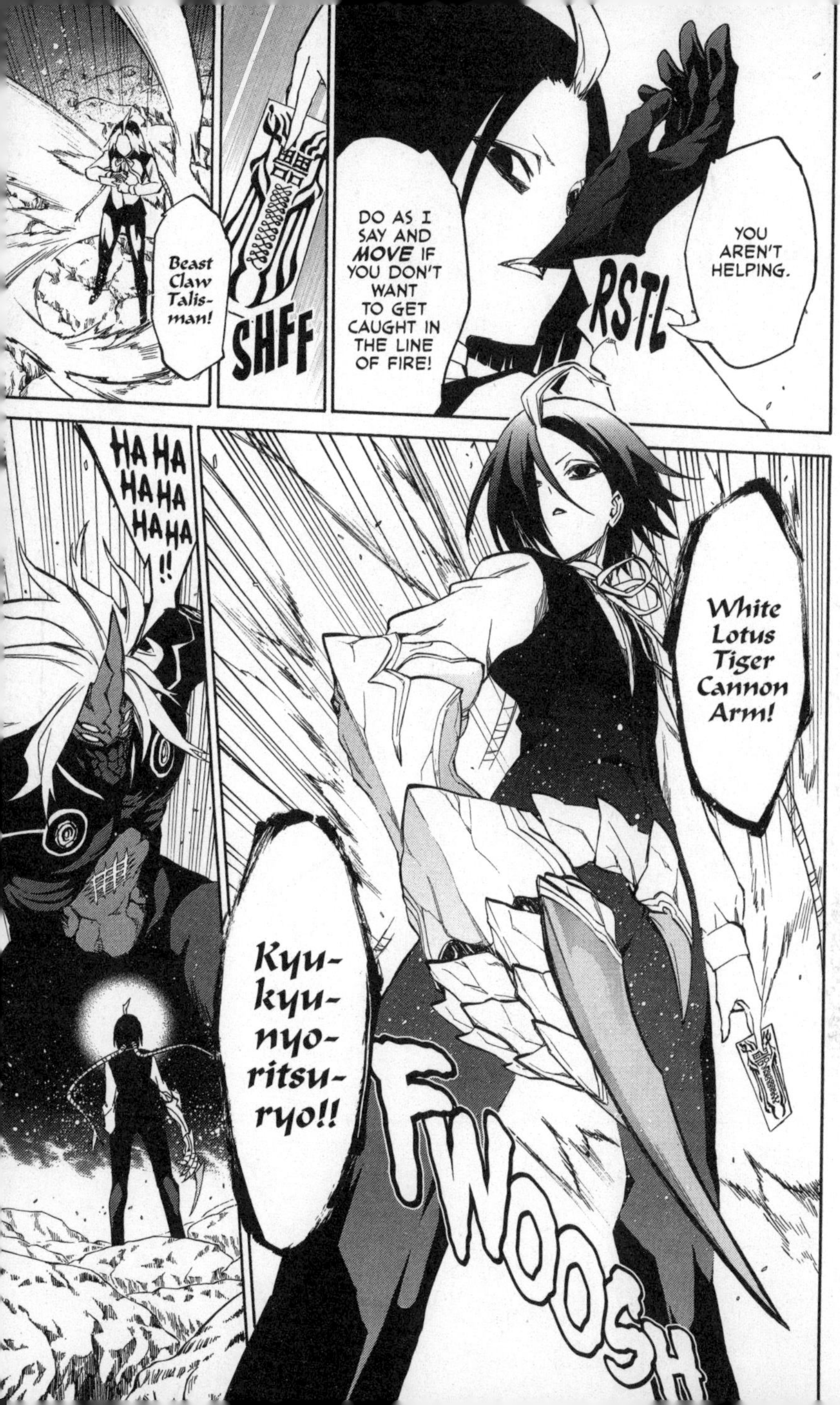
YOU AREN'T HELPING.
RSTL
DO AS I SAY AND *MOVE* IF YOU DON'T WANT TO GET CAUGHT IN THE LINE OF FIRE!
SHFF
Beast Claw Talis-man!
White Lotus Tiger Cannon Arm!
Kyu-kyu-nyo-ritsu-ryo!!
WOOSH
HA HA HA HA HA HA HA!!

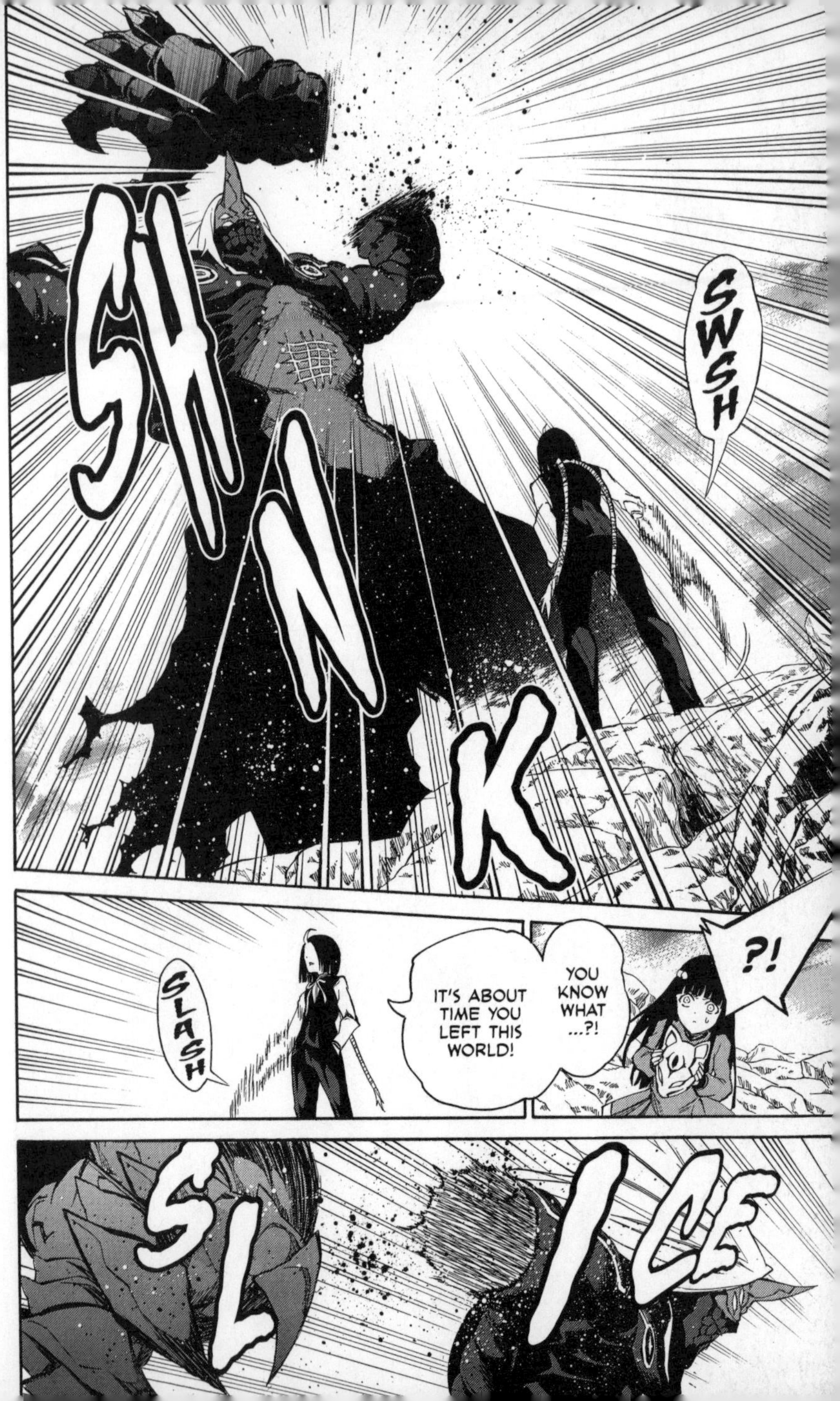
SWSH
SHNK
?!
YOU KNOW WHAT ...?!
IT'S ABOUT TIME YOU LEFT THIS WORLD!
SLASH
SLICE

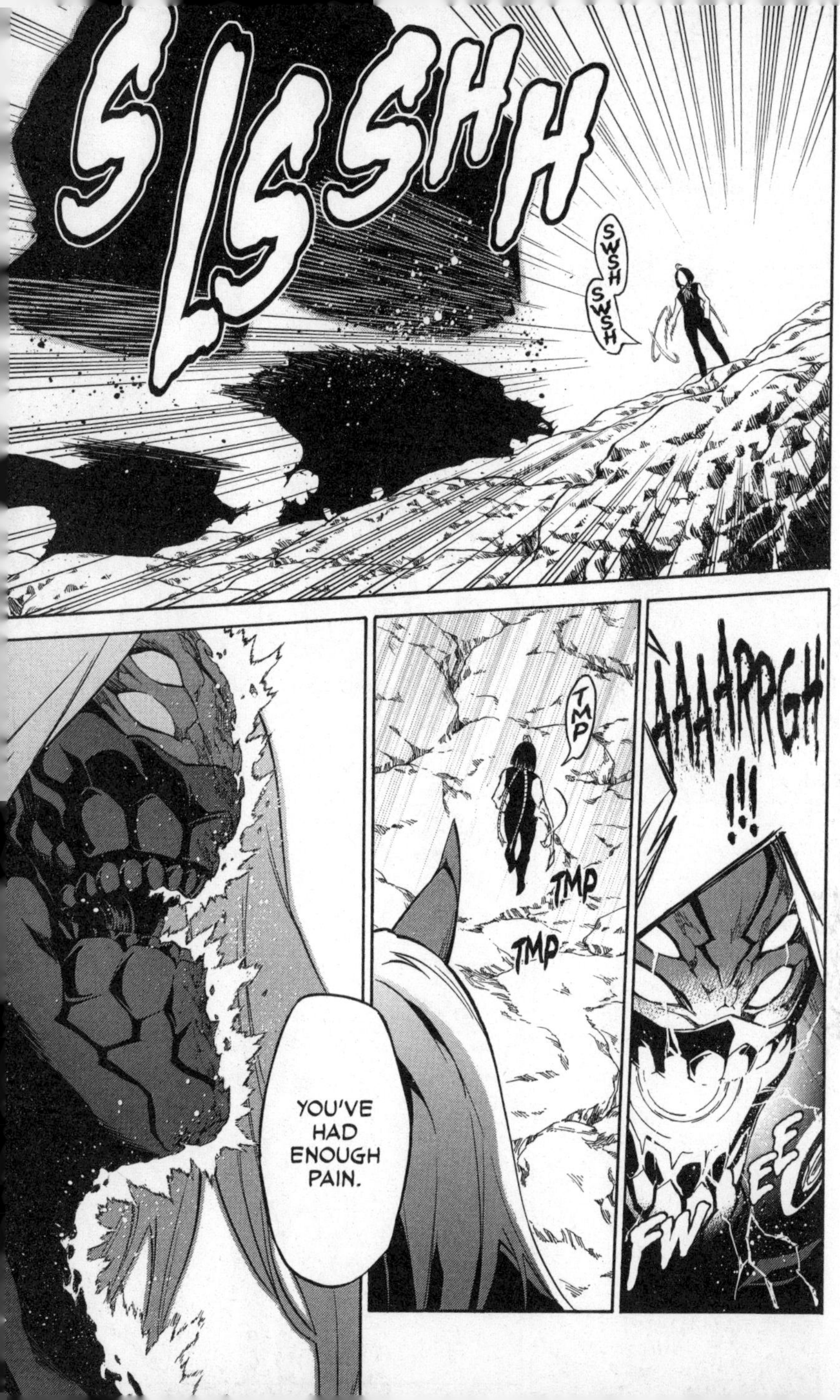
SLSSHH
SWSH SWSH
AAAARRGH!!!
FWEE
TMP
TMP
TMP
YOU'VE HAD ENOUGH PAIN.

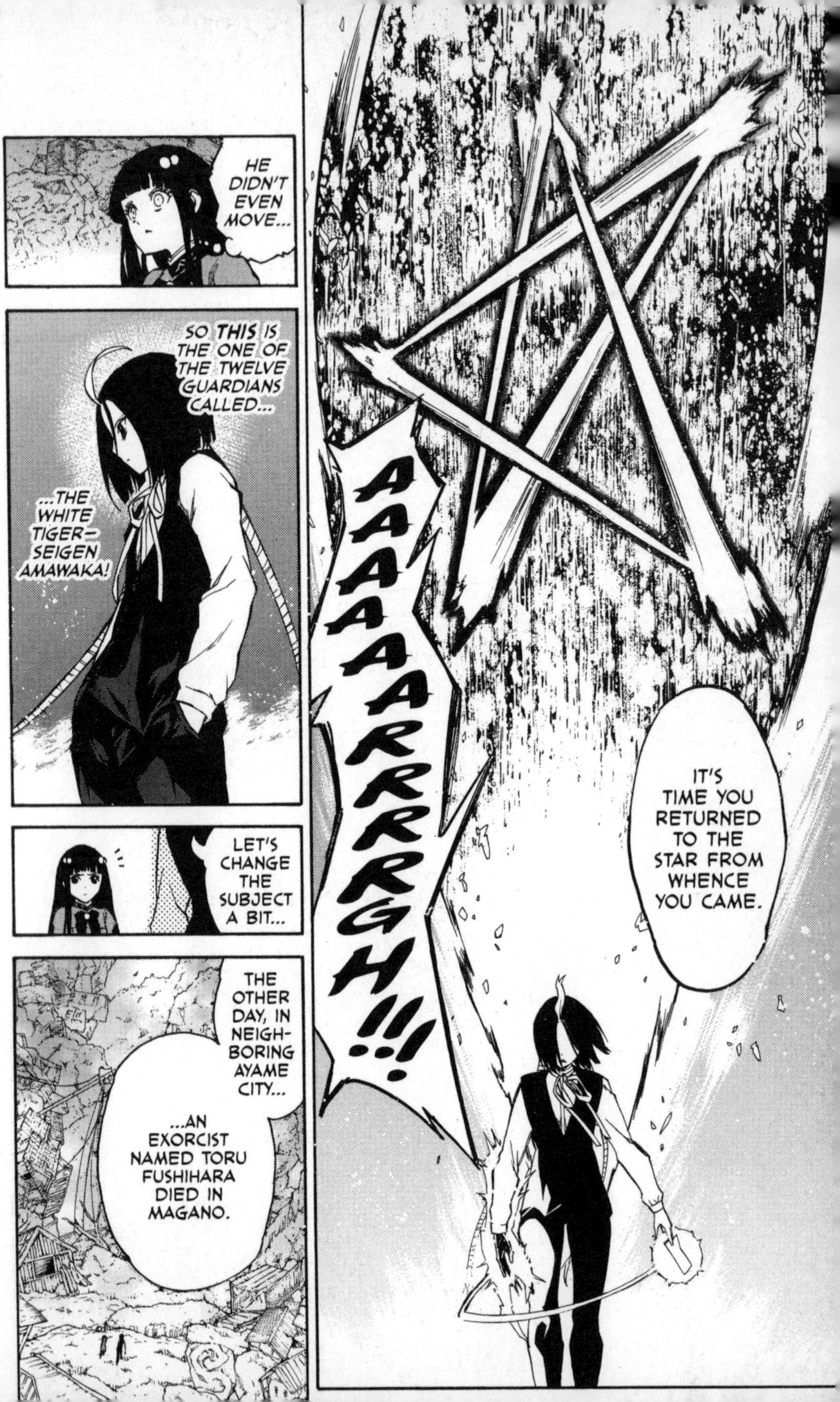
AAAAAARRRRGH!!!
IT'S TIME YOU RETURNED TO THE STAR FROM WHENCE YOU CAME.
HE DIDN'T EVEN MOVE...
SO THIS IS THE ONE OF THE TWELVE GUARDIANS CALLED...
...THE WHITE TIGER— SEIGEN AMAWAKA!
LET'S CHANGE THE SUBJECT A BIT...
THE OTHER DAY, IN NEIGHBORING AYAME CITY...
...AN EXORCIST NAMED TORU FUSHIHARA DIED IN MAGANO.

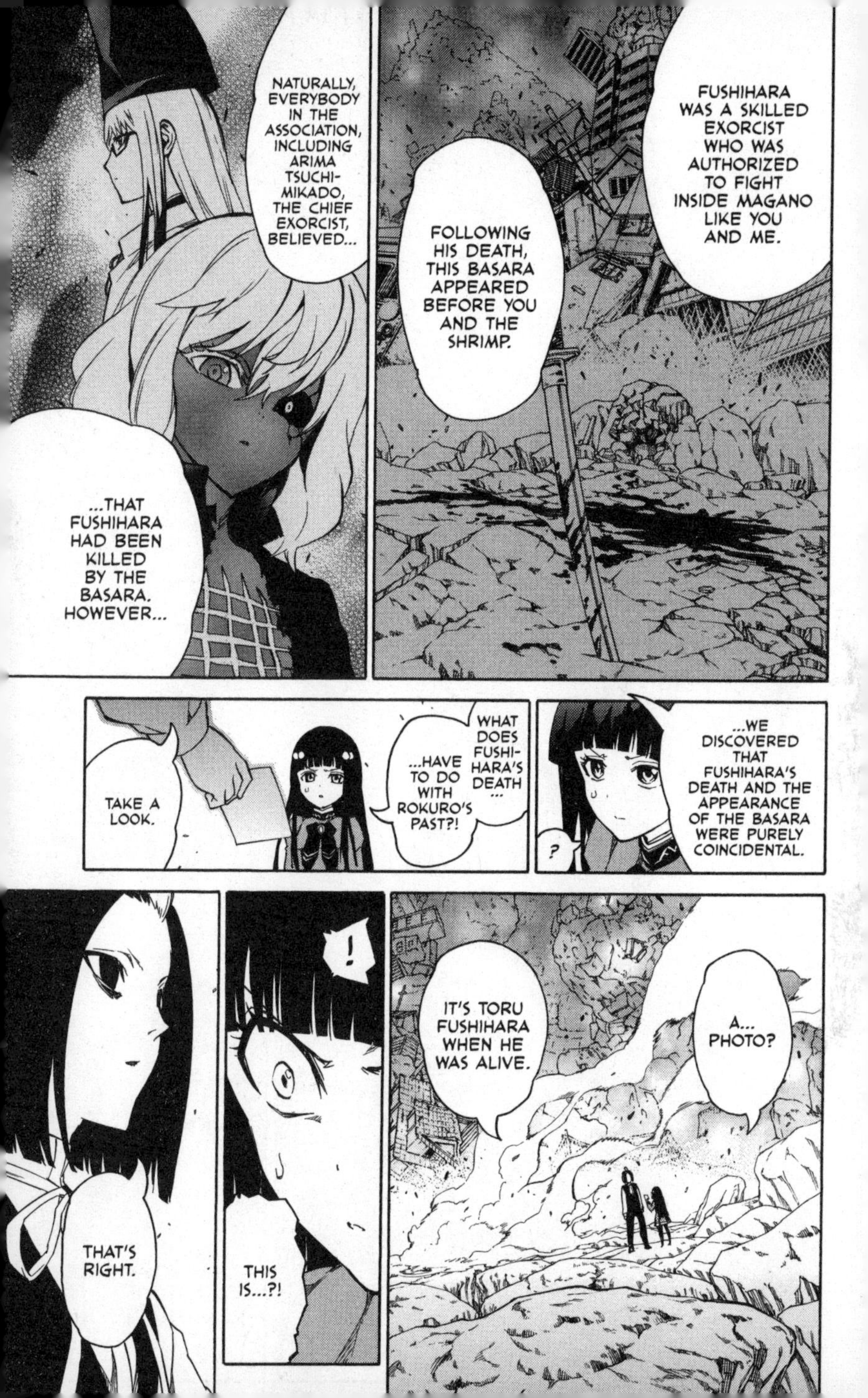
FUSHIHARA WAS A SKILLED EXORCIST WHO WAS AUTHORIZED TO FIGHT INSIDE MAGANO LIKE YOU AND ME.
FOLLOWING HIS DEATH, THIS BASARA APPEARED BEFORE YOU AND THE SHRIMP.
NATURALLY, EVERYBODY IN THE ASSOCIATION, INCLUDING ARIMA TSUCHI-MIKADO, THE CHIEF EXORCIST, BELIEVED...
...THAT FUSHIHARA HAD BEEN KILLED BY THE BASARA. HOWEVER...
...WE DISCOVERED THAT FUSHIHARA'S DEATH AND THE APPEARANCE OF THE BASARA WERE PURELY COINCIDENTAL.
?
WHAT DOES FUSHI-HARA'S DEATH...
...HAVE TO DO WITH ROKURO'S PAST?!
TAKE A LOOK.
A... PHOTO?
IT'S TORU FUSHIHARA WHEN HE WAS ALIVE.
!
THIS IS...?!
THAT'S RIGHT.

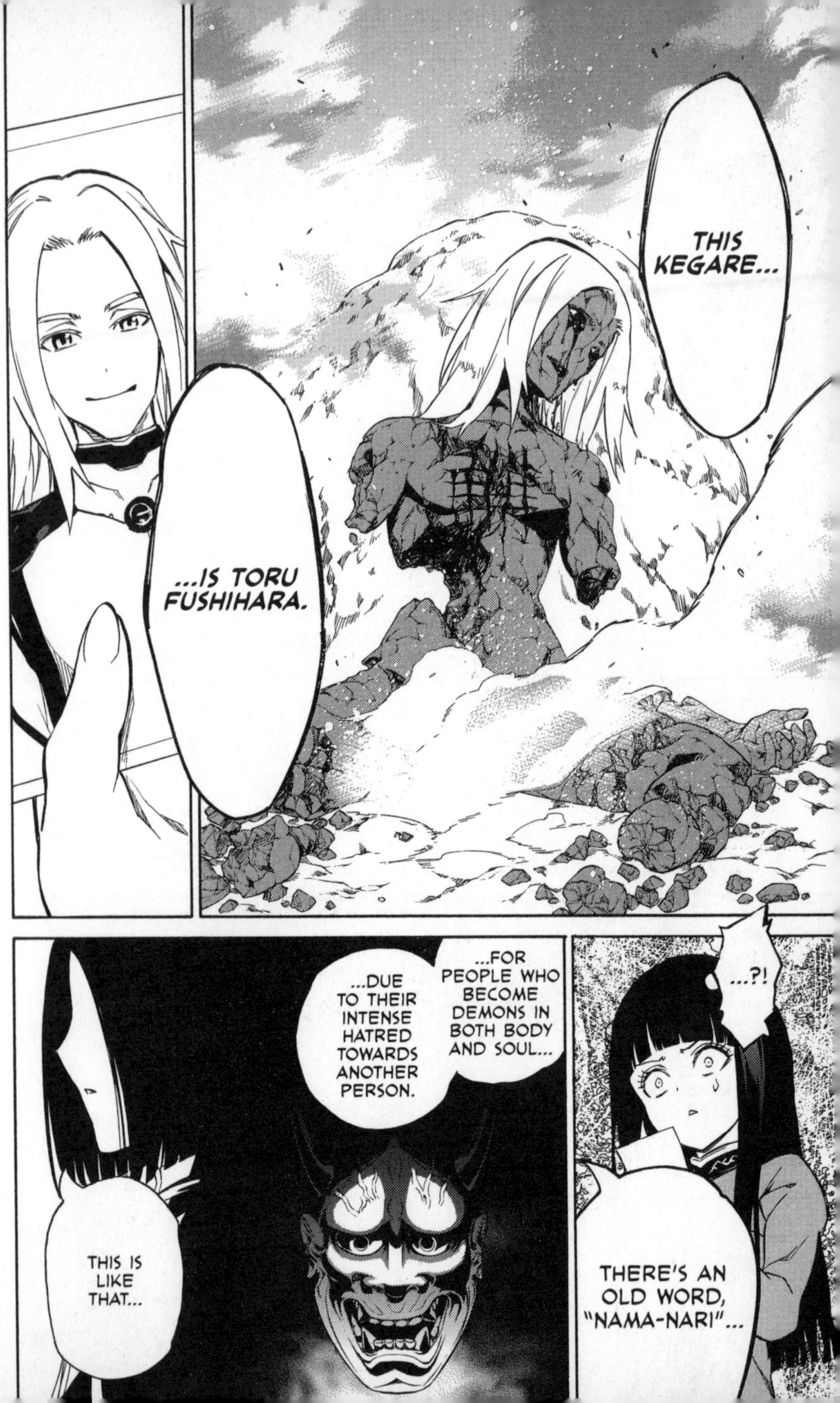
THIS KEGARE...
...IS TORU FUSHIHARA.
...?!
THERE'S AN OLD WORD, "NAMA-NARI"...
...FOR PEOPLE WHO BECOME DEMONS IN BOTH BODY AND SOUL...
...DUE TO THEIR INTENSE HATRED TOWARDS ANOTHER PERSON.
THIS IS LIKE THAT...

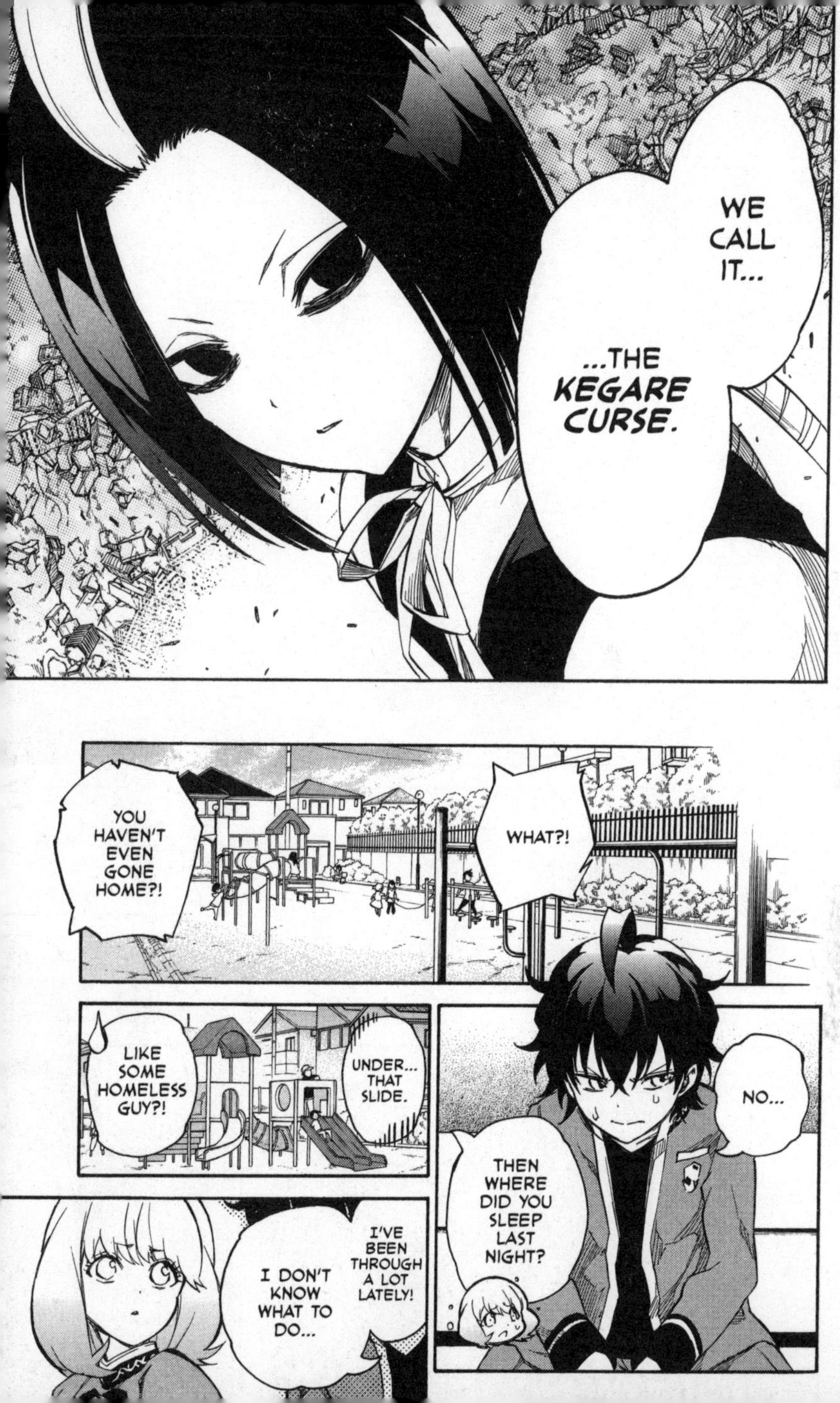

WE CALL IT...
...THE KEGARE CURSE.
WHAT?!
YOU HAVEN'T EVEN GONE HOME?!
NO...
THEN WHERE DID YOU SLEEP LAST NIGHT?
UNDER... THAT SLIDE.
LIKE SOME HOMELESS GUY?!
I'VE BEEN THROUGH A LOT LATELY!
I DON'T KNOW WHAT TO DO...

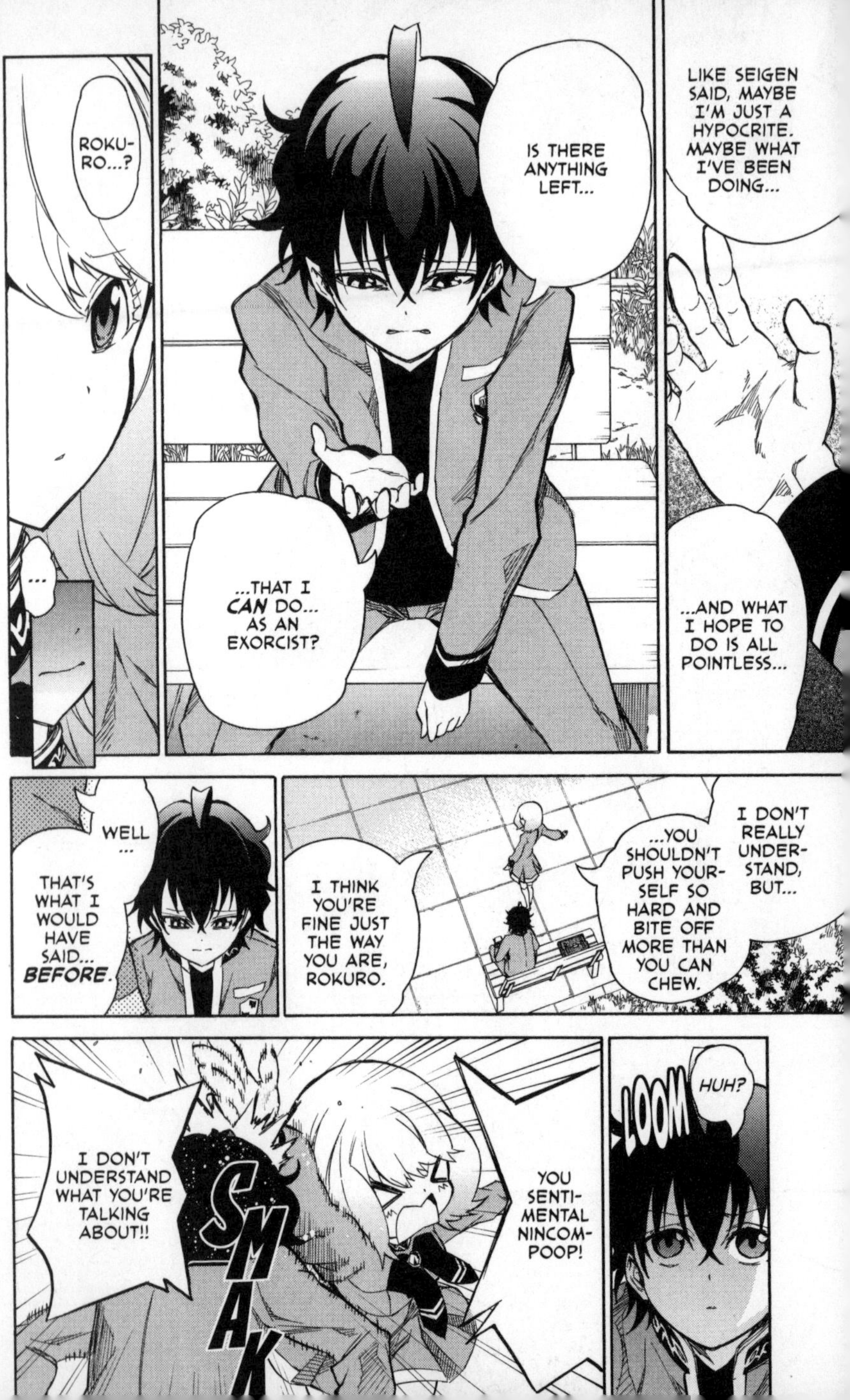
LIKE SEIGEN SAID, MAYBE I'M JUST A HYPOCRITE. MAYBE WHAT I'VE BEEN DOING...
...AND WHAT I HOPE TO DO IS ALL POINTLESS...
IS THERE ANYTHING LEFT...
...THAT I CAN DO... AS AN EXORCIST?
ROKURO...?
...
I DON'T REALLY UNDERSTAND, BUT...
...YOU SHOULDN'T PUSH YOURSELF SO HARD AND BITE OFF MORE THAN YOU CAN CHEW.
I THINK YOU'RE FINE JUST THE WAY YOU ARE, ROKURO.
WELL...
THAT'S WHAT I WOULD HAVE SAID... BEFORE.
LOOM
HUH?
YOU SENTIMENTAL NINCOMPOOP!
SMAK
I DON'T UNDERSTAND WHAT YOU'RE TALKING ABOUT!!

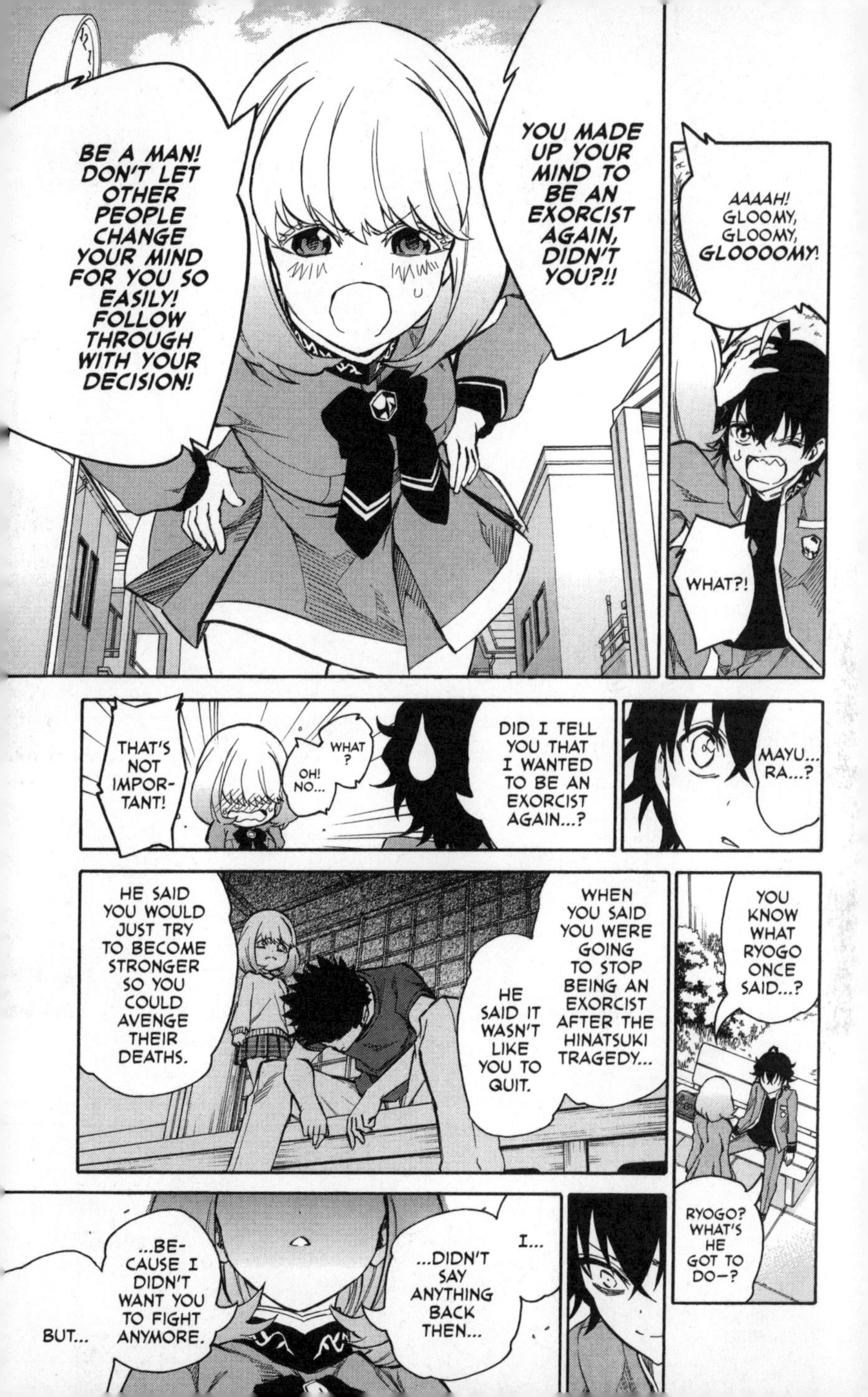
AAAAH! GLOOMY, GLOOMY, GLOOOOOMY!
WHAT?!
YOU MADE UP YOUR MIND TO BE AN EXORCIST AGAIN, DIDN'T YOU?!!
BE A MAN! DON'T LET OTHER PEOPLE CHANGE YOUR MIND FOR YOU SO EASILY! FOLLOW THROUGH WITH YOUR DECISION!
MAYU... RA...?
DID I TELL YOU THAT I WANTED TO BE AN EXORCIST AGAIN...?
WHAT ?
OH! NO...
THAT'S NOT IMPOR-TANT!
YOU KNOW WHAT RYOGO ONCE SAID...?
RYOGO? WHAT'S HE GOT TO DO—?
WHEN YOU SAID YOU WERE GOING TO STOP BEING AN EXORCIST AFTER THE HINATSUKI TRAGEDY...
HE SAID IT WASN'T LIKE YOU TO QUIT.
HE SAID YOU WOULD JUST TRY TO BECOME STRONGER SO YOU COULD AVENGE THEIR DEATHS.
I...
...DIDN'T SAY ANYTHING BACK THEN...
...BE-CAUSE I DIDN'T WANT YOU TO FIGHT ANYMORE.
BUT...

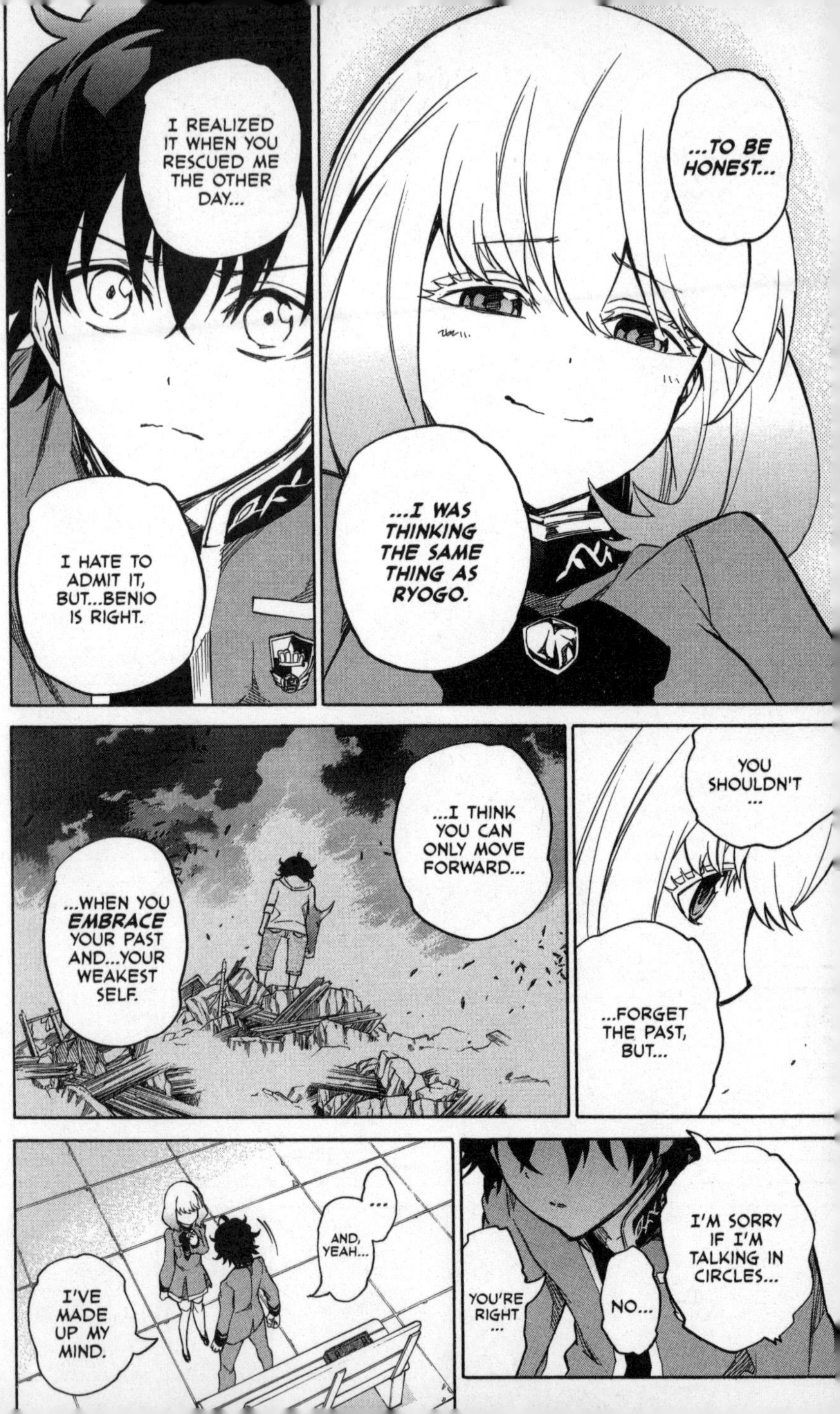
...TO BE HONEST...
...I WAS THINKING THE SAME THING AS RYOGO.
I REALIZED IT WHEN YOU RESCUED ME THE OTHER DAY...
I HATE TO ADMIT IT, BUT...BENIO IS RIGHT.
YOU SHOULDN'T ...
...FORGET THE PAST, BUT...
...I THINK YOU CAN ONLY MOVE FORWARD...
...WHEN YOU *EMBRACE* YOUR PAST AND...YOUR WEAKEST SELF.
I'M SORRY IF I'M TALKING IN CIRCLES...
NO...
YOU'RE RIGHT ...
...
AND, YEAH...
I'VE MADE UP MY MIND.

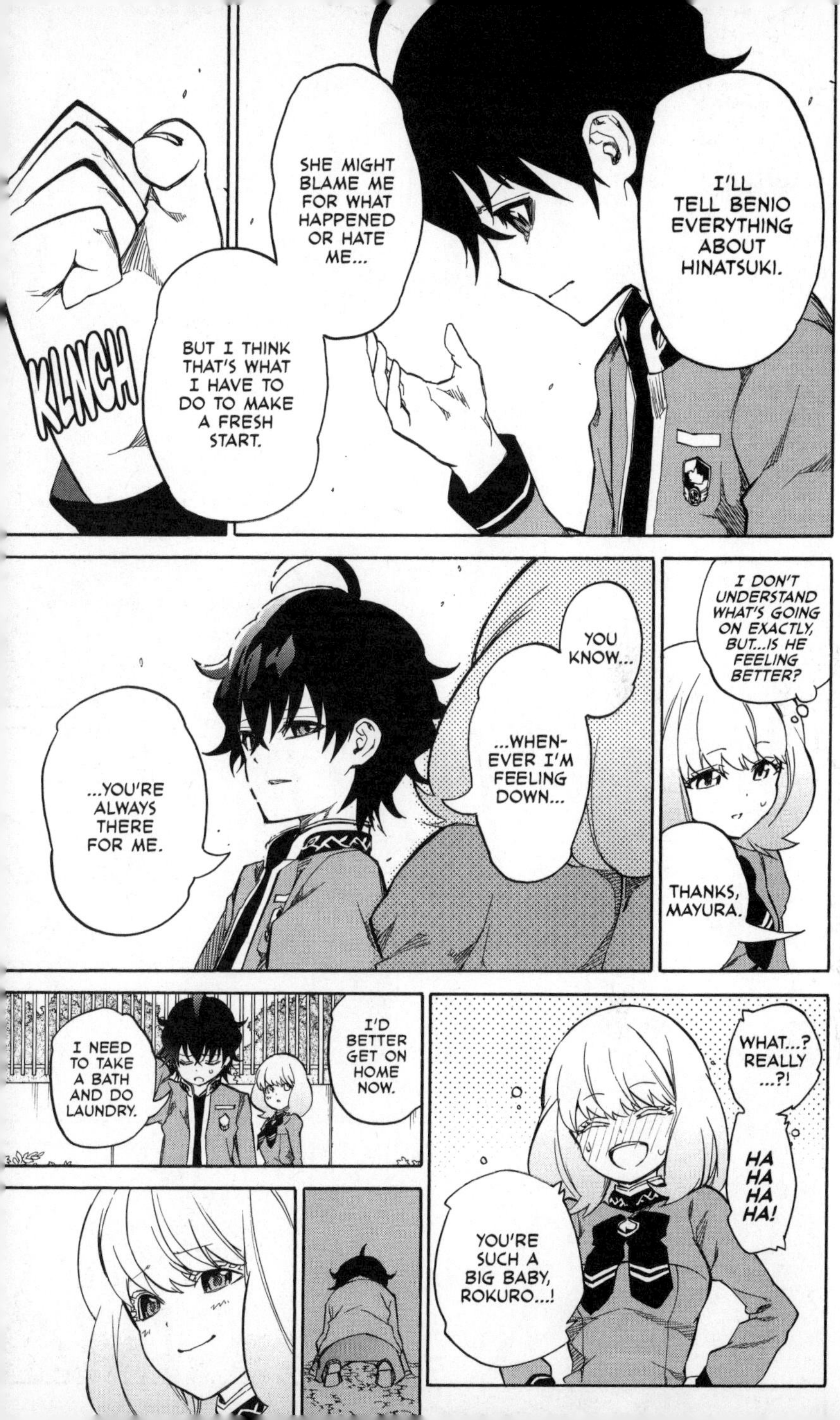

I'LL TELL BENIO EVERYTHING ABOUT HINATSUKI.
SHE MIGHT BLAME ME FOR WHAT HAPPENED OR HATE ME...
BUT I THINK THAT'S WHAT I HAVE TO DO TO MAKE A FRESH START.
KLNCH
I DON'T UNDERSTAND WHAT'S GOING ON EXACTLY, BUT...IS HE FEELING BETTER?
THANKS, MAYURA.
YOU KNOW...
...WHENEVER I'M FEELING DOWN...
...YOU'RE ALWAYS THERE FOR ME.
WHAT...? REALLY ...?!
HA HA HA HA!
YOU'RE SUCH A BIG BABY, ROKURO...!
I'D BETTER GET ON HOME NOW.
I NEED TO TAKE A BATH AND DO LAUNDRY.

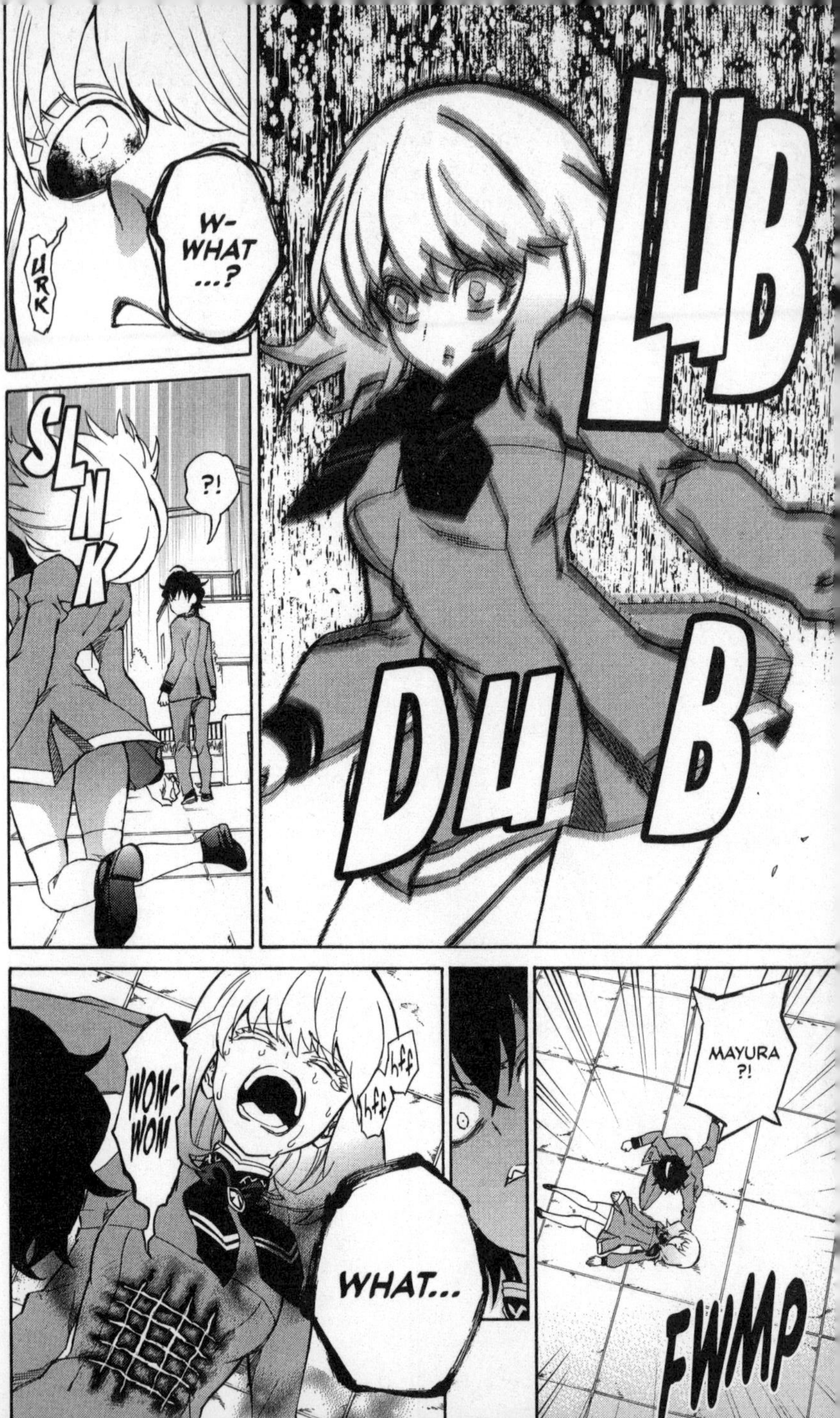
LUB
DUB
W-WHAT ...?
URK
SLNK
?!
MAYURA ?!
FWMP
hff hff
WOM-WOM
WHAT...

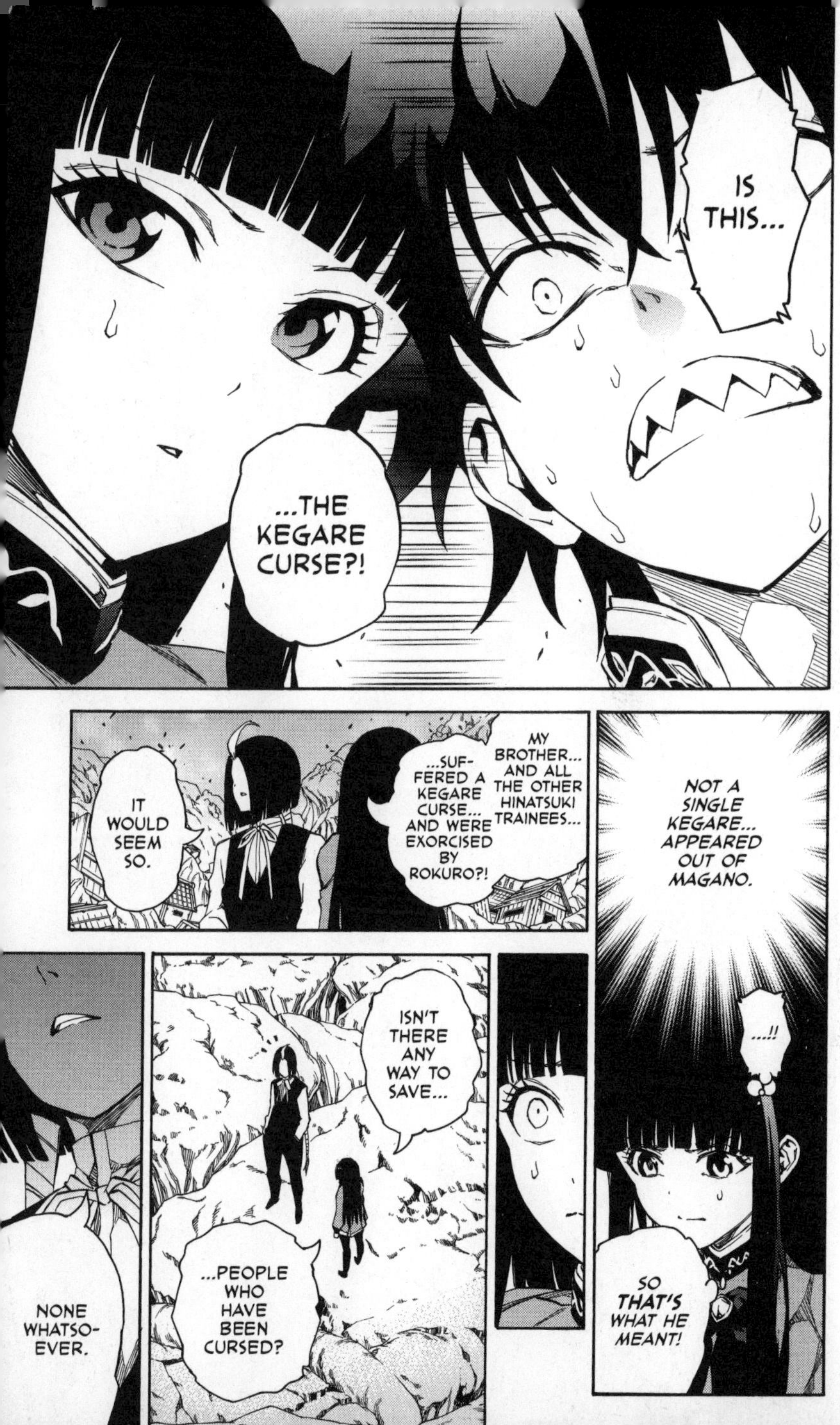
IS THIS...
...THE KEGARE CURSE?!
NOT A SINGLE KEGARE... APPEARED OUT OF MAGANO.
...!!
SO *THAT'S* WHAT HE MEANT!
MY BROTHER... AND ALL THE OTHER HINATSUKI TRAINEES...
...SUF-FERED A KEGARE CURSE... AND WERE EXORCISED BY ROKURO?!
IT WOULD SEEM SO.
ISN'T THERE ANY WAY TO SAVE...
...PEOPLE WHO HAVE BEEN CURSED?
NONE WHATSO-EVER.

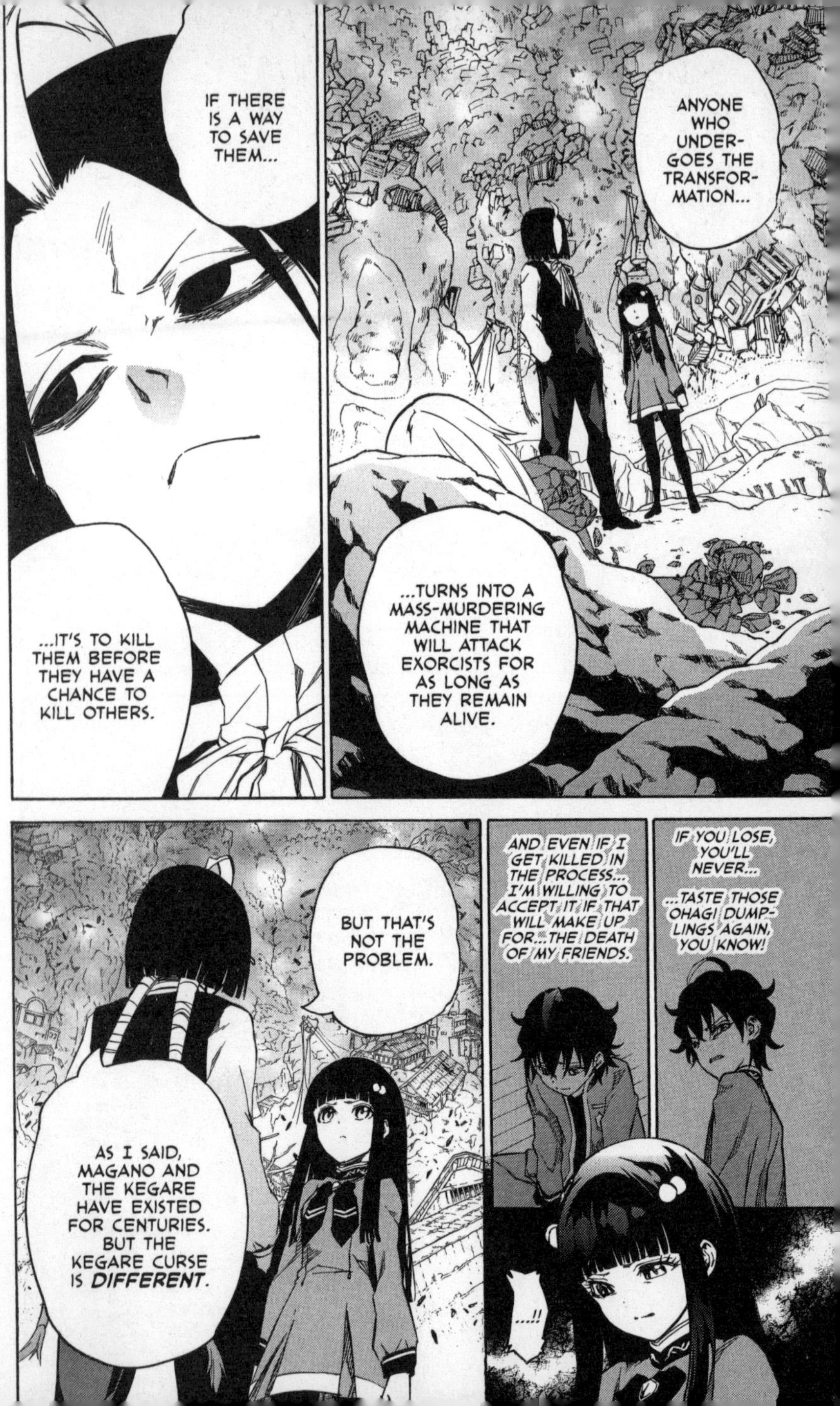
ANYONE WHO UNDER-GOES THE TRANSFOR-MATION...
...TURNS INTO A MASS-MURDERING MACHINE THAT WILL ATTACK EXORCISTS FOR AS LONG AS THEY REMAIN ALIVE.
IF THERE IS A WAY TO SAVE THEM...
...IT'S TO KILL THEM BEFORE THEY HAVE A CHANCE TO KILL OTHERS.
IF YOU LOSE, YOU'LL NEVER...
...TASTE THOSE OHAGI DUMP-LINGS AGAIN, YOU KNOW!
AND EVEN IF I GET KILLED IN THE PROCESS... I'M WILLING TO ACCEPT IT IF THAT WILL MAKE UP FOR...THE DEATH OF MY FRIENDS.
....!!
BUT THAT'S NOT THE PROBLEM.
AS I SAID, MAGANO AND THE KEGARE HAVE EXISTED FOR CENTURIES. BUT THE KEGARE CURSE IS *DIFFERENT*.

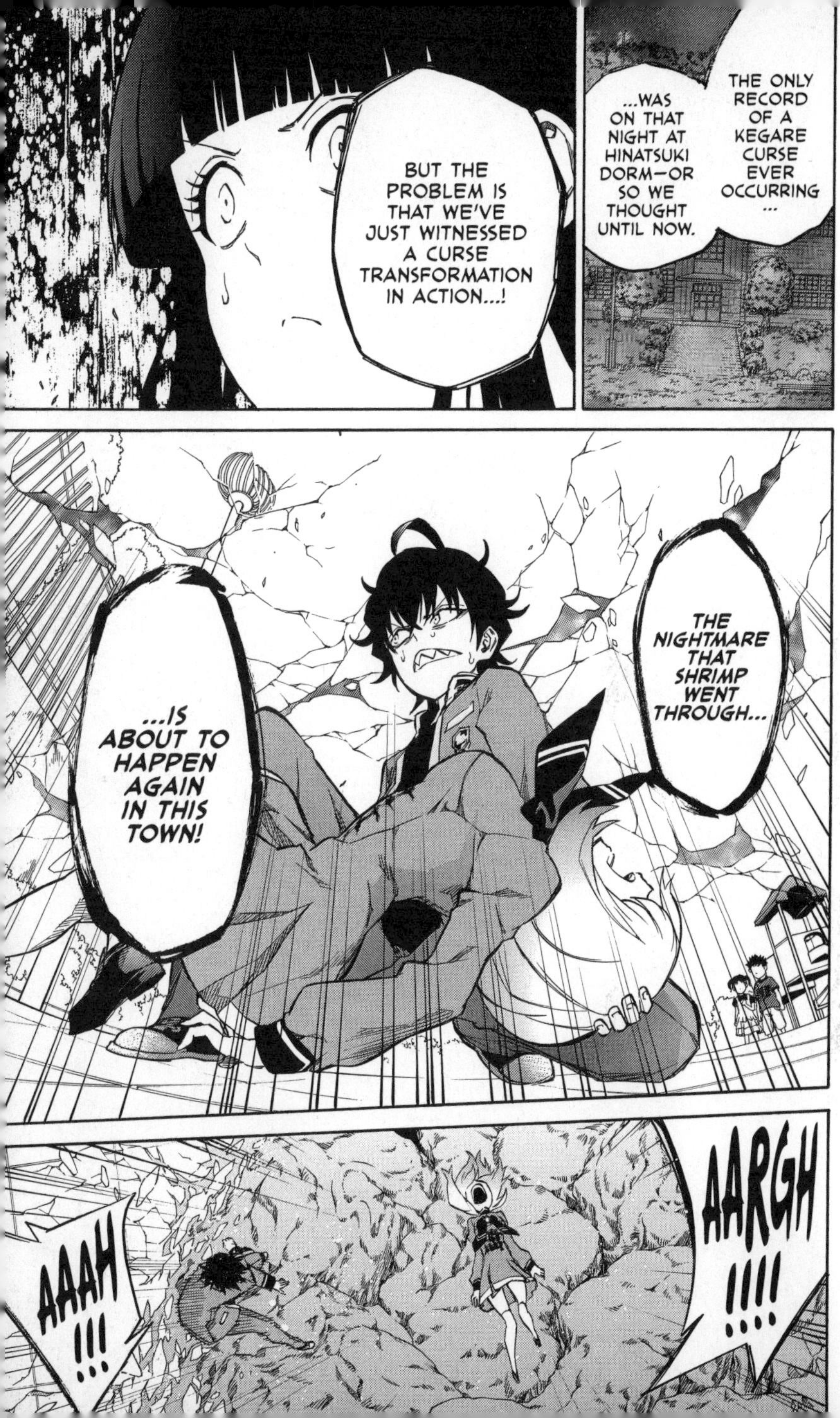
THE ONLY RECORD OF A KEGARE CURSE EVER OCCURRING ...
...WAS ON THAT NIGHT AT HINATSUKI DORM—OR SO WE THOUGHT UNTIL NOW.
BUT THE PROBLEM IS THAT WE'VE JUST WITNESSED A CURSE TRANSFORMATION IN ACTION...!
THE NIGHTMARE THAT SHRIMP WENT THROUGH...
...IS ABOUT TO HAPPEN AGAIN IN THIS TOWN!
AARGH !!!!
AAAH !!!

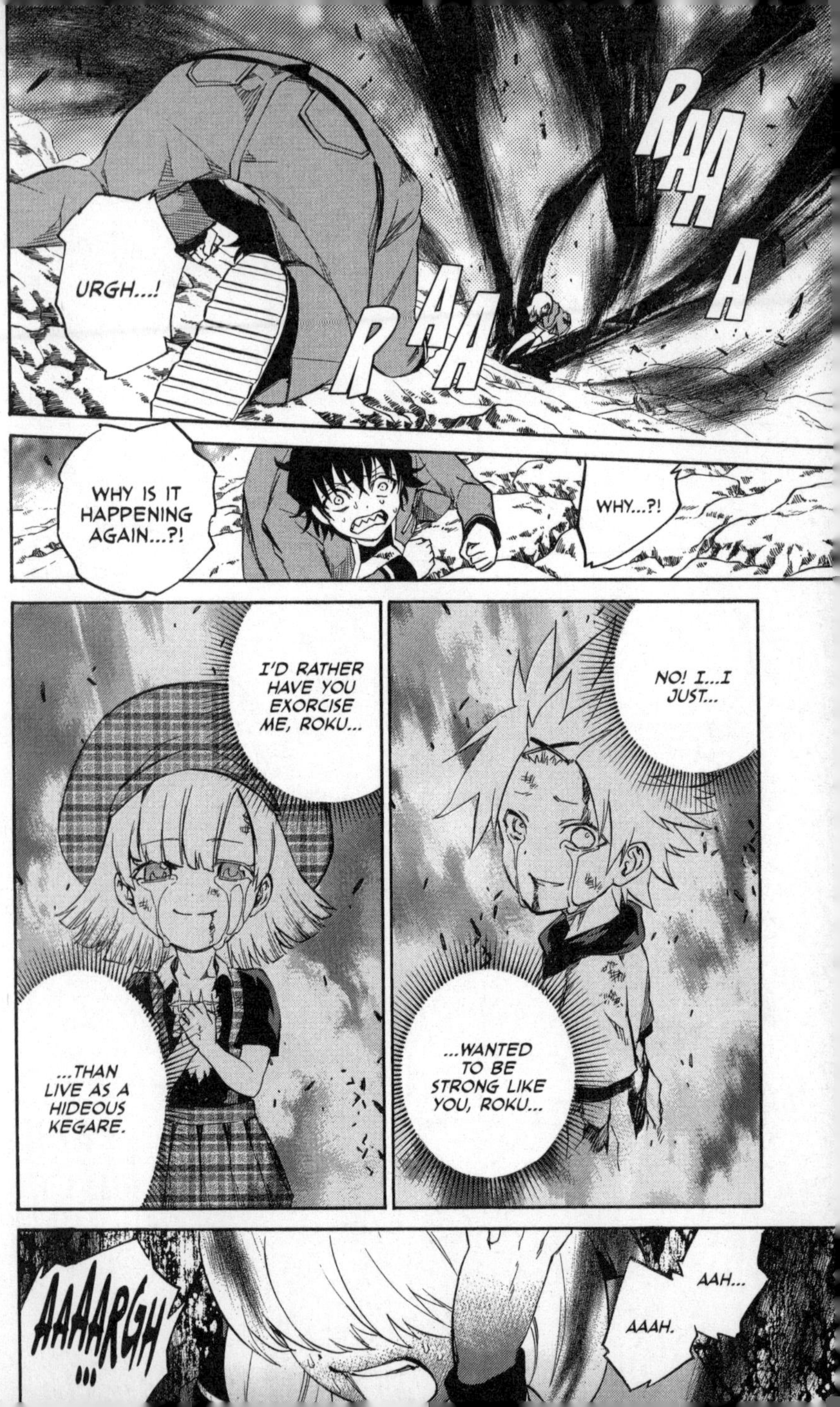
RAAAA
RAA
URGH...!
WHY...?!
WHY IS IT HAPPENING AGAIN...?!
NO! I...I JUST...
...WANTED TO BE STRONG LIKE YOU, ROKU...
I'D RATHER HAVE YOU EXORCISE ME, ROKU...
...THAN LIVE AS A HIDEOUS KEGARE.
AAH...
AAAH.
AAAARGH...

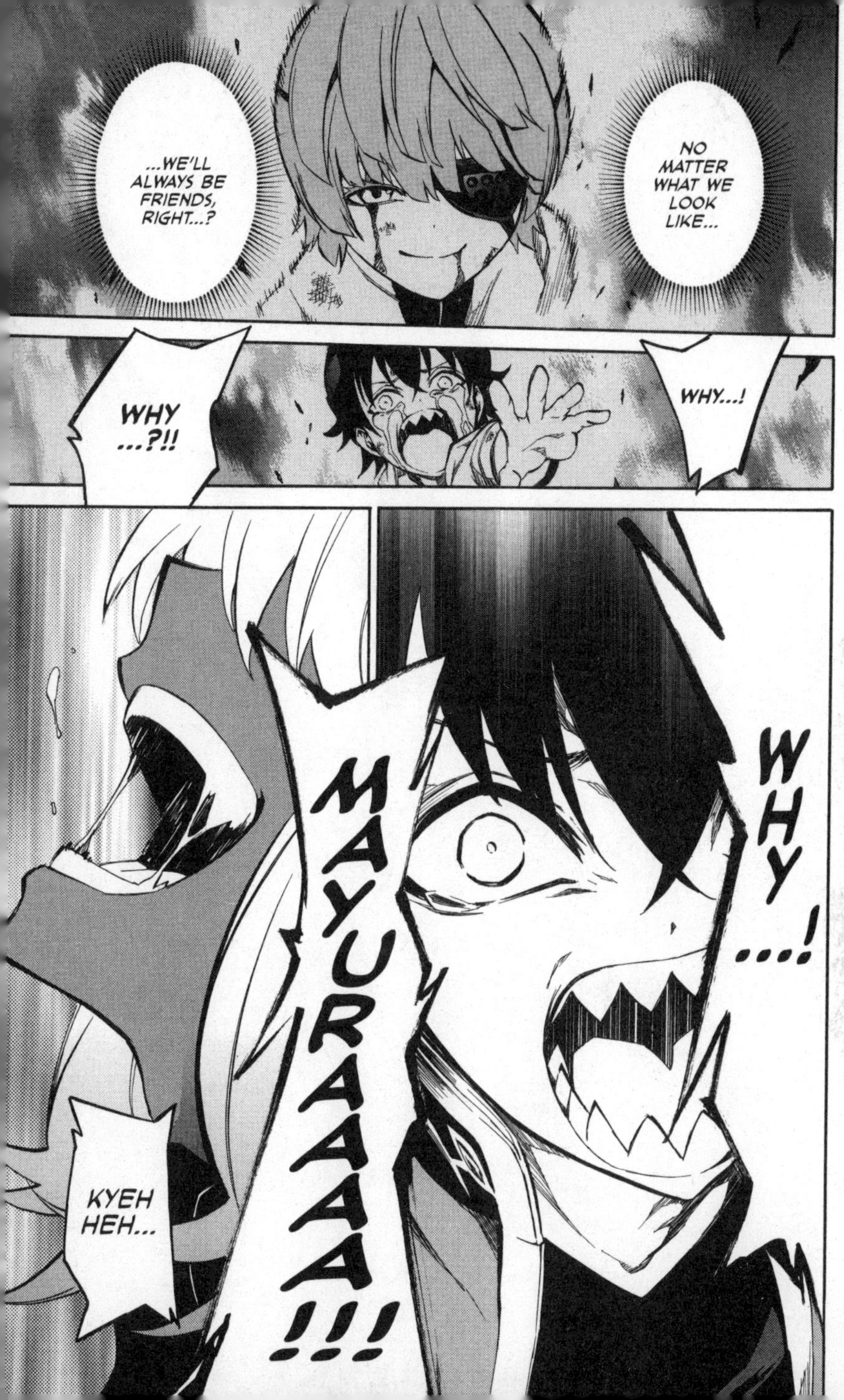
NO MATTER WHAT WE LOOK LIKE...
...WE'LL ALWAYS BE FRIENDS, RIGHT...?
WHY...!
WHY ...?!!
WHY ...!
MAYURAAAAA!!!
KYEH HEH...

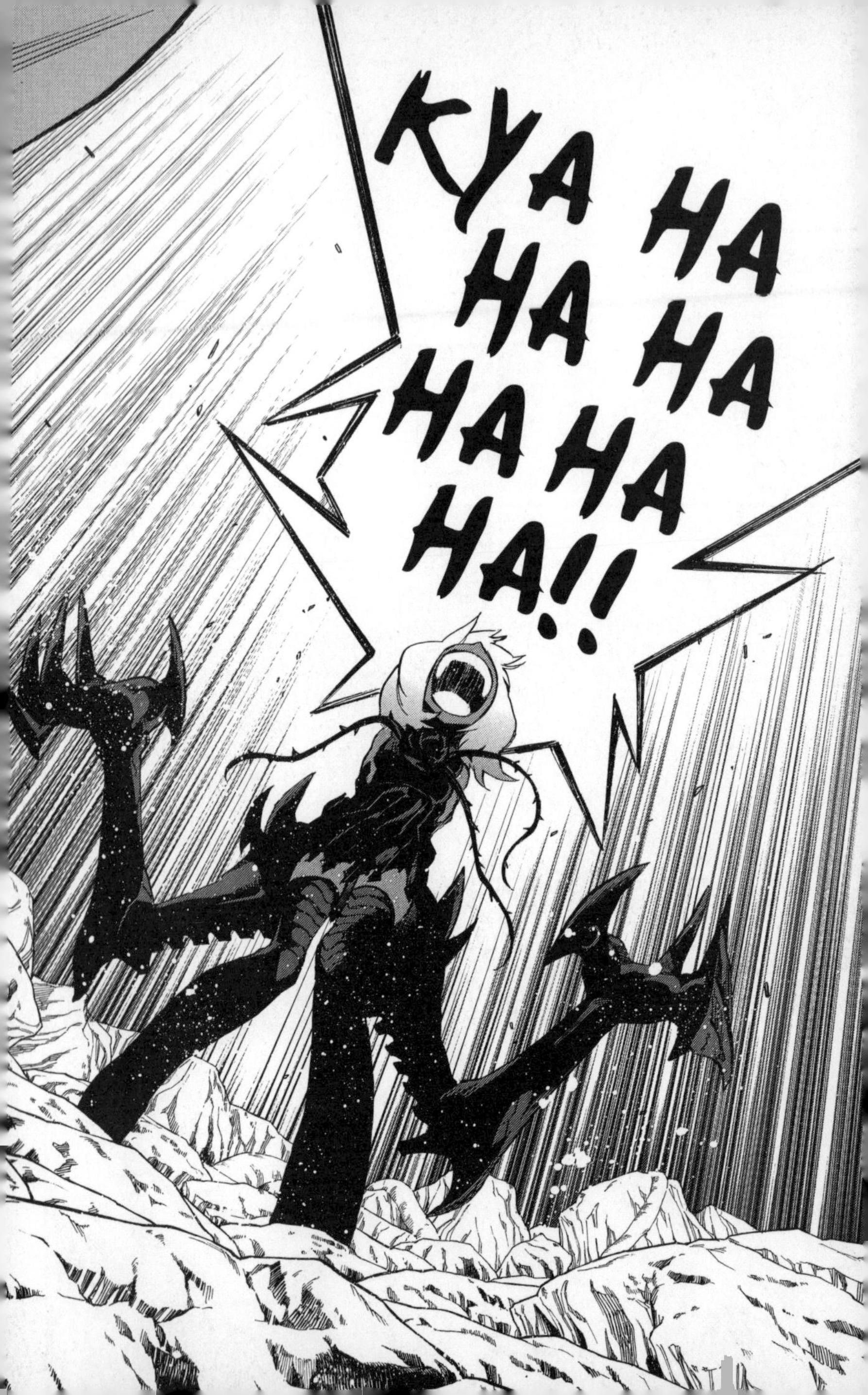
KYA HA HA HA HA HA HA HA HA!!

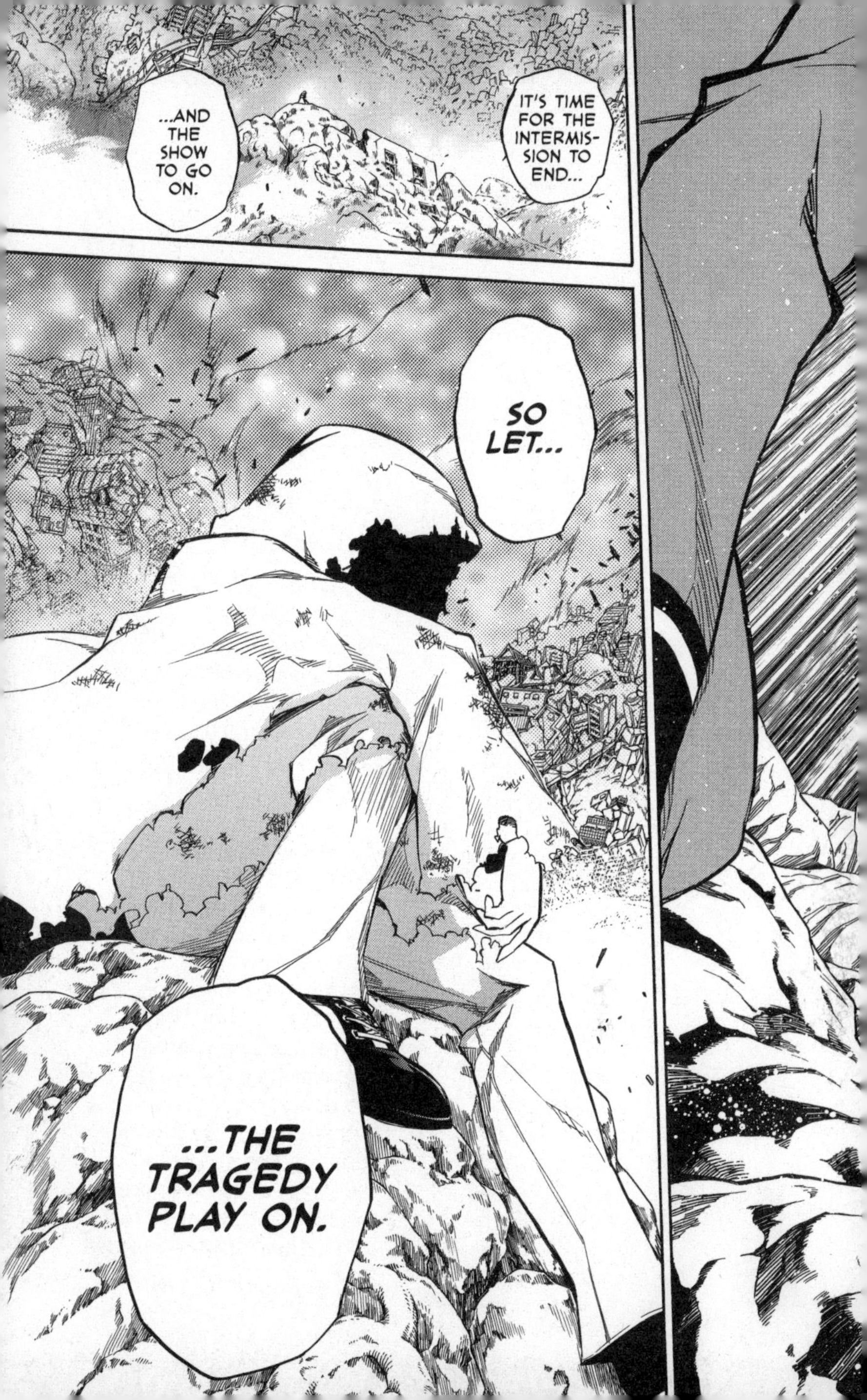
IT'S TIME FOR THE INTERMISSION TO END...
...AND THE SHOW TO GO ON.
SO LET...
...THE TRAGEDY PLAY ON.

Column 6: Shikigami (Spirit Servants)

A Shikigami or Spirit Servant is the term for the demon minions exorcists control. *Shiki* means "to make use of." It doesn't mean there was a god named "Shikigami."

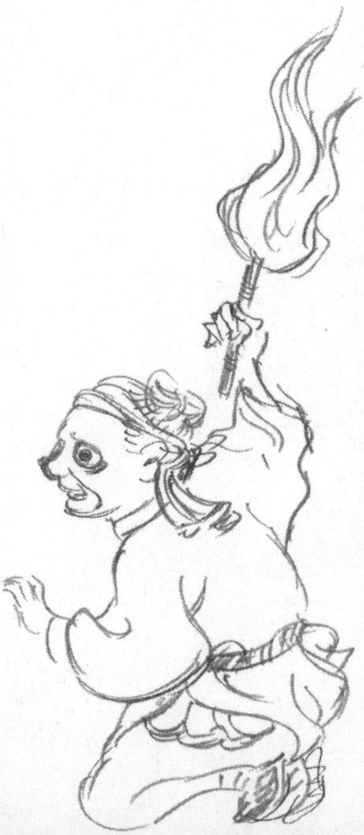

People usually imagine these Spirit Servants as creatures to summon, but they are portrayed differently in various documents and works. Sometimes they are summoned as spiritual entities to curse an enemy to death, whereas in other records they are merely depicted as servants summoned to do chores and look after the home while their master is away.

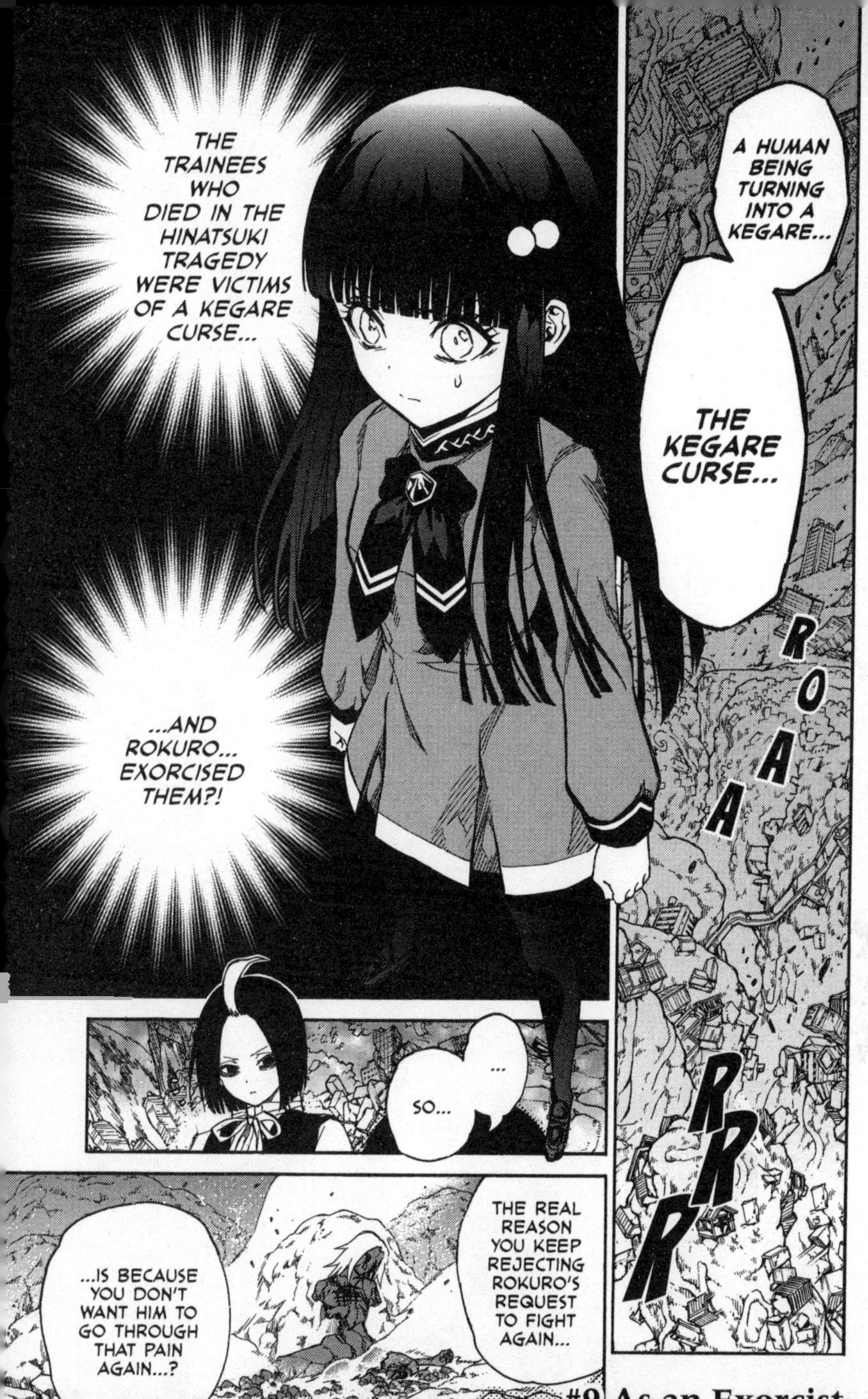
A HUMAN BEING TURNING INTO A KEGARE...
THE KEGARE CURSE...
ROAAARRR
THE TRAINEES WHO DIED IN THE HINATSUKI TRAGEDY WERE VICTIMS OF A KEGARE CURSE...
...AND ROKURO... EXORCISED THEM?!
...
SO...
THE REAL REASON YOU KEEP REJECTING ROKURO'S REQUEST TO FIGHT AGAIN...
...IS BECAUSE YOU DON'T WANT HIM TO GO THROUGH THAT PAIN AGAIN...?

#9 As an Exorcist

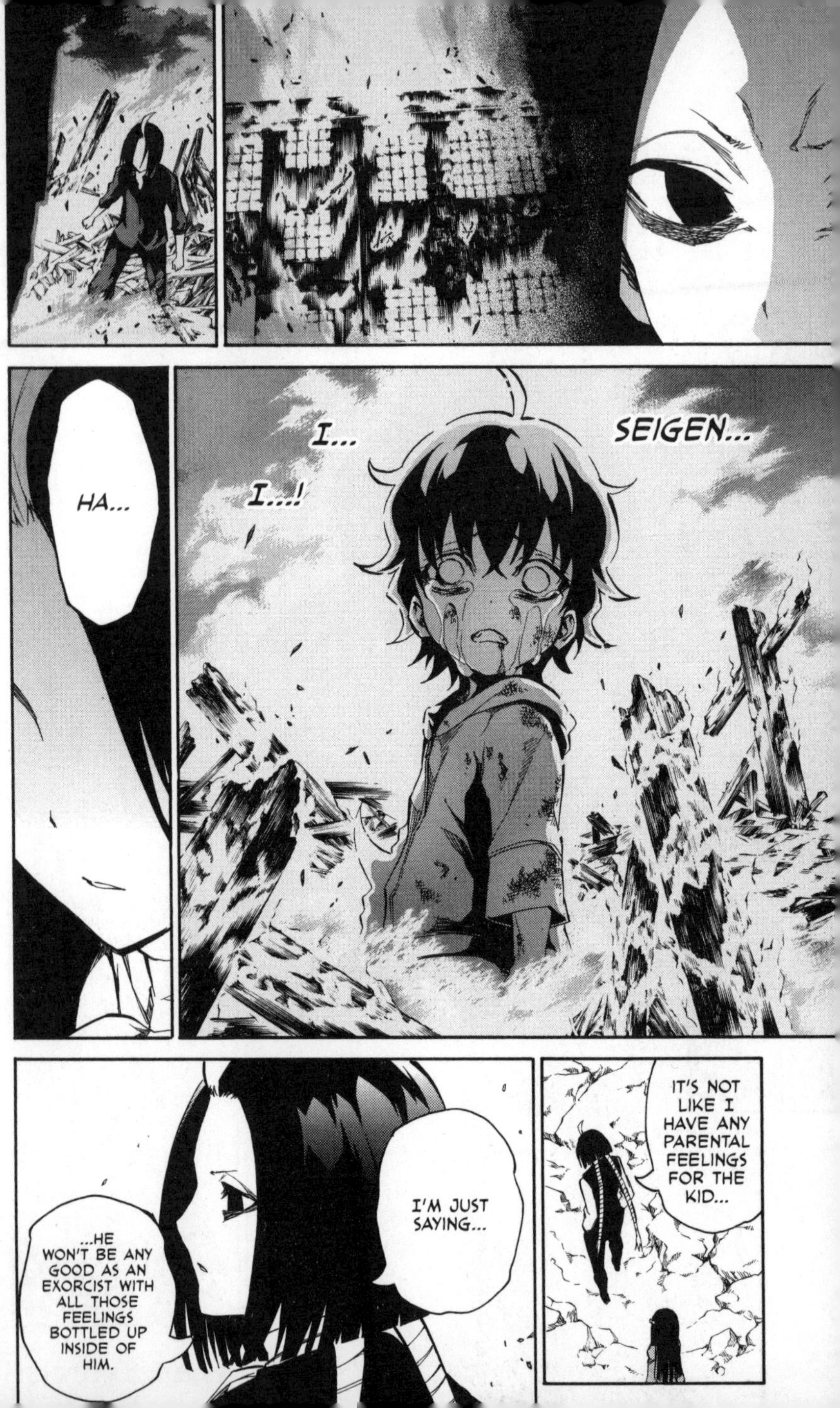
SEIGEN...
I...
I...!
HA...
IT'S NOT LIKE I HAVE ANY PARENTAL FEELINGS FOR THE KID...
I'M JUST SAYING...
...HE WON'T BE ANY GOOD AS AN EXORCIST WITH ALL THOSE FEELINGS BOTTLED UP INSIDE OF HIM.

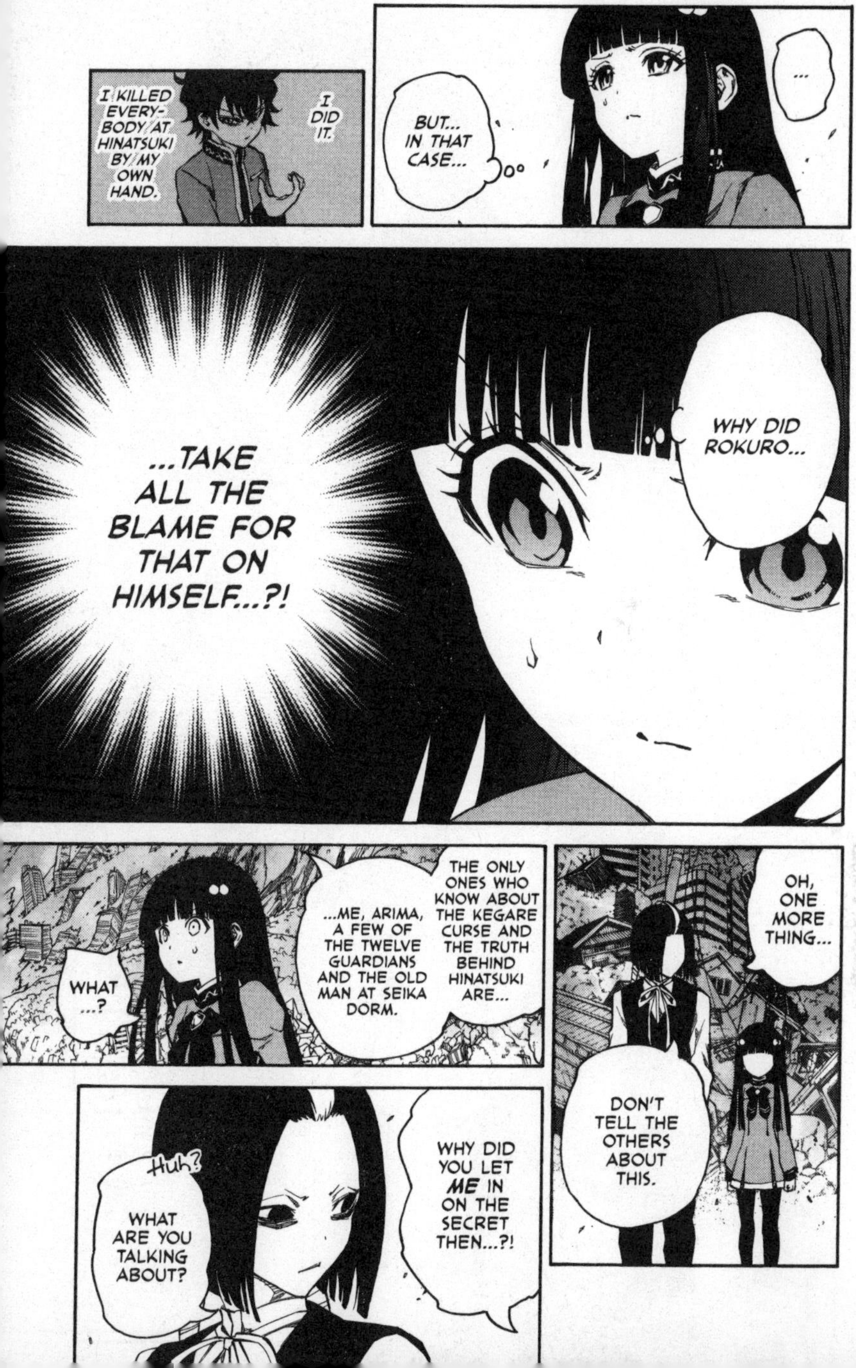
...
BUT... IN THAT CASE...
I DID IT.
I KILLED EVERYBODY AT HINATSUKI BY MY OWN HAND.
WHY DID ROKURO...
...TAKE ALL THE BLAME FOR THAT ON HIMSELF...?!
OH, ONE MORE THING...
DON'T TELL THE OTHERS ABOUT THIS.
THE ONLY ONES WHO KNOW ABOUT THE KEGARE CURSE AND THE TRUTH BEHIND HINATSUKI ARE...
...ME, ARIMA, A FEW OF THE TWELVE GUARDIANS AND THE OLD MAN AT SEIKA DORM.
WHAT ...?
WHY DID YOU LET ME IN ON THE SECRET THEN...?!
Huh?
WHAT ARE YOU TALKING ABOUT?

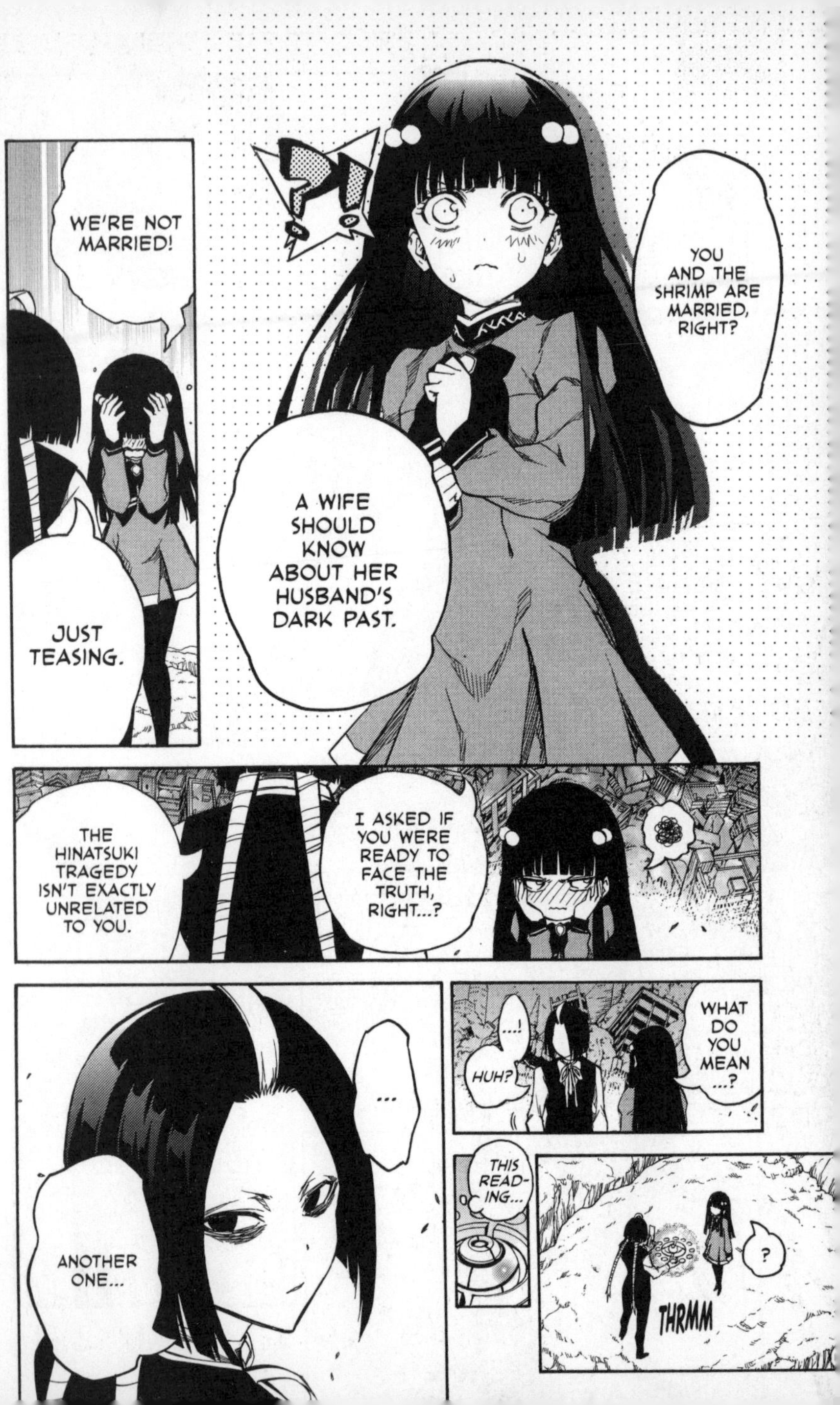
YOU AND THE SHRIMP ARE MARRIED, RIGHT?
A WIFE SHOULD KNOW ABOUT HER HUSBAND'S DARK PAST.
WE'RE NOT MARRIED!
JUST TEASING.
I ASKED IF YOU WERE READY TO FACE THE TRUTH, RIGHT...?
THE HINATSUKI TRAGEDY ISN'T EXACTLY UNRELATED TO YOU.
WHAT DO YOU MEAN ...?
...!
HUH?
?
THRMM
THIS READING...
...
ANOTHER ONE...

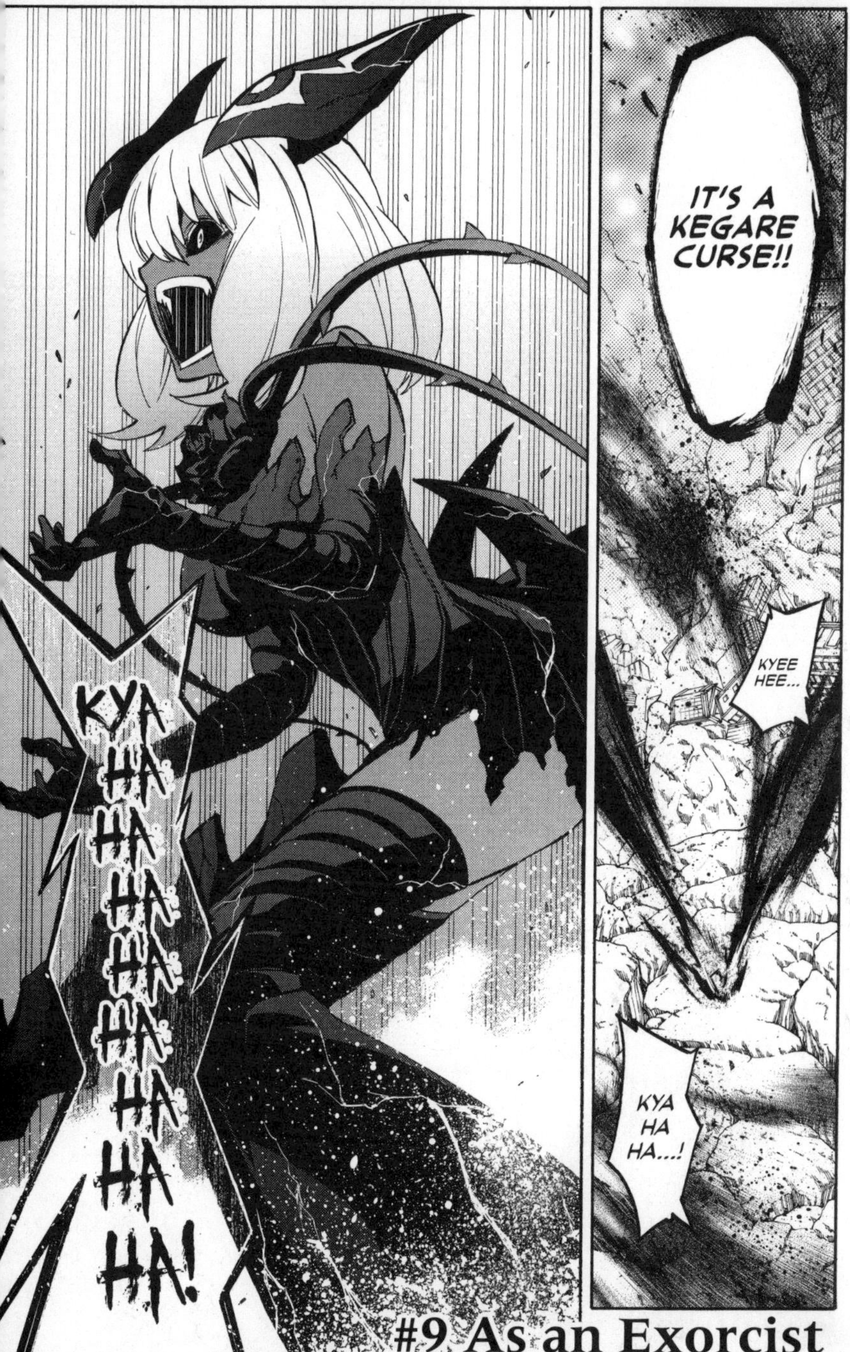
IT'S A KEGARE CURSE!!
KYEE HEE...
KYA HA HA...!
KYA HA HA HA HA HA HA HA HA!

#9 As an Exorcist

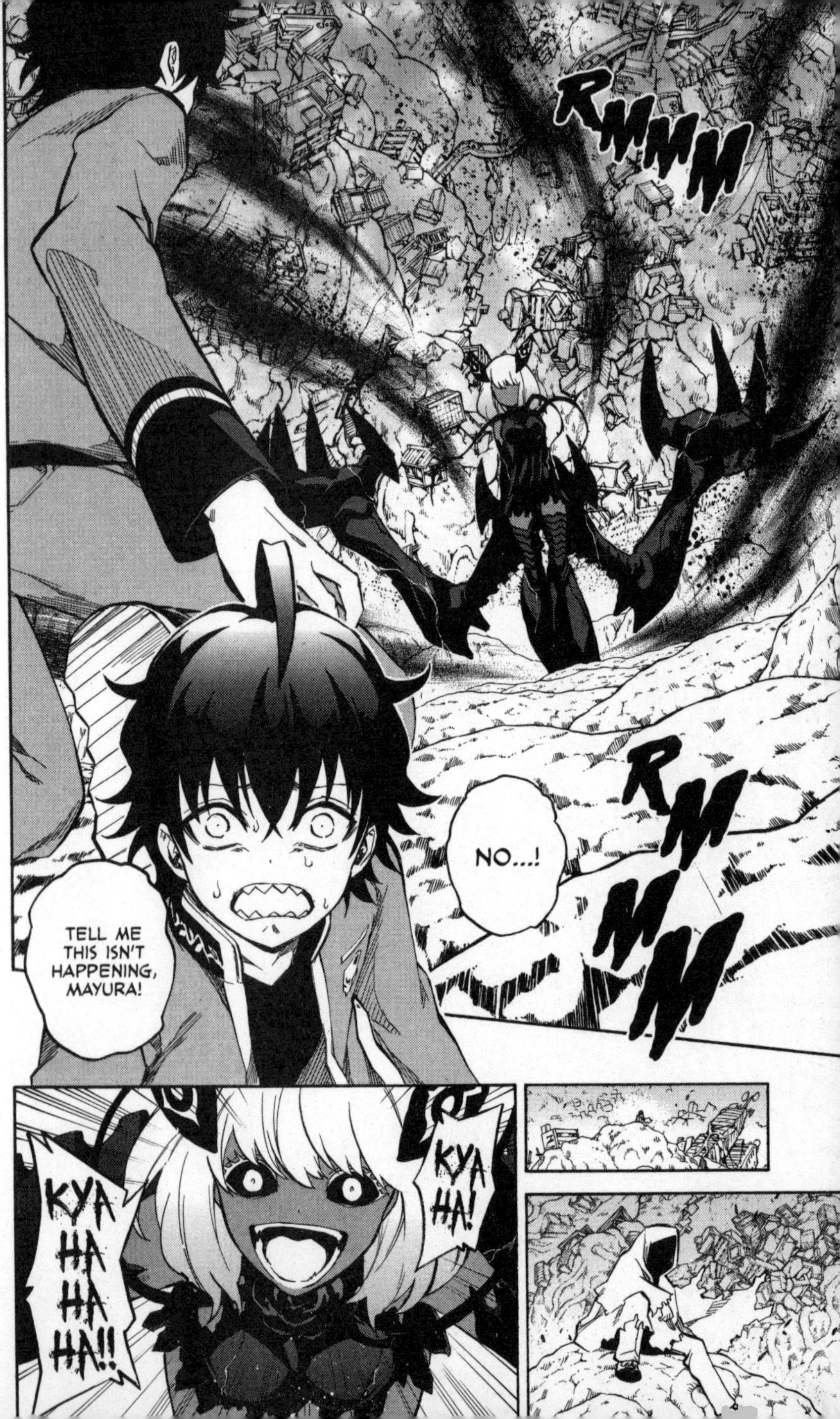
RMMM
RMMMM
NO...!
TELL ME THIS ISN'T HAPPENING, MAYURA!
KYA HA!
KYA HA HA HA HA!!

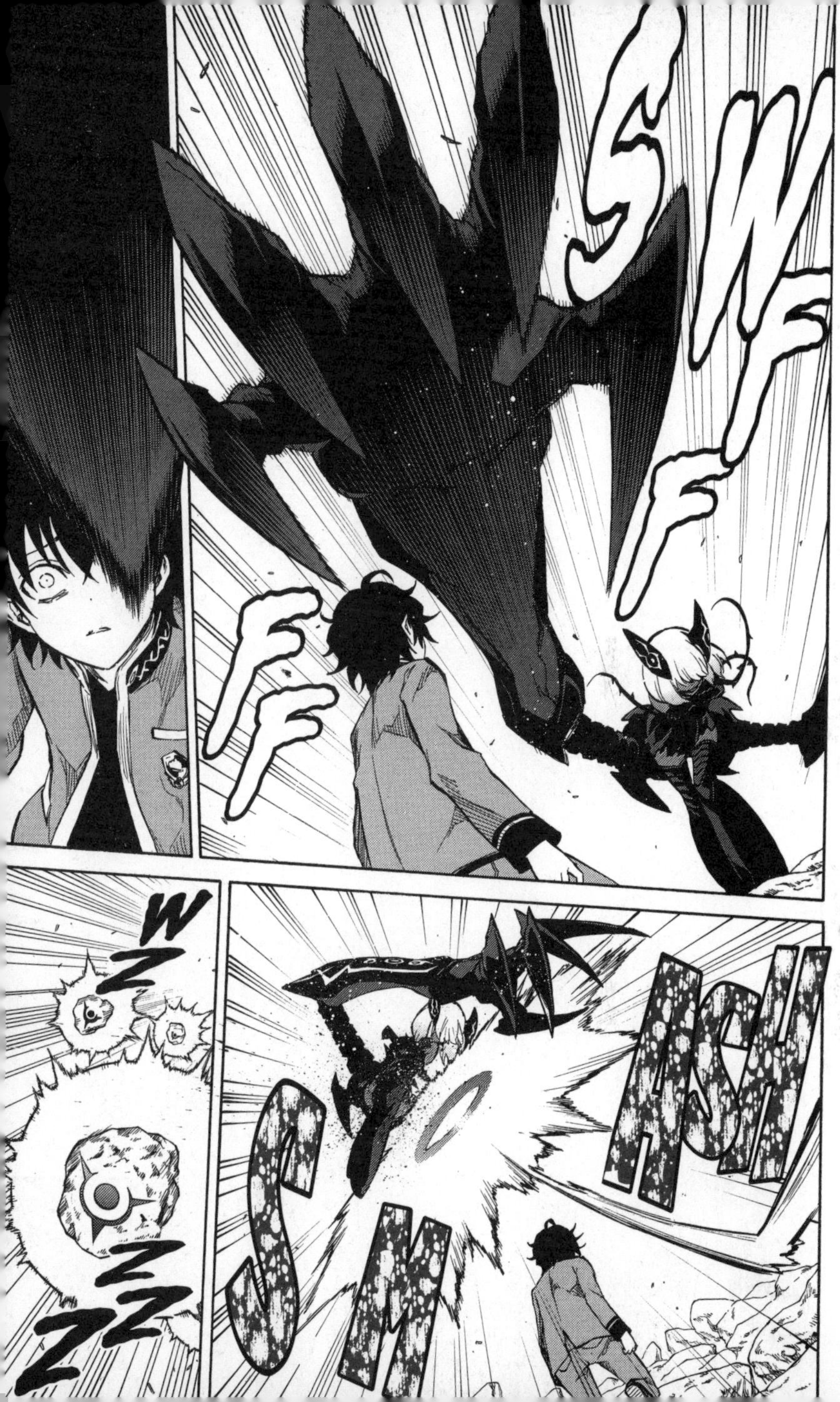
SWFF
SMASH
WZZZZZ

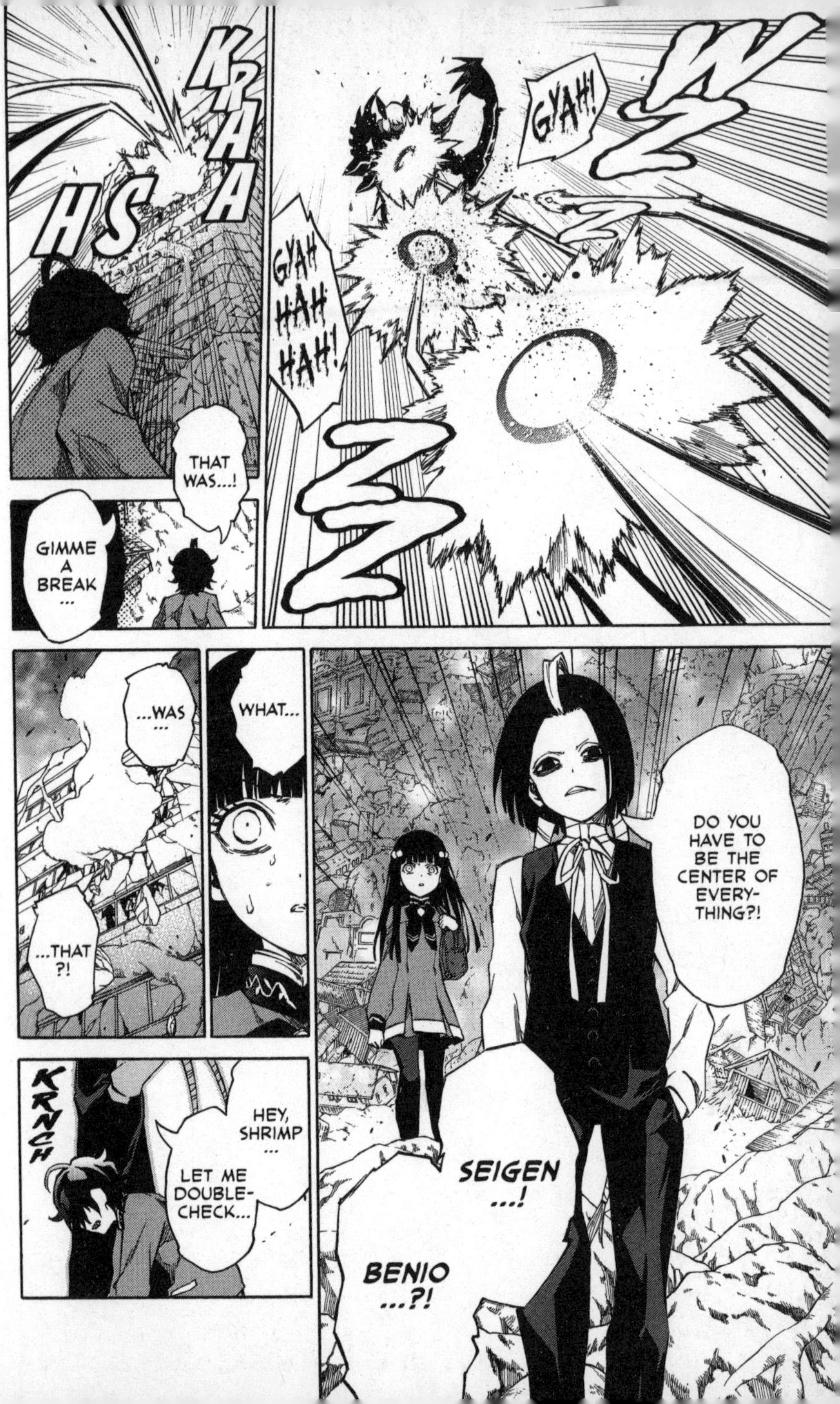
WZ
GYAH!
GYAH HAH HAH!
ZZ
KRAAA
HS
THAT WAS...!
GIMME A BREAK...
DO YOU HAVE TO BE THE CENTER OF EVERYTHING?!
SEIGEN...!
BENIO...?!
WHAT...
...WAS...
...THAT?!
KRNCH
HEY, SHRIMP...
LET ME DOUBLE-CHECK...

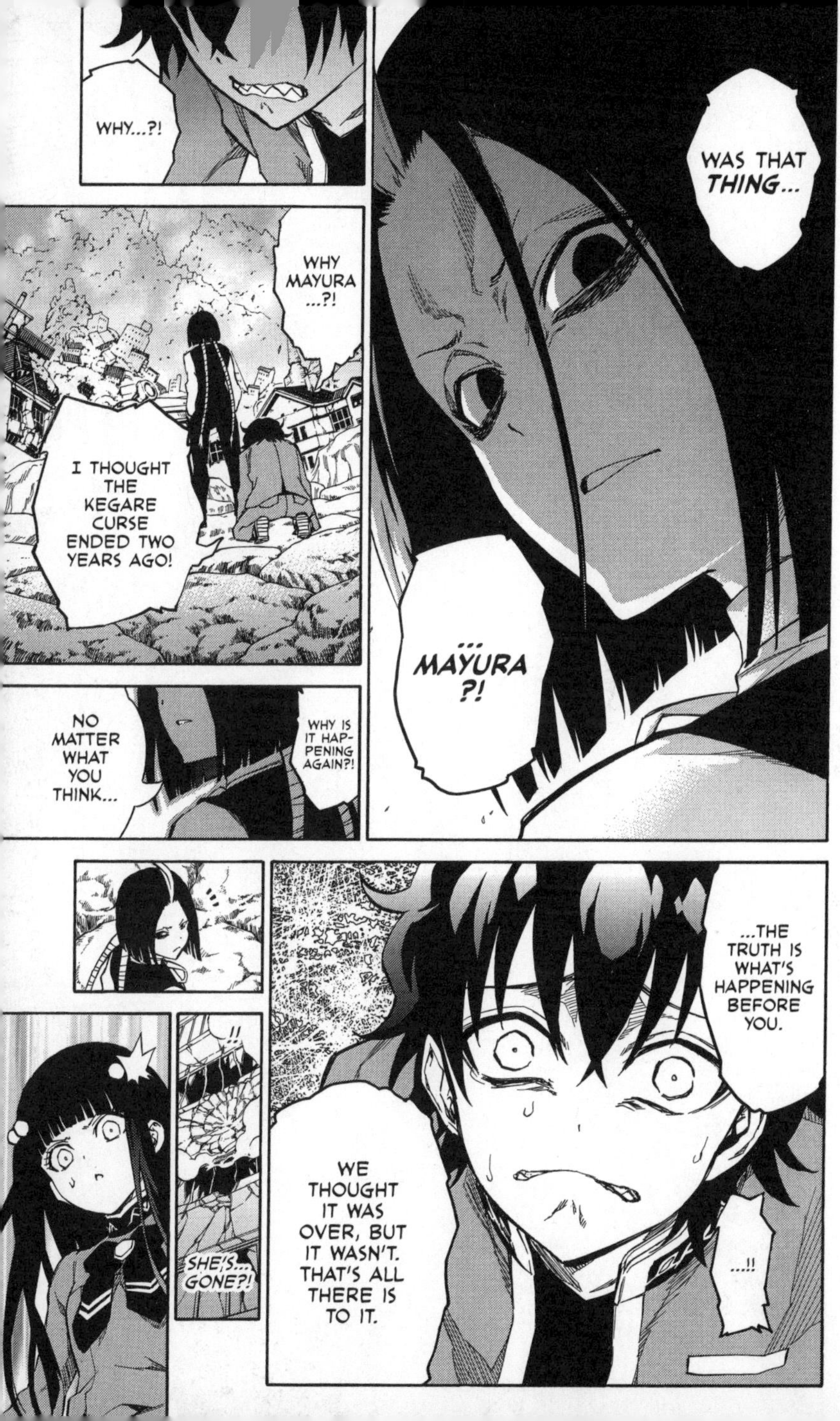
WAS THAT THING...
...MAYURA?!
WHY...?!
WHY MAYURA...?!
I THOUGHT THE KEGARE CURSE ENDED TWO YEARS AGO!
WHY IS IT HAPPENING AGAIN?!
NO MATTER WHAT YOU THINK...
...THE TRUTH IS WHAT'S HAPPENING BEFORE YOU.
WE THOUGHT IT WAS OVER, BUT IT WASN'T. THAT'S ALL THERE IS TO IT.
...!!
!!
SHE'S... GONE?!

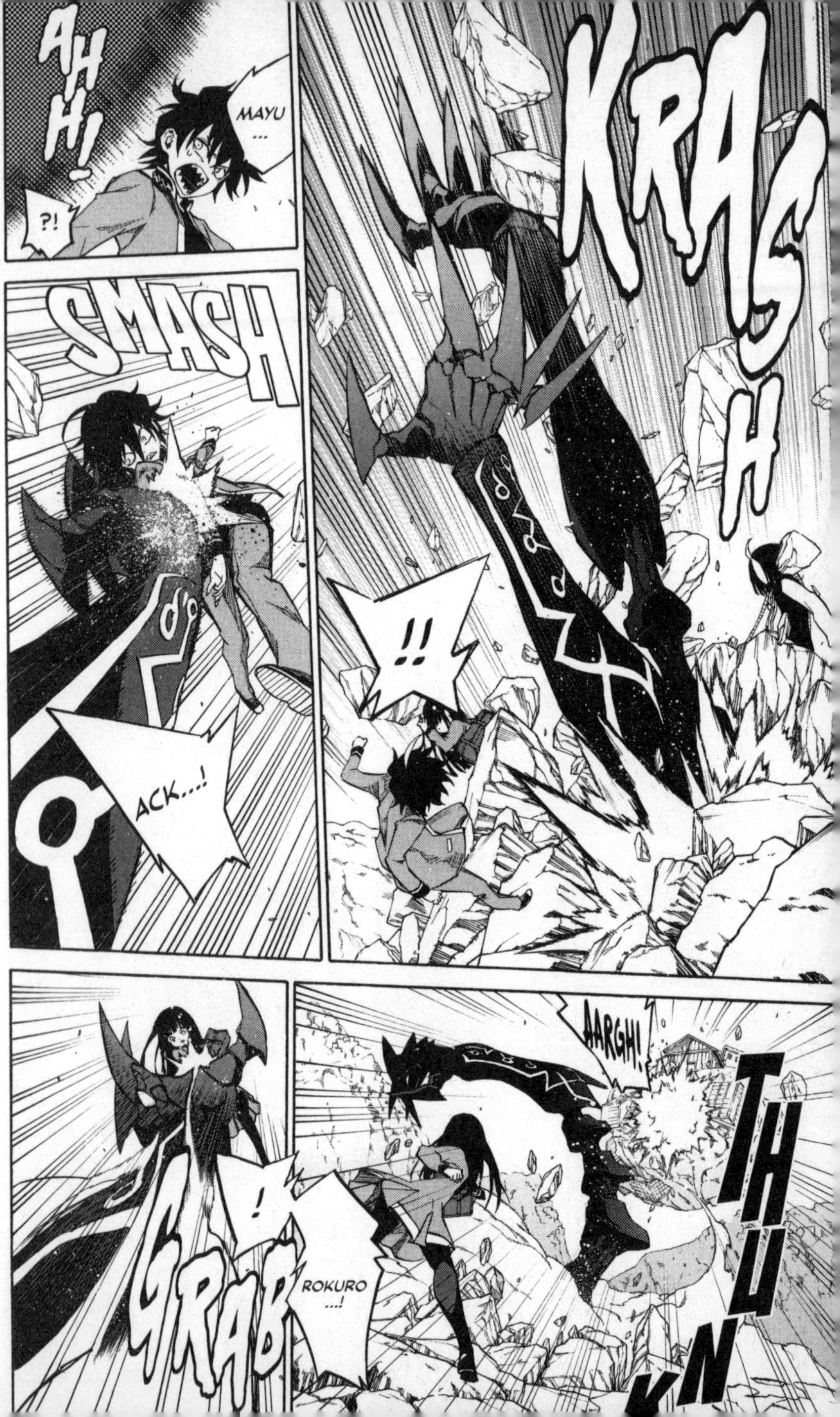
KRASSH
!!
MAYU ...
AHH!
?!
SMASH
ACK...!
THUNK
AARGH!
ROKURO ...!
!
GRAB

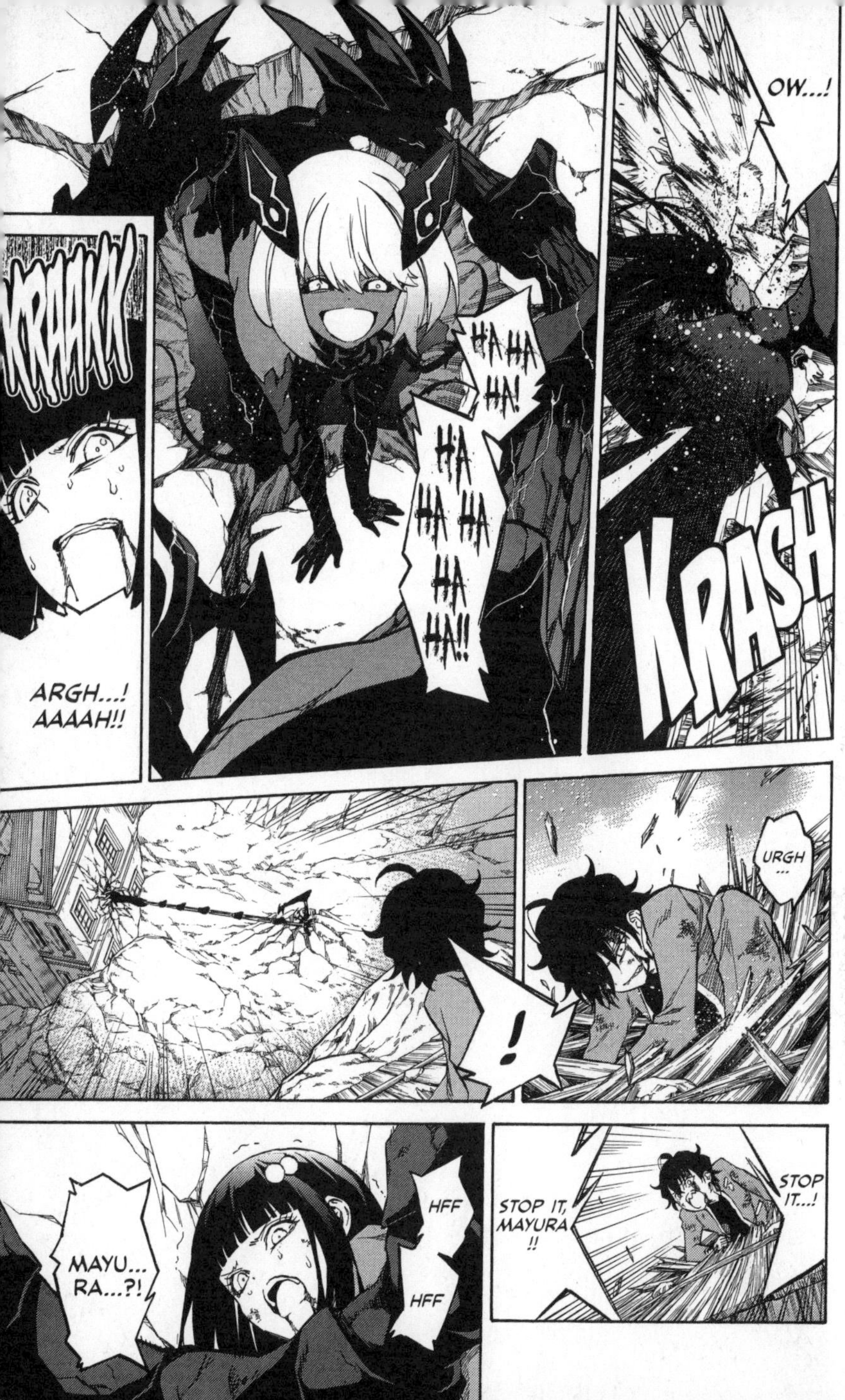
OW...!
KRASH!!
HA HA HA!
HA HA HA HA HA HA!!
KRAAKK
ARGH...! AAAAH!!
URGH...
!
STOP IT...!
STOP IT, MAYURA!!
HFF
MAYU... RA...?!
HFF

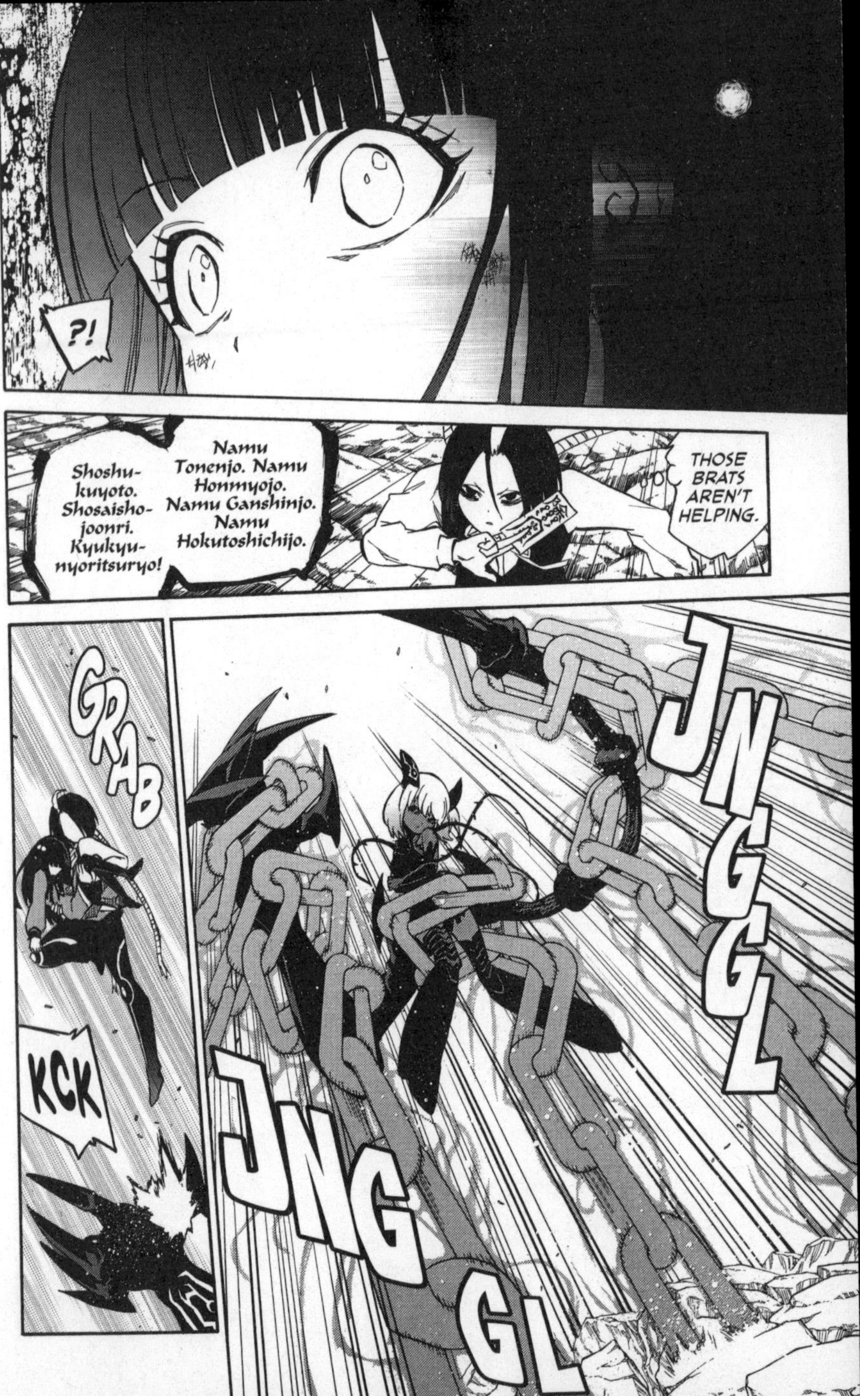
?!
THOSE BRATS AREN'T HELPING.
Namu Tonenjo. Namu Honmyojo. Namu Ganshinjo. Namu Hokutoshichijo.
Shoshukuyoto. Shosaishojoonri. Kyukyunyoritsuryo!
JINGGL
JNG GL
GRAB
KCK

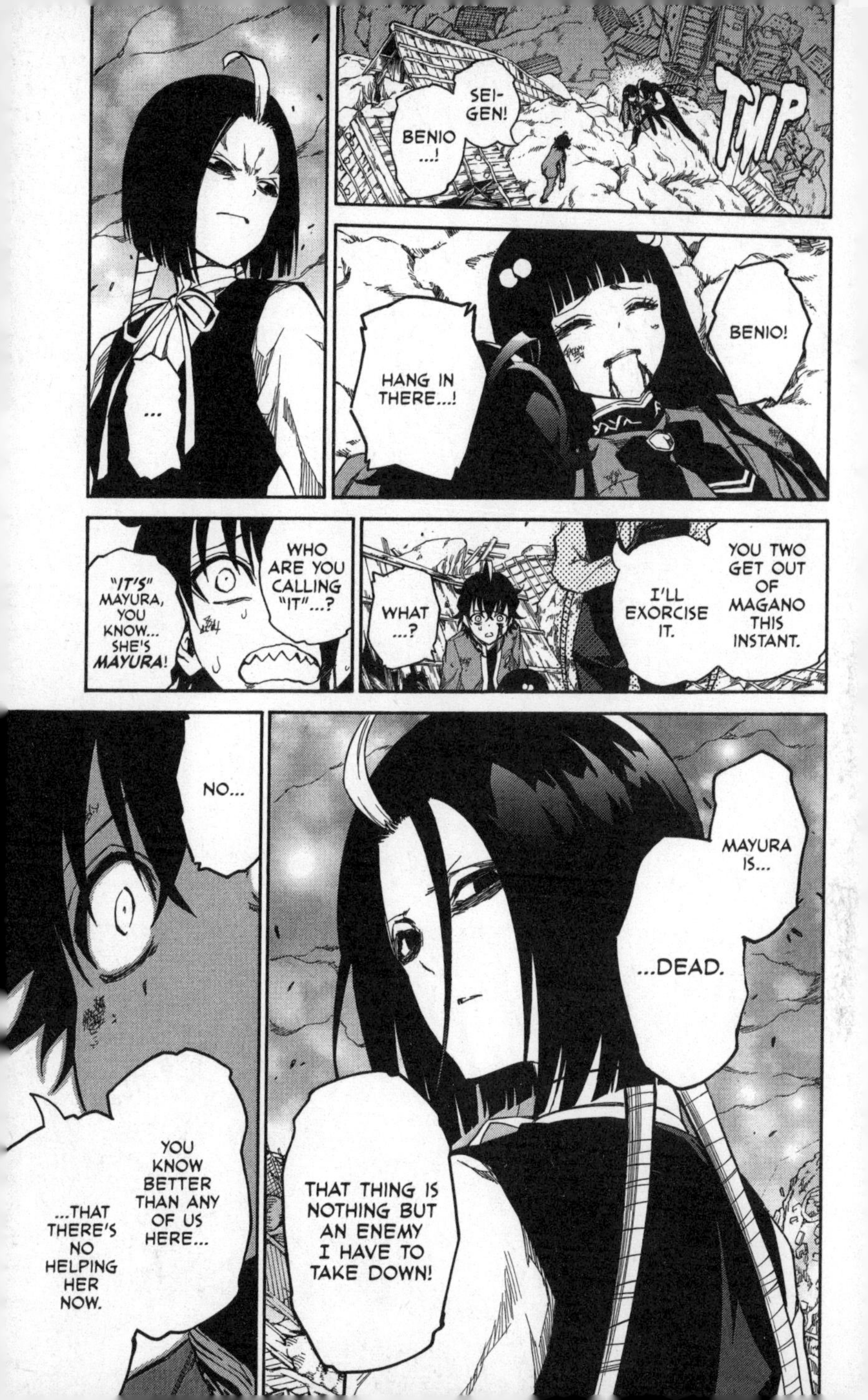
TMP
SEI-GEN!
BENIO ...!
BENIO!
HANG IN THERE...!
...
YOU TWO GET OUT OF MAGANO THIS INSTANT.
I'LL EXORCISE IT.
WHAT ...?
WHO ARE YOU CALLING "IT"...?
"*IT'S*" MAYURA, YOU KNOW... SHE'S ***MAYURA***!
MAYURA IS...
...DEAD.
THAT THING IS NOTHING BUT AN ENEMY I HAVE TO TAKE DOWN!
NO...
YOU KNOW BETTER THAN ANY OF US HERE...
...THAT THERE'S NO HELPING HER NOW.

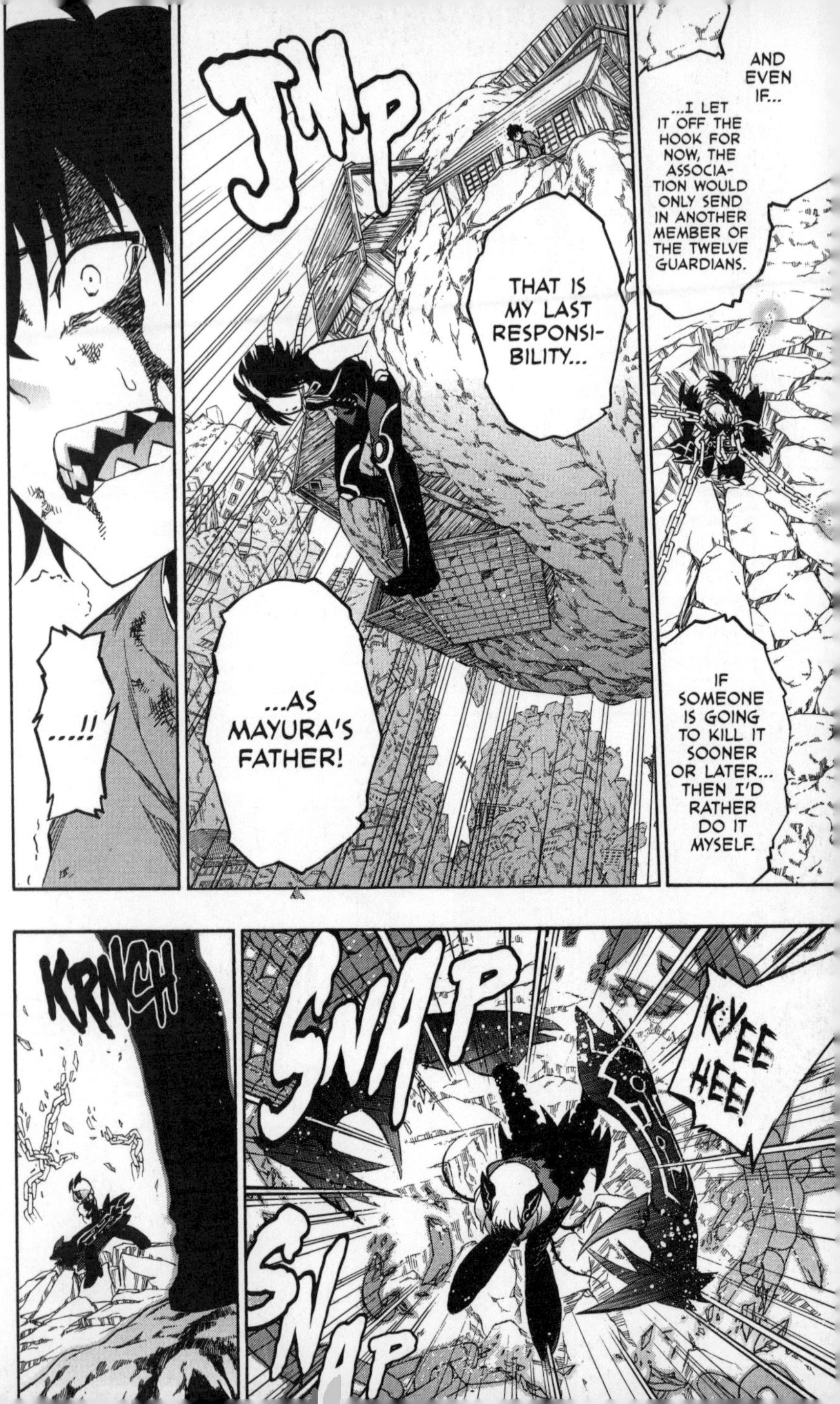
AND EVEN IF...
...I LET IT OFF THE HOOK FOR NOW, THE ASSOCIA-TION WOULD ONLY SEND IN ANOTHER MEMBER OF THE TWELVE GUARDIANS.
IF SOMEONE IS GOING TO KILL IT SOONER OR LATER... THEN I'D RATHER DO IT MYSELF.
JMP
THAT IS MY LAST RESPONSI-BILITY...
...AS MAYURA'S FATHER!
...!!
KYEE HEE!
SNAP
SNAP
SNAP
KRNCH

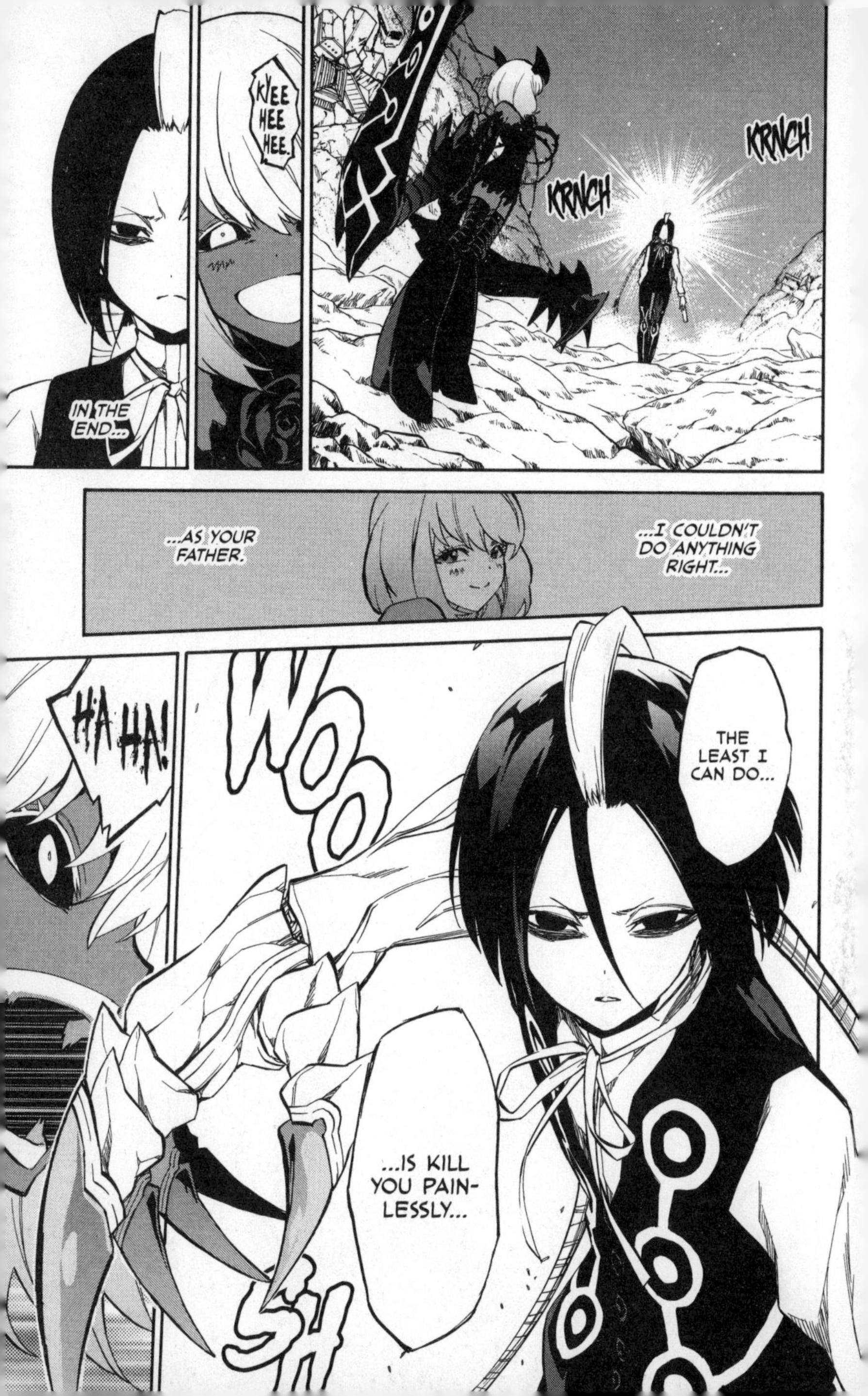
KRNCH
KRNCH
KYEE HEE HEE.
IN THE END...
...I COULDN'T DO ANYTHING RIGHT...
...AS YOUR FATHER.
THE LEAST I CAN DO...
...IS KILL YOU PAINLESSLY...
WOOOSH
HA HA!

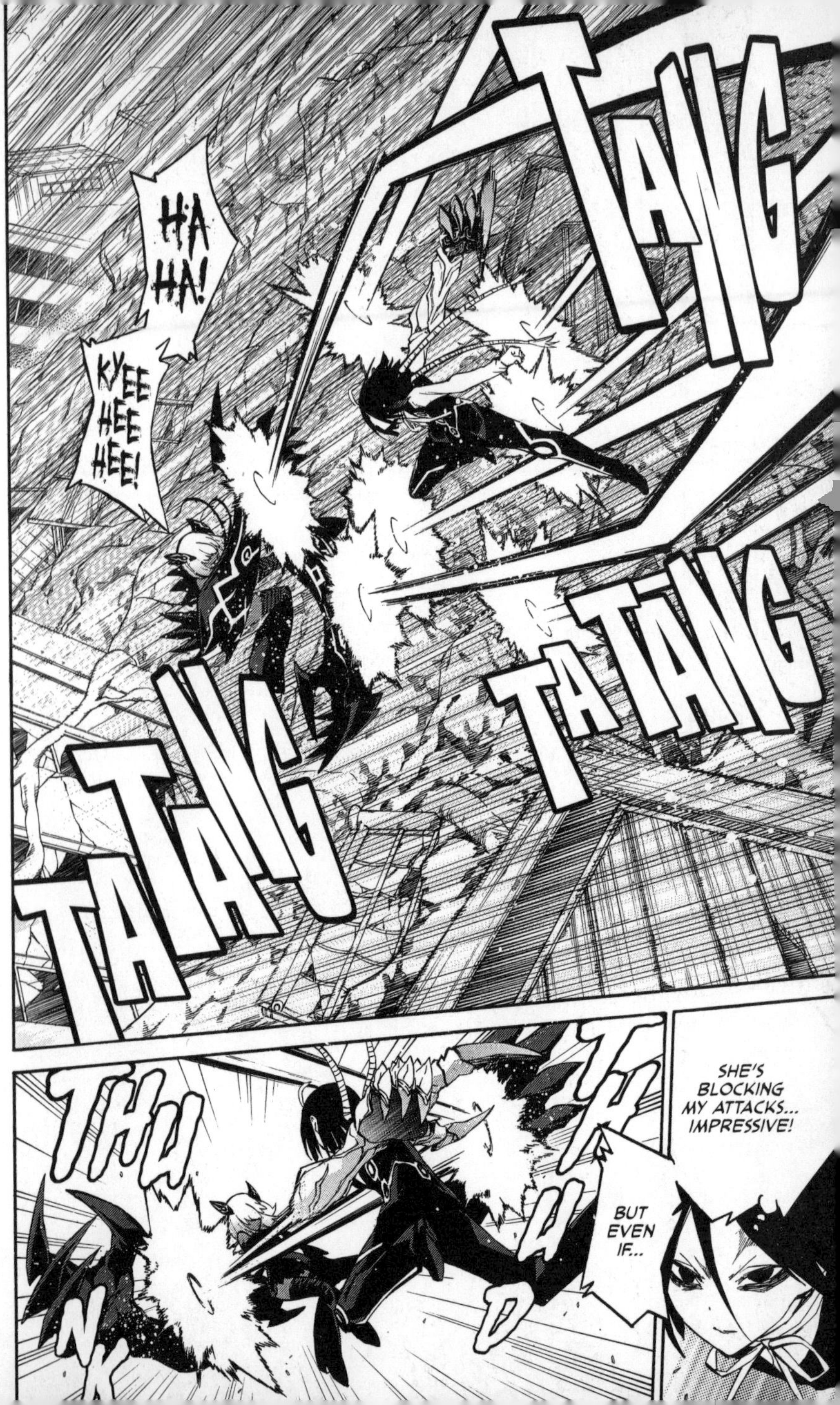
TANG
HA HA!
KYEE HEE HEE HEE!
TA TANG
TA TANG
SHE'S BLOCKING MY ATTACKS... IMPRESSIVE!
THUD
BUT EVEN IF...
THUNK

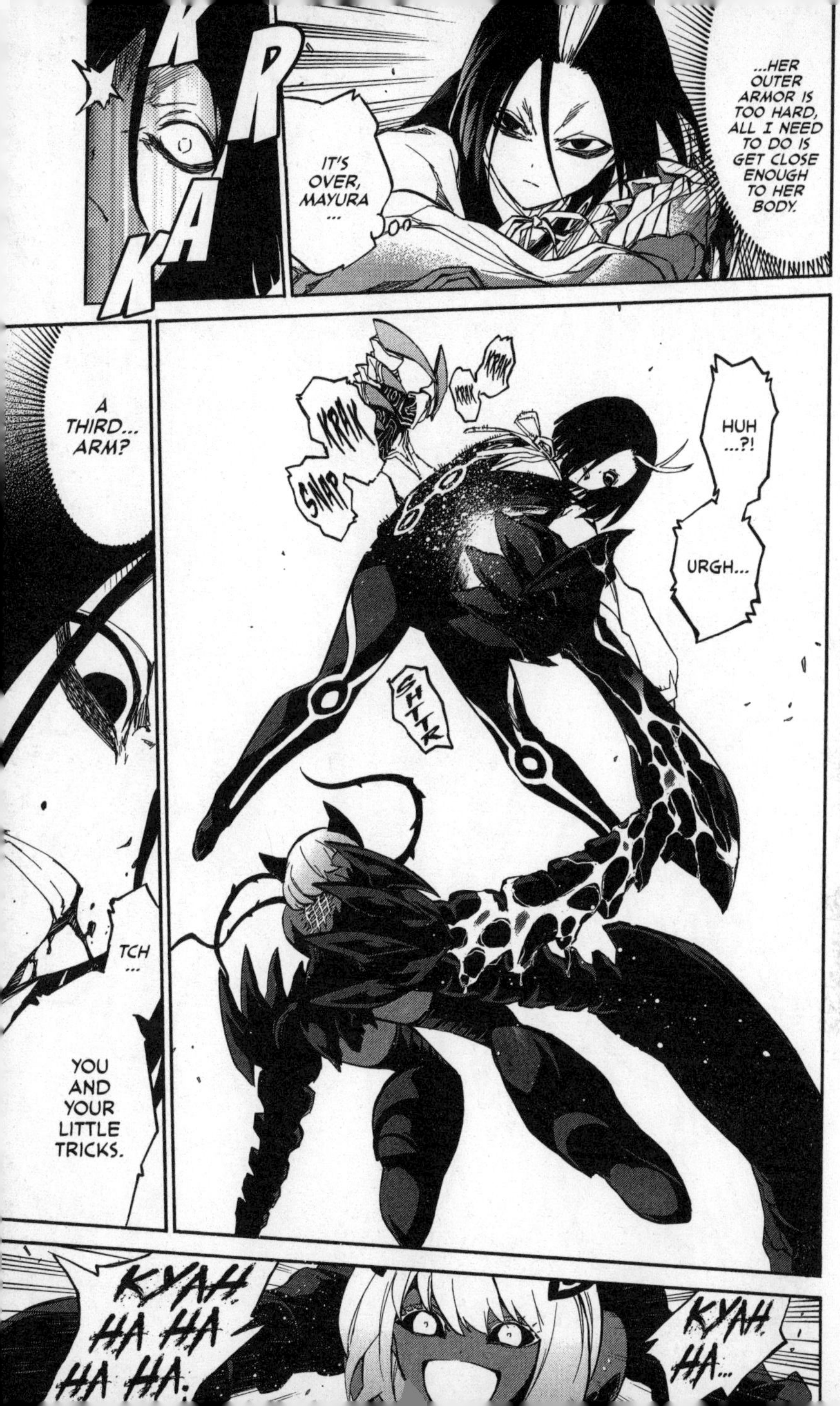
...HER OUTER ARMOR IS TOO HARD, ALL I NEED TO DO IS GET CLOSE ENOUGH TO HER BODY.
IT'S OVER, MAYURA...
KRAKK
KRAK
KRAK
KRAK
SNAP
HUH...?!
URGH...
SHTTK
A THIRD... ARM?
TCH...
YOU AND YOUR LITTLE TRICKS.
KYAH HA...
KYAH HA HA HA HA HA.

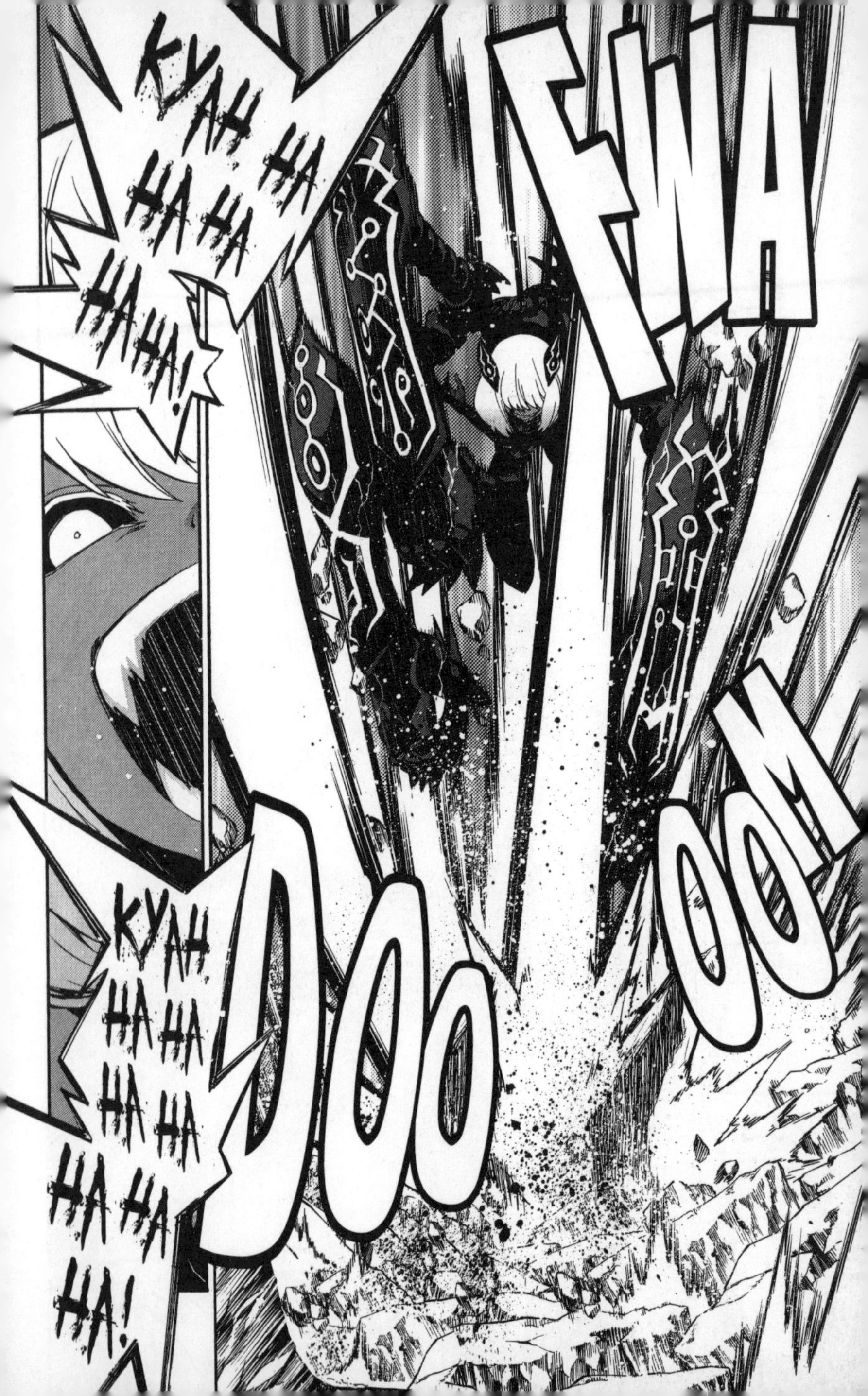
FWA
KYAH HA HA HA HA HA!
DOOOOOM!
KYAH HA HA HA HA HA HA HA!

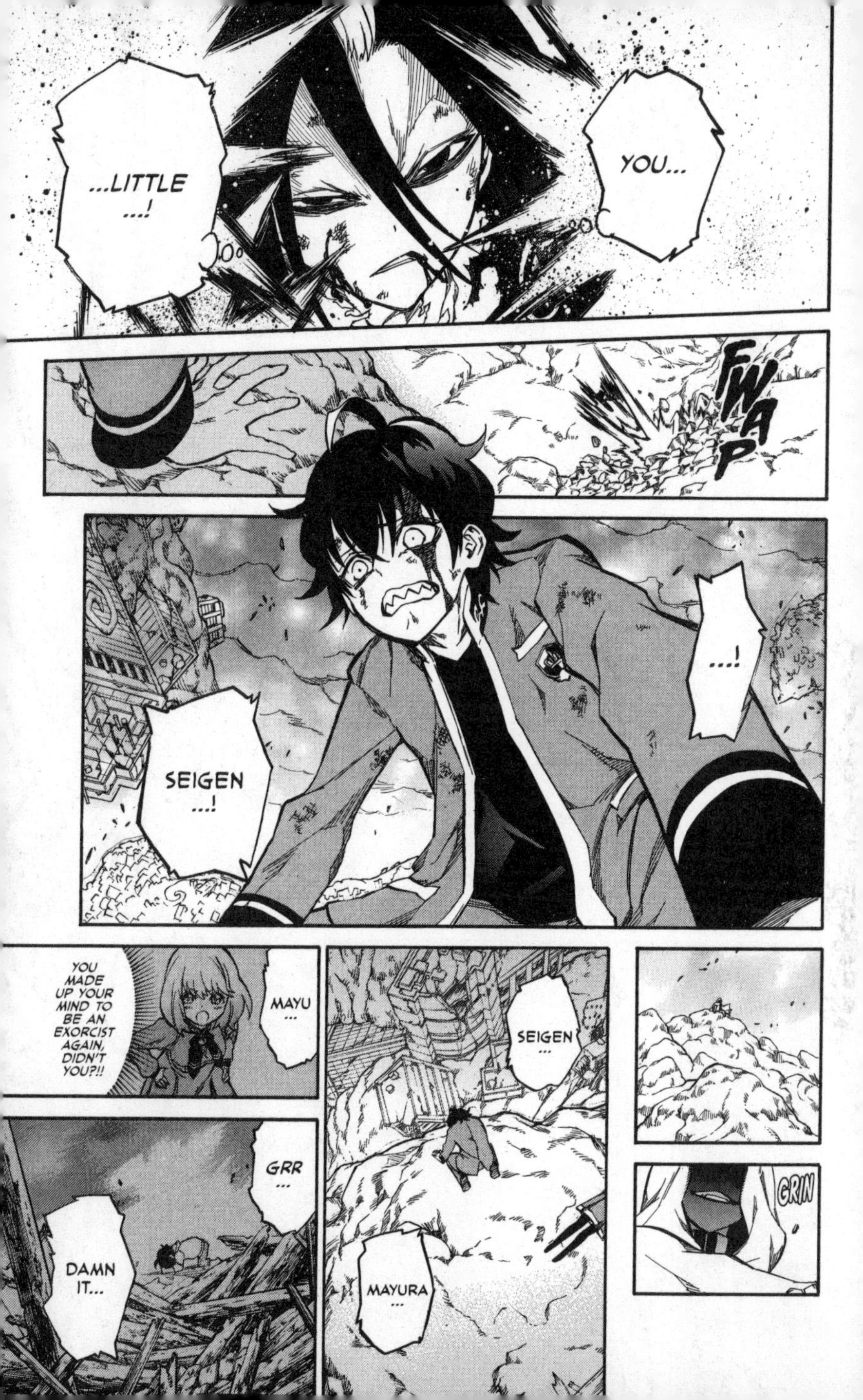
YOU...
...LITTLE ...!
FWAP
...!
SEIGEN ...!
GRIN
SEIGEN ...
MAYURA ...
MAYU ...
YOU MADE UP YOUR MIND TO BE AN EXORCIST AGAIN, DIDN'T YOU?!!
GRR ...
DAMN IT...

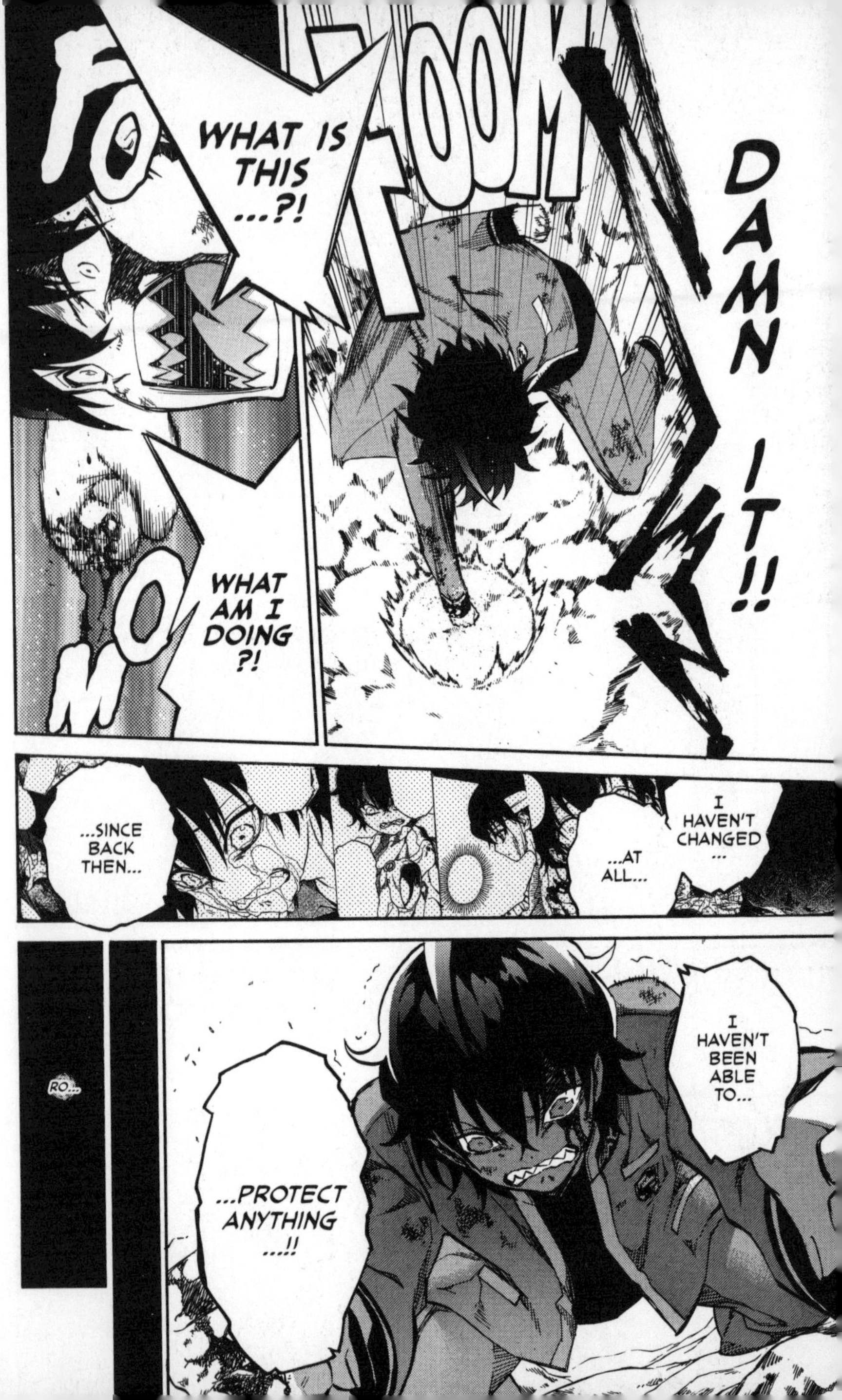

FOOM
DAMN IT!!
WHAT IS THIS ...?!
WHAT AM I DOING ?!
I HAVEN'T CHANGED ...
...AT ALL...
...SINCE BACK THEN...
I HAVEN'T BEEN ABLE TO...
...PROTECT ANYTHING ...!!
RO...

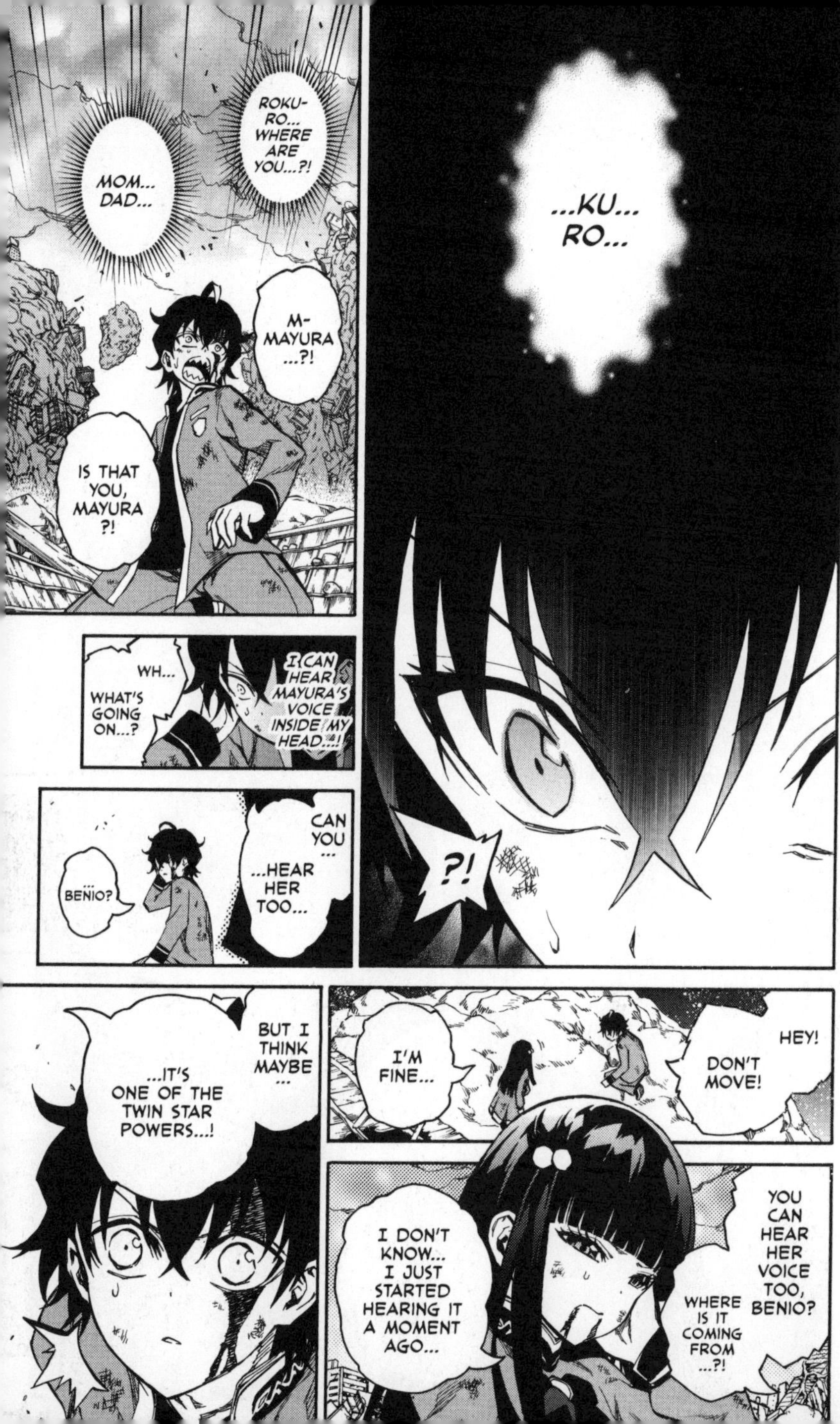
...KU... RO...
?!
ROKURO... WHERE ARE YOU...?!
MOM... DAD...
M-MAYURA...?!
IS THAT YOU, MAYURA?!
I CAN HEAR MAYURA'S VOICE INSIDE MY HEAD...!
WH... WHAT'S GOING ON...?
CAN YOU ...HEAR HER TOO...
...BENIO?
HEY! DON'T MOVE!
I'M FINE...
YOU CAN HEAR HER VOICE TOO, BENIO?
WHERE IS IT COMING FROM...?!
I DON'T KNOW... I JUST STARTED HEARING IT A MOMENT AGO...
BUT I THINK MAYBE...
...IT'S ONE OF THE TWIN STAR POWERS...!

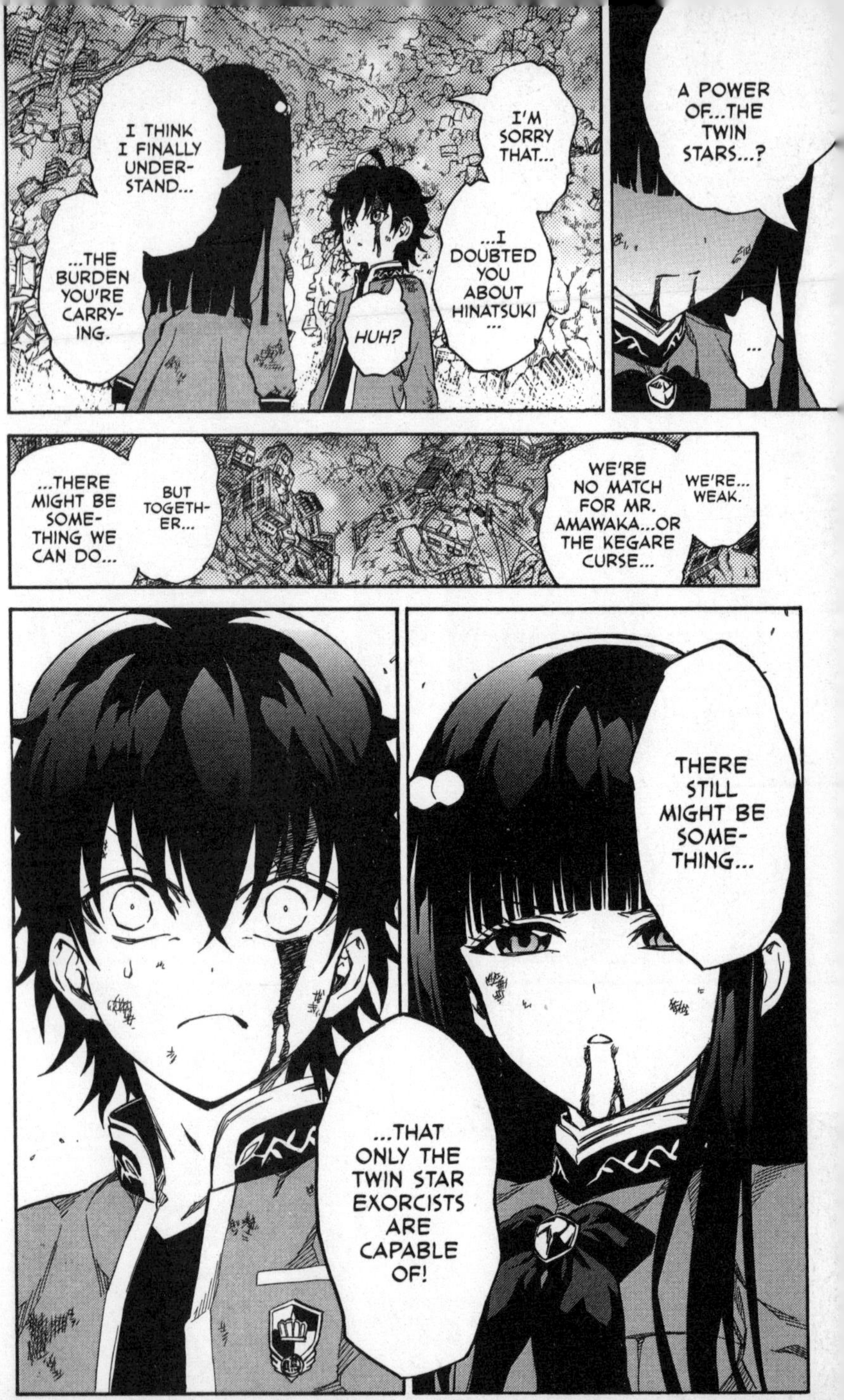

A POWER OF...THE TWIN STARS...?
...
I'M SORRY THAT...
...I DOUBTED YOU ABOUT HINATSUKI ...
HUH?
I THINK I FINALLY UNDER-STAND...
...THE BURDEN YOU'RE CARRY-ING.
WE'RE... WEAK.
WE'RE NO MATCH FOR MR. AMAWAKA...OR THE KEGARE CURSE...
BUT TOGETH-ER...
...THERE MIGHT BE SOME-THING WE CAN DO...
THERE STILL MIGHT BE SOME-THING...
...THAT ONLY THE TWIN STAR EXORCISTS ARE CAPABLE OF!

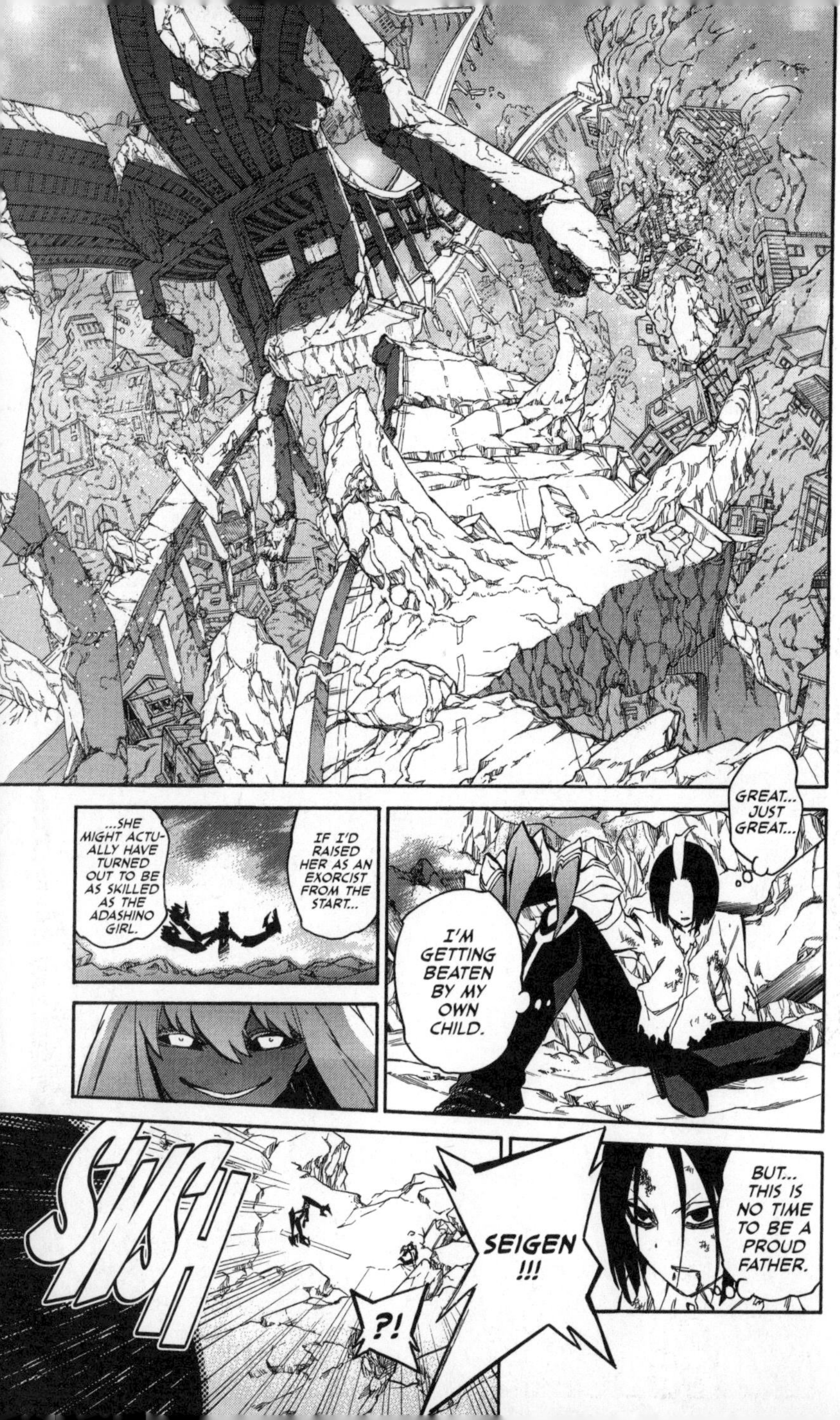
GREAT... JUST GREAT...
I'M GETTING BEATEN BY MY OWN CHILD.
IF I'D RAISED HER AS AN EXORCIST FROM THE START...
...SHE MIGHT ACTU-ALLY HAVE TURNED OUT TO BE AS SKILLED AS THE ADASHINO GIRL.
BUT... THIS IS NO TIME TO BE A PROUD FATHER.
SEIGEN !!!
?!
SWSH

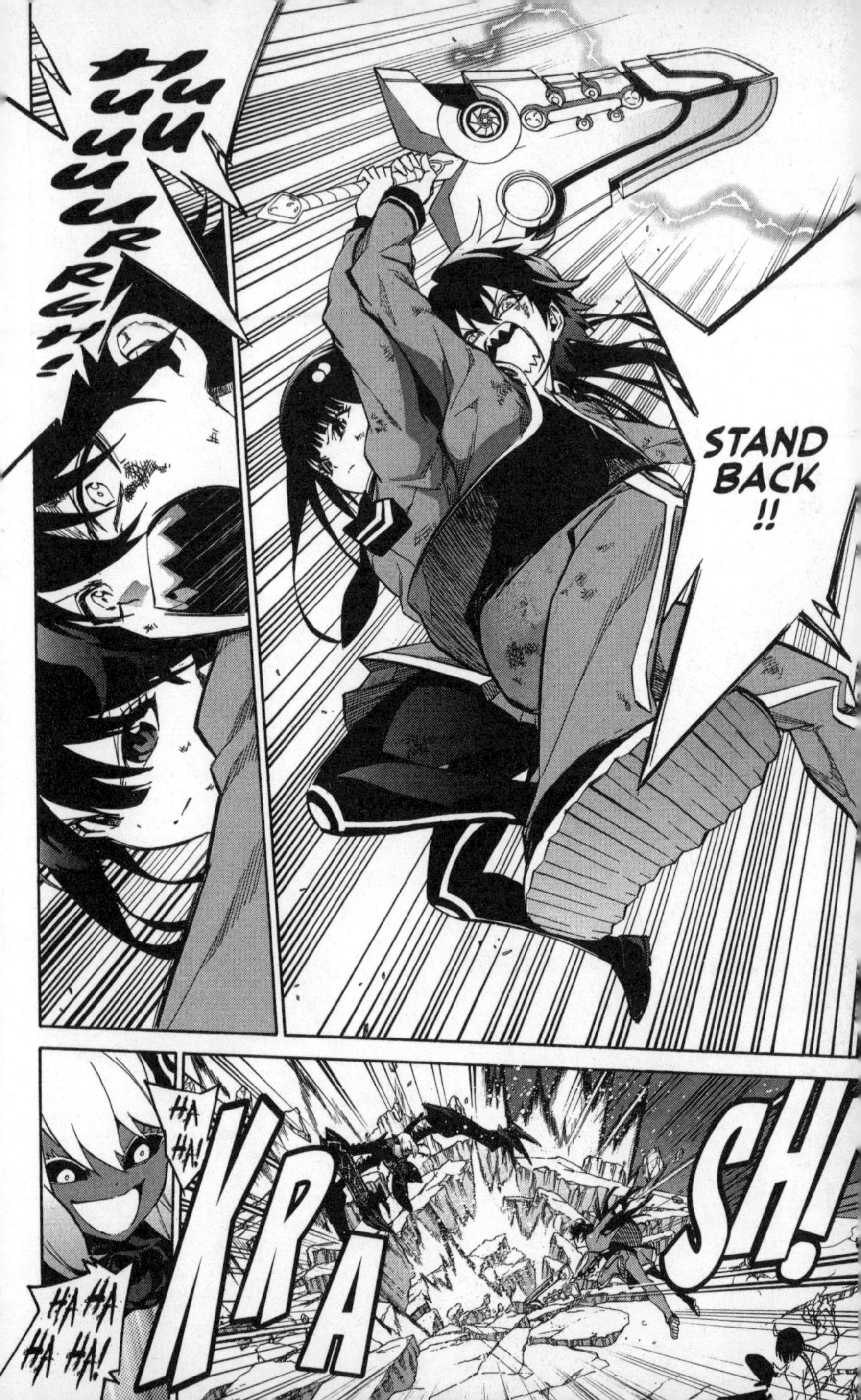
STAND BACK !!
HUUUUURRGH!!
KRASH!
HA HA!
HA HA HA HA!

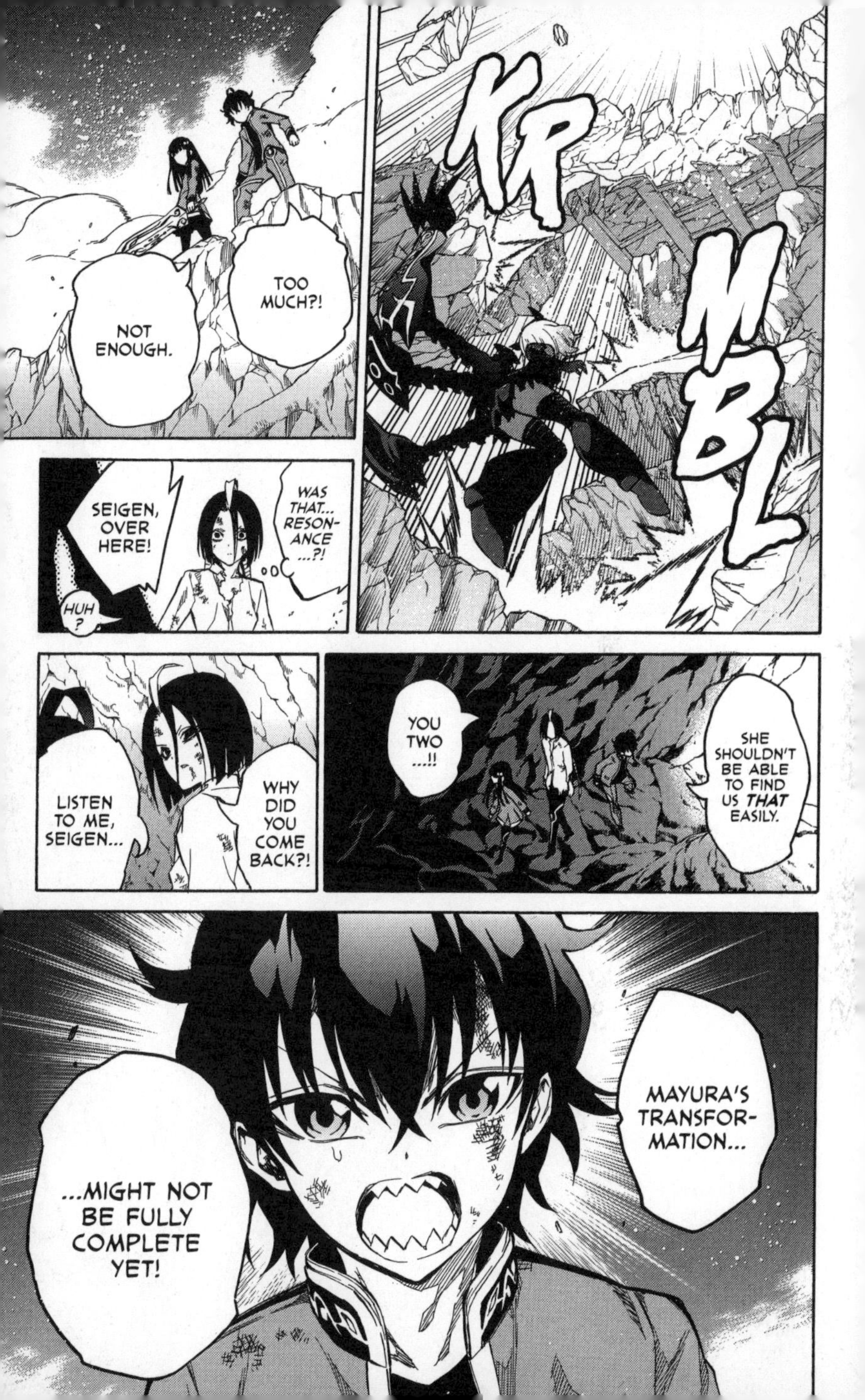
KRMBL
TOO MUCH?!
NOT ENOUGH.
WAS THAT... RESONANCE...?!
SEIGEN, OVER HERE!
HUH?
SHE SHOULDN'T BE ABLE TO FIND US *THAT* EASILY.
YOU TWO...!!
WHY DID YOU COME BACK?!
LISTEN TO ME, SEIGEN...
MAYURA'S TRANSFORMATION...
...MIGHT NOT BE FULLY COMPLETE YET!

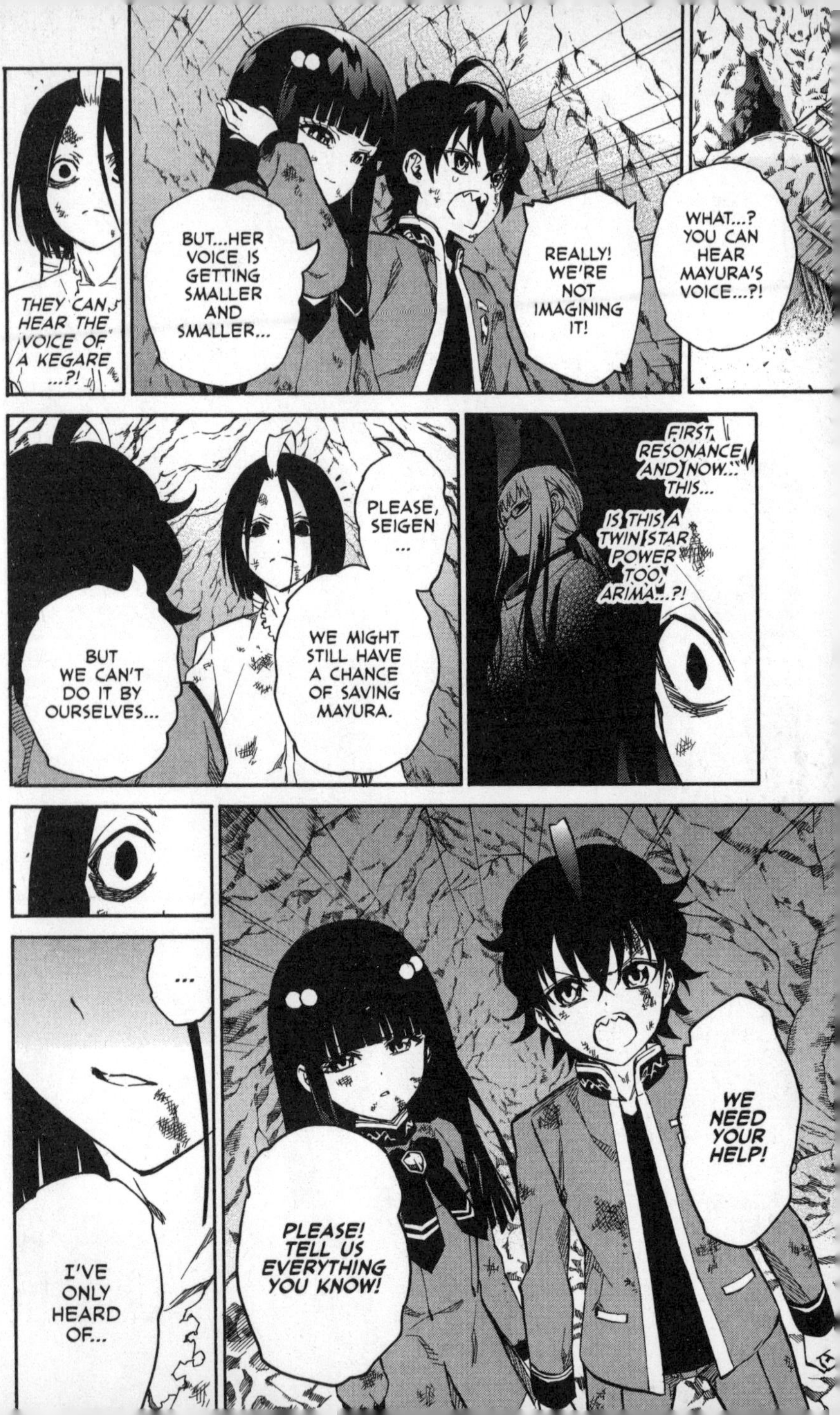
WHAT...? YOU CAN HEAR MAYURA'S VOICE...?!
REALLY! WE'RE NOT IMAGINING IT!
BUT...HER VOICE IS GETTING SMALLER AND SMALLER...
THEY CAN HEAR THE VOICE OF A KEGARE ...?!
FIRST, RESONANCE AND NOW... THIS...
IS THIS A TWIN STAR POWER TOO, ARIMA...?!
PLEASE, SEIGEN ...
WE MIGHT STILL HAVE A CHANCE OF SAVING MAYURA.
BUT WE CAN'T DO IT BY OURSELVES...
WE NEED YOUR HELP!
PLEASE! TELL US EVERYTHING YOU KNOW!
...
I'VE ONLY HEARD OF...

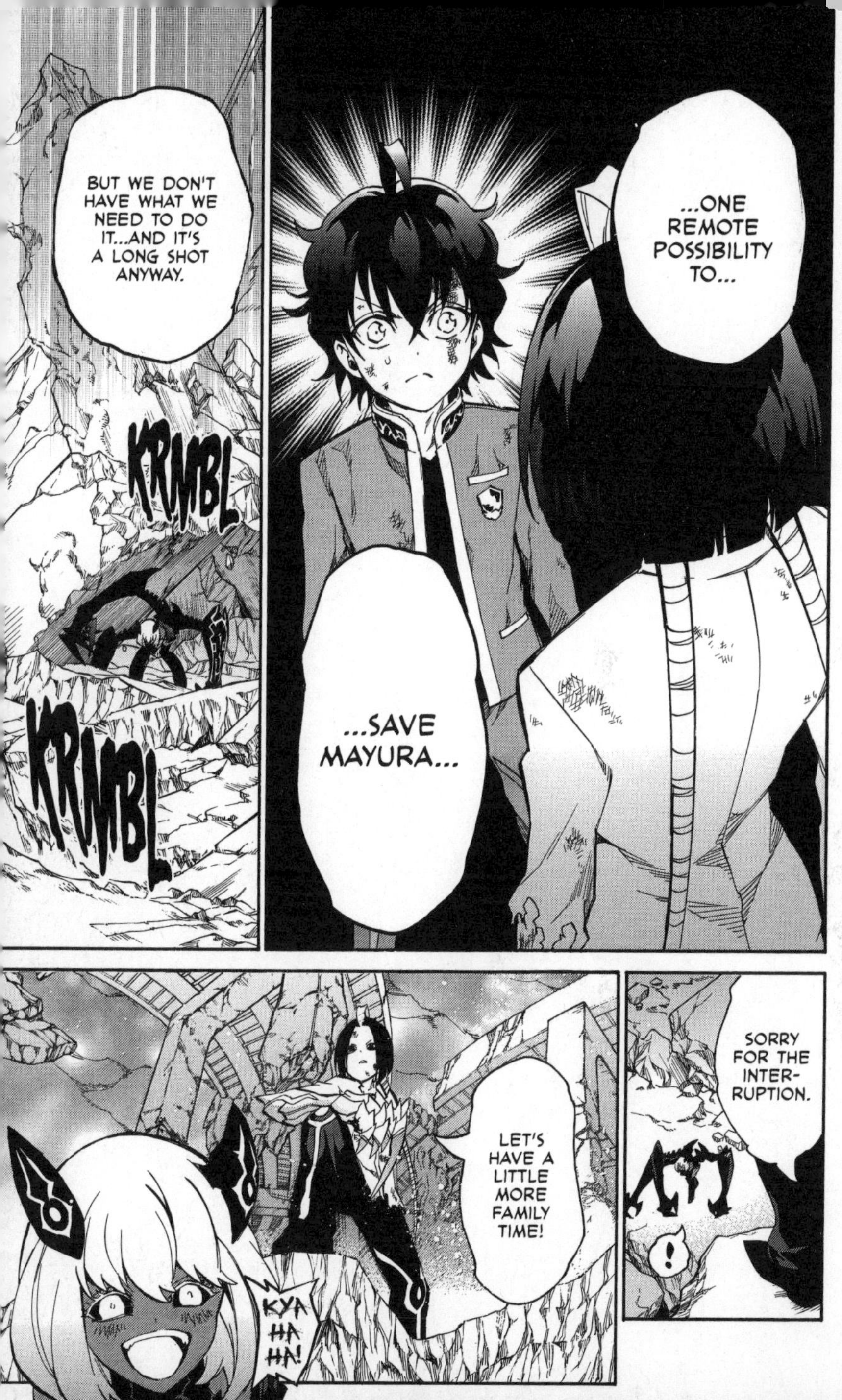
...ONE REMOTE POSSIBILITY TO...
...SAVE MAYURA...
BUT WE DON'T HAVE WHAT WE NEED TO DO IT...AND IT'S A LONG SHOT ANYWAY.
KRMBL
KRMBL
SORRY FOR THE INTER-RUPTION.
!
LET'S HAVE A LITTLE MORE FAMILY TIME!
KYA HA HA!

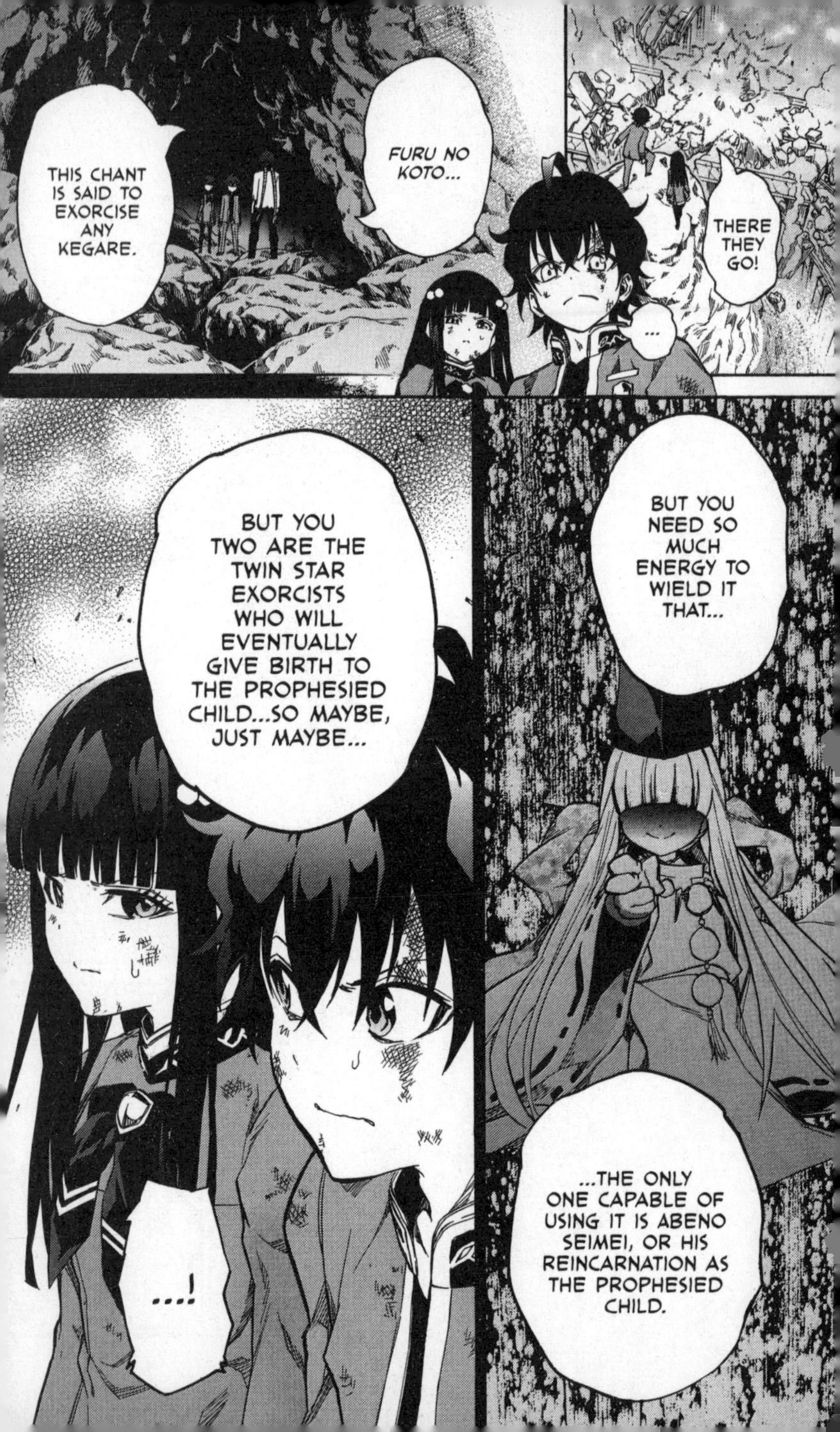
THERE THEY GO!
...
FURU NO KOTO...
THIS CHANT IS SAID TO EXORCISE ANY KEGARE.
BUT YOU NEED SO MUCH ENERGY TO WIELD IT THAT...
...THE ONLY ONE CAPABLE OF USING IT IS ABENO SEIMEI, OR HIS REINCARNATION AS THE PROPHESIED CHILD.
BUT YOU TWO ARE THE TWIN STAR EXORCISTS WHO WILL EVENTUALLY GIVE BIRTH TO THE PROPHESIED CHILD...SO MAYBE, JUST MAYBE...
...!

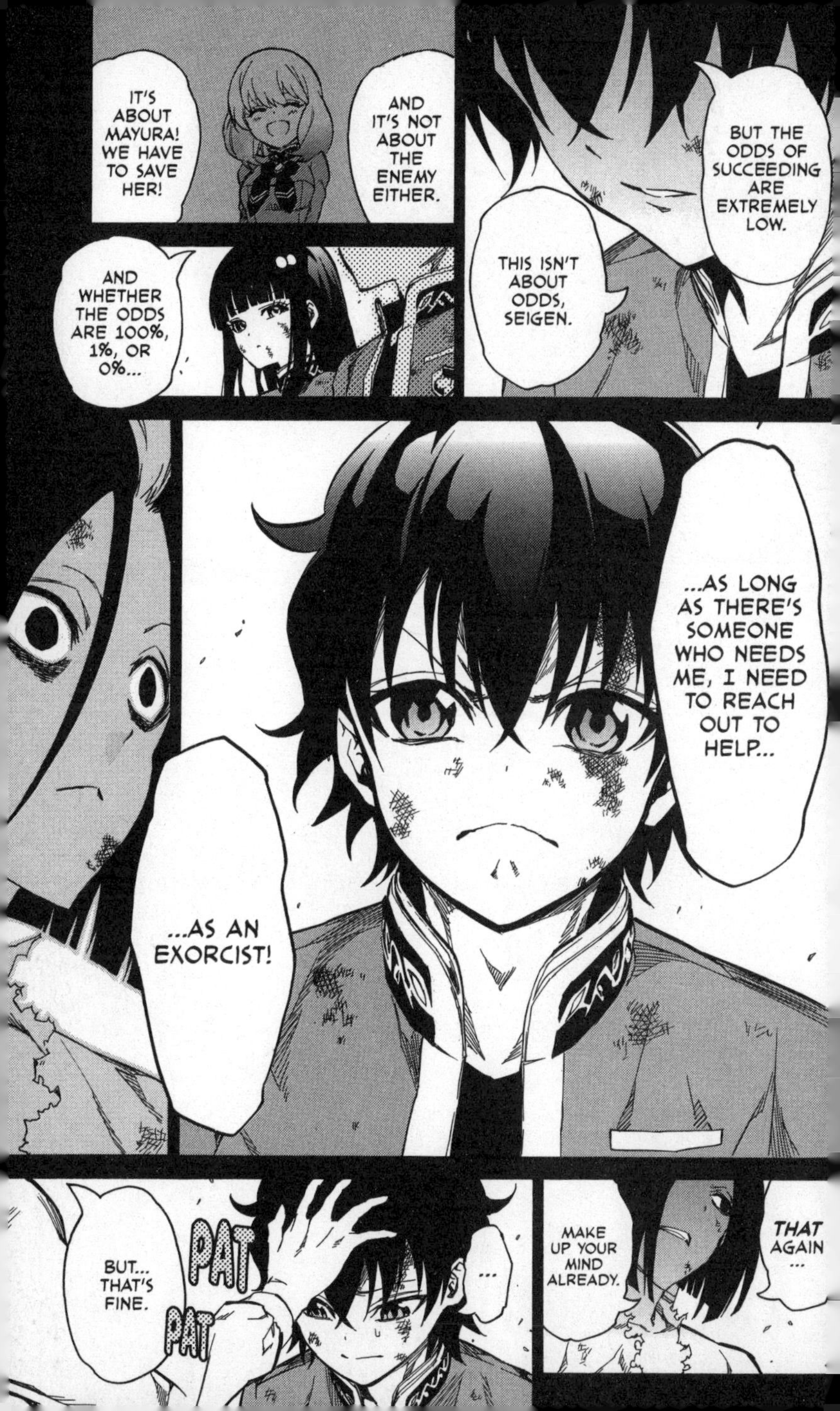
BUT THE ODDS OF SUCCEEDING ARE EXTREMELY LOW.
THIS ISN'T ABOUT ODDS, SEIGEN.
AND IT'S NOT ABOUT THE ENEMY EITHER.
IT'S ABOUT MAYURA! WE HAVE TO SAVE HER!
AND WHETHER THE ODDS ARE 100%, 1%, OR 0%...
...AS LONG AS THERE'S SOMEONE WHO NEEDS ME, I NEED TO REACH OUT TO HELP...
...AS AN EXORCIST!
THAT AGAIN ...
MAKE UP YOUR MIND ALREADY.
...
PAT
PAT
BUT... THAT'S FINE.

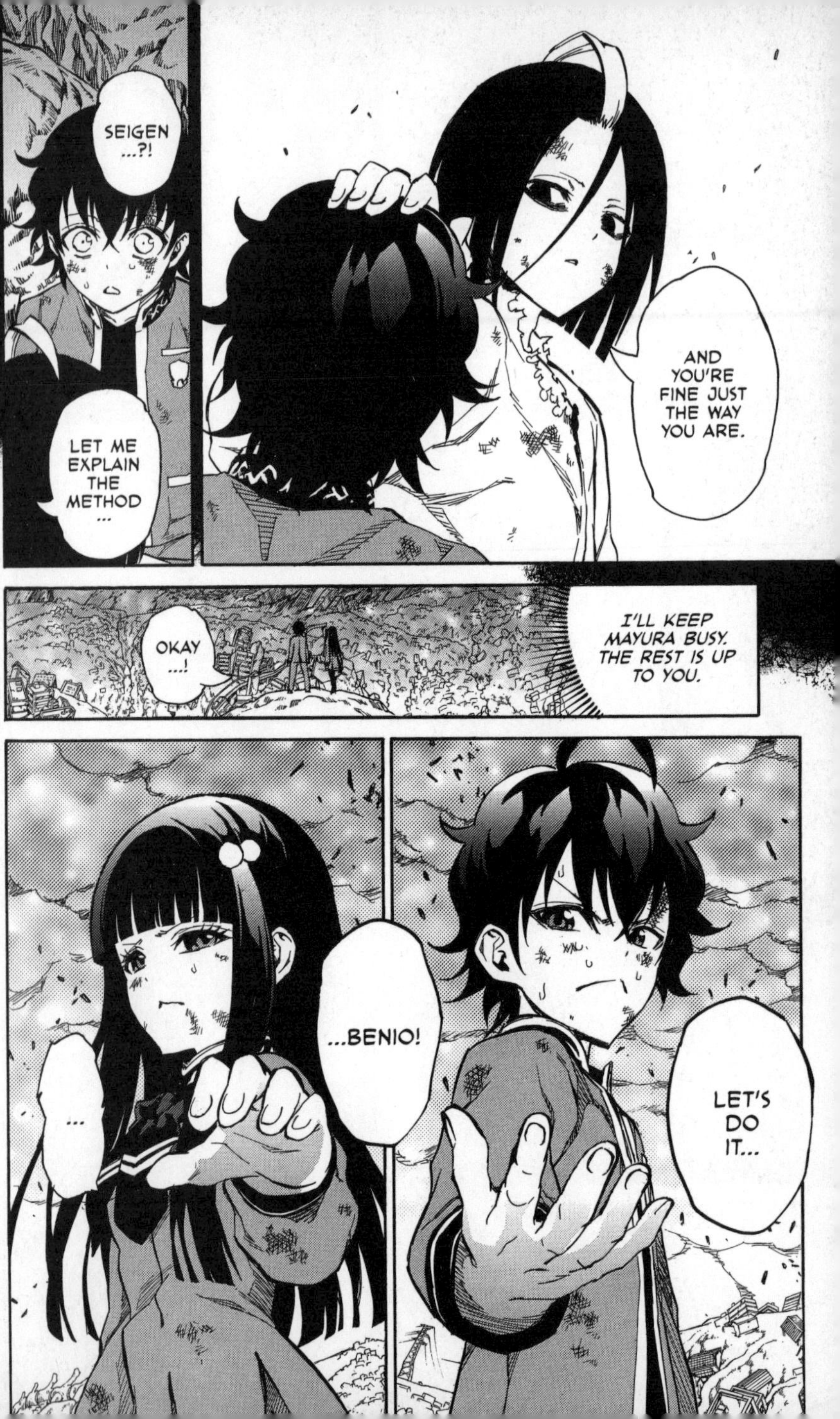
AND YOU'RE FINE JUST THE WAY YOU ARE.
SEIGEN ...?!
LET ME EXPLAIN THE METHOD ...
I'LL KEEP MAYURA BUSY. THE REST IS UP TO YOU.
OKAY ...!
LET'S DO IT...
...BENIO!
...

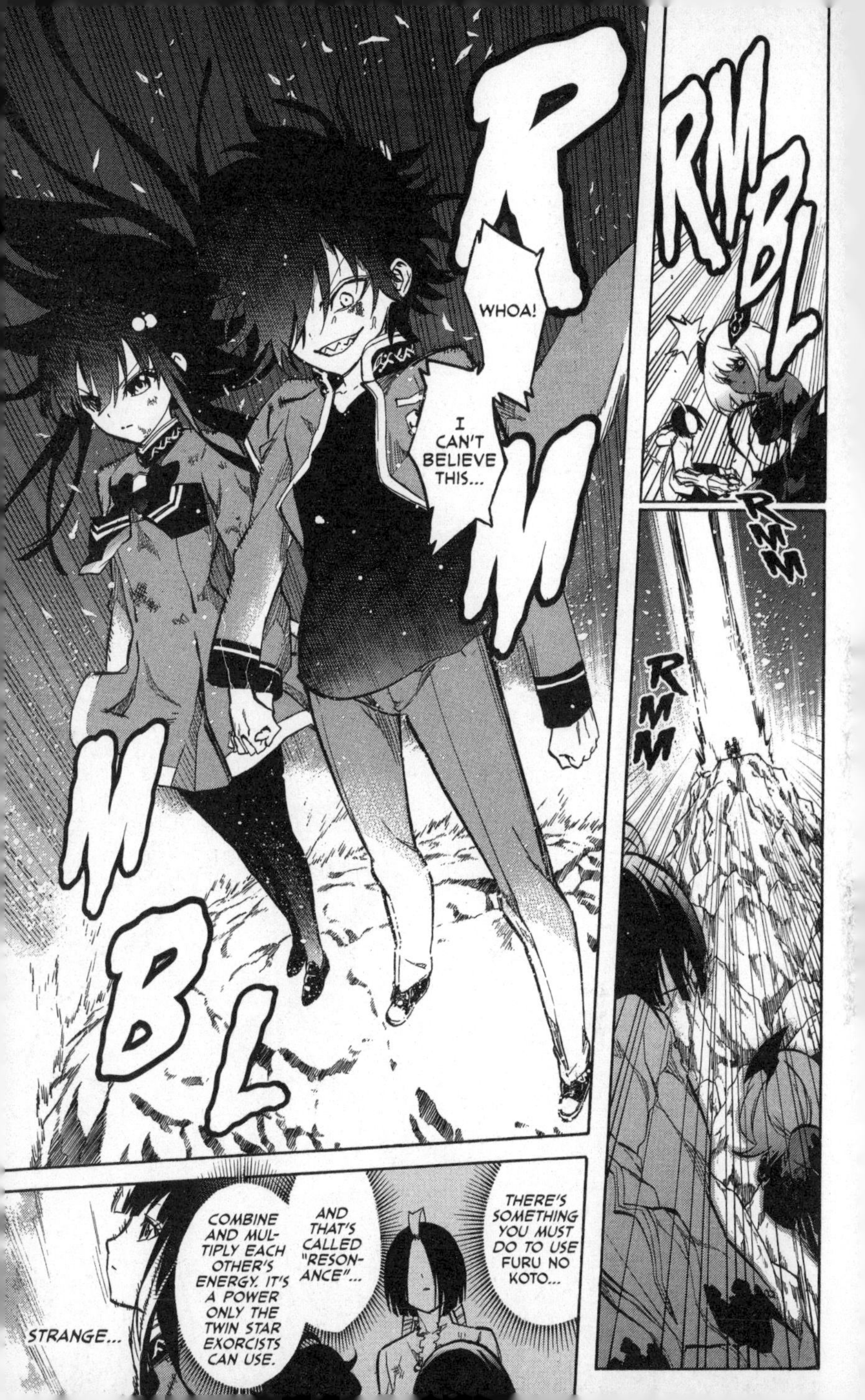
RMBL
RMM
RMM
RMMBL
WHOA!
I CAN'T BELIEVE THIS...
THERE'S SOMETHING YOU MUST DO TO USE FURU NO KOTO...
AND THAT'S CALLED "RESONANCE"...
COMBINE AND MULTIPLY EACH OTHER'S ENERGY. IT'S A POWER ONLY THE TWIN STAR EXORCISTS CAN USE.
STRANGE...

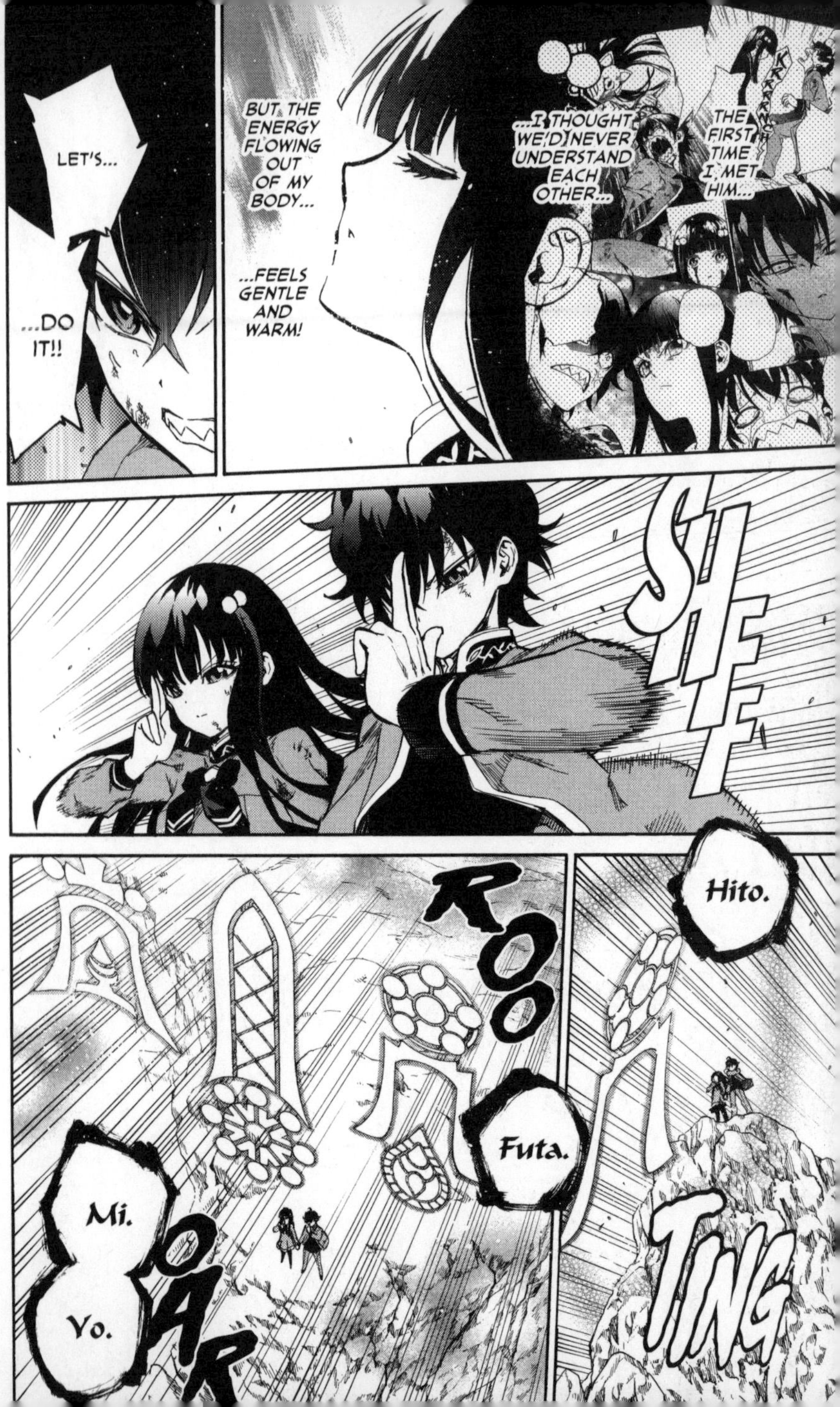
KRRRRNCH
THE FIRST TIME I MET HIM...
...I THOUGHT WE'D NEVER UNDERSTAND EACH OTHER...
BUT THE ENERGY FLOWING OUT OF MY BODY...
...FEELS GENTLE AND WARM!
LET'S...
...DO IT!!
SHFF
Hito.
TING
ROO
Futa.
Mi.
Yo.
OAR

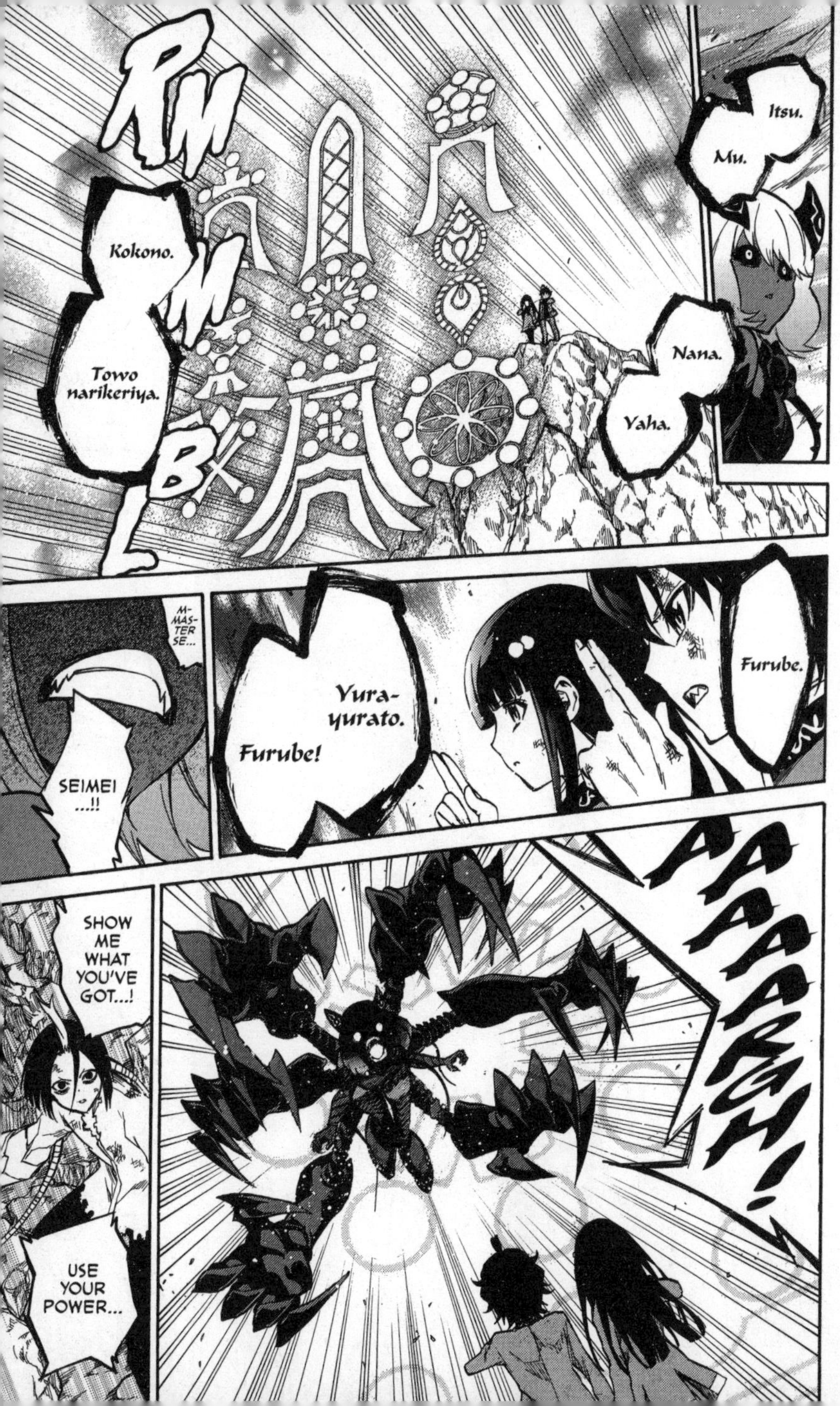
Itsu.
Mu.
Nana.
Yaha.
Kokono.
Towo narikeriya.
Furube.
Yura-yurato.
Furube!
M-MASTER SE...
SEIMEI ...!!
SHOW ME WHAT YOU'VE GOT...!
USE YOUR POWER...

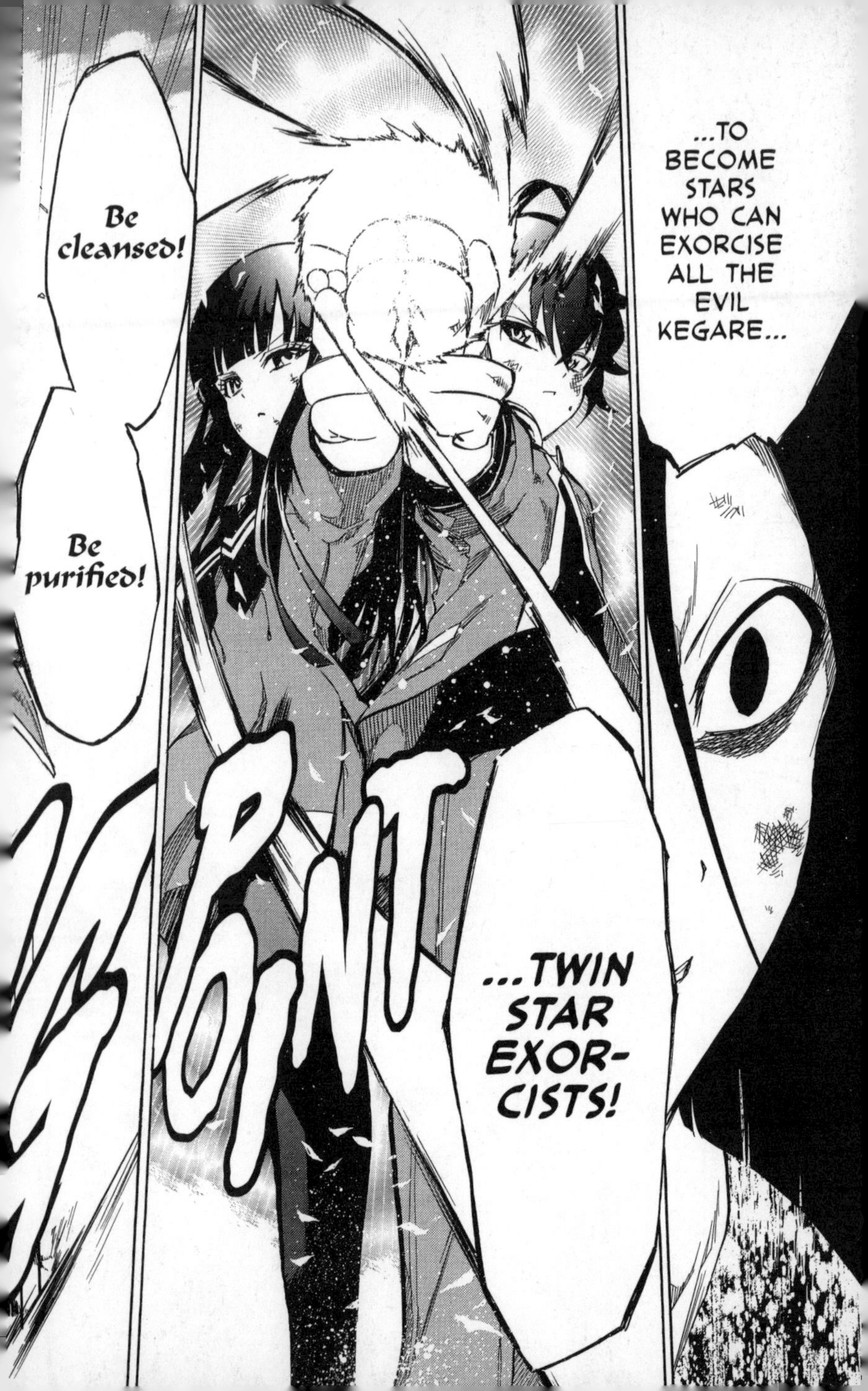
...TO BECOME STARS WHO CAN EXORCISE ALL THE EVIL KEGARE...
...TWIN STAR EXOR-CISTS!
Be cleansed!
Be purified!

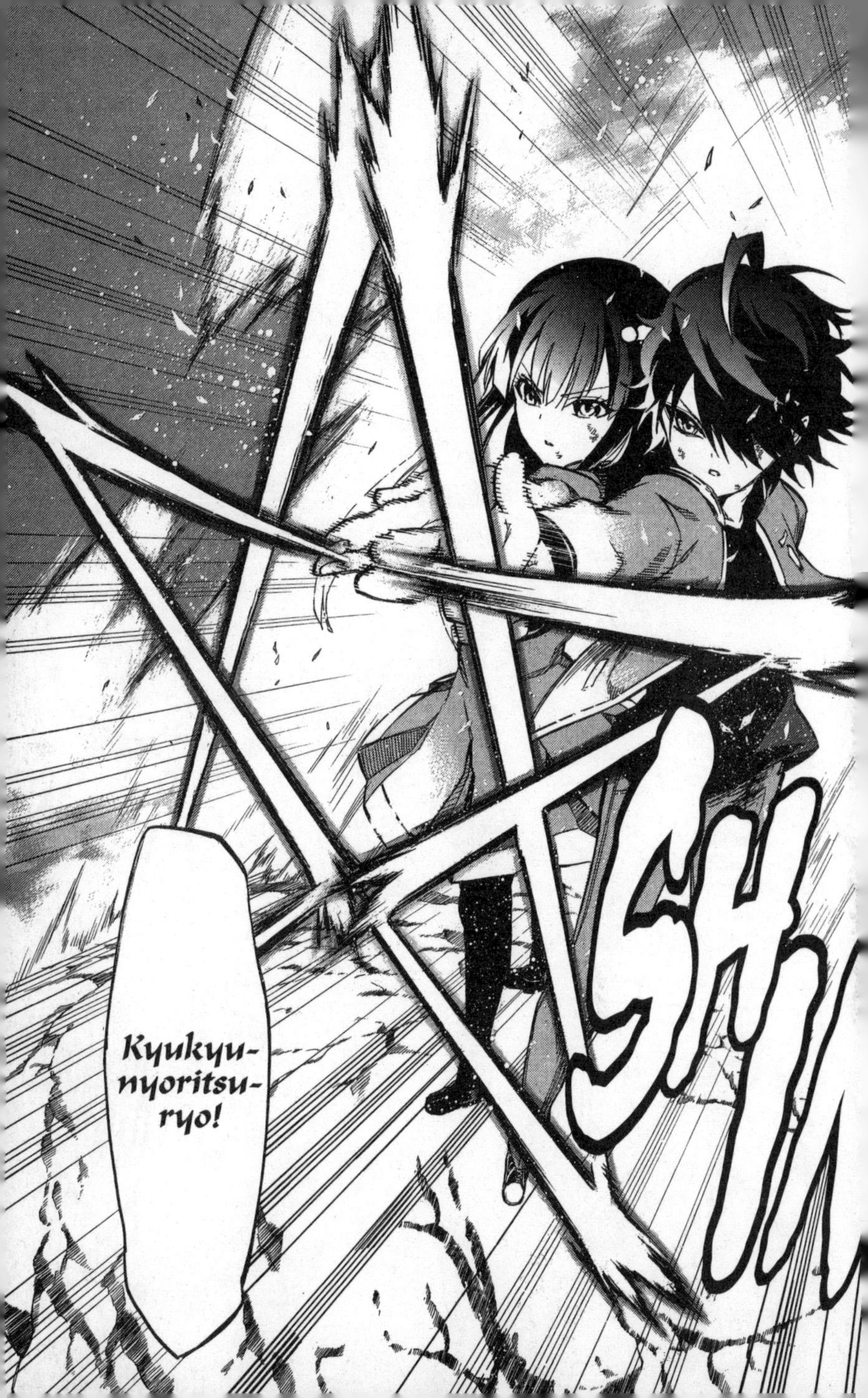
Kyukyu-nyoritsu-ryo!
SHH

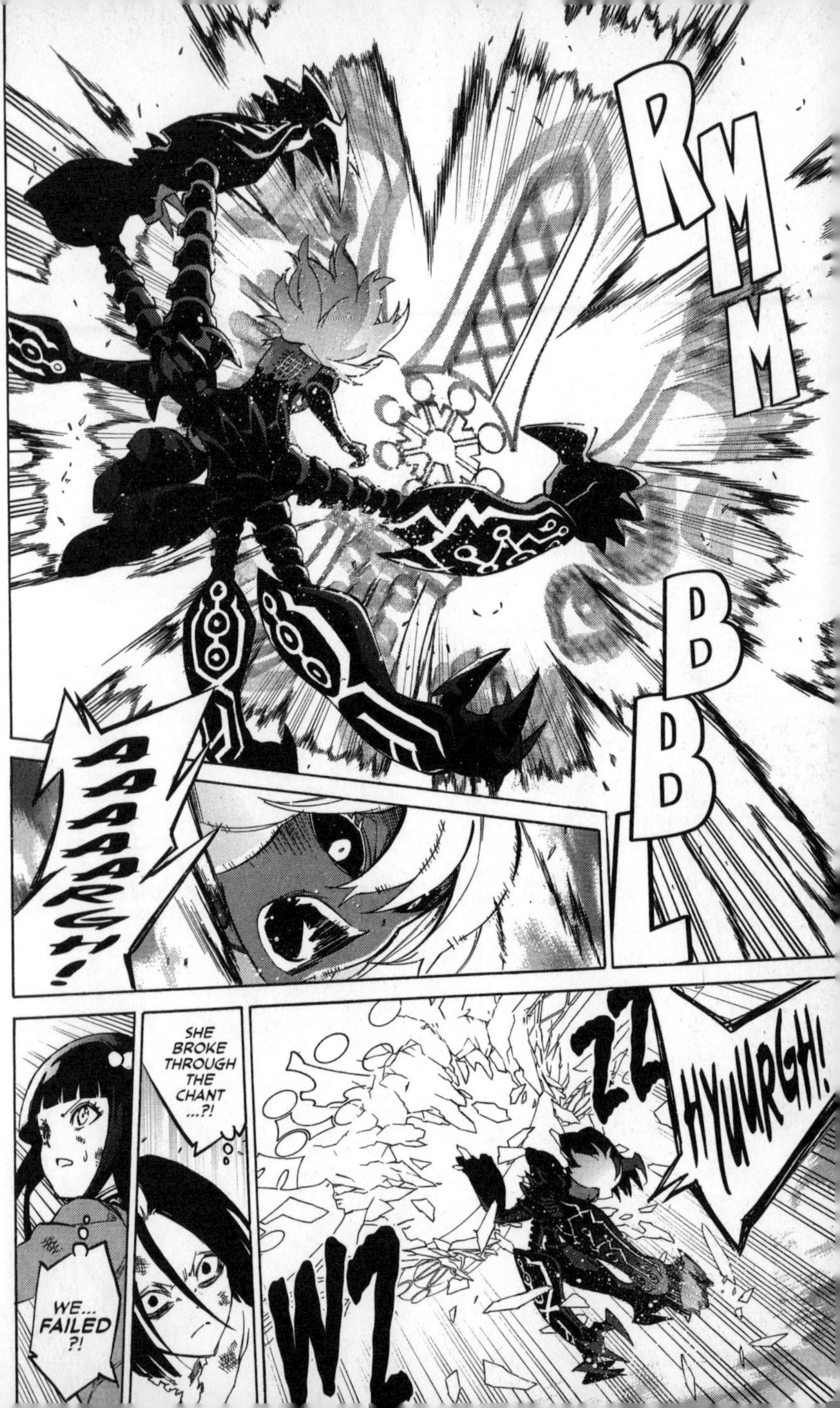
RMMM
BBL
AAAAAARGH!
ZZ
HYUURGH!
WZ
SHE BROKE THROUGH THE CHANT ...?!
WE... FAILED ?!

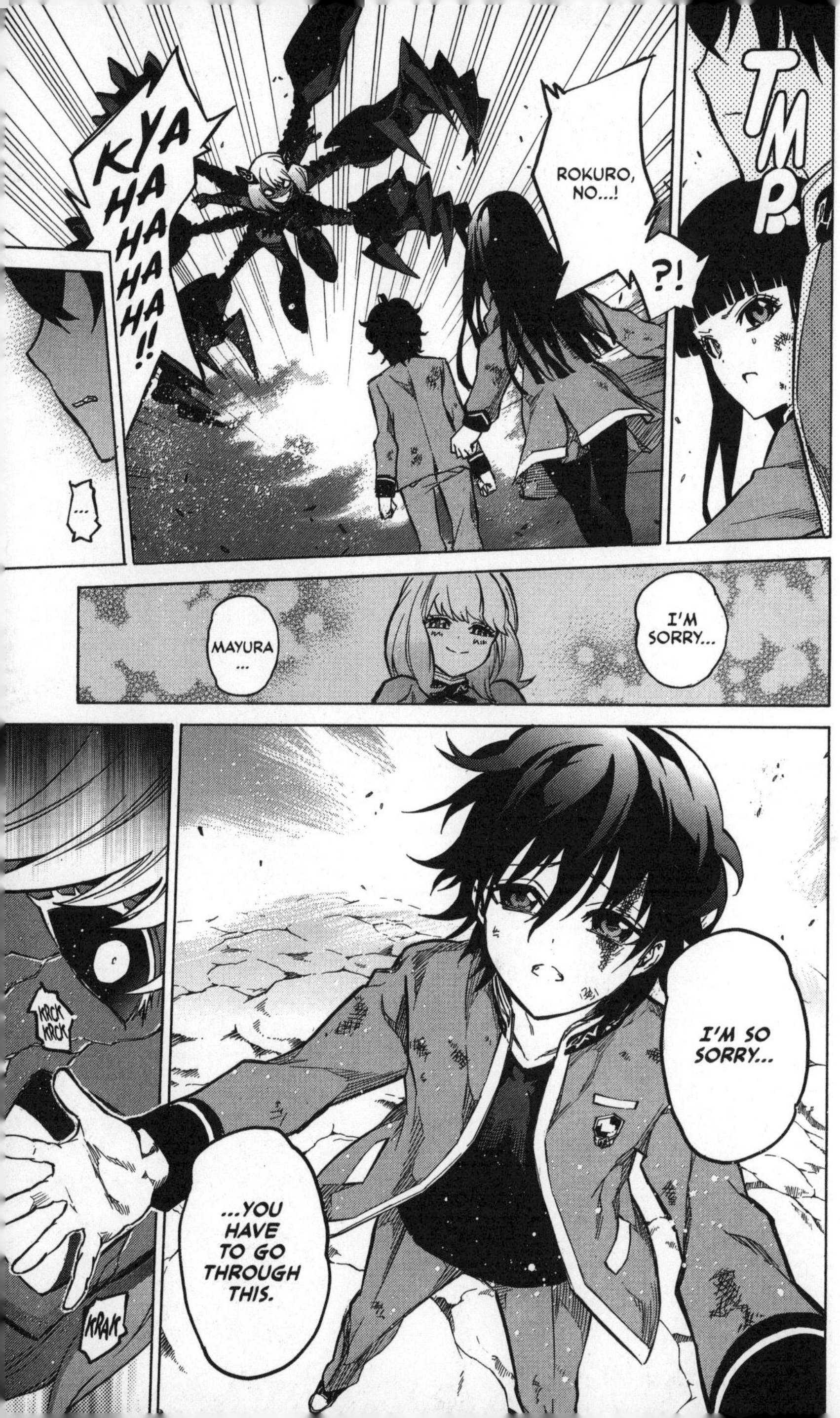
TMP
?!
ROKURO, NO...!
KYAHAHAHAHAHA!!
...
I'M SORRY...
MAYURA...
I'M SO SORRY...
...YOU HAVE TO GO THROUGH THIS.
KRCK KRCK
KRAK

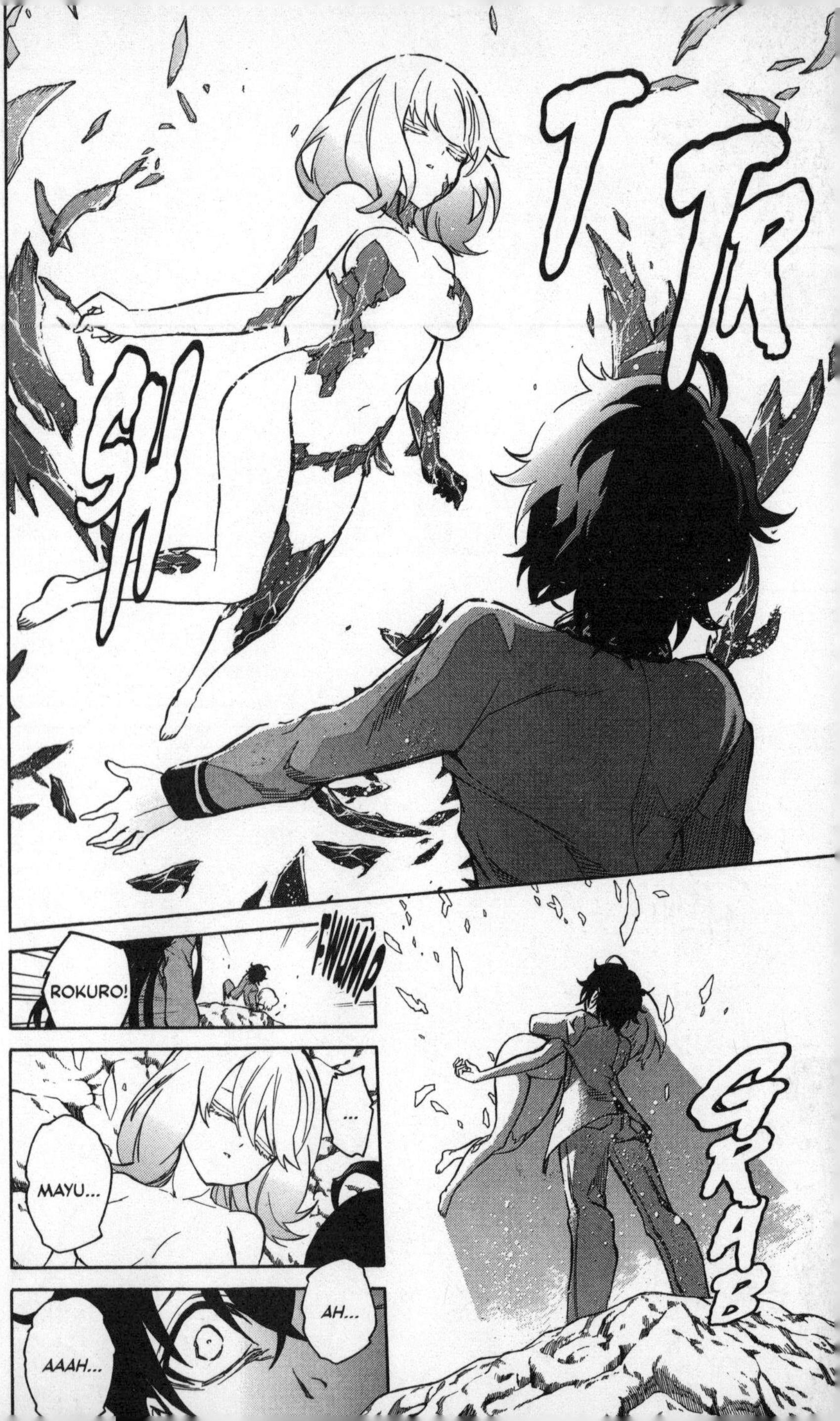
TR
T
SH
GRAB
FWUMP
ROKURO!
...
MAYU...
AH...
AAAH...

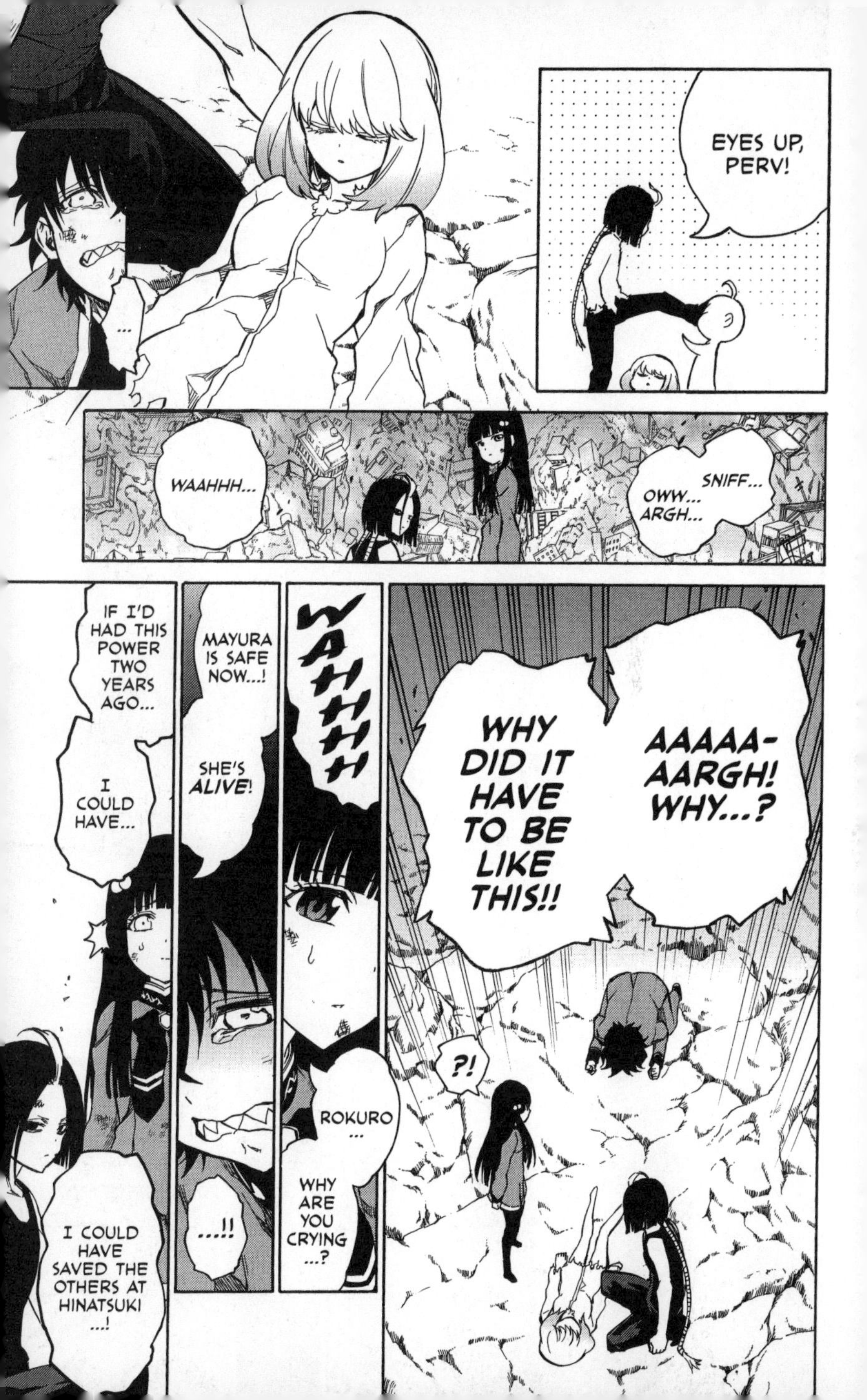
EYES UP, PERV!
...
SNIFF... OWW... ARGH...
WAAHHH...
AAAAA-AARGH! WHY...?
WHY DID IT HAVE TO BE LIKE THIS!!
?!
WAHHHHH
ROKURO ...
WHY ARE YOU CRYING ...?
MAYURA IS SAFE NOW...!
SHE'S ALIVE!
...!!
IF I'D HAD THIS POWER TWO YEARS AGO...
I COULD HAVE...
I COULD HAVE SAVED THE OTHERS AT HINATSUKI ...!

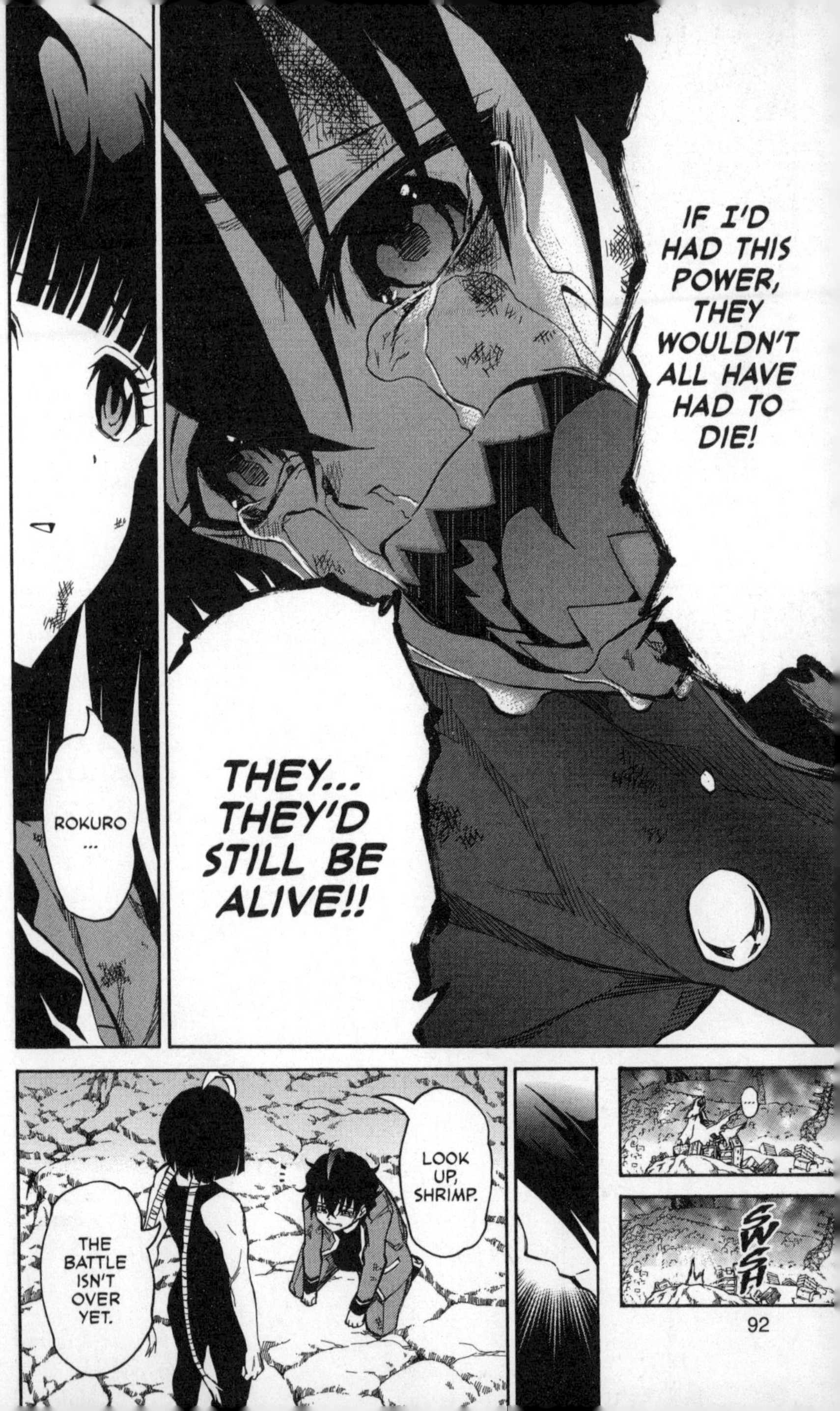
IF I'D HAD THIS POWER, THEY WOULDN'T ALL HAVE HAD TO DIE!
THEY... THEY'D STILL BE ALIVE!!
ROKURO ...
...
SWSH
LOOK UP, SHRIMP.
THE BATTLE ISN'T OVER YET.

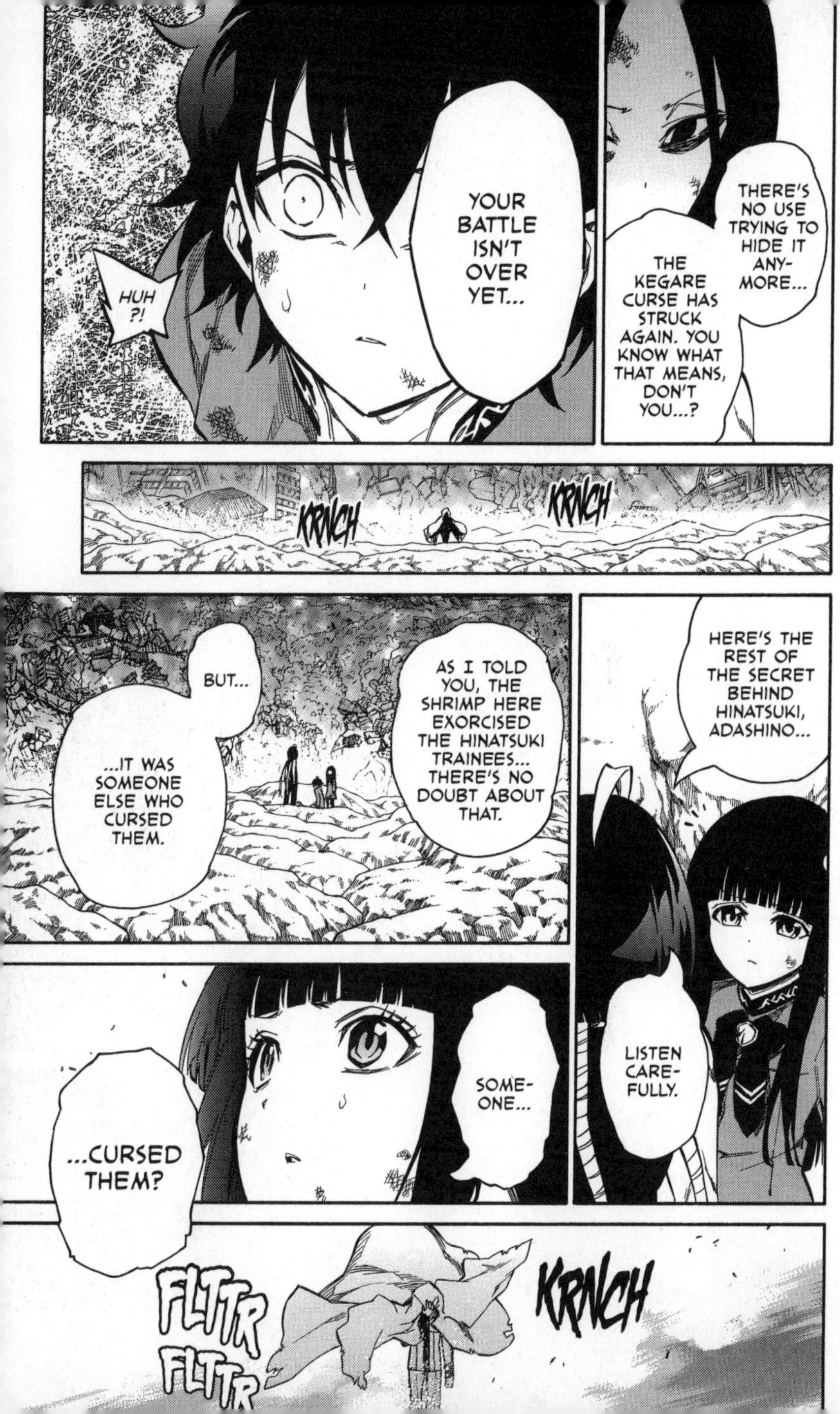
THERE'S NO USE TRYING TO HIDE IT ANY-MORE...
THE KEGARE CURSE HAS STRUCK AGAIN. YOU KNOW WHAT THAT MEANS, DON'T YOU...?
YOUR BATTLE ISN'T OVER YET...
HUH ?!
KRNCH
KRNCH
HERE'S THE REST OF THE SECRET BEHIND HINATSUKI, ADASHINO...
LISTEN CARE-FULLY.
AS I TOLD YOU, THE SHRIMP HERE EXORCISED THE HINATSUKI TRAINEES... THERE'S NO DOUBT ABOUT THAT.
BUT...
...IT WAS SOMEONE ELSE WHO CURSED THEM.
SOME-ONE...
...CURSED THEM?
KRNCH
FLTTR FLTTR

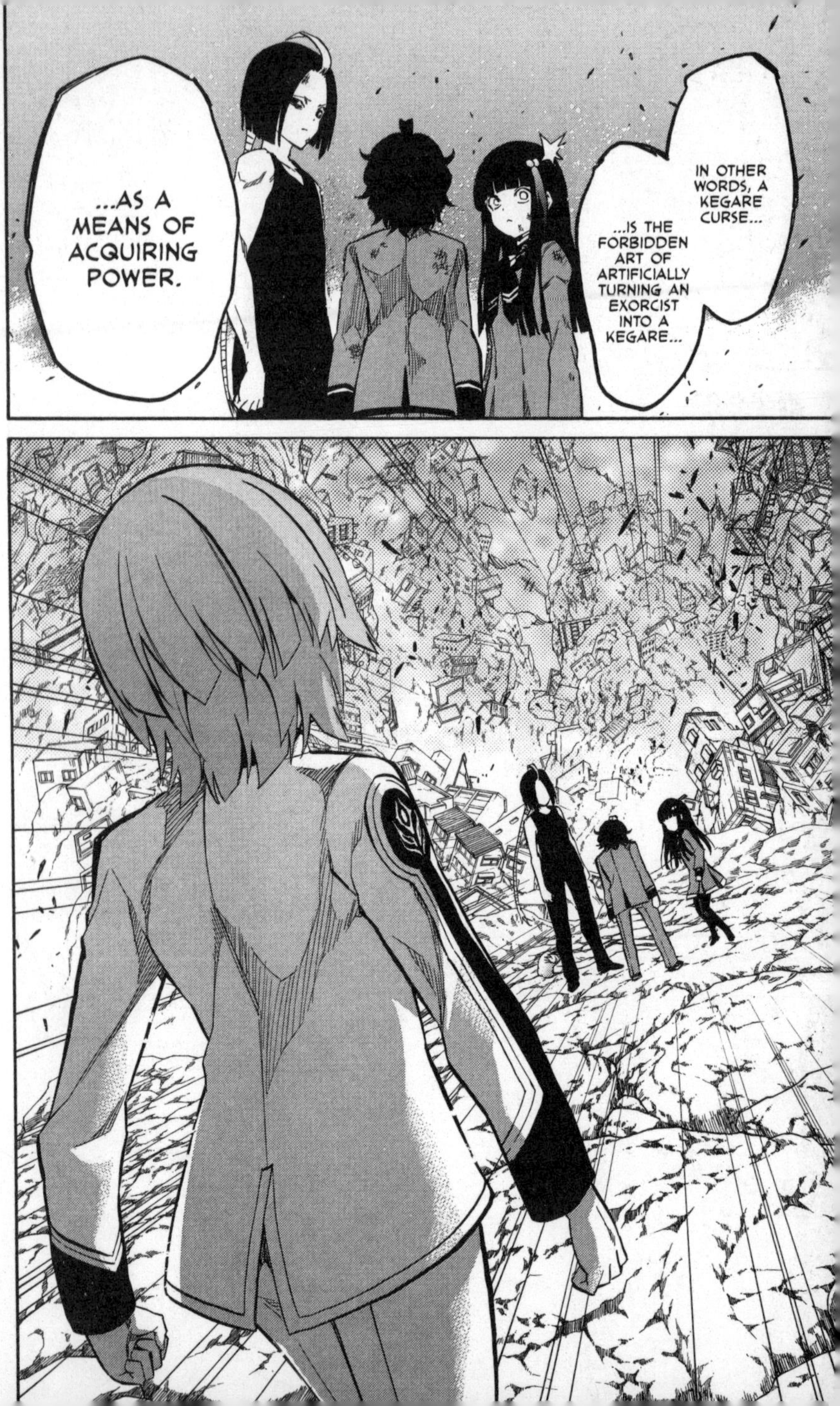
IN OTHER WORDS, A KEGARE CURSE...
...IS THE FORBIDDEN ART OF ARTIFICIALLY TURNING AN EXORCIST INTO A KEGARE...
...AS A MEANS OF ACQUIRING POWER.

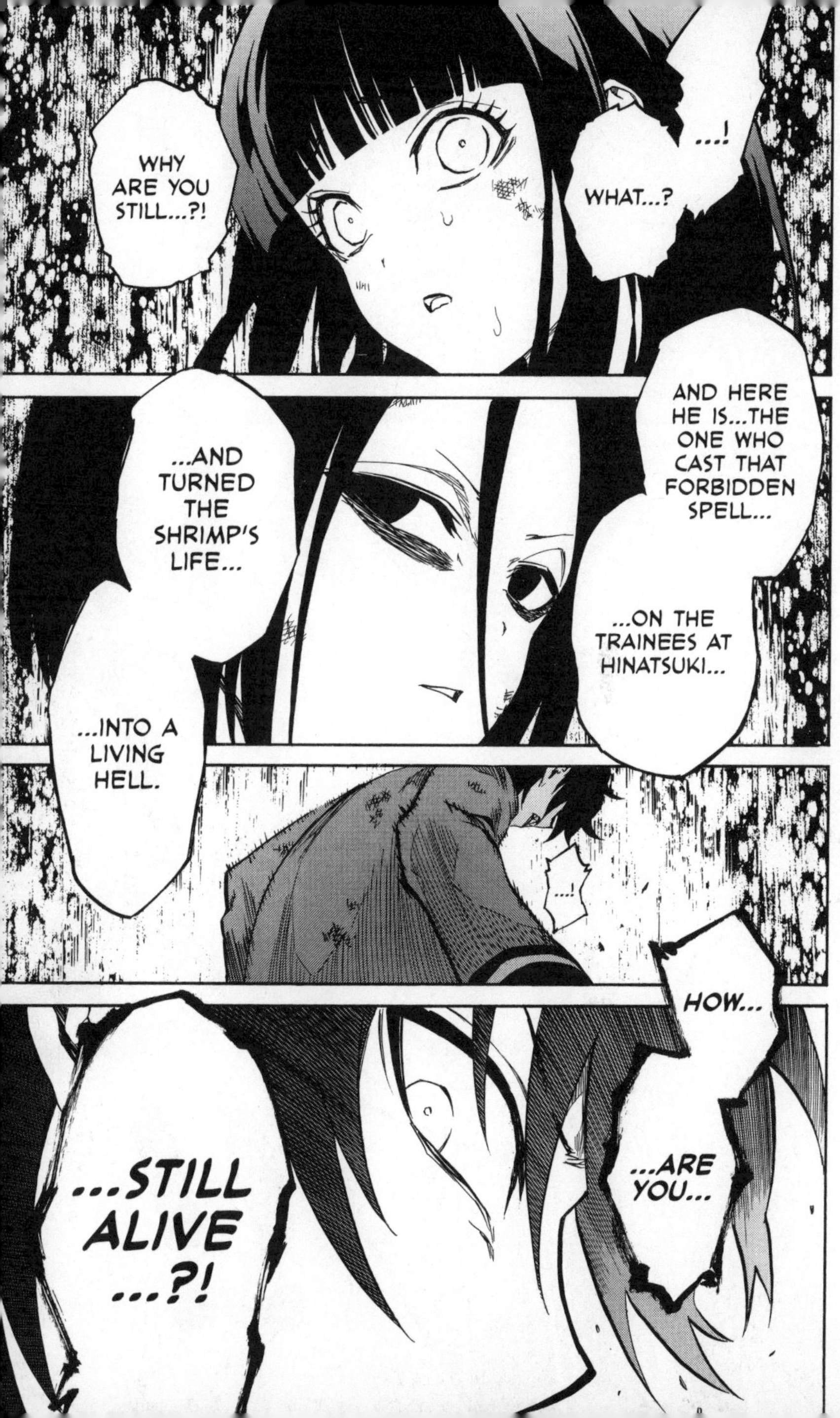
...!
WHAT...?
WHY ARE YOU STILL...?!
AND HERE HE IS...THE ONE WHO CAST THAT FORBIDDEN SPELL...
...ON THE TRAINEES AT HINATSUKI...
...AND TURNED THE SHRIMP'S LIFE...
...INTO A LIVING HELL.
...!
HOW...
...ARE YOU...
...STILL ALIVE ...?!

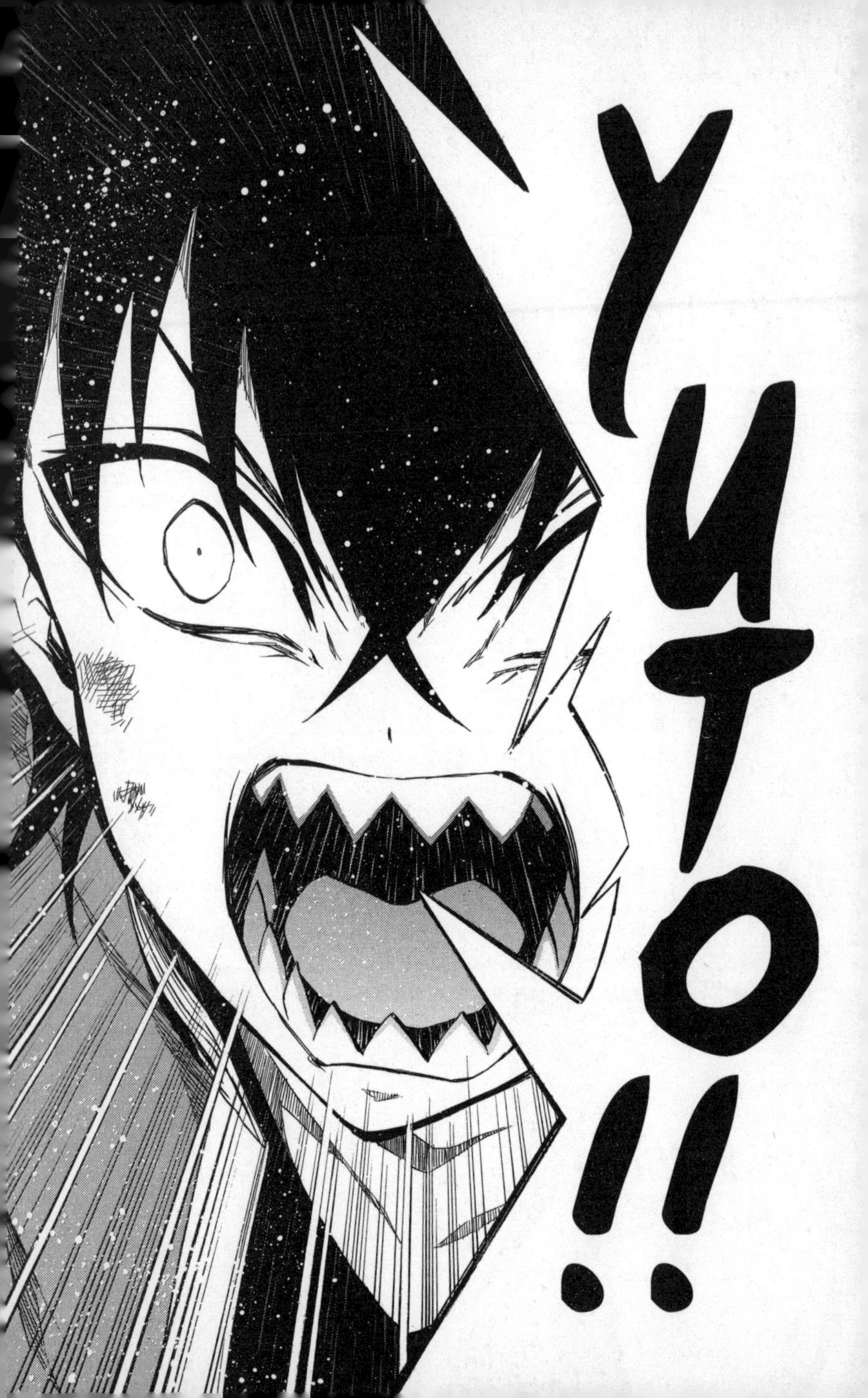
YUTO!!

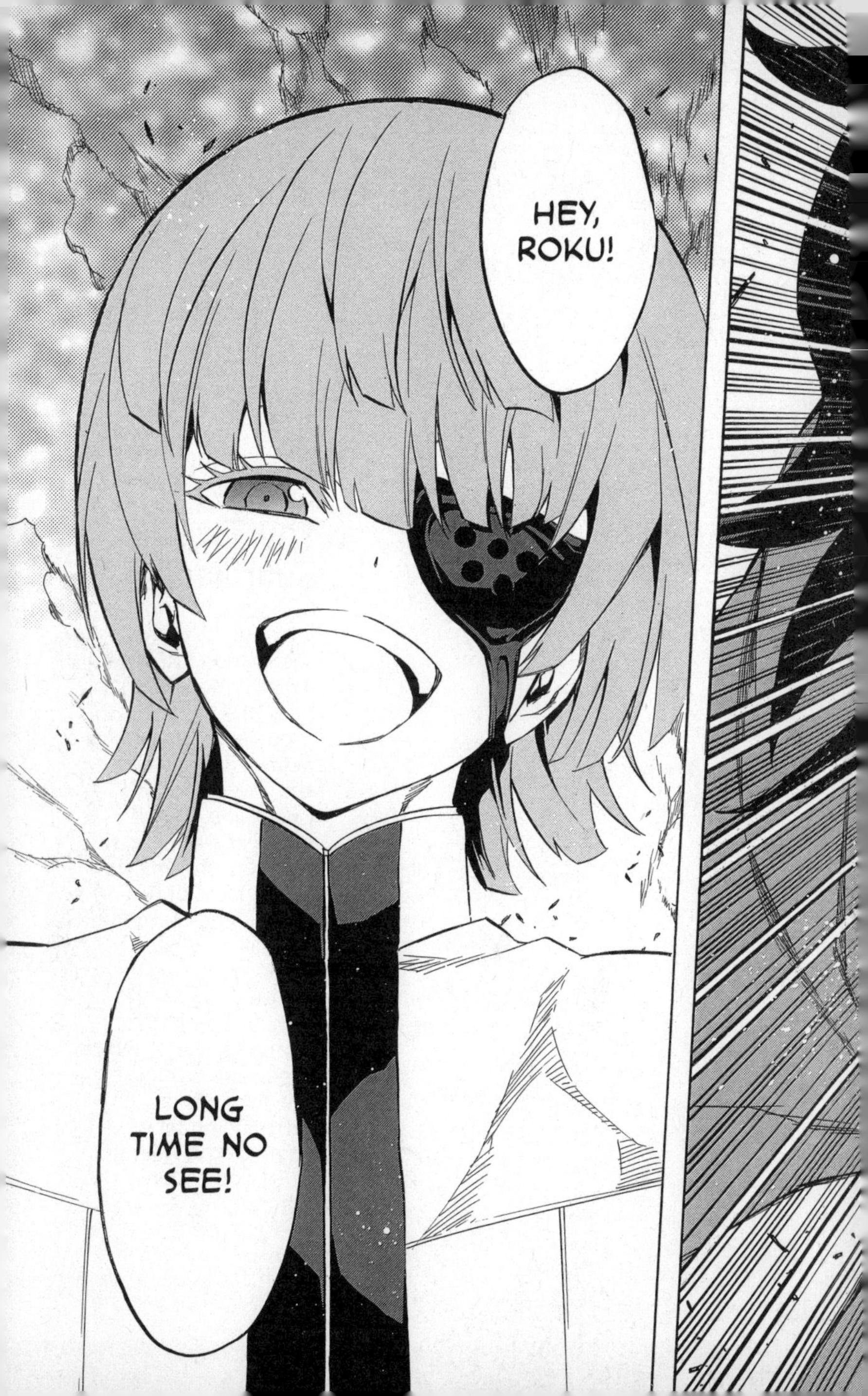
HEY, ROKU!
LONG TIME NO SEE!

Column 7: The Twelve Guardians

I've already briefly introduced them in the manga, but the most famous Spirit Servants that the great exorcist Abeno Seimei oversaw are the Twelve Guardians. These guardians appear in exorcist prophecies. Their names are Kijin, Flying Serpent, Vermillion Bird, Rikugo, Kochin, Azure Dragon, Tenko, Daion, Black Tortoise, Taijo, White Tiger and Tenku. I'm thinking of introducing all of them in the manga... but I don't know when...

#10 Evil

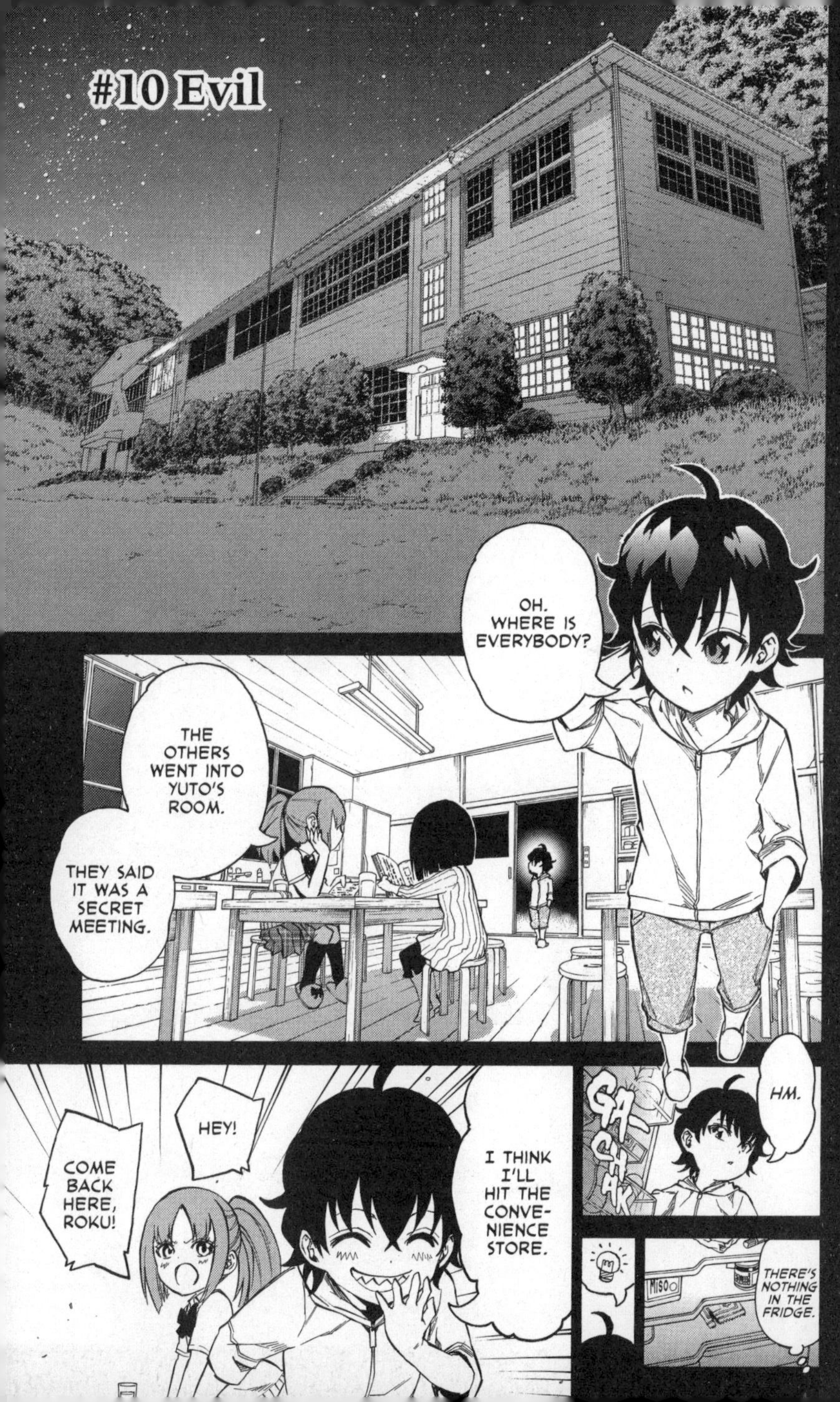
OH. WHERE IS EVERYBODY?
THE OTHERS WENT INTO YUTO'S ROOM.
THEY SAID IT WAS A SECRET MEETING.
GA-CHAK
HM.
MISO
THERE'S NOTHING IN THE FRIDGE.
I THINK I'LL HIT THE CONVE-NIENCE STORE.
HEY!
COME BACK HERE, ROKU!

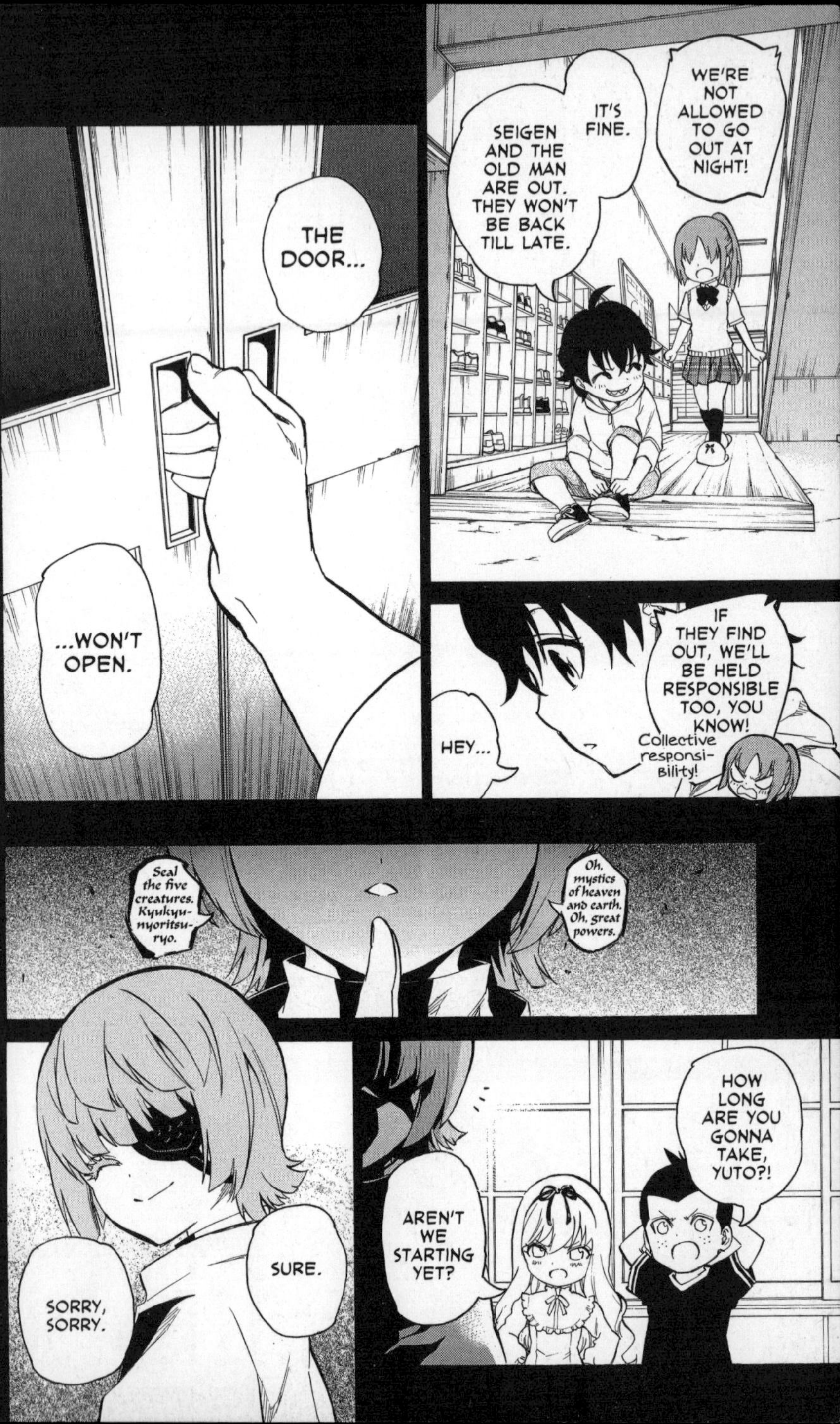
WE'RE NOT ALLOWED TO GO OUT AT NIGHT!
IT'S FINE.
SEIGEN AND THE OLD MAN ARE OUT. THEY WON'T BE BACK TILL LATE.
IF THEY FIND OUT, WE'LL BE HELD RESPONSIBLE TOO, YOU KNOW!
Collective responsi-bility!
HEY...
THE DOOR...
...WON'T OPEN.
Oh, mystics of heaven and earth. Oh, great powers.
Seal the five creatures. Kyukyu-nyoritsu-ryo.
HOW LONG ARE YOU GONNA TAKE, YUTO?!
AREN'T WE STARTING YET?
...
SURE.
SORRY, SORRY.

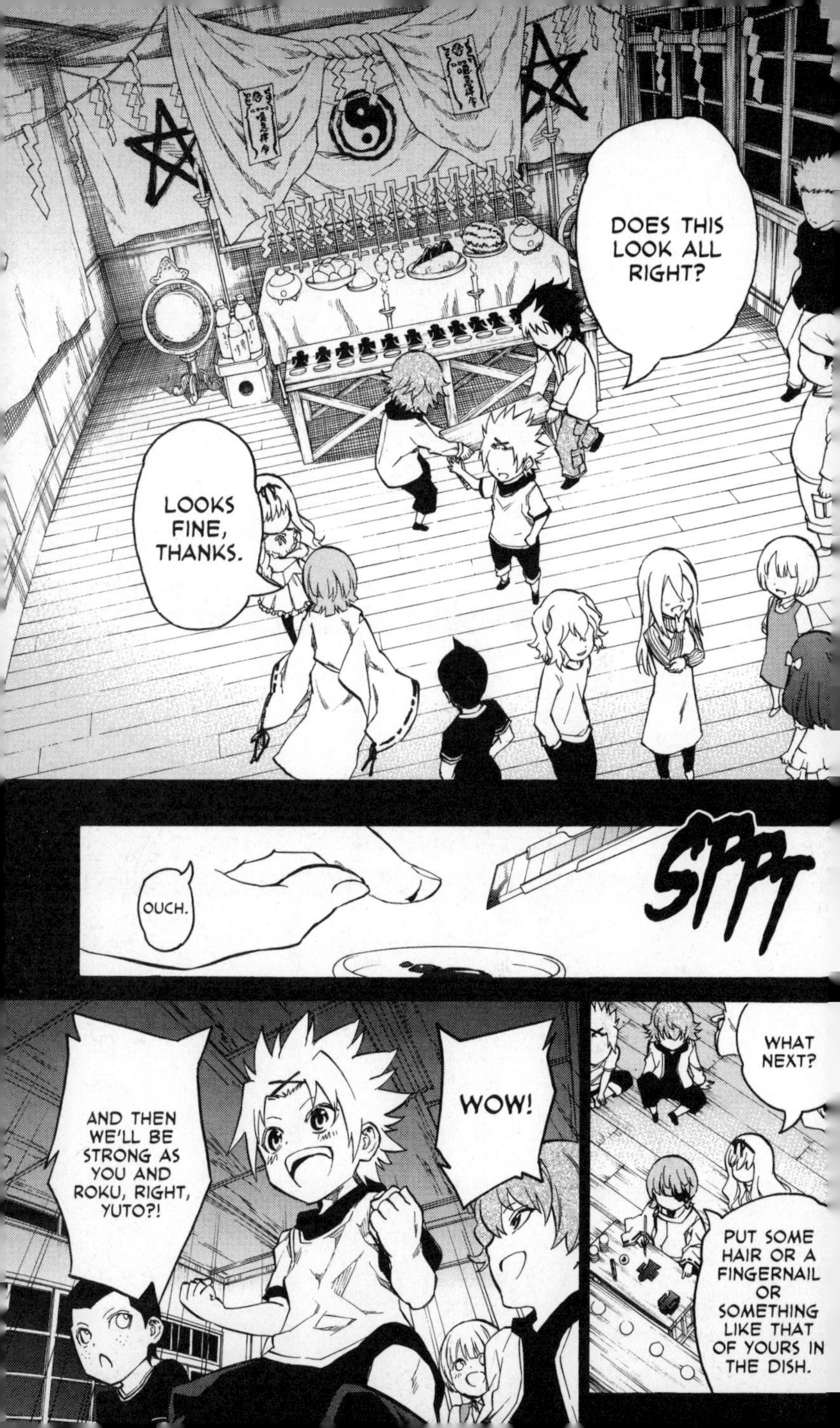
DOES THIS LOOK ALL RIGHT?
LOOKS FINE, THANKS.
SPPT
OUCH.
WHAT NEXT?
PUT SOME HAIR OR A FINGERNAIL OR SOMETHING LIKE THAT OF YOURS IN THE DISH.
WOW!
AND THEN WE'LL BE STRONG AS YOU AND ROKU, RIGHT, YUTO?!

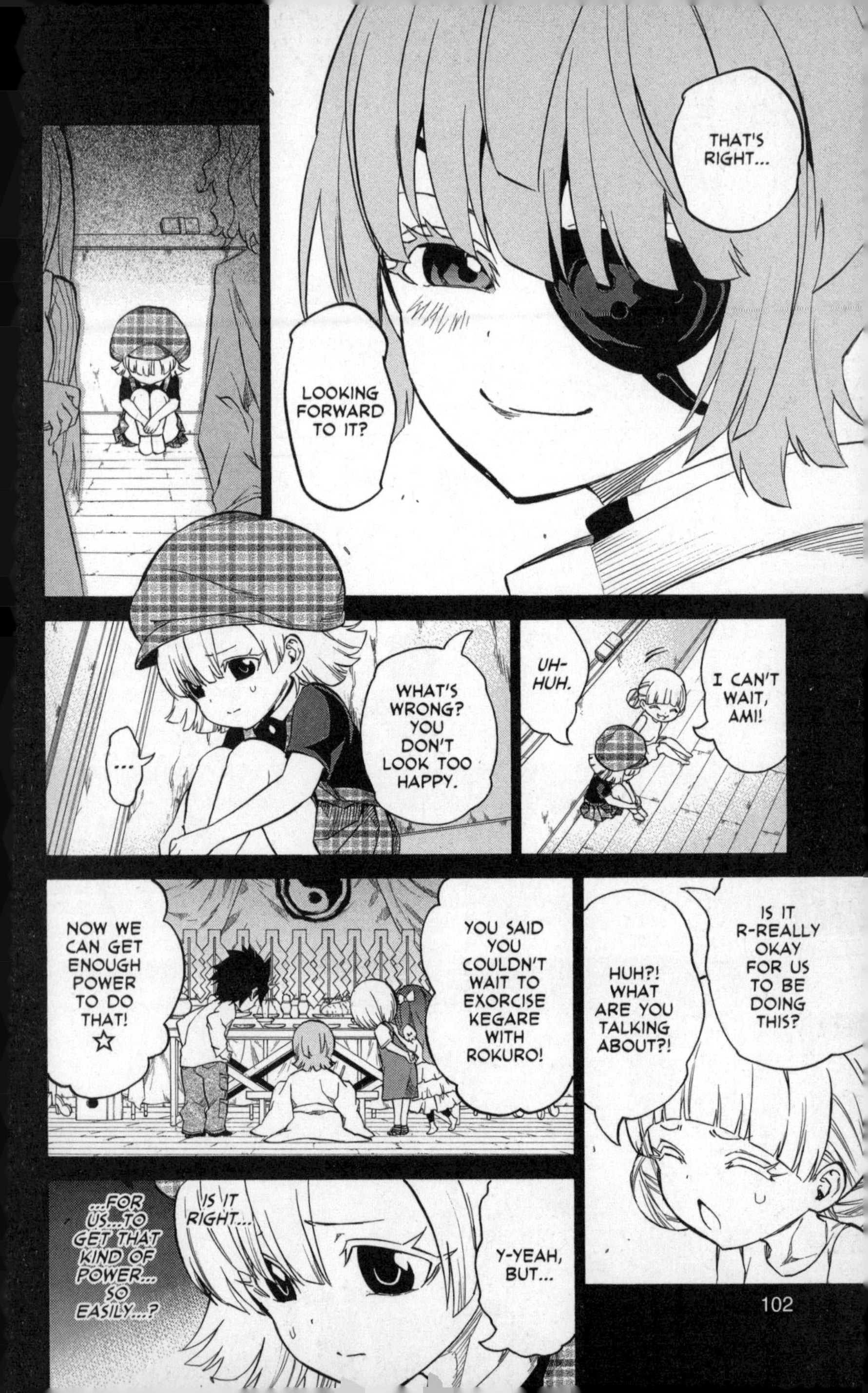
THAT'S RIGHT...
LOOKING FORWARD TO IT?
I CAN'T WAIT, AMI!
UH-HUH.
WHAT'S WRONG? YOU DON'T LOOK TOO HAPPY.
...
IS IT R-REALLY OKAY FOR US TO BE DOING THIS?
HUH?! WHAT ARE YOU TALKING ABOUT?!
YOU SAID YOU COULDN'T WAIT TO EXORCISE KEGARE WITH ROKURO!
NOW WE CAN GET ENOUGH POWER TO DO THAT! ☆
Y-YEAH, BUT...
IS IT RIGHT...
...FOR US...TO GET THAT KIND OF POWER... SO EASILY...?

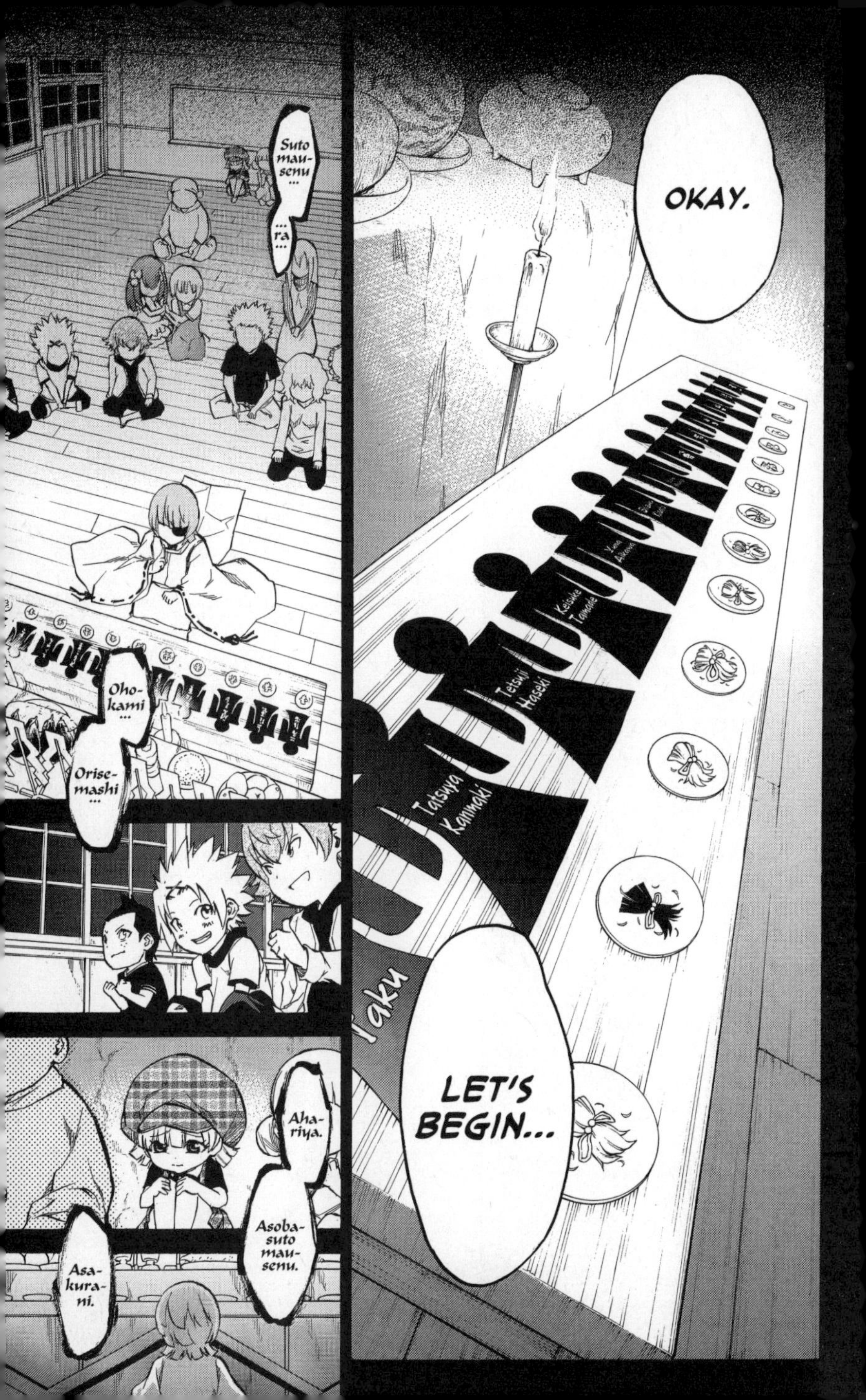
OKAY.
LET'S BEGIN...
Tetsuji Haseki
Keisuke Tamade
Tatsuya Kanmaki
Suto mausenu...
...ra...
Ohokami...
Orisemashi...
Ahariya.
Asobasuto mausenu.
Asakurani.

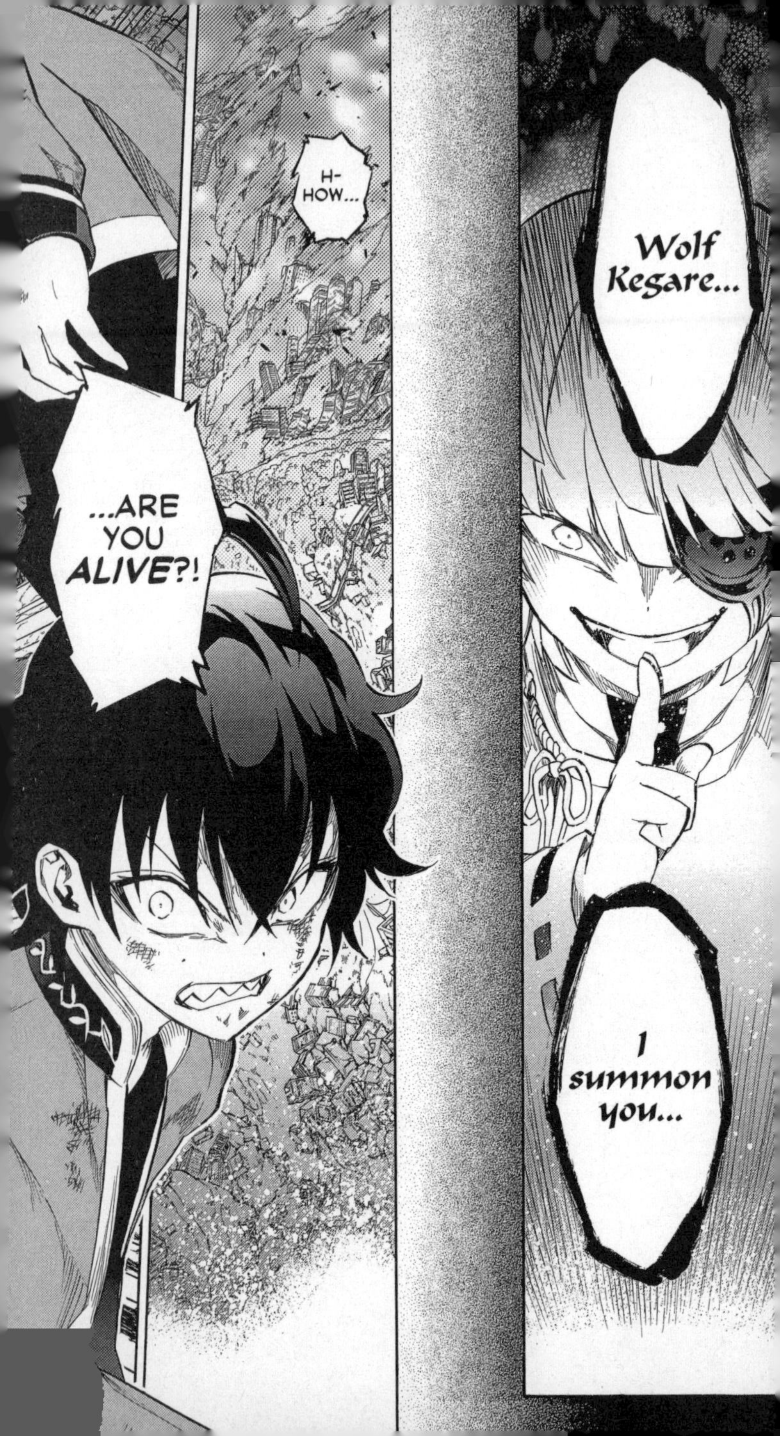
Wolf Kegare...
I summon you...
H-HOW...
...ARE YOU ALIVE?!

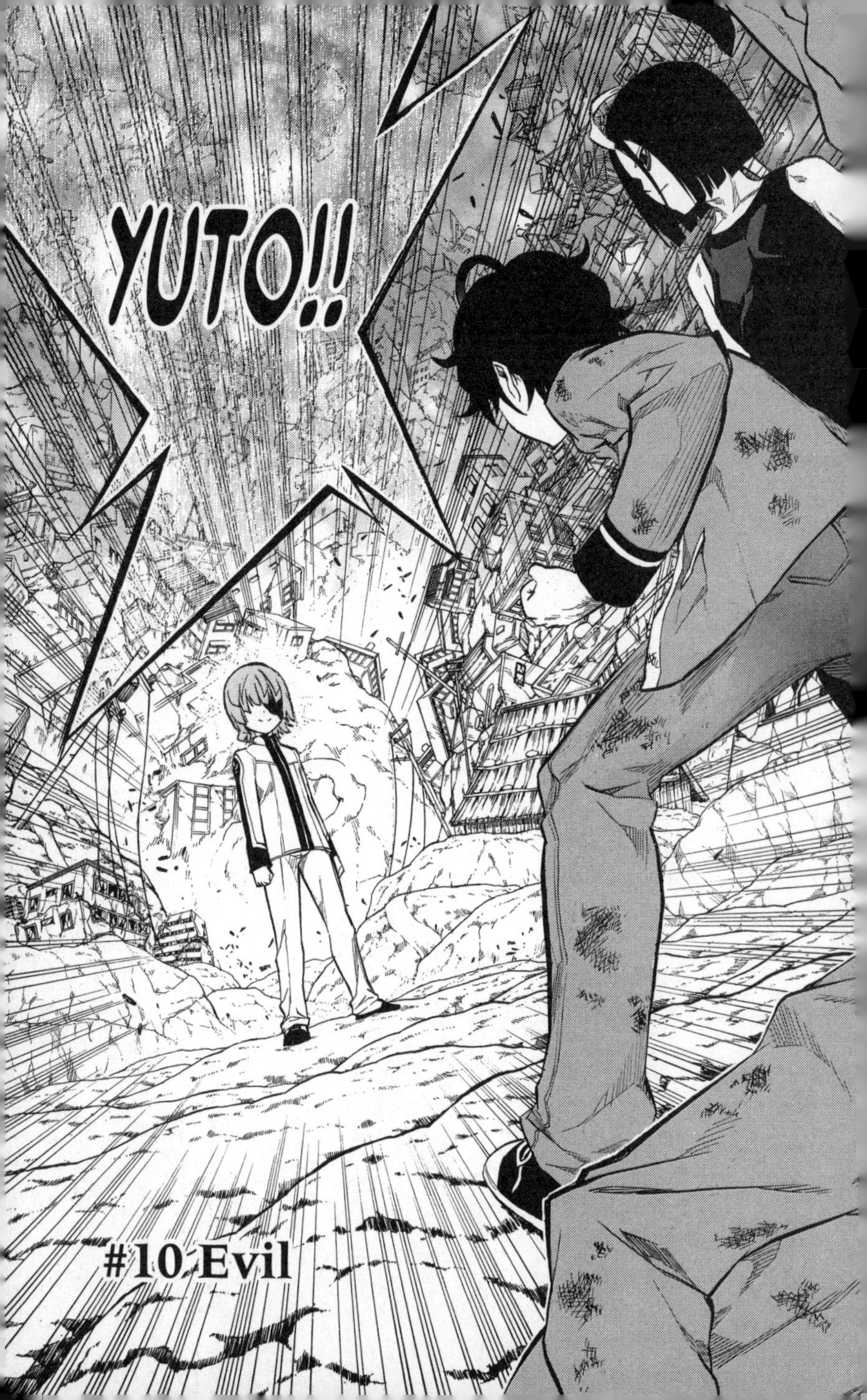
YUTO!!
#10 Evil

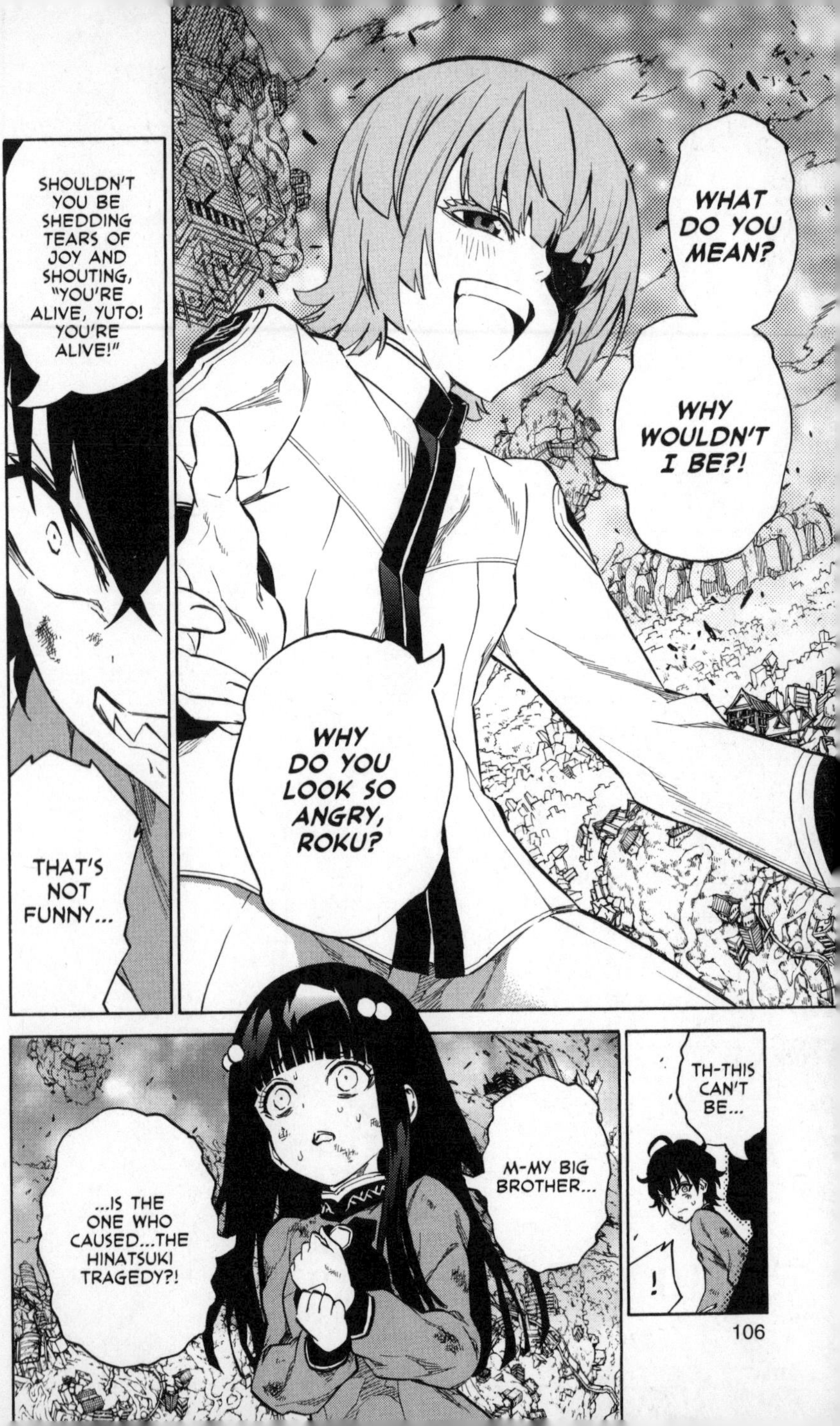
WHAT DO YOU MEAN?
WHY WOULDN'T I BE?!
WHY DO YOU LOOK SO ANGRY, ROKU?
SHOULDN'T YOU BE SHEDDING TEARS OF JOY AND SHOUTING, "YOU'RE ALIVE, YUTO! YOU'RE ALIVE!"
THAT'S NOT FUNNY...
TH-THIS CAN'T BE...
!
M-MY BIG BROTHER...
...IS THE ONE WHO CAUSED...THE HINATSUKI TRAGEDY?!

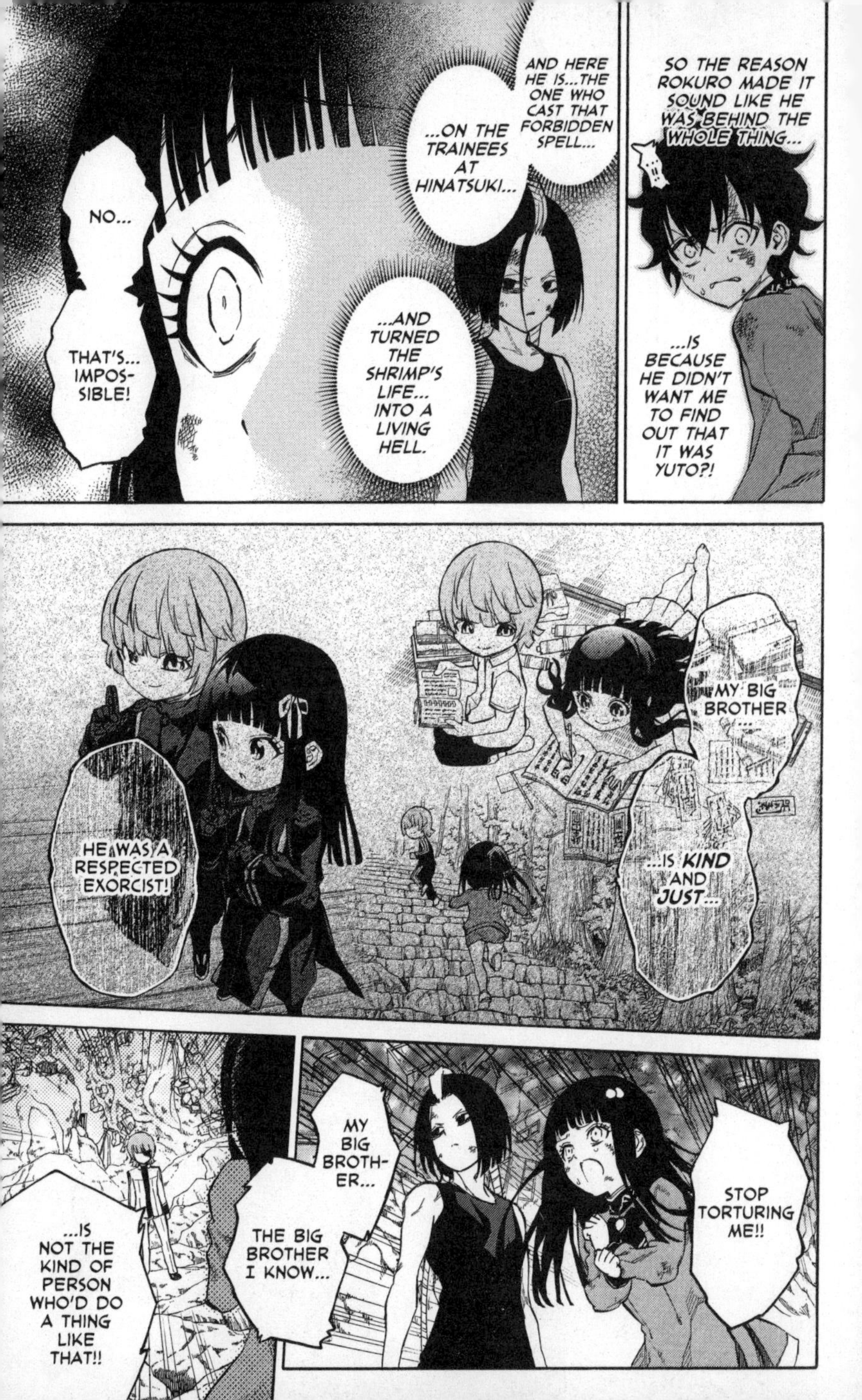
SO THE REASON ROKURO MADE IT SOUND LIKE HE WAS BEHIND THE WHOLE THING...
...IS BECAUSE HE DIDN'T WANT ME TO FIND OUT THAT IT WAS YUTO?!
AND HERE HE IS...THE ONE WHO CAST THAT FORBIDDEN SPELL...
...ON THE TRAINEES AT HINATSUKI...
...AND TURNED THE SHRIMP'S LIFE... INTO A LIVING HELL.
NO...
THAT'S... IMPOSSIBLE!
MY BIG BROTHER...
...IS **KIND** AND **JUST**...
HE WAS A RESPECTED EXORCIST!
STOP TORTURING ME!!
MY BIG BROTHER...
THE BIG BROTHER I KNOW...
...IS NOT THE KIND OF PERSON WHO'D DO A THING LIKE THAT!!

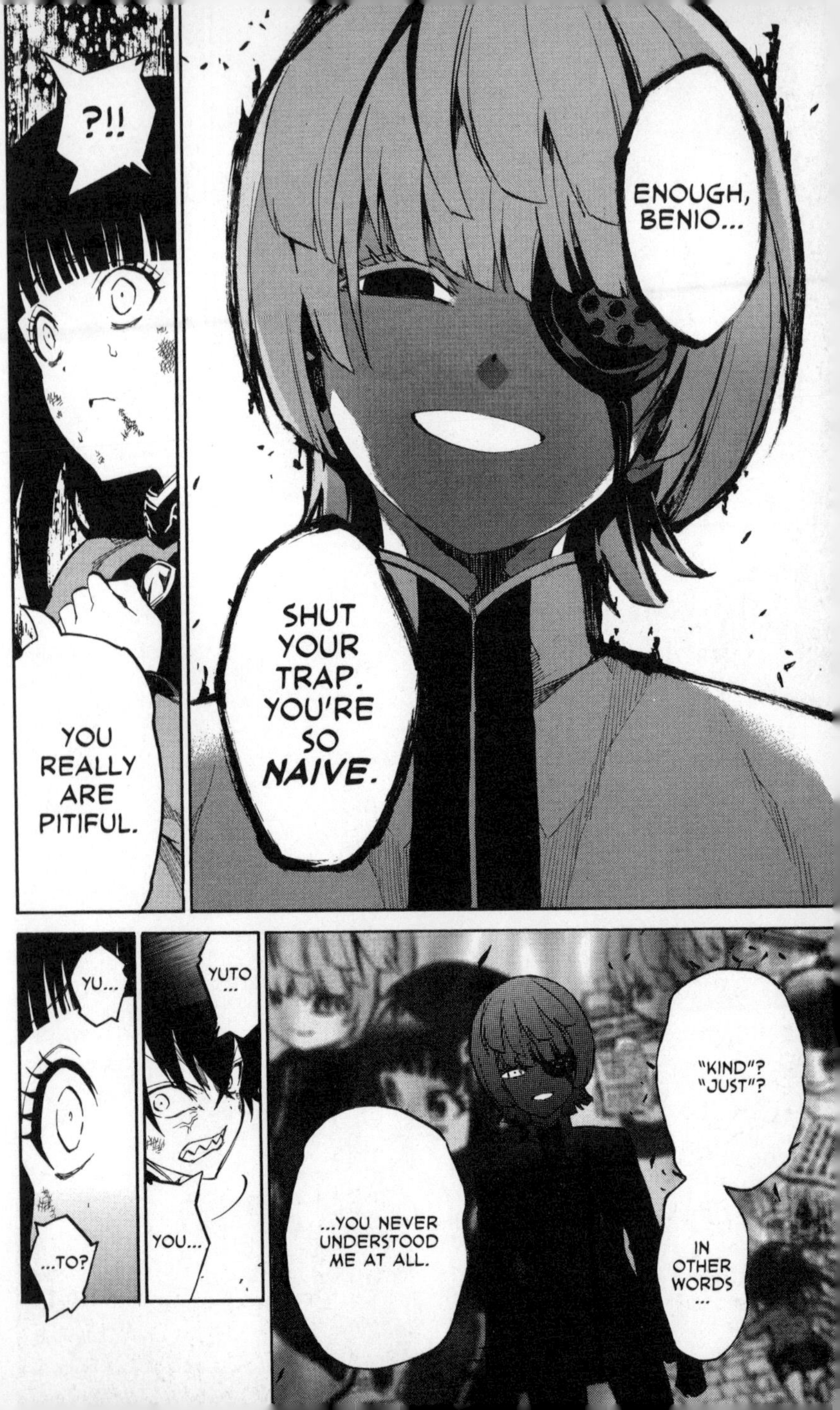
ENOUGH, BENIO...
SHUT YOUR TRAP. YOU'RE SO *NAIVE*.
?!!
YOU REALLY ARE PITIFUL.
"KIND"? "JUST"?
IN OTHER WORDS...
...YOU NEVER UNDERSTOOD ME AT ALL.
YUTO...
YOU...
YU...
...TO?

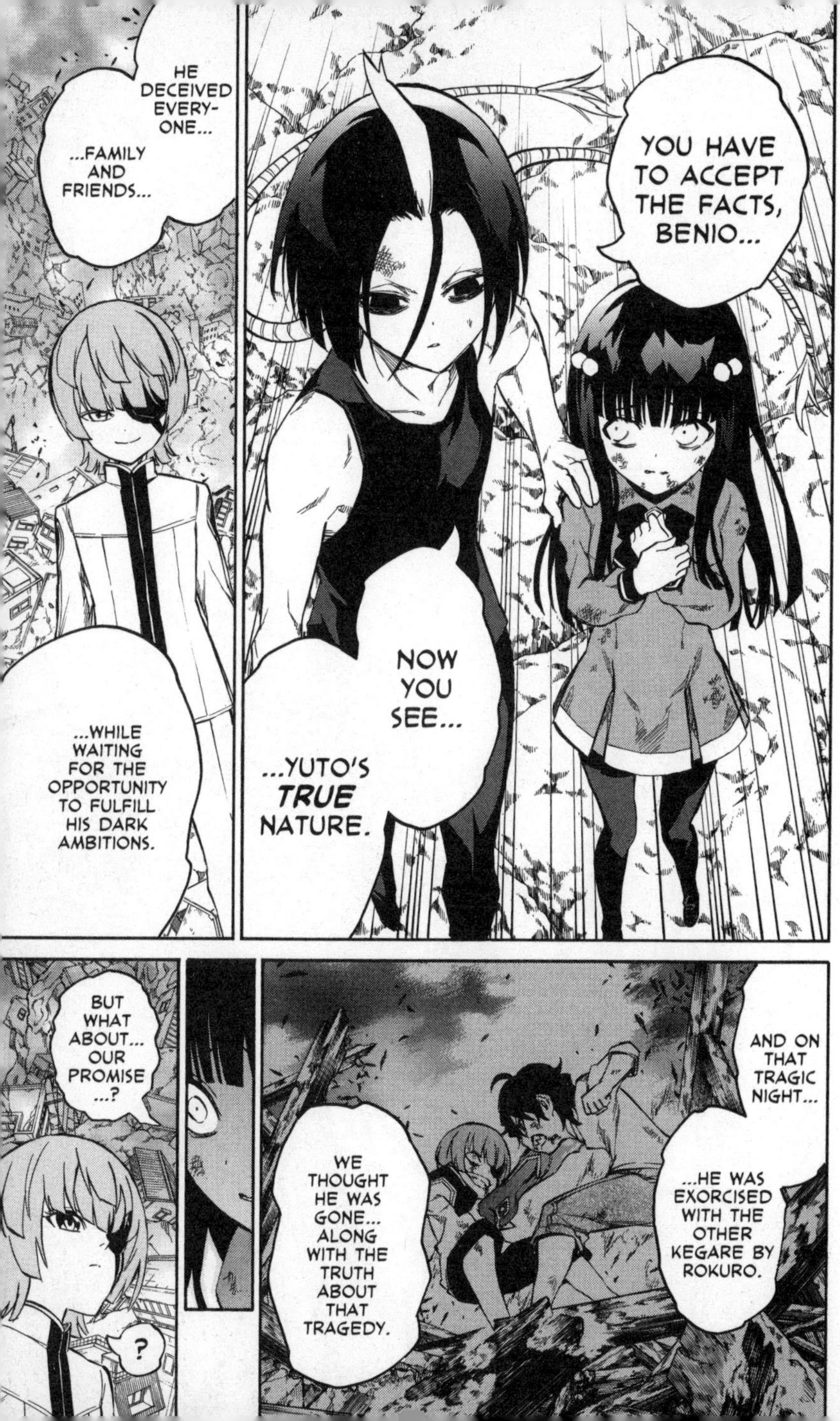
YOU HAVE TO ACCEPT THE FACTS, BENIO...
NOW YOU SEE...
...YUTO'S *TRUE* NATURE.
HE DECEIVED EVERYONE...
...FAMILY AND FRIENDS...
...WHILE WAITING FOR THE OPPORTUNITY TO FULFILL HIS DARK AMBITIONS.
AND ON THAT TRAGIC NIGHT...
...HE WAS EXORCISED WITH THE OTHER KEGARE BY ROKURO.
WE THOUGHT HE WAS GONE... ALONG WITH THE TRUTH ABOUT THAT TRAGEDY.
BUT WHAT ABOUT... OUR PROMISE ...?
?

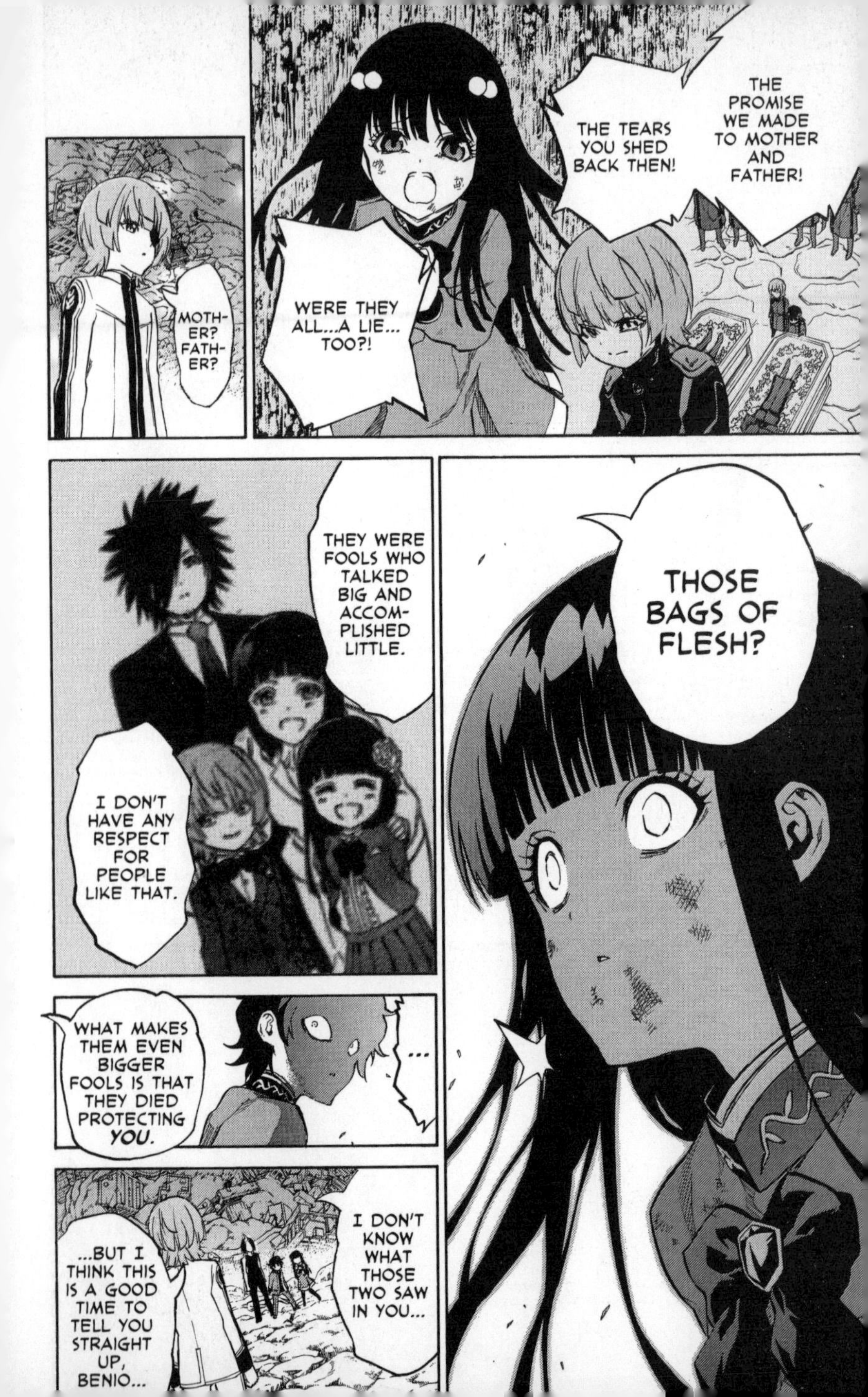
THE PROMISE WE MADE TO MOTHER AND FATHER!
THE TEARS YOU SHED BACK THEN!
WERE THEY ALL...A LIE... TOO?!
MOTH-ER? FATH-ER?
THOSE BAGS OF FLESH?
THEY WERE FOOLS WHO TALKED BIG AND ACCOM-PLISHED LITTLE.
I DON'T HAVE ANY RESPECT FOR PEOPLE LIKE THAT.
...
WHAT MAKES THEM EVEN BIGGER FOOLS IS THAT THEY DIED PROTECTING *YOU*.
I DON'T KNOW WHAT THOSE TWO SAW IN YOU...
...BUT I THINK THIS IS A GOOD TIME TO TELL YOU STRAIGHT UP, BENIO...

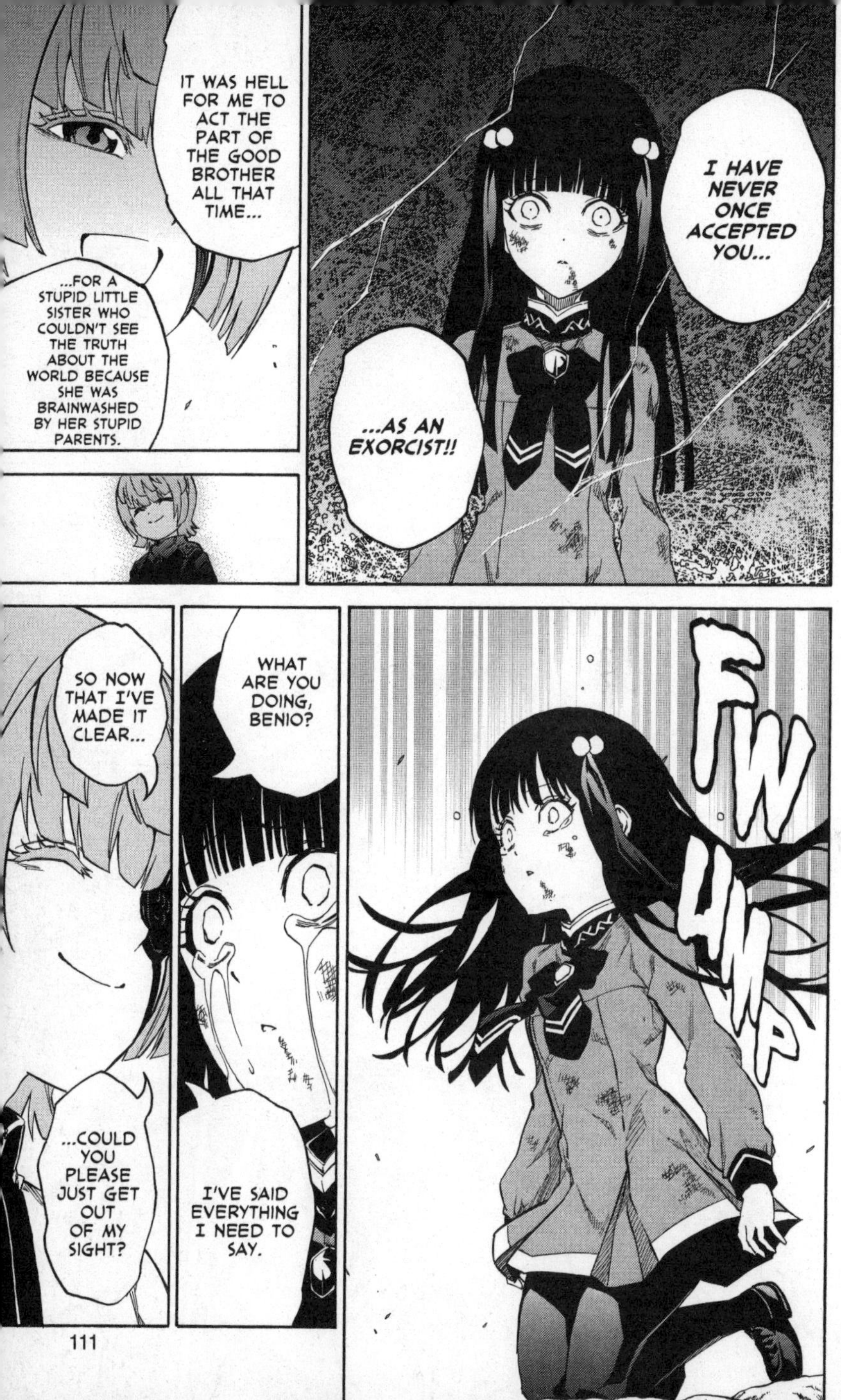
I HAVE NEVER ONCE ACCEPTED YOU...
...AS AN EXORCIST!!
IT WAS HELL FOR ME TO ACT THE PART OF THE GOOD BROTHER ALL THAT TIME...
...FOR A STUPID LITTLE SISTER WHO COULDN'T SEE THE TRUTH ABOUT THE WORLD BECAUSE SHE WAS BRAINWASHED BY HER STUPID PARENTS.
FWUMP
WHAT ARE YOU DOING, BENIO?
I'VE SAID EVERYTHING I NEED TO SAY.
SO NOW THAT I'VE MADE IT CLEAR...
...COULD YOU PLEASE JUST GET OUT OF MY SIGHT?

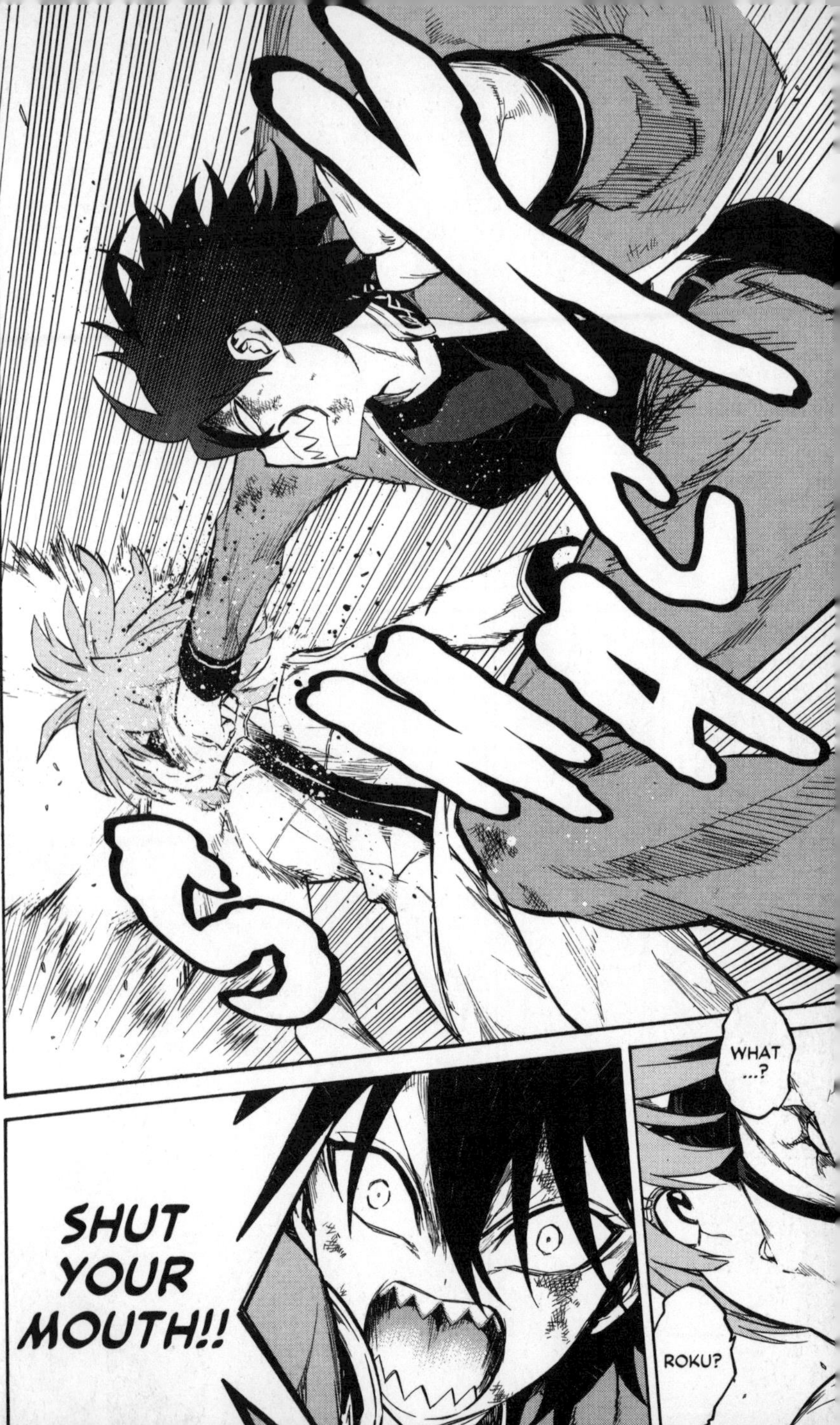
SMACK
WHAT ...?
ROKU?
SHUT YOUR MOUTH!!

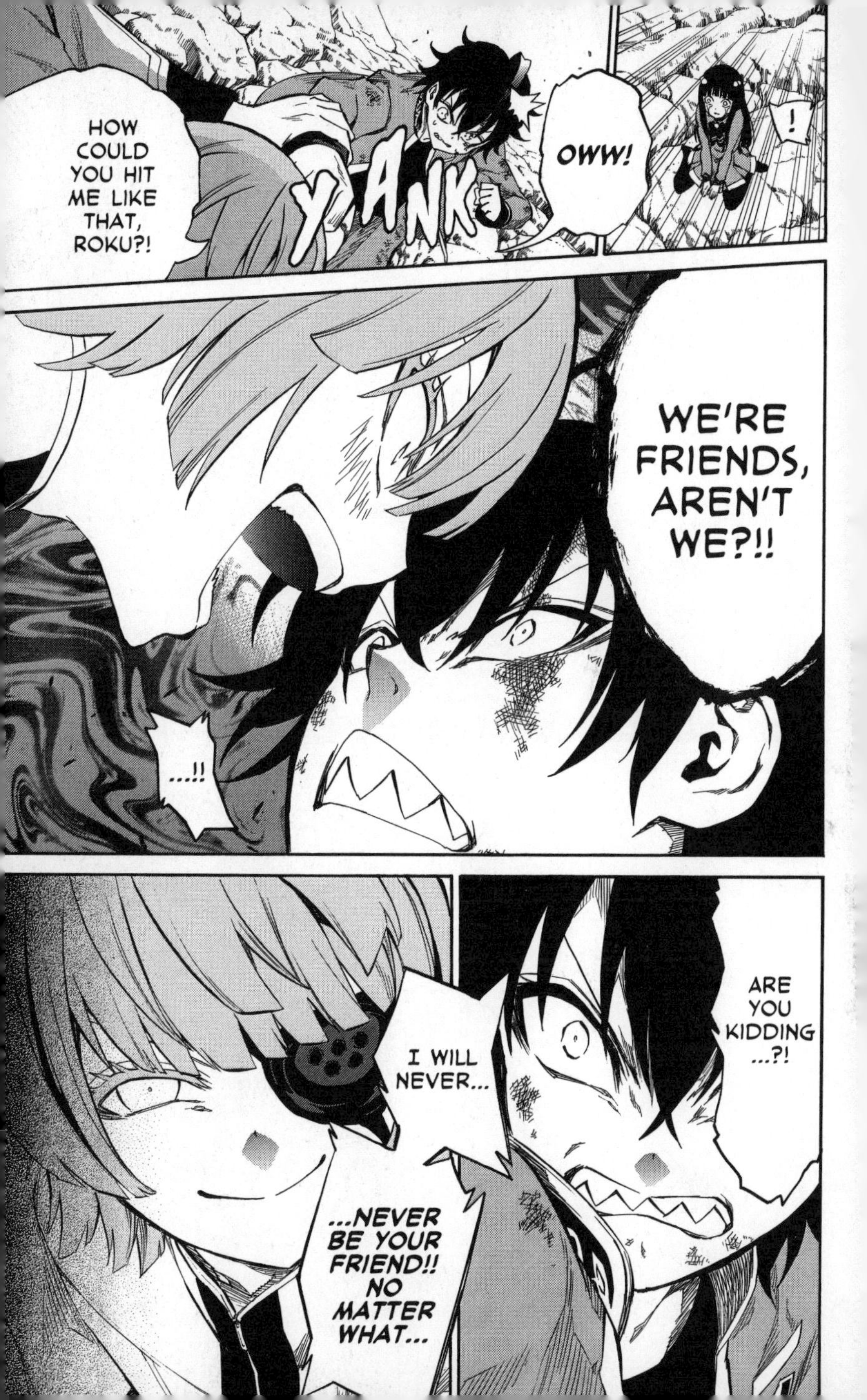
!
OWW!
YANK
HOW COULD YOU HIT ME LIKE THAT, ROKU?!
WE'RE FRIENDS, AREN'T WE?!!
...!!
ARE YOU KIDDING...?!
I WILL NEVER...
...NEVER BE YOUR FRIEND!! NO MATTER WHAT...

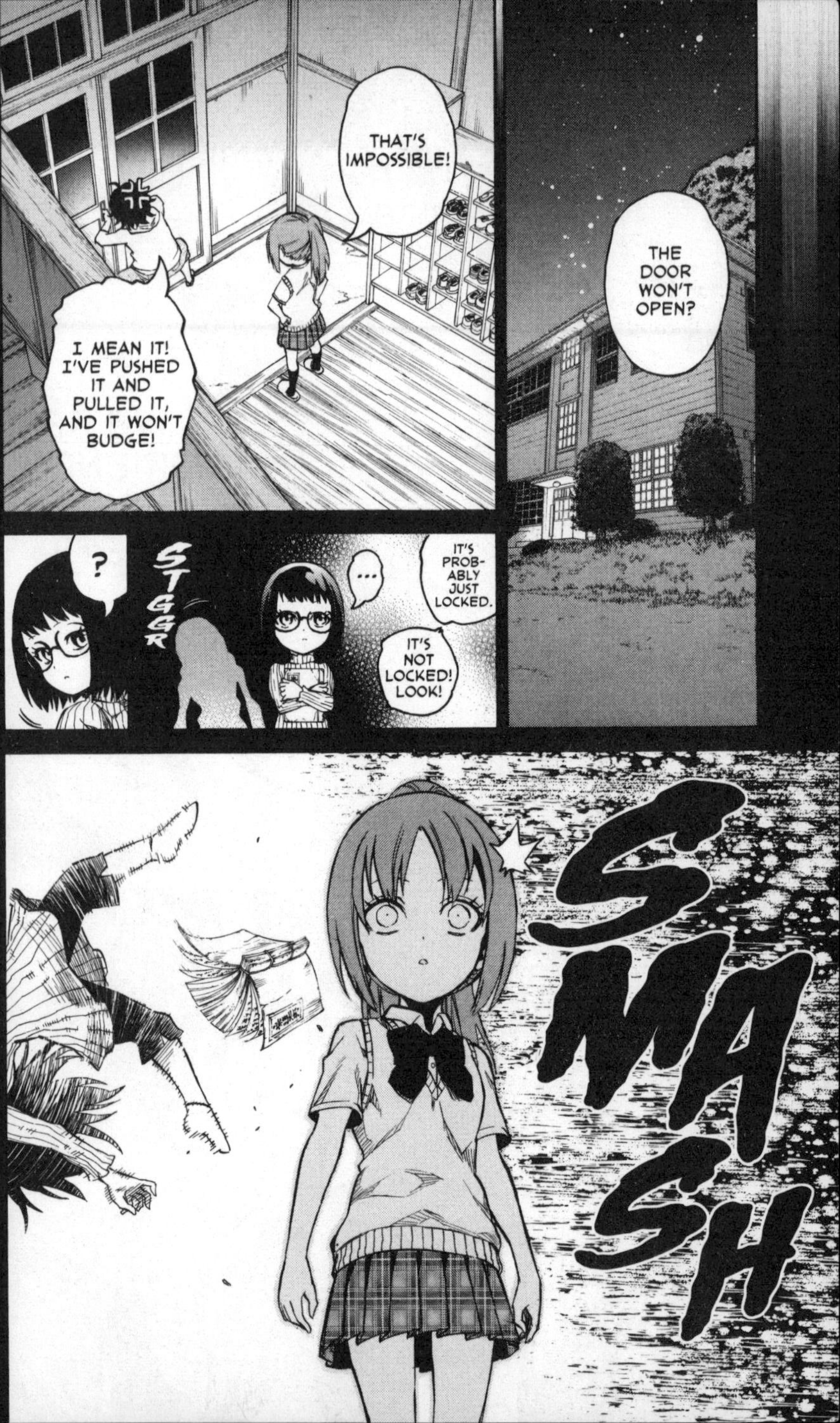
THE DOOR WON'T OPEN?
THAT'S IMPOSSIBLE!
I MEAN IT! I'VE PUSHED IT AND PULLED IT, AND IT WON'T BUDGE!
IT'S PROB-ABLY JUST LOCKED.
...
IT'S NOT LOCKED! LOOK!
STGGR
?
SMASH

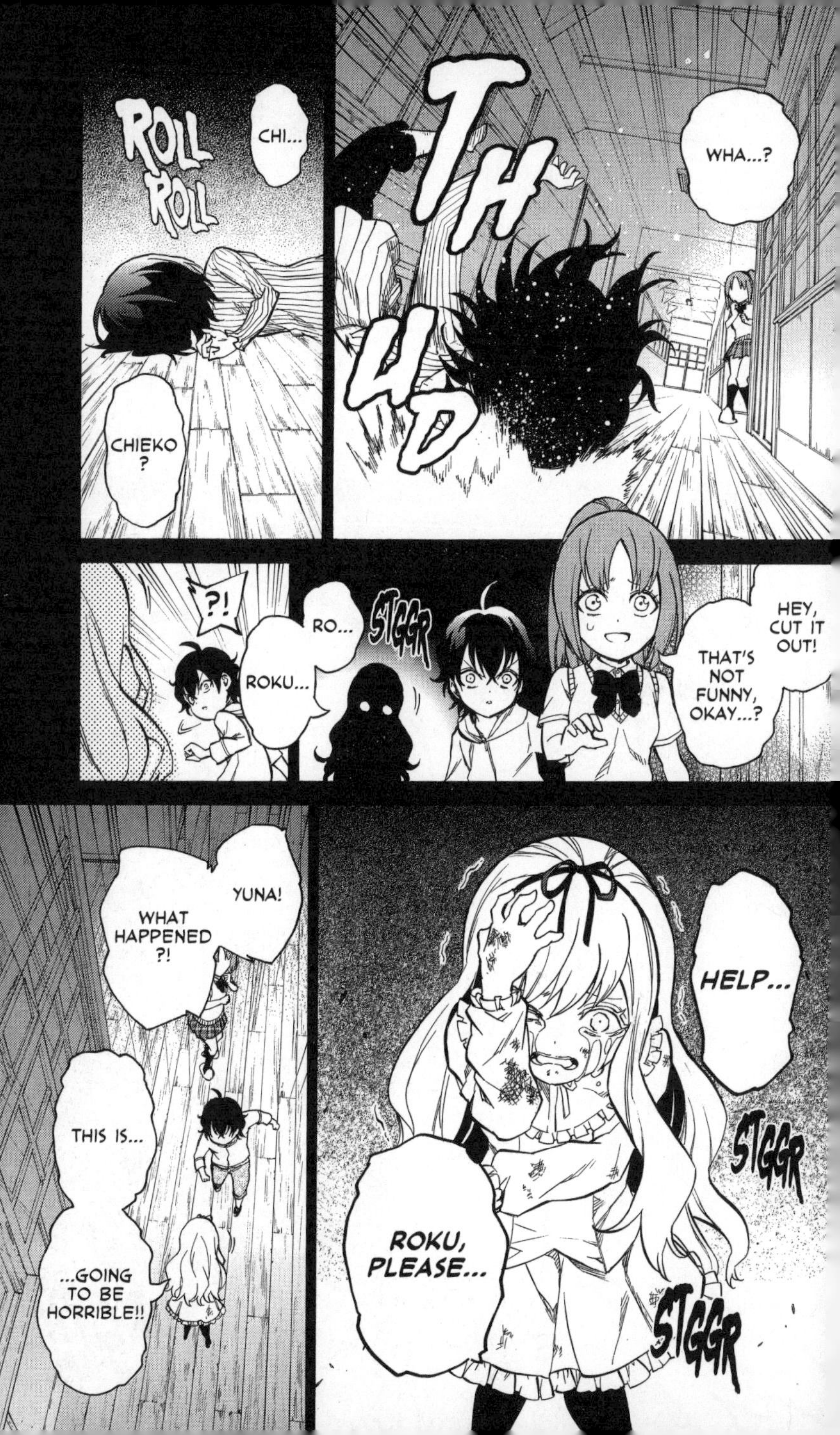
WHA...?
THUD
CHI...
ROLL ROLL
CHIEKO?
HEY, CUT IT OUT!
THAT'S NOT FUNNY, OKAY...?
STGGR
RO...
ROKU...
?!
HELP...
STGGR
ROKU, PLEASE...
STGGR
YUNA!
WHAT HAPPENED?!
THIS IS...
...GOING TO BE HORRIBLE!!

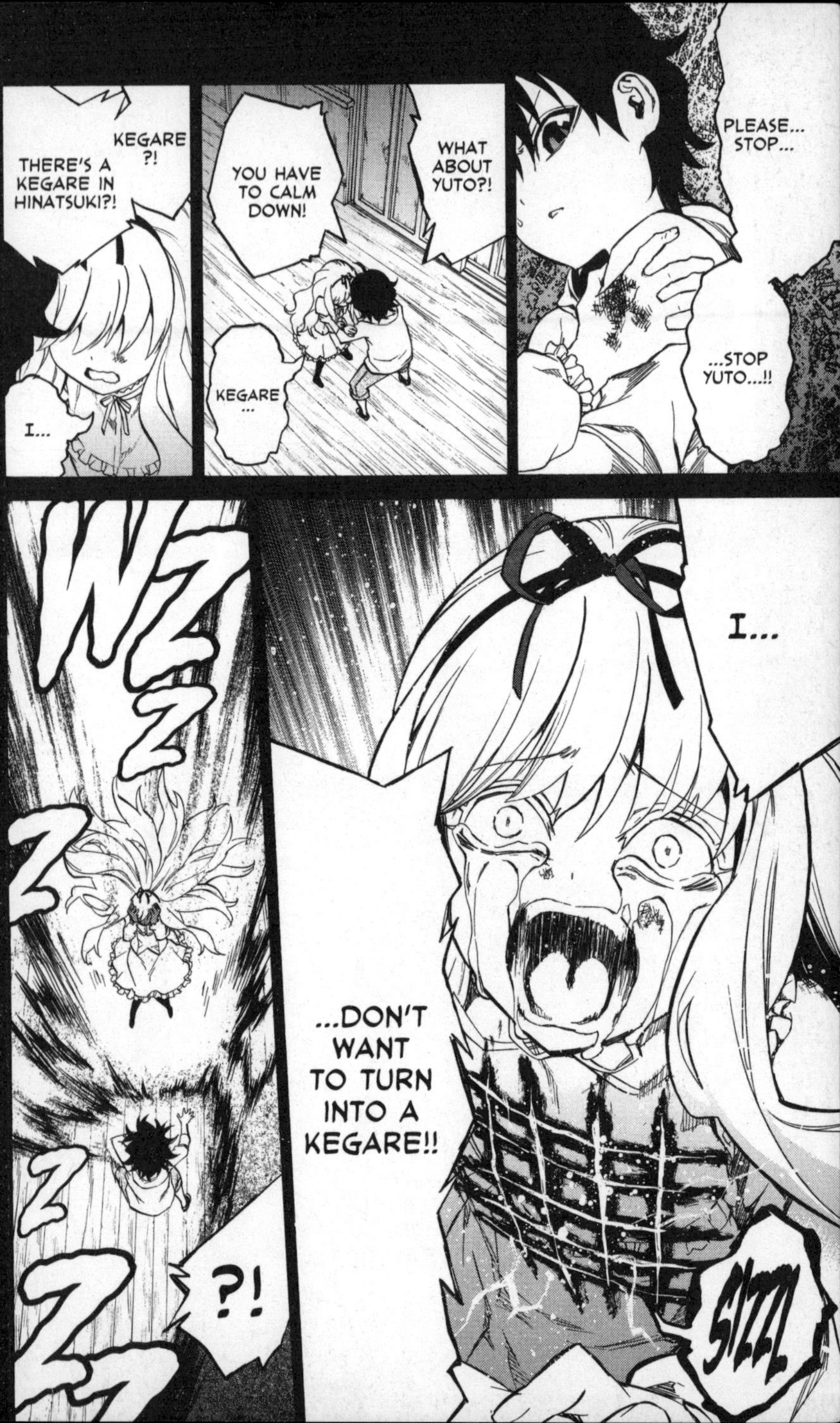
PLEASE... STOP...
...STOP YUTO...!!
WHAT ABOUT YUTO?!
YOU HAVE TO CALM DOWN!
KEGARE ...
KEGARE ?!
THERE'S A KEGARE IN HINATSUKI?!
I...
I...
...DON'T WANT TO TURN INTO A KEGARE!!
SIZZL
WZZZZZ
?!

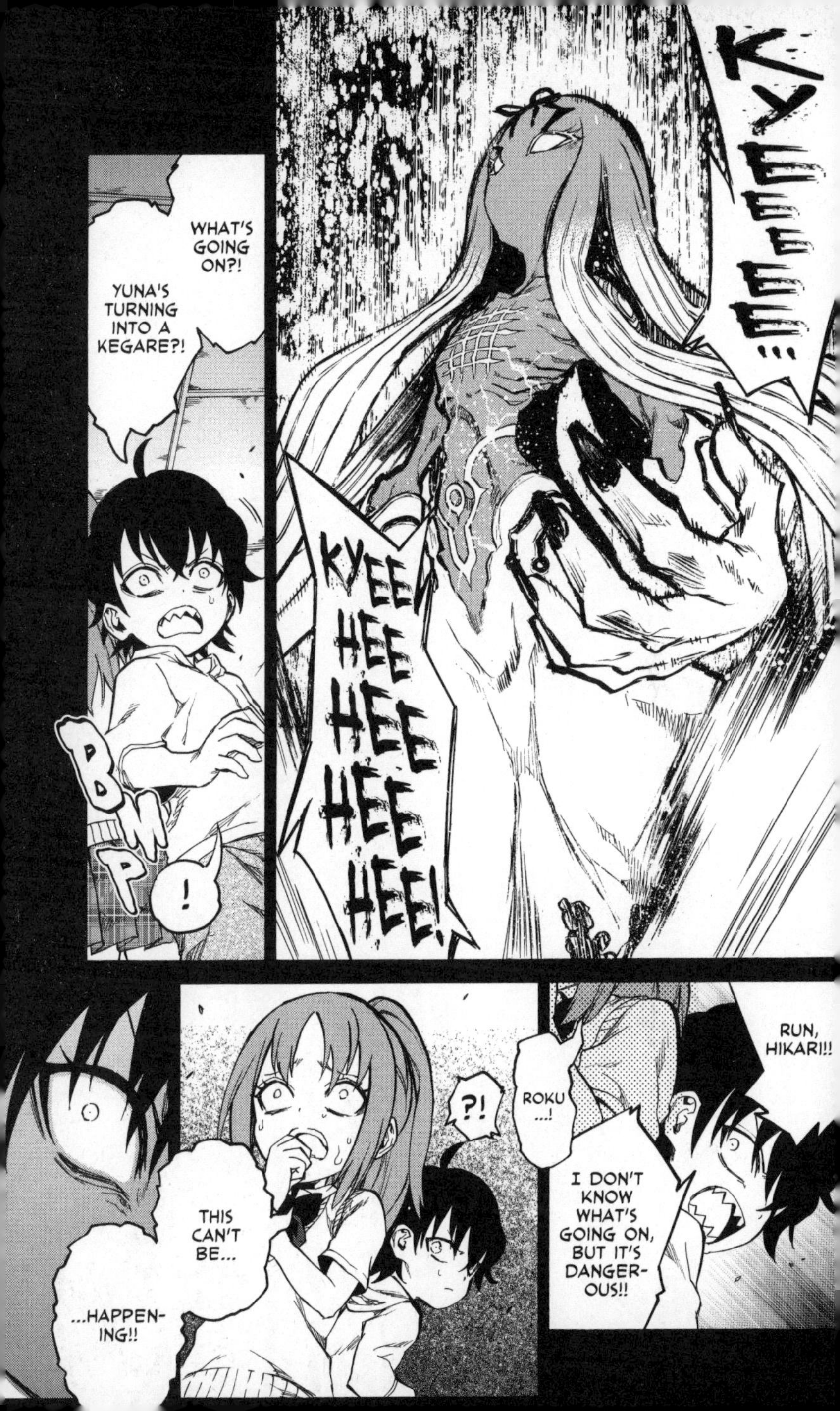
KYEEEEEE...
KYEEN HEE HEE HEE HEE!
WHAT'S GOING ON?!
YUNA'S TURNING INTO A KEGARE?!
BMP
!
RUN, HIKARI!!
ROKU ...!
I DON'T KNOW WHAT'S GOING ON, BUT IT'S DANGER-OUS!!
?!
THIS CAN'T BE...
...HAPPEN-ING!!

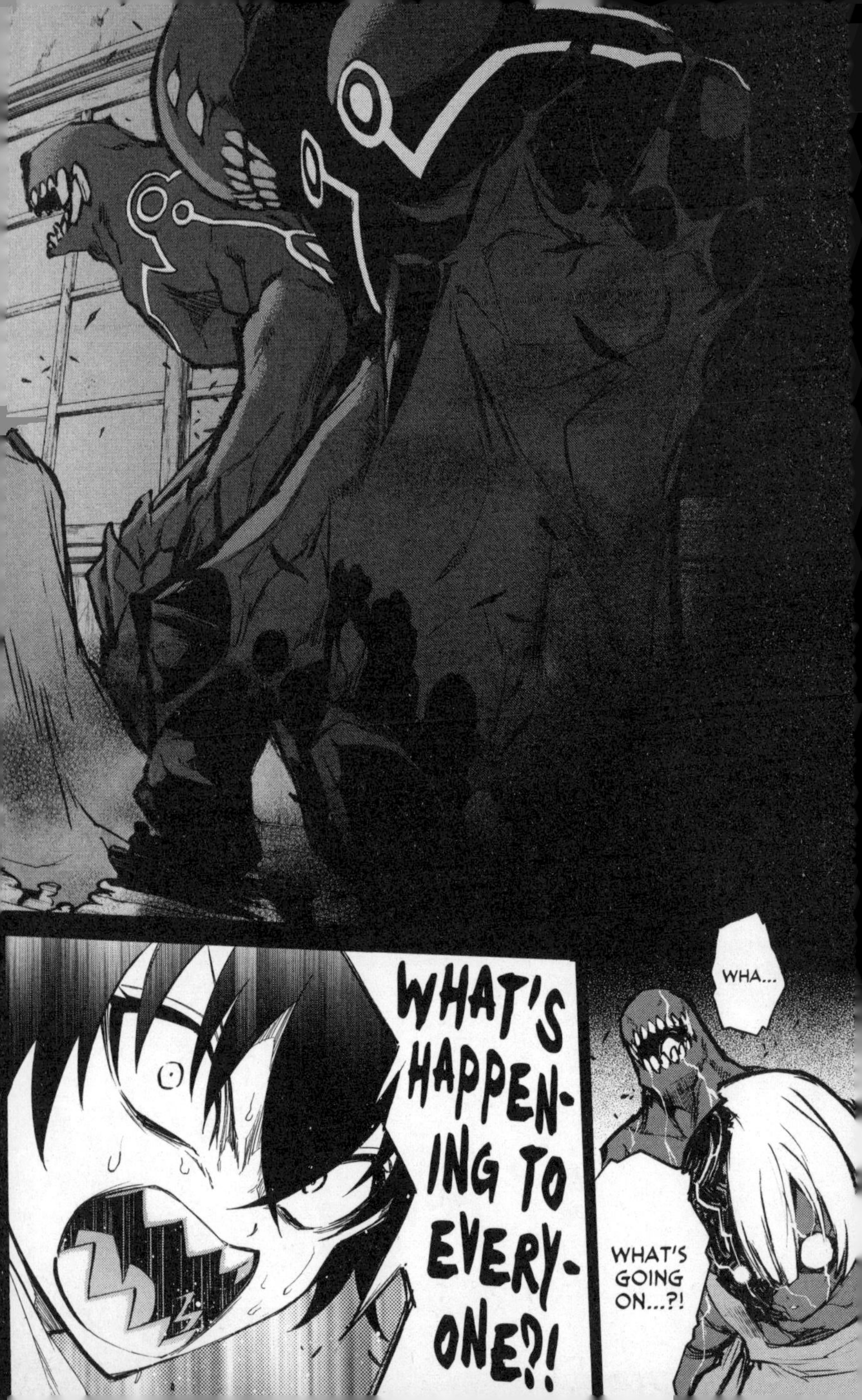
WHA...
WHAT'S GOING ON...?!
WHAT'S HAPPEN-ING TO EVERY-ONE?!

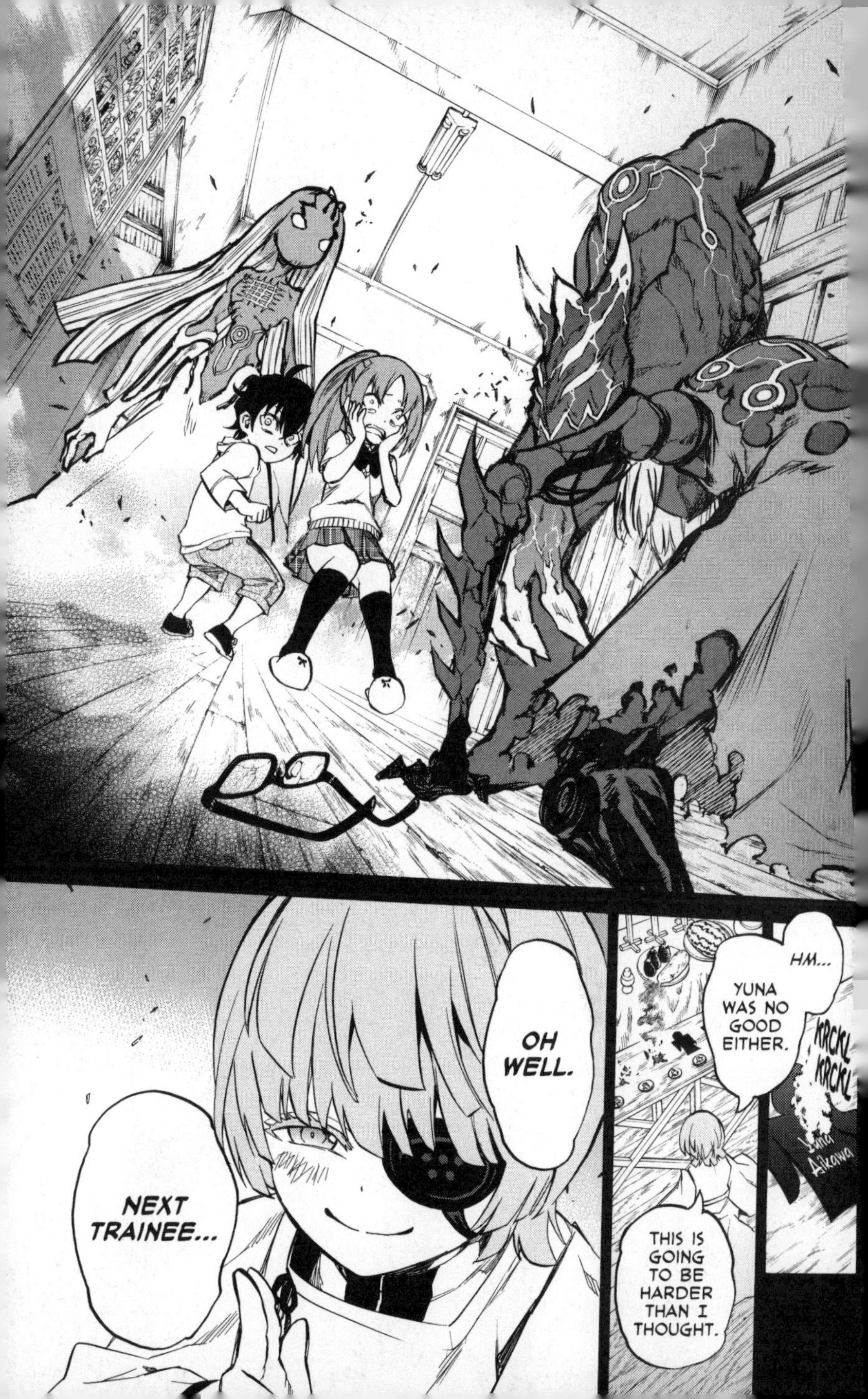
HM... YUNA WAS NO GOOD EITHER.
KRCKL KRCKL
THIS IS GOING TO BE HARDER THAN I THOUGHT.
OH WELL.
NEXT TRAINEE...

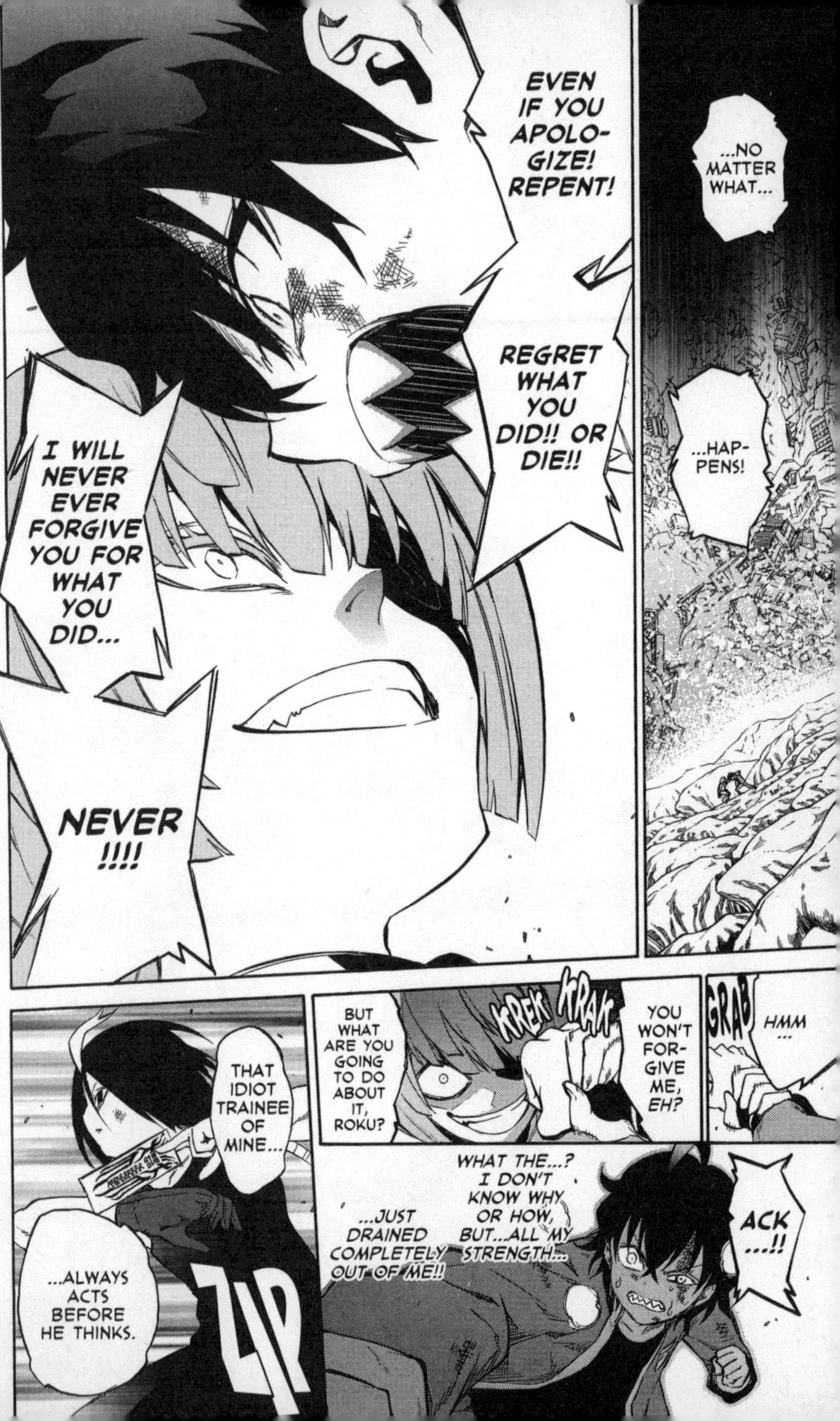
...NO MATTER WHAT...
...HAP-PENS!
EVEN IF YOU APOLO-GIZE! REPENT!
REGRET WHAT YOU DID!! OR DIE!!
I WILL NEVER EVER FORGIVE YOU FOR WHAT YOU DID...
NEVER !!!!
GRAB
HMM ...
KREK KRAK
YOU WON'T FOR-GIVE ME, EH?
BUT WHAT ARE YOU GOING TO DO ABOUT IT, ROKU?
ACK ...!!
WHAT THE...? I DON'T KNOW WHY OR HOW, BUT...ALL MY STRENGTH...
...JUST DRAINED COMPLETELY OUT OF ME!!
THAT IDIOT TRAINEE OF MINE...
ZIP
...ALWAYS ACTS BEFORE HE THINKS.

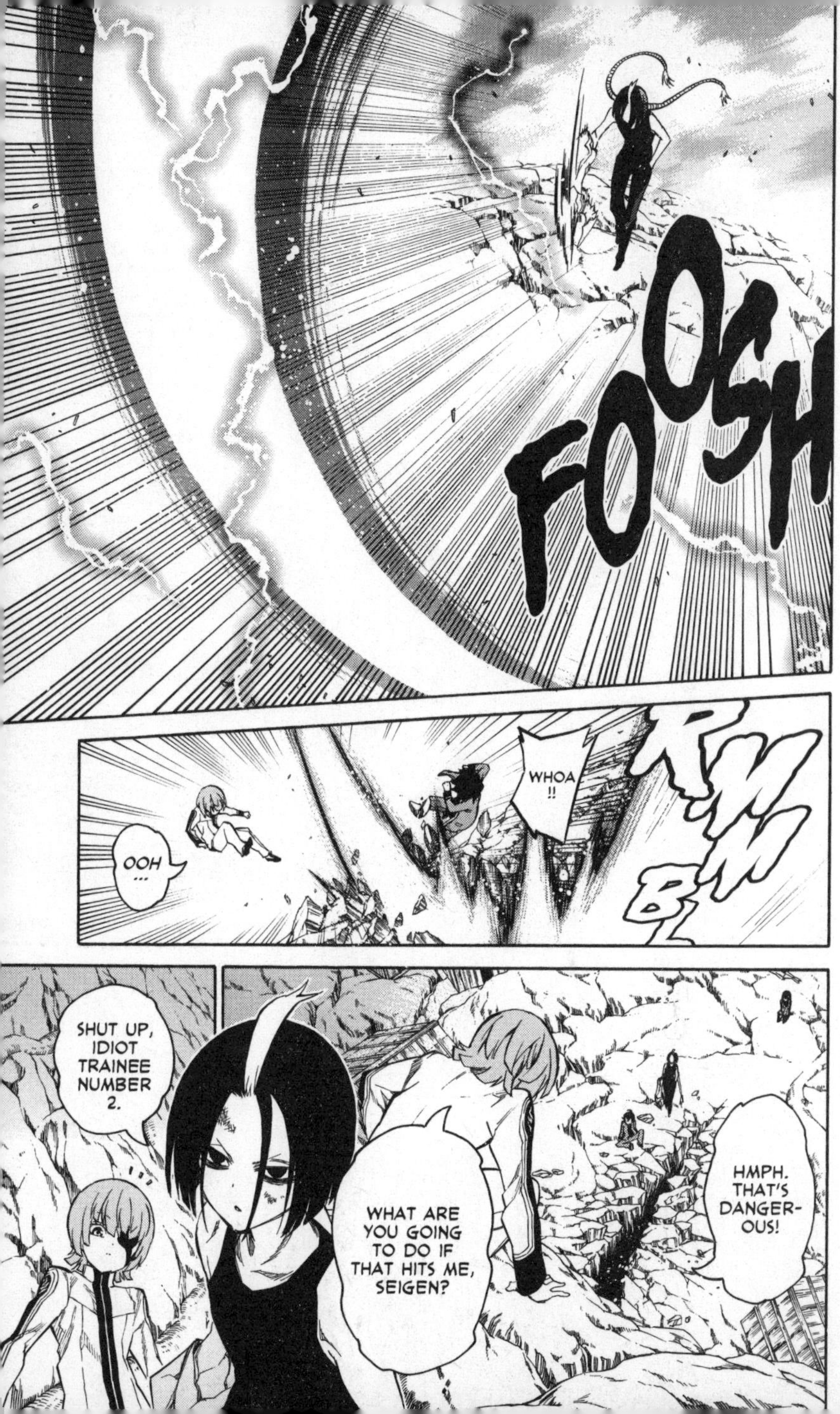
FOOSH
RMMBL
WHOA!!
OOH...
HMPH. THAT'S DANGER-OUS!
WHAT ARE YOU GOING TO DO IF THAT HITS ME, SEIGEN?
SHUT UP, IDIOT TRAINEE NUMBER 2.

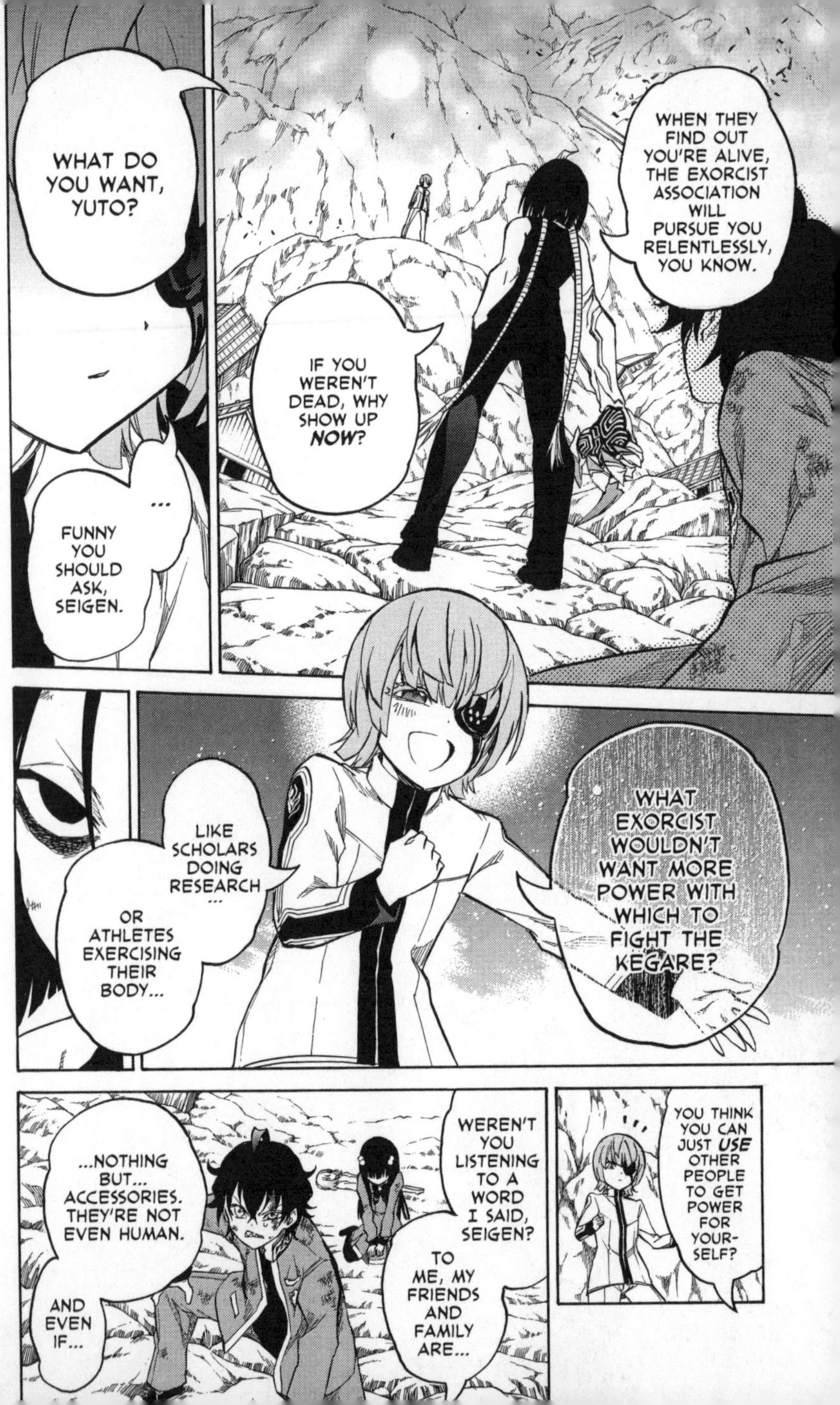
WHEN THEY FIND OUT YOU'RE ALIVE, THE EXORCIST ASSOCIATION WILL PURSUE YOU RELENTLESSLY, YOU KNOW.
IF YOU WEREN'T DEAD, WHY SHOW UP *NOW*?
WHAT DO YOU WANT, YUTO?
...
FUNNY YOU SHOULD ASK, SEIGEN.
WHAT EXORCIST WOULDN'T WANT MORE POWER WITH WHICH TO FIGHT THE KEGARE?
LIKE SCHOLARS DOING RESEARCH...
OR ATHLETES EXERCISING THEIR BODY...
YOU THINK YOU CAN JUST *USE* OTHER PEOPLE TO GET POWER FOR YOUR-SELF?
WEREN'T YOU LISTENING TO A WORD I SAID, SEIGEN?
TO ME, MY FRIENDS AND FAMILY ARE...
...NOTHING BUT... ACCESSORIES. THEY'RE NOT EVEN HUMAN.
AND EVEN IF...

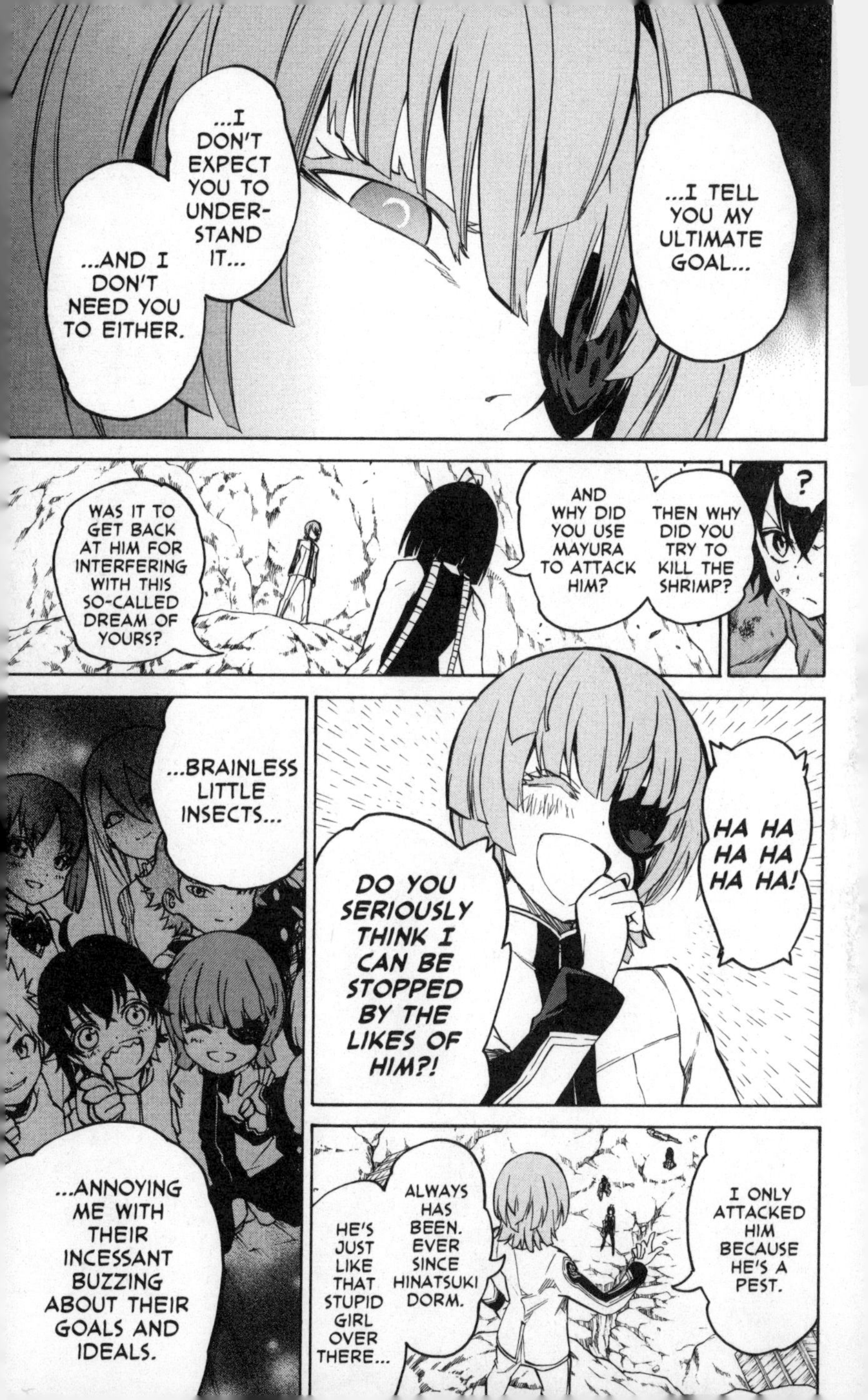
...I TELL YOU MY ULTIMATE GOAL...
...I DON'T EXPECT YOU TO UNDER-STAND IT...
...AND I DON'T NEED YOU TO EITHER.
?
THEN WHY DID YOU TRY TO KILL THE SHRIMP?
AND WHY DID YOU USE MAYURA TO ATTACK HIM?
WAS IT TO GET BACK AT HIM FOR INTERFERING WITH THIS SO-CALLED DREAM OF YOURS?
HA HA HA HA HA HA!
DO YOU SERIOUSLY THINK I CAN BE STOPPED BY THE LIKES OF HIM?!
I ONLY ATTACKED HIM BECAUSE HE'S A PEST.
ALWAYS HAS BEEN. EVER SINCE HINATSUKI DORM.
HE'S JUST LIKE THAT STUPID GIRL OVER THERE...
...BRAINLESS LITTLE INSECTS...
...ANNOYING ME WITH THEIR INCESSANT BUZZING ABOUT THEIR GOALS AND IDEALS.

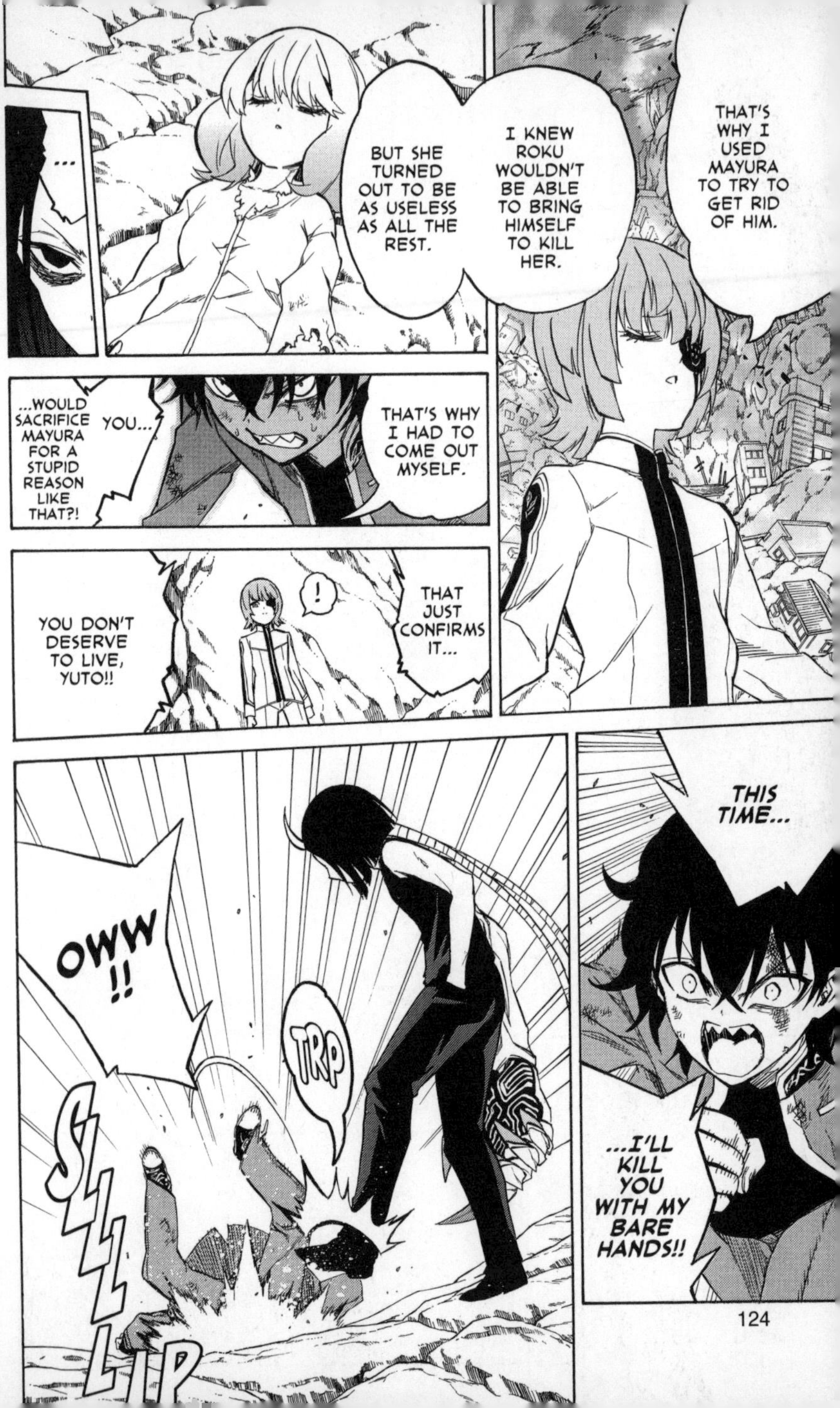

THAT'S WHY I USED MAYURA TO TRY TO GET RID OF HIM.
I KNEW ROKU WOULDN'T BE ABLE TO BRING HIMSELF TO KILL HER.
BUT SHE TURNED OUT TO BE AS USELESS AS ALL THE REST.
...
THAT'S WHY I HAD TO COME OUT MYSELF.
YOU...
...WOULD SACRIFICE MAYURA FOR A STUPID REASON LIKE THAT?!
THAT JUST CONFIRMS IT...
!
YOU DON'T DESERVE TO LIVE, YUTO!!
THIS TIME...
...I'LL KILL YOU WITH MY BARE HANDS!!
TRP
OWW!!
SLLLIP

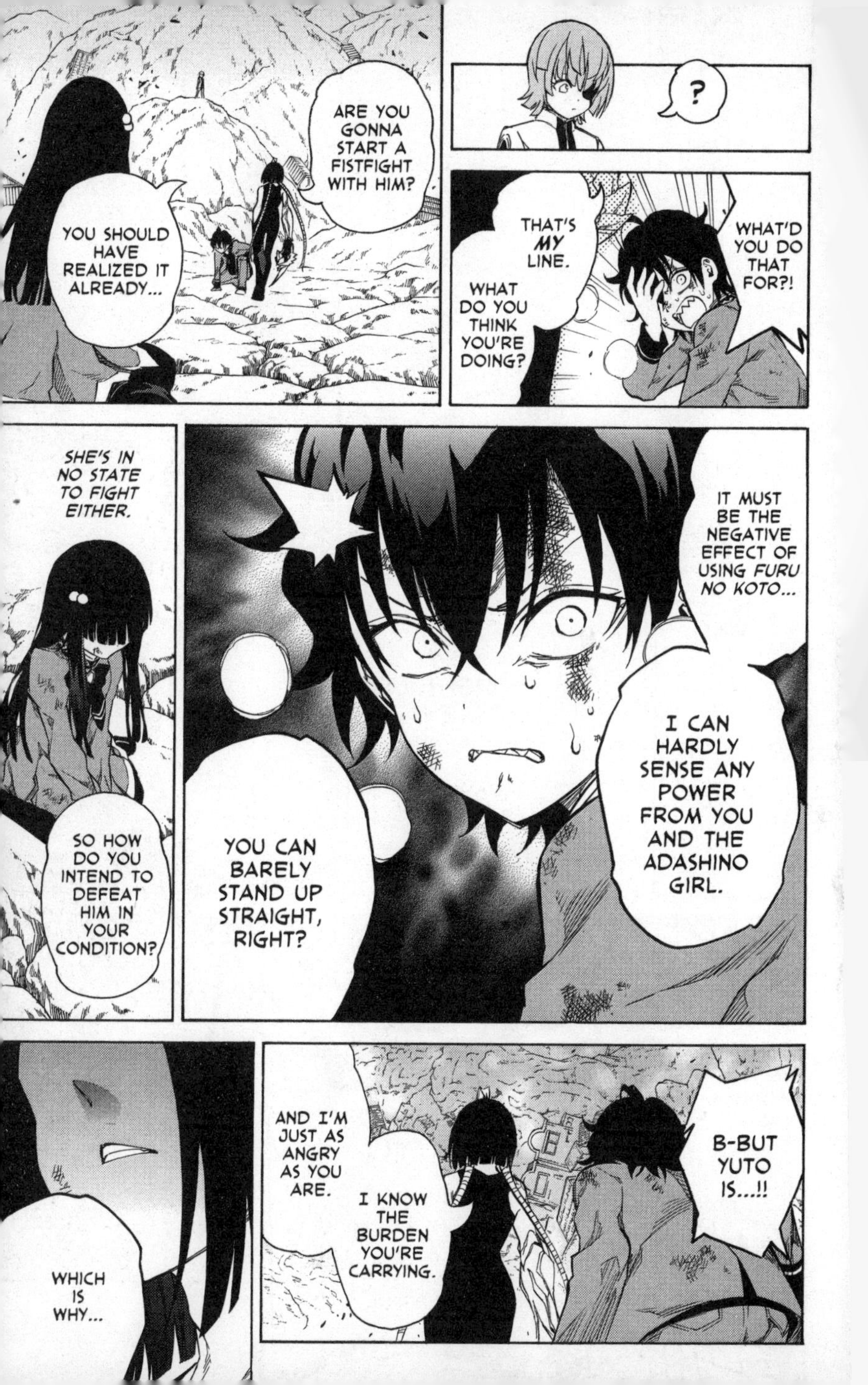
?
WHAT'D YOU DO THAT FOR?!
THAT'S *MY* LINE.
WHAT DO YOU THINK YOU'RE DOING?
ARE YOU GONNA START A FISTFIGHT WITH HIM?
YOU SHOULD HAVE REALIZED IT ALREADY...
IT MUST BE THE NEGATIVE EFFECT OF USING *FURU NO KOTO*...
I CAN HARDLY SENSE ANY POWER FROM YOU AND THE ADASHINO GIRL.
YOU CAN BARELY STAND UP STRAIGHT, RIGHT?
SHE'S IN NO STATE TO FIGHT EITHER.
SO HOW DO YOU INTEND TO DEFEAT HIM IN YOUR CONDITION?
B-BUT YUTO IS...!!
AND I'M JUST AS ANGRY AS YOU ARE.
I KNOW THE BURDEN YOU'RE CARRYING.
WHICH IS WHY...

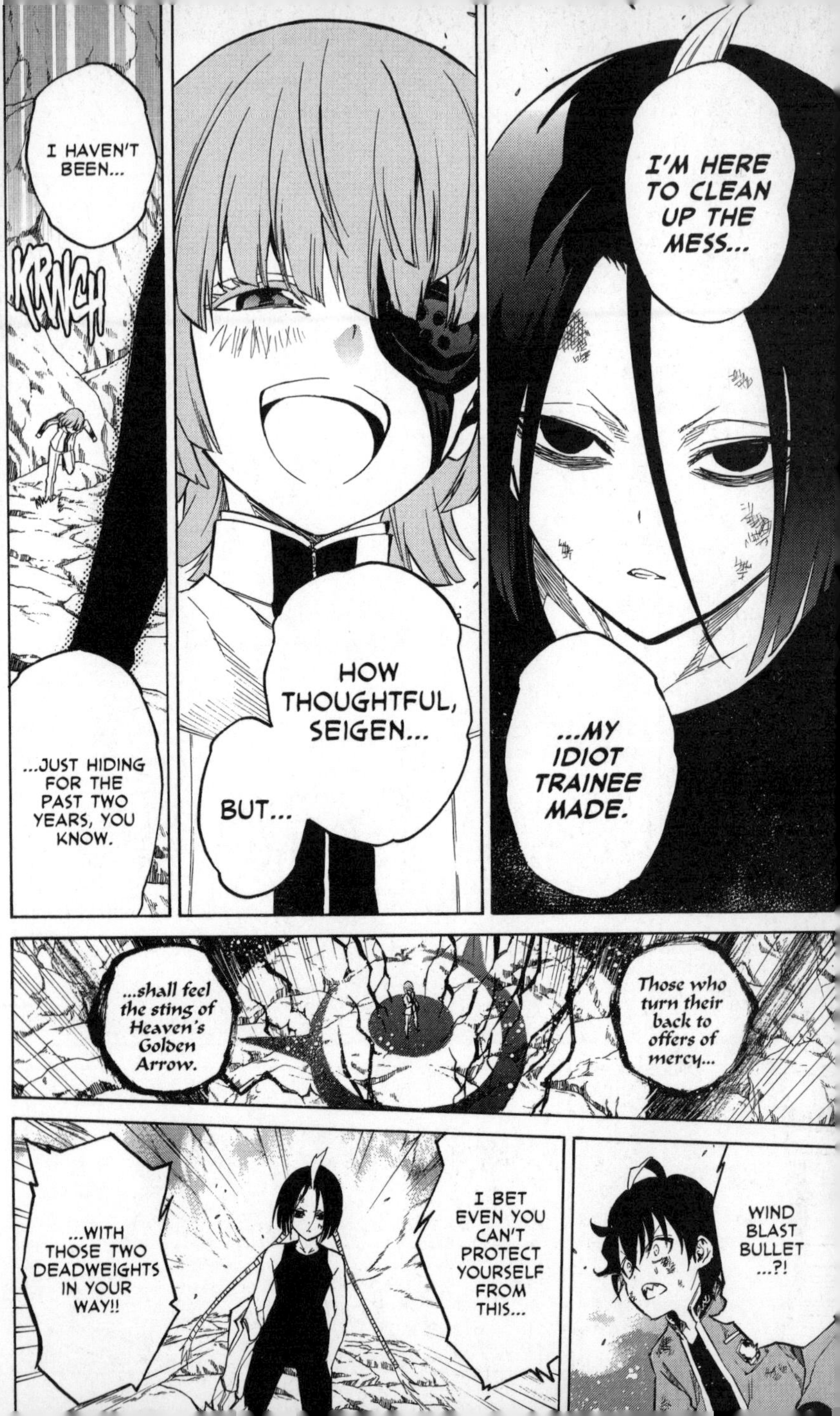
I'M HERE TO CLEAN UP THE MESS...
...MY IDIOT TRAINEE MADE.
HOW THOUGHTFUL, SEIGEN...
BUT...
I HAVEN'T BEEN...
KRWCH
...JUST HIDING FOR THE PAST TWO YEARS, YOU KNOW.
Those who turn their back to offers of mercy...
...shall feel the sting of Heaven's Golden Arrow.
WIND BLAST BULLET ...?!
I BET EVEN YOU CAN'T PROTECT YOURSELF FROM THIS...
...WITH THOSE TWO DEADWEIGHTS IN YOUR WAY!!

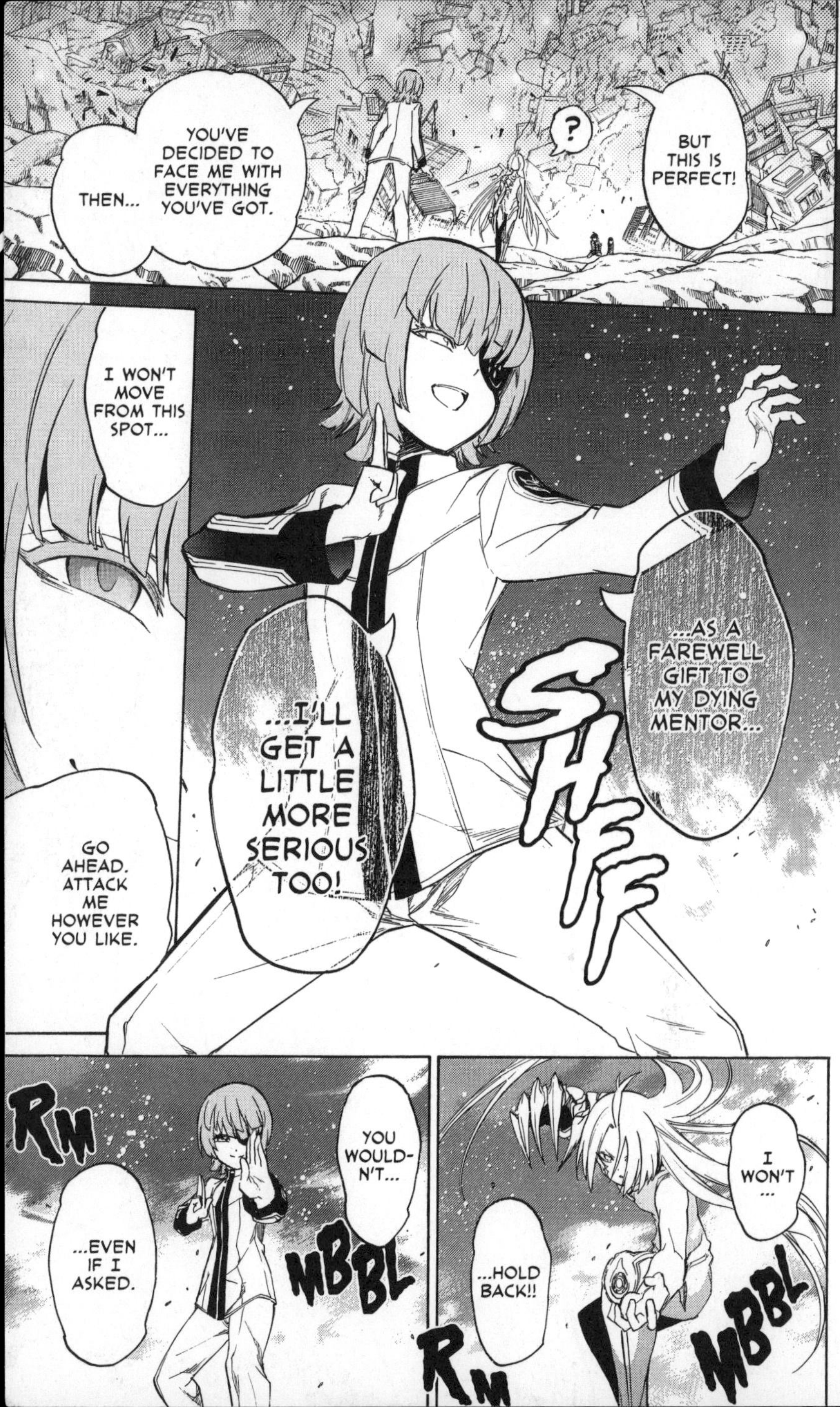
BUT THIS IS PERFECT!
?
THEN...
YOU'VE DECIDED TO FACE ME WITH EVERYTHING YOU'VE GOT.
...AS A FAREWELL GIFT TO MY DYING MENTOR...
SHFF
...I'LL GET A LITTLE MORE SERIOUS TOO!
I WON'T MOVE FROM THIS SPOT...
GO AHEAD. ATTACK ME HOWEVER YOU LIKE.
I WON'T ...
...HOLD BACK!!
RMMBBL
RMMBBL
YOU WOULDN'T...
...EVEN IF I ASKED.
RMMBBL

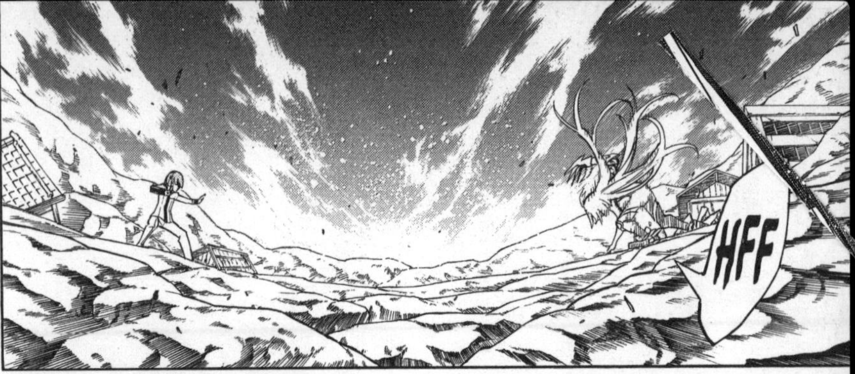
HFF
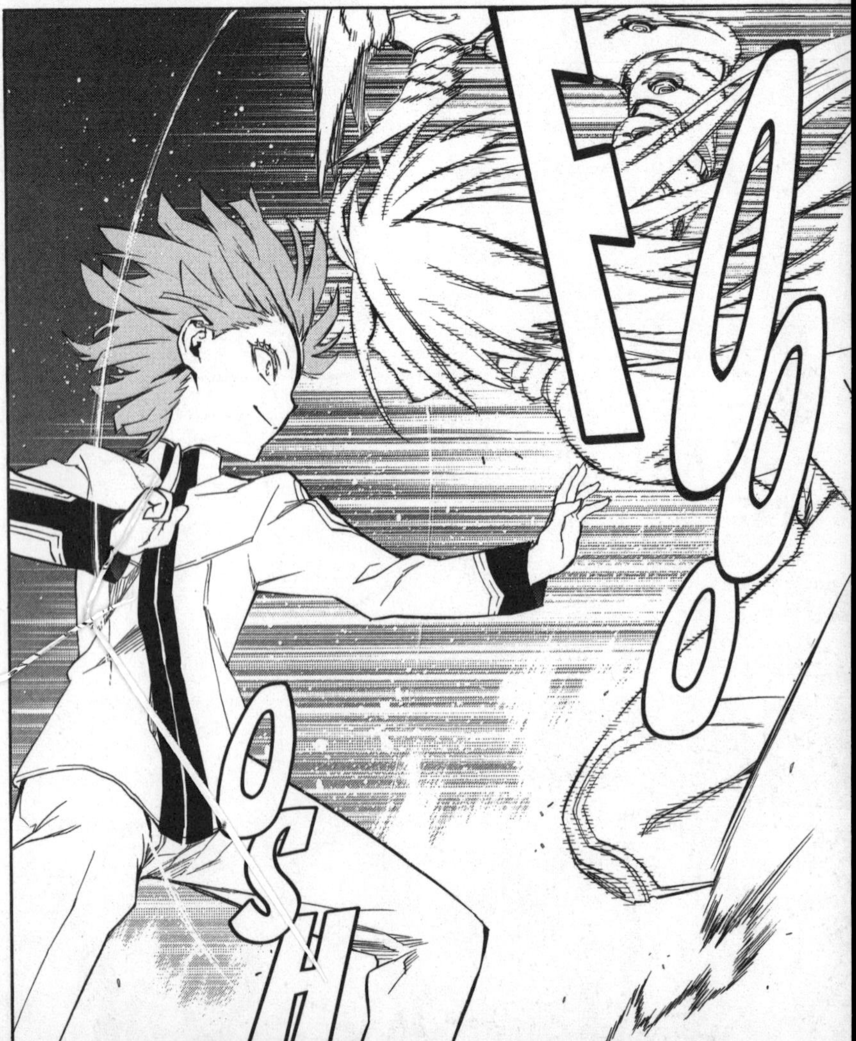
FOOOOOOSH

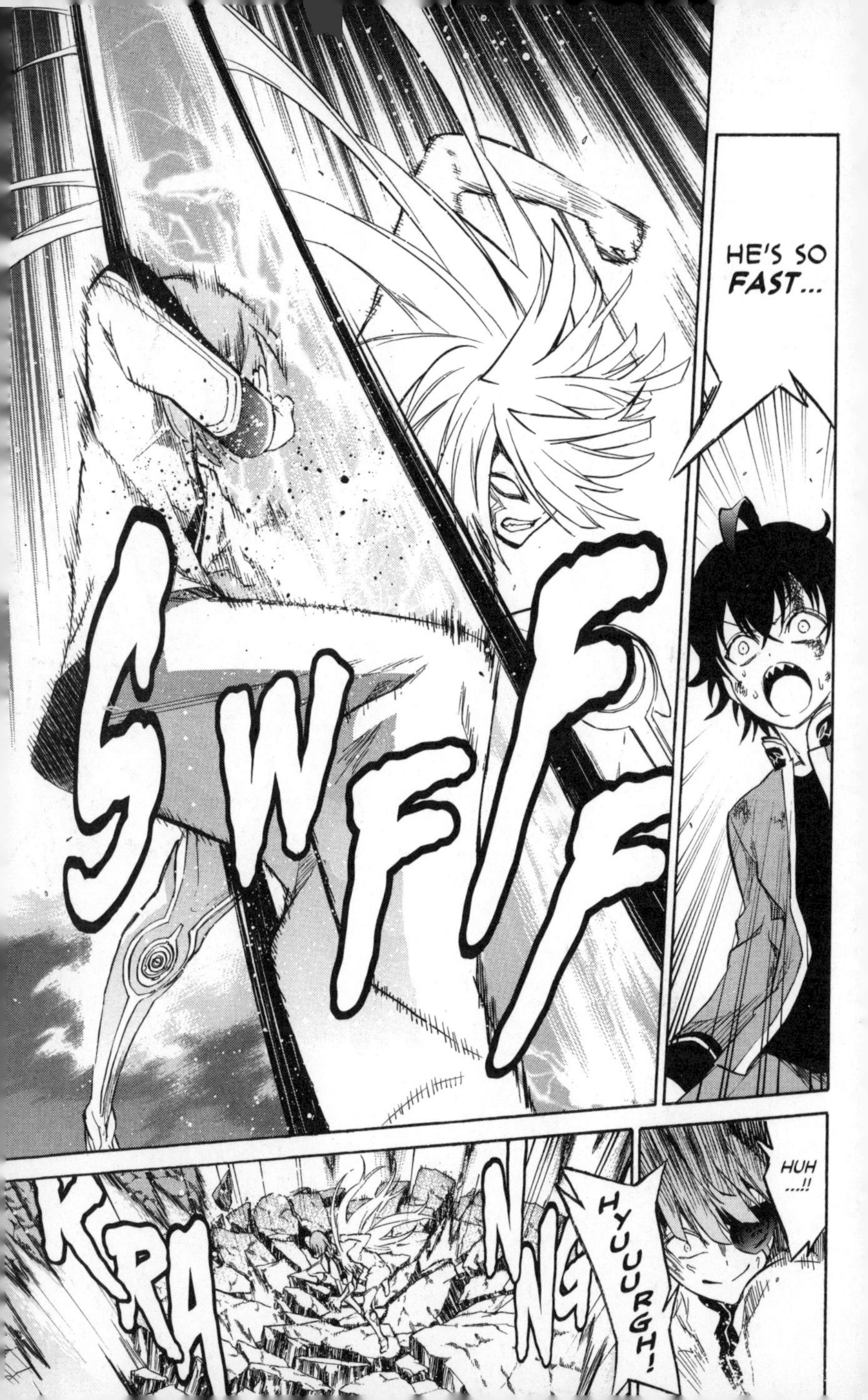
HE'S SO FAST...
SWFF
HUH ...!!
HYUUURGH!
KPANNG

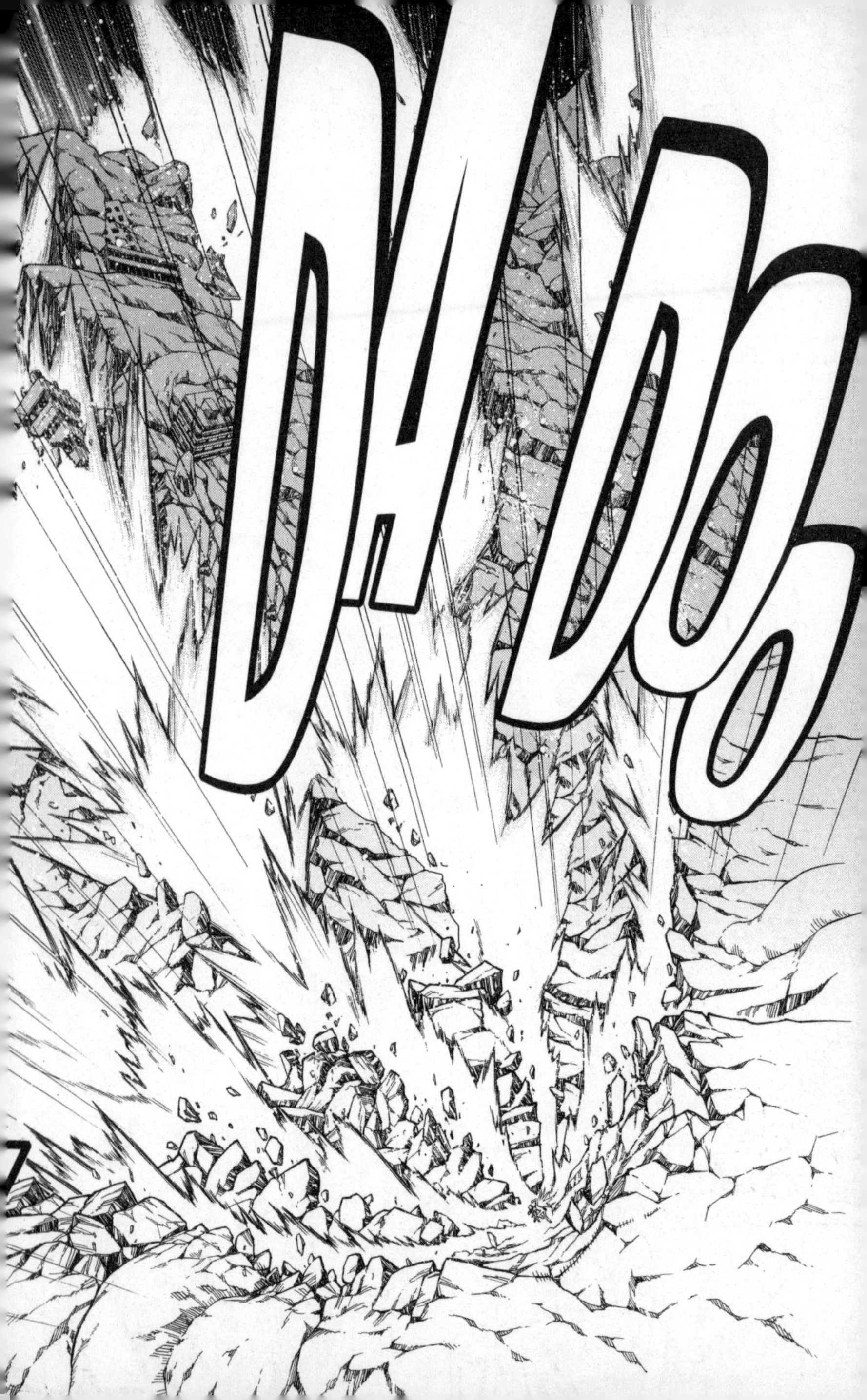
DHDO

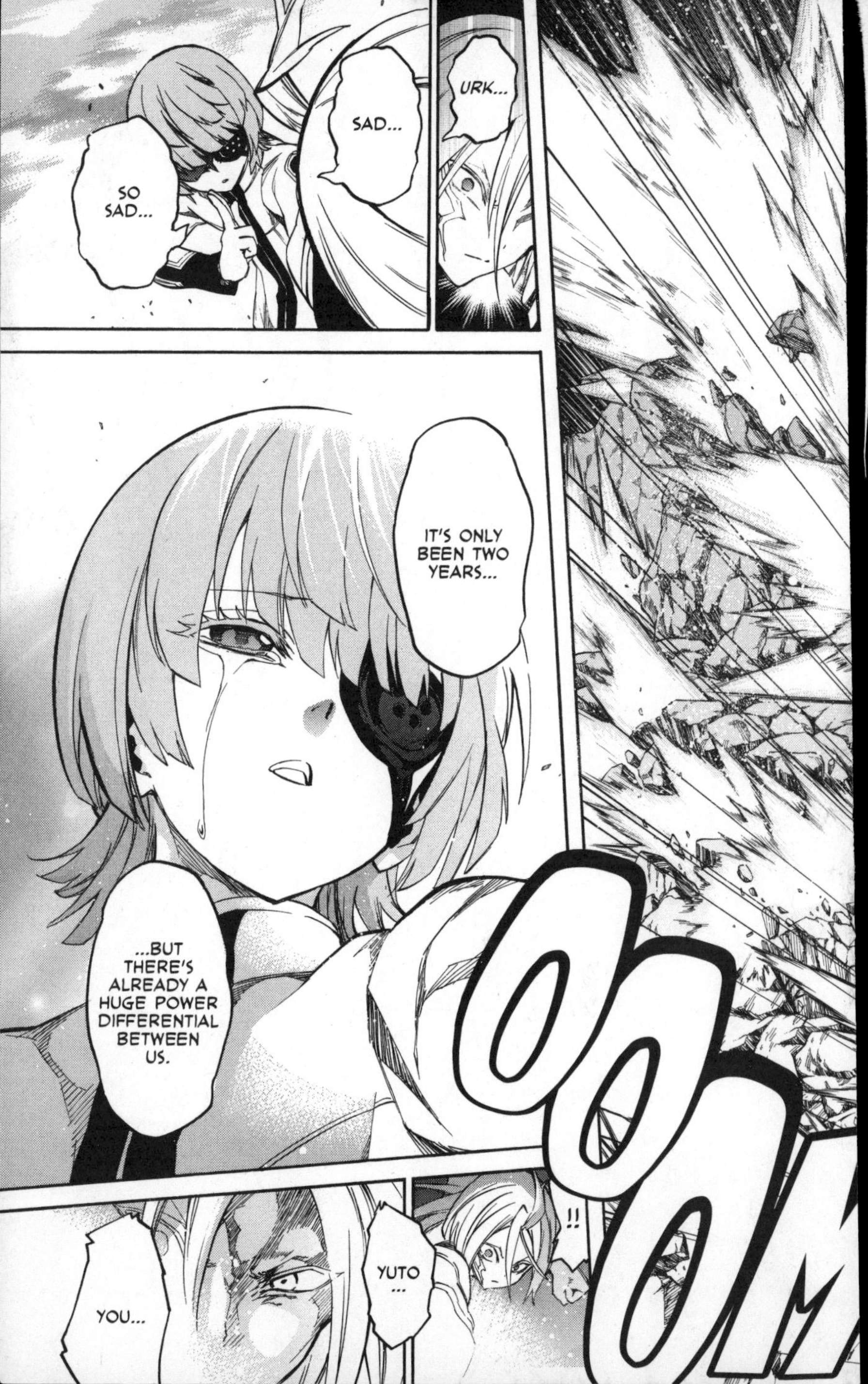
URK...
SAD...
SO SAD...
IT'S ONLY BEEN TWO YEARS...
...BUT THERE'S ALREADY A HUGE POWER DIFFERENTIAL BETWEEN US.
!!
YUTO ...
YOU...

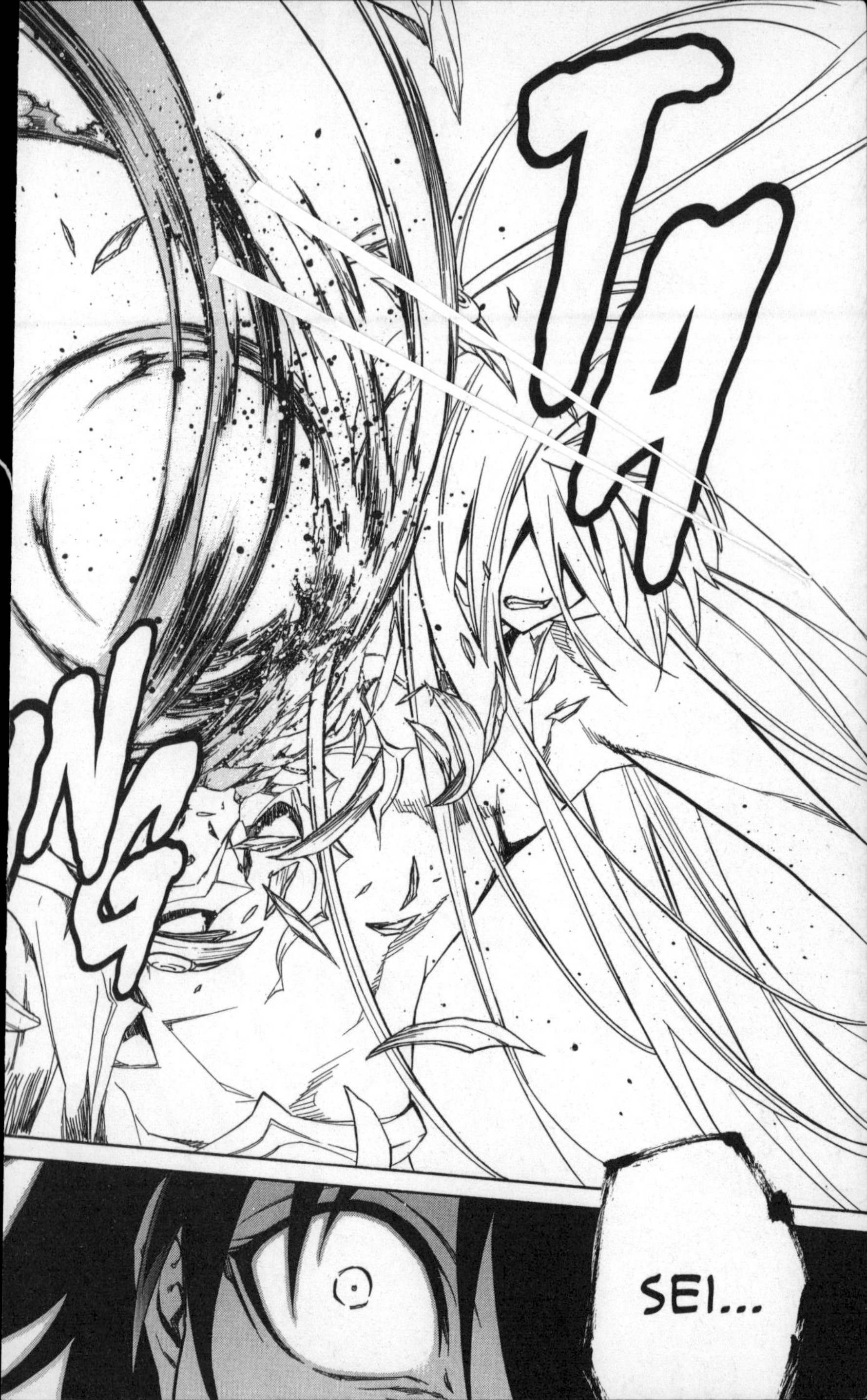
SEI...

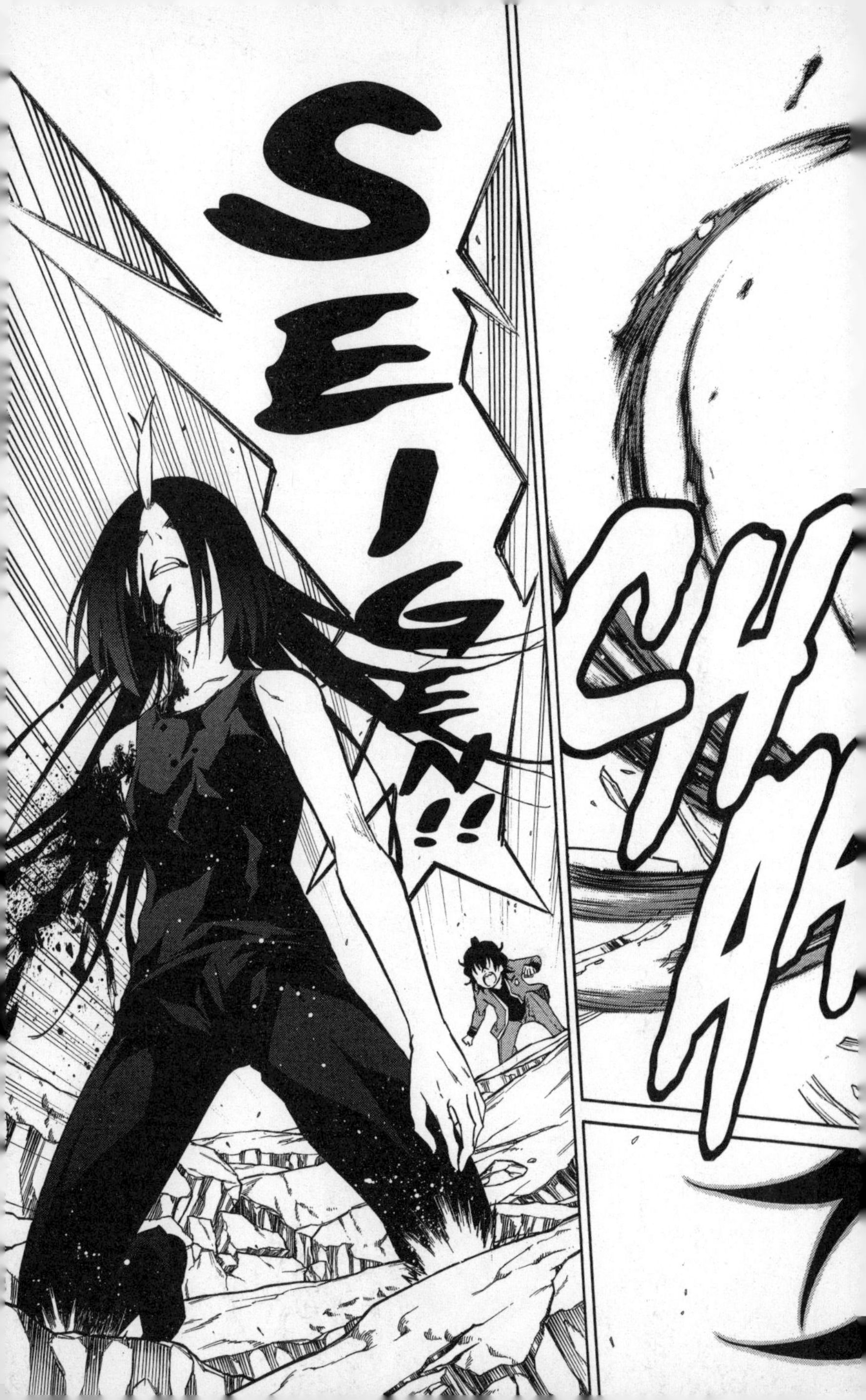
CHA
SEIGEN!!

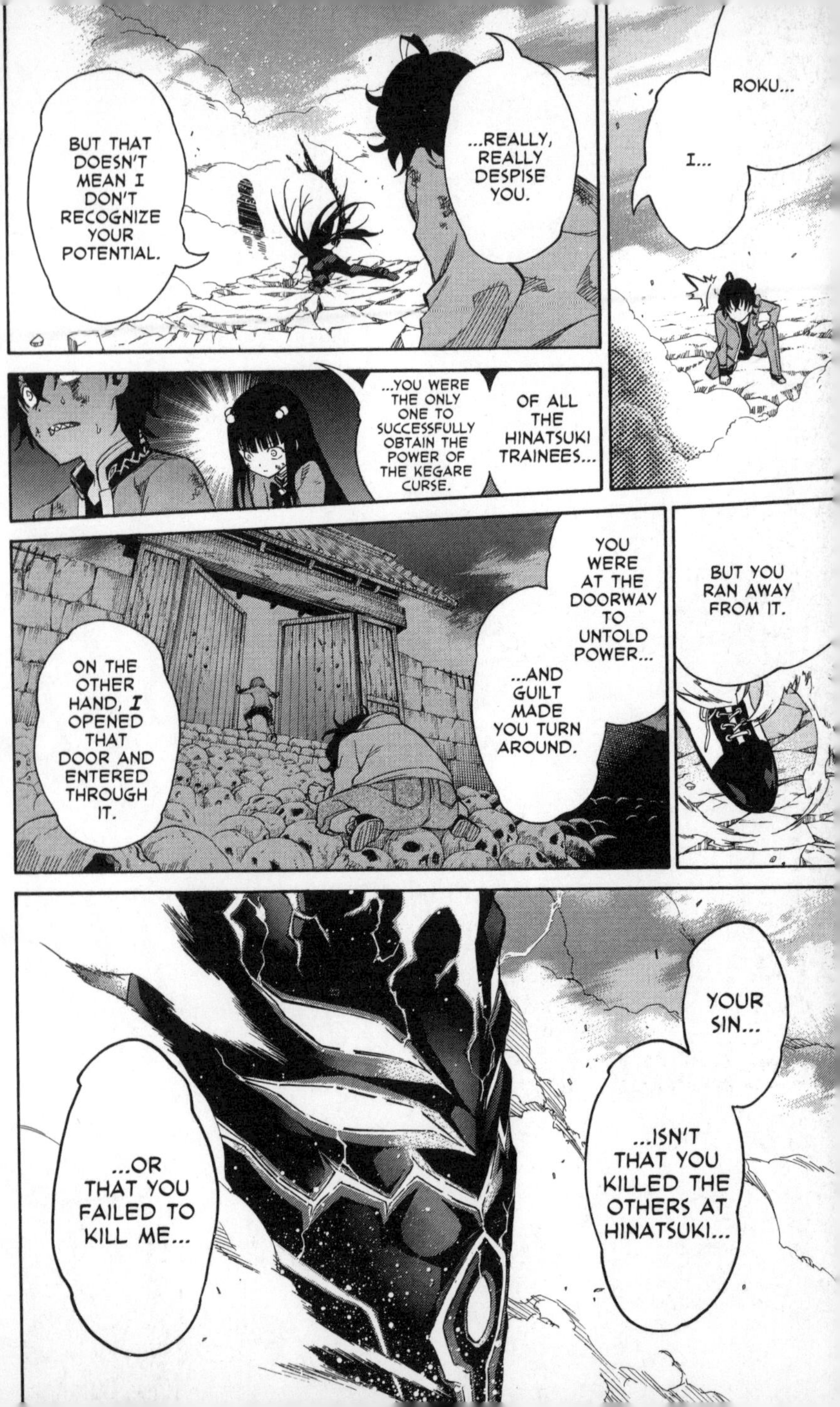
ROKU...
I...
...REALLY, REALLY DESPISE YOU.
BUT THAT DOESN'T MEAN I DON'T RECOGNIZE YOUR POTENTIAL.
OF ALL THE HINATSUKI TRAINEES...
...YOU WERE THE ONLY ONE TO SUCCESSFULLY OBTAIN THE POWER OF THE KEGARE CURSE.
BUT YOU RAN AWAY FROM IT.
YOU WERE AT THE DOORWAY TO UNTOLD POWER...
...AND GUILT MADE YOU TURN AROUND.
ON THE OTHER HAND, *I* OPENED THAT DOOR AND ENTERED THROUGH IT.
YOUR SIN...
...ISN'T THAT YOU KILLED THE OTHERS AT HINATSUKI...
...OR THAT YOU FAILED TO KILL ME...

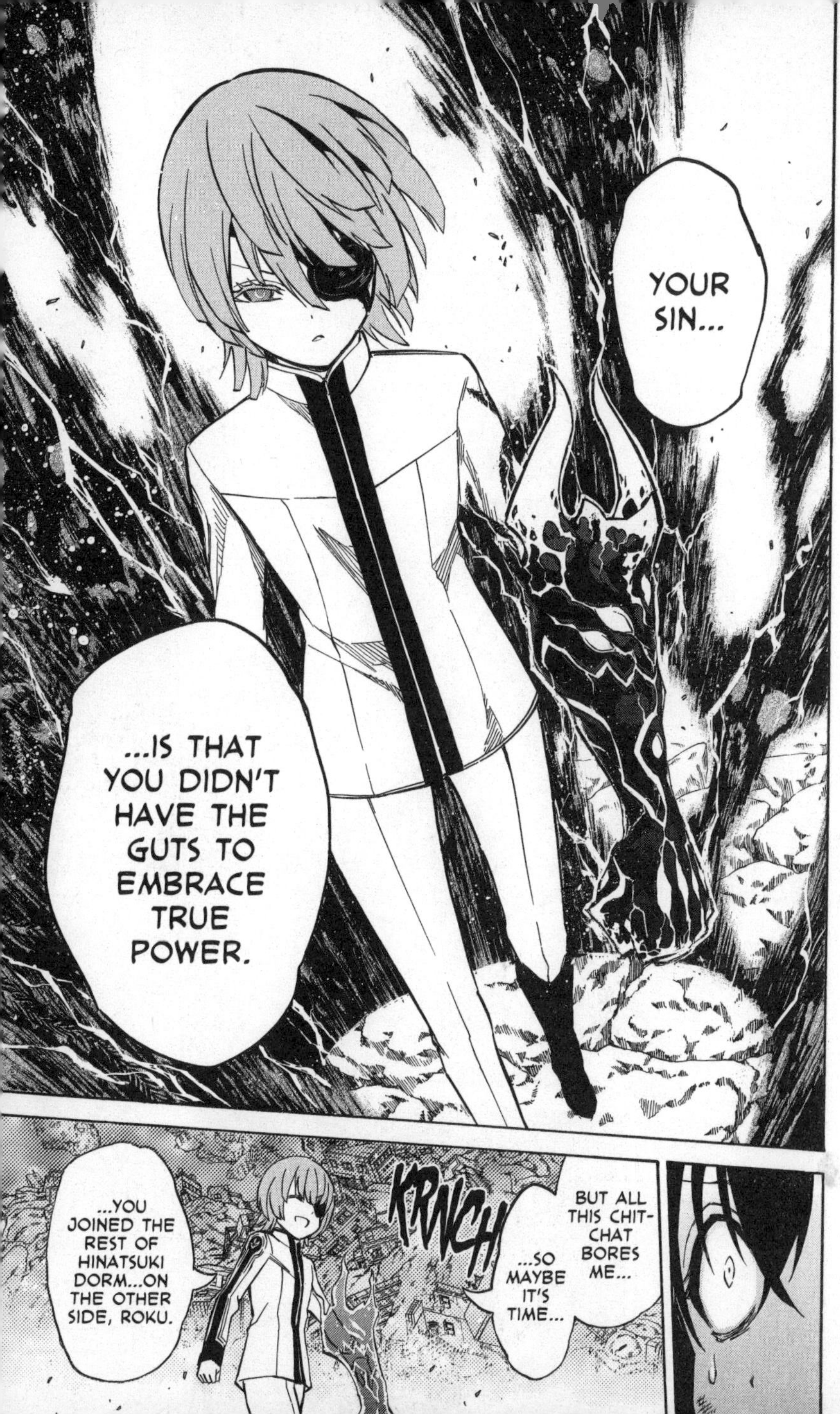
YOUR SIN...
...IS THAT YOU DIDN'T HAVE THE GUTS TO EMBRACE TRUE POWER.
BUT ALL THIS CHIT-CHAT BORES ME...
...SO MAYBE IT'S TIME...
KRNCH
...YOU JOINED THE REST OF HINATSUKI DORM...ON THE OTHER SIDE, ROKU.

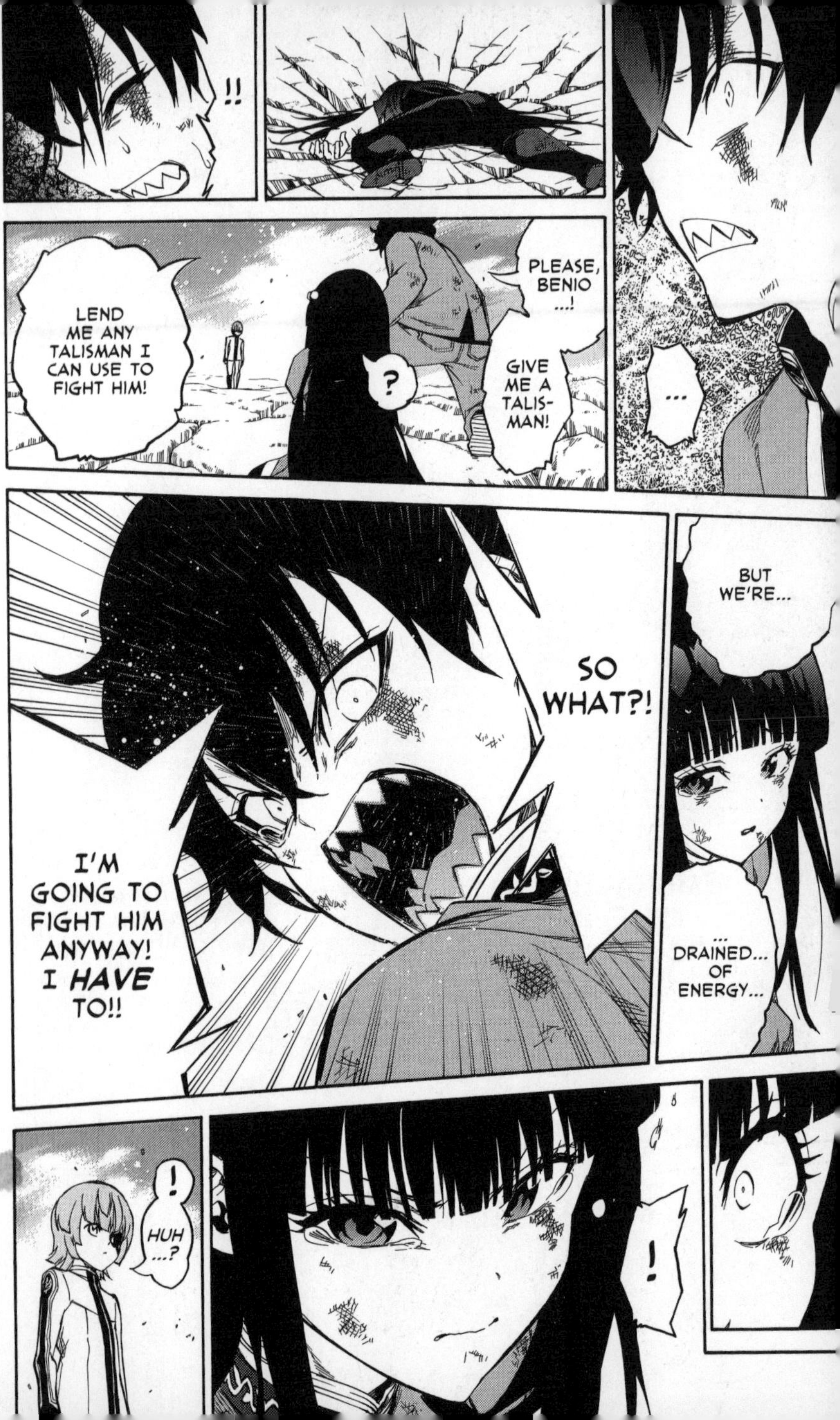
...
!!
PLEASE, BENIO ...!
GIVE ME A TALISMAN!
?
LEND ME ANY TALISMAN I CAN USE TO FIGHT HIM!
BUT WE'RE...
... DRAINED... OF ENERGY...
SO WHAT?!
I'M GOING TO FIGHT HIM ANYWAY! I *HAVE* TO!!
!
!
HUH ...?

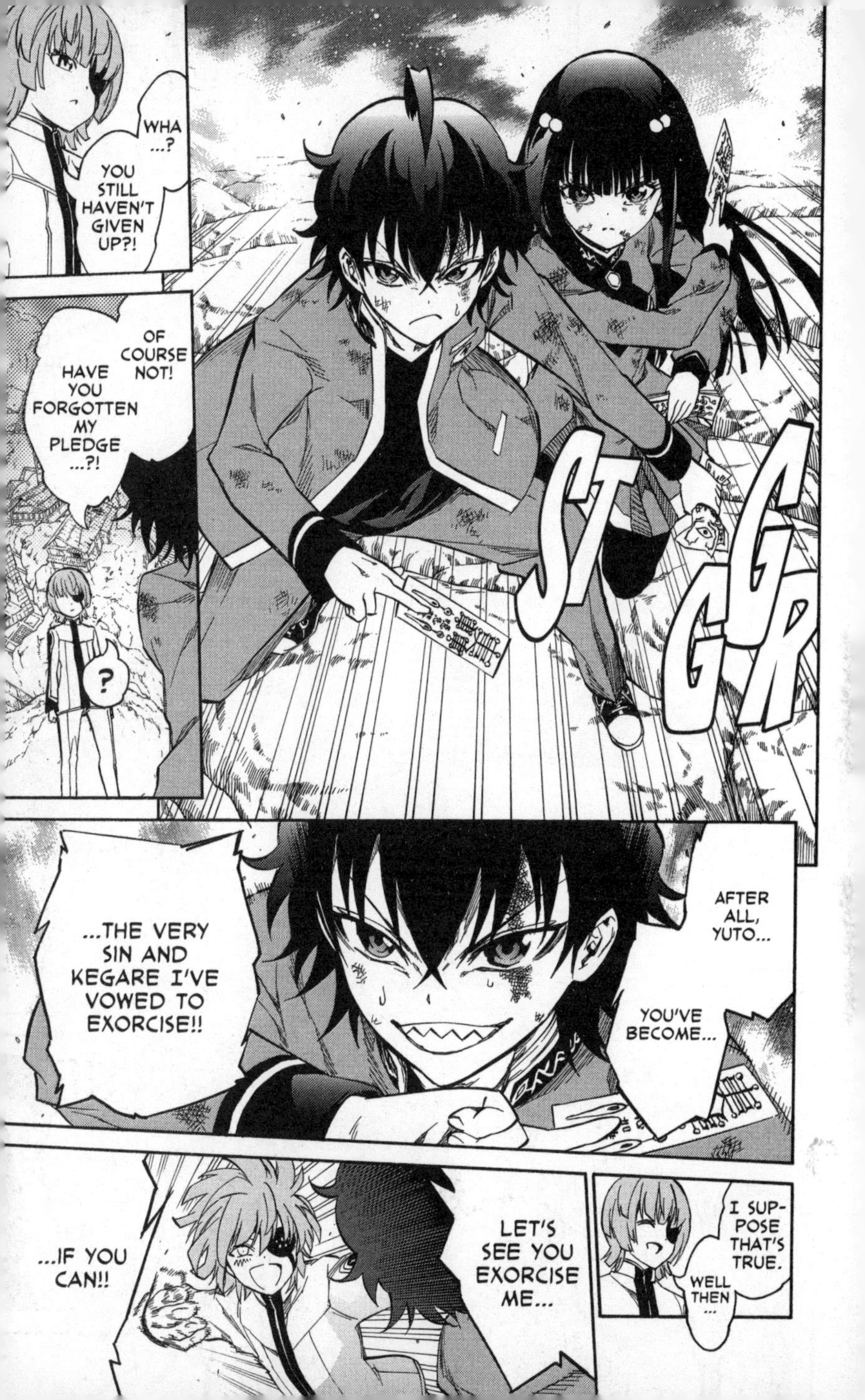
WHA ...?
YOU STILL HAVEN'T GIVEN UP?!
OF COURSE NOT!
HAVE YOU FORGOTTEN MY PLEDGE ...?!
?
AFTER ALL, YUTO...
YOU'VE BECOME...
...THE VERY SIN AND KEGARE I'VE VOWED TO EXORCISE!!
I SUP-POSE THAT'S TRUE.
WELL THEN ...
LET'S SEE YOU EXORCISE ME...
...IF YOU CAN!!

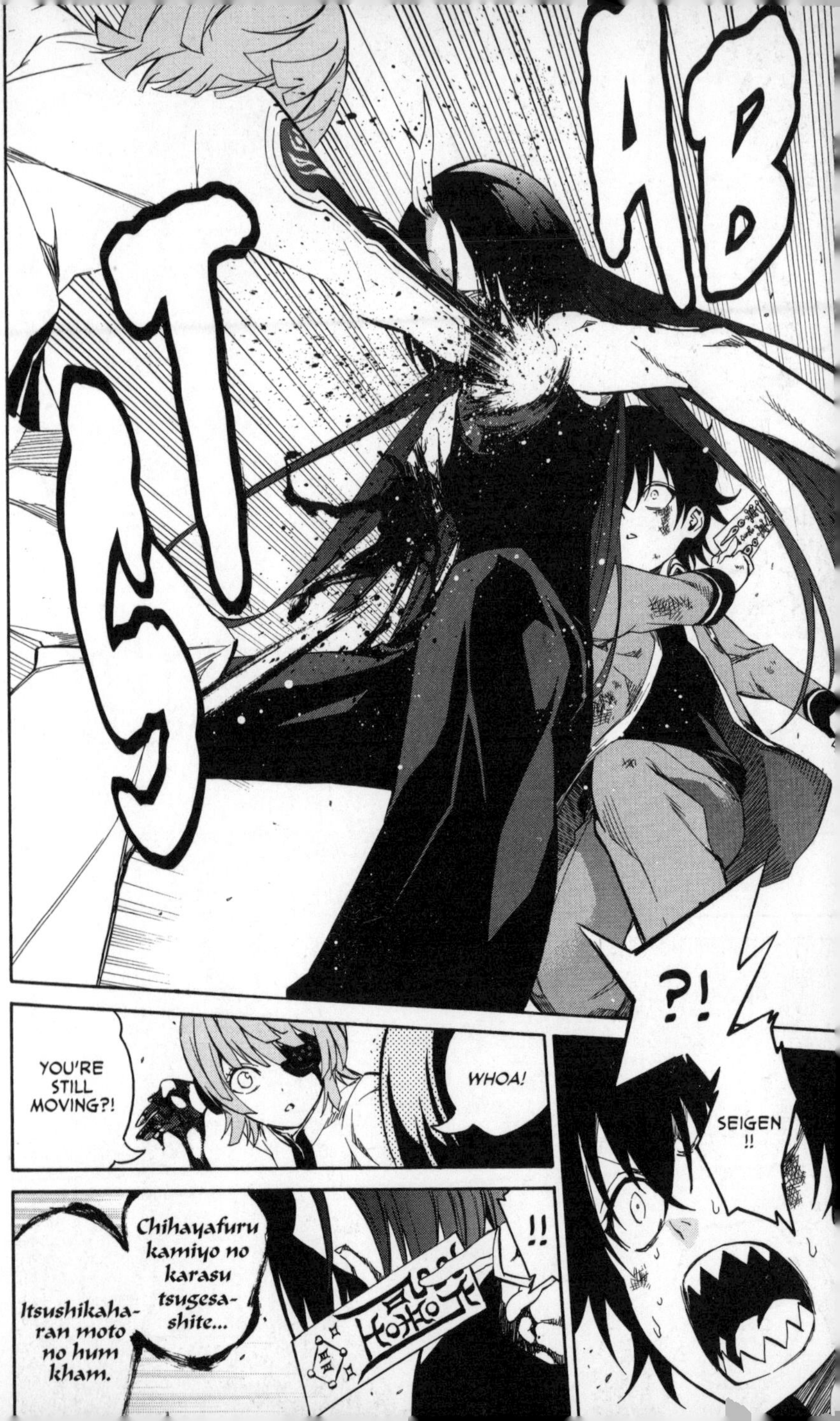
AB
?!
SEIGEN !!
WHOA!
YOU'RE STILL MOVING?!
!!
Chihayafuru kamiyo no karasu tsugesa-shite...
Itsushikahara-ran moto no hum kham.

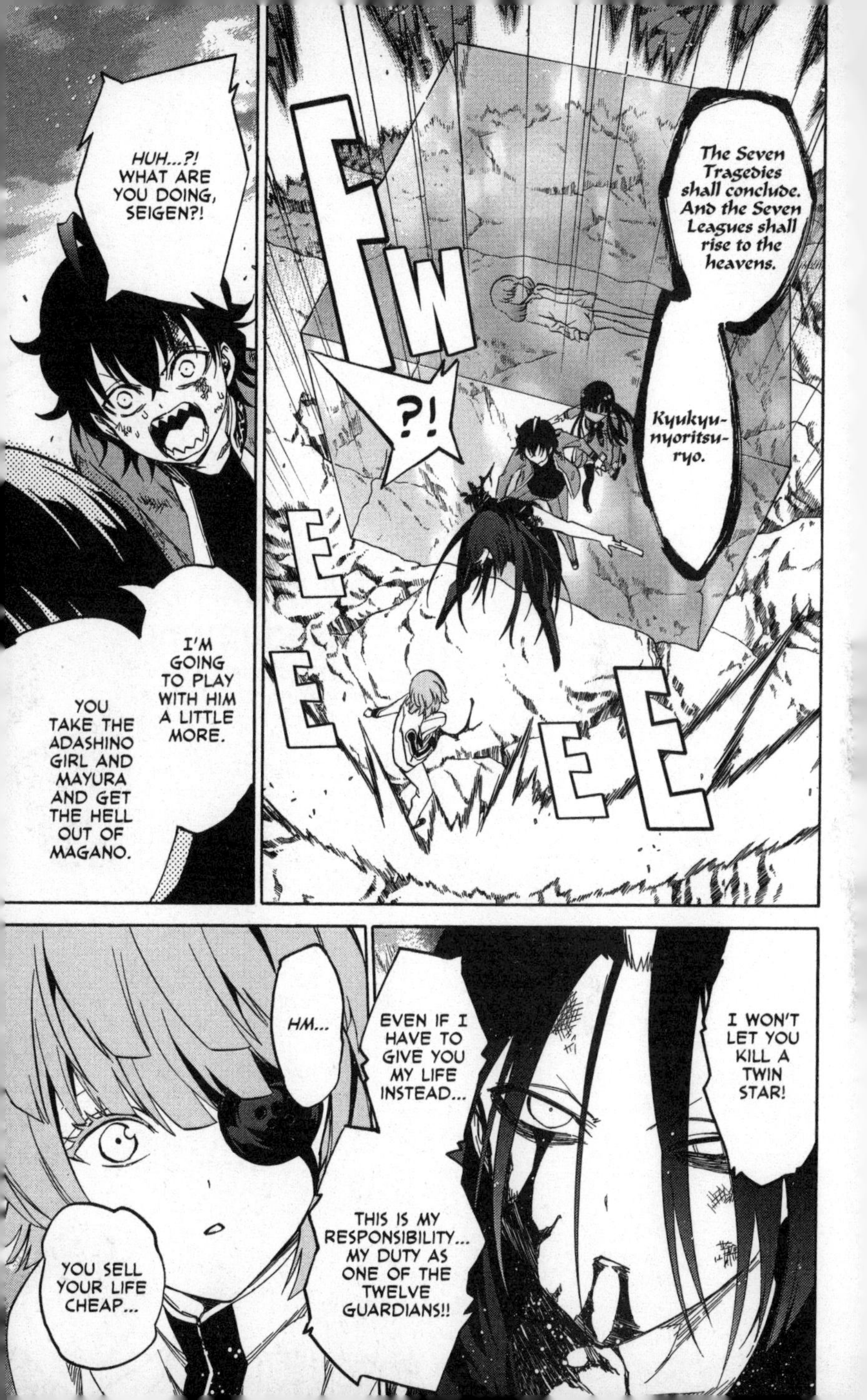
The Seven Tragedies shall conclude. And the Seven Leagues shall rise to the heavens.
Kyukyu-nyoritsu-ryo.
FIWEEEE
?!
HUH...?! WHAT ARE YOU DOING, SEIGEN?!
I'M GOING TO PLAY WITH HIM A LITTLE MORE.
YOU TAKE THE ADASHINO GIRL AND MAYURA AND GET THE HELL OUT OF MAGANO.
I WON'T LET YOU KILL A TWIN STAR!
EVEN IF I HAVE TO GIVE YOU MY LIFE INSTEAD...
THIS IS MY RESPONSIBILITY... MY DUTY AS ONE OF THE TWELVE GUARDIANS!!
HM...
YOU SELL YOUR LIFE CHEAP...

Column 8: Nademono

Otherwise known as Hitogata or Katashiro, these wood or paper dolls are used to represent the person you place a curse upon. Driving a nail into a straw doll is another method. These effigies can also be used as scapegoats to receive a curse your enemy has tried to place upon you. This series was introduced in the *Jump* magazine TV show before it started, and they had an exorcist on the program who said he used these methods in real life. So, you know...things like this are true!!

#11 As If a New Star Were Born

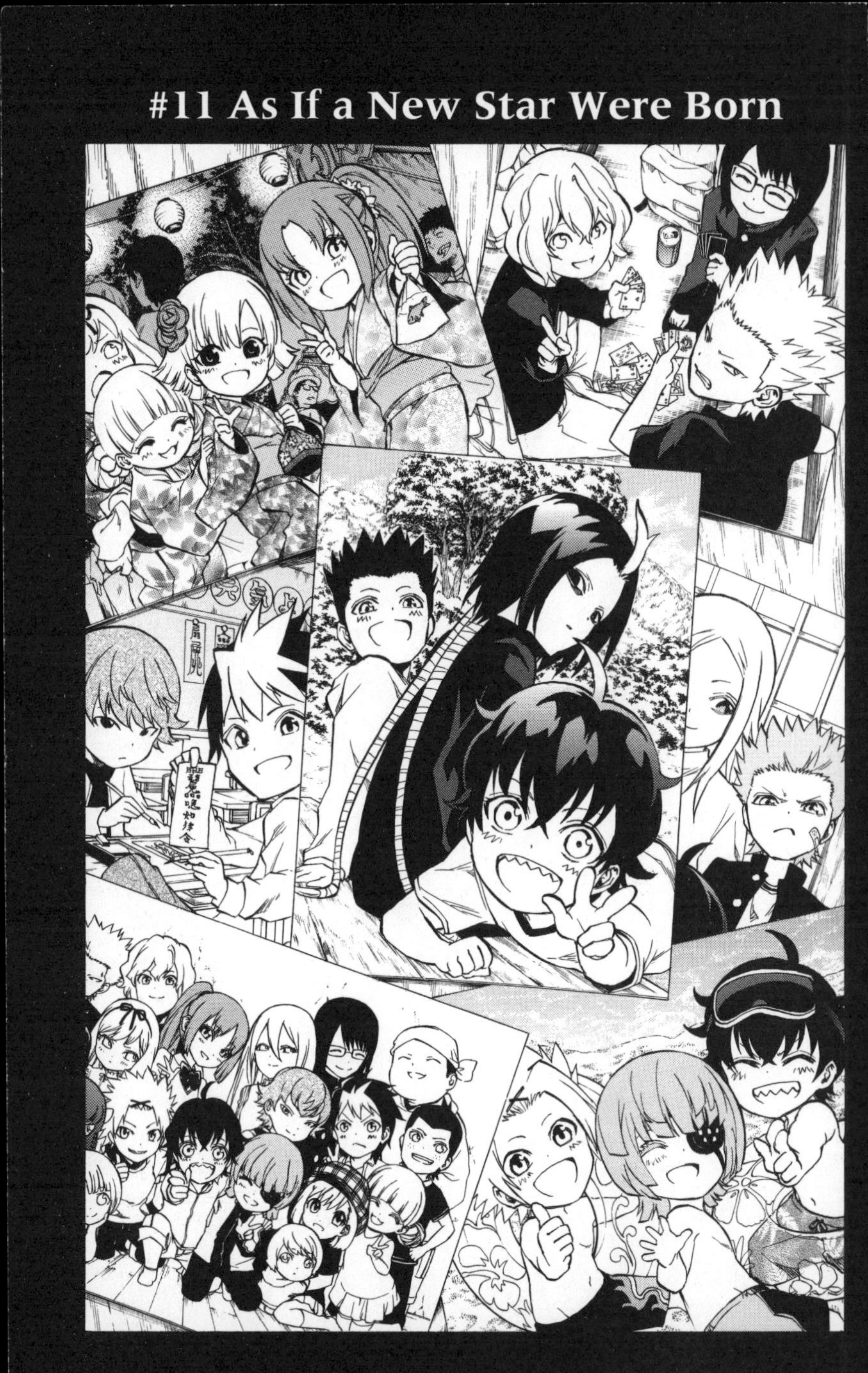

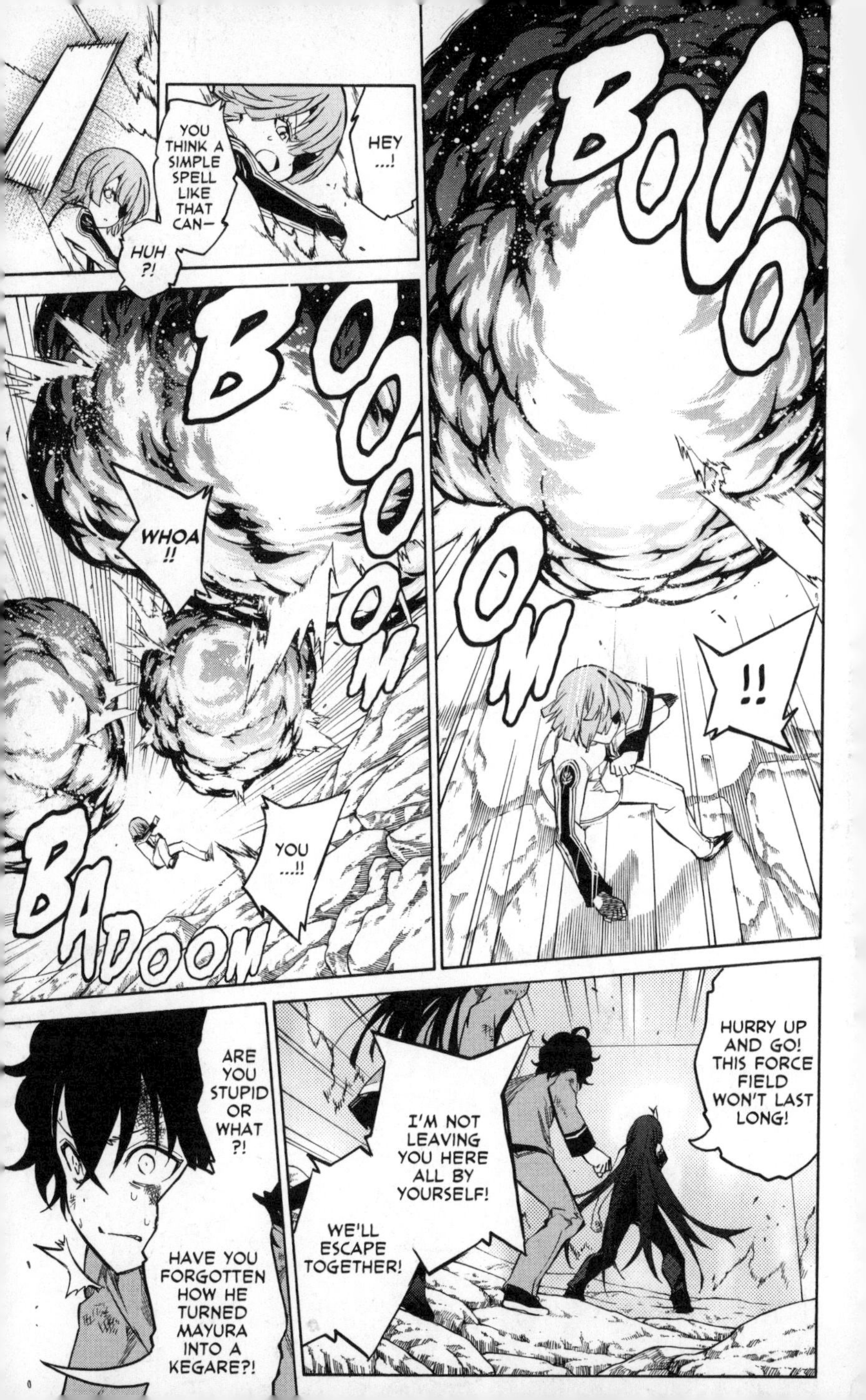
BOOOOOOM
!!
HEY ...!
YOU THINK A SIMPLE SPELL LIKE THAT CAN—
HUH ?!
BOOOOOOM
WHOA !!
YOU ...!!
BADOOM
HURRY UP AND GO! THIS FORCE FIELD WON'T LAST LONG!
I'M NOT LEAVING YOU HERE ALL BY YOURSELF!
WE'LL ESCAPE TOGETHER!
ARE YOU STUPID OR WHAT ?!
HAVE YOU FORGOTTEN HOW HE TURNED MAYURA INTO A KEGARE?!

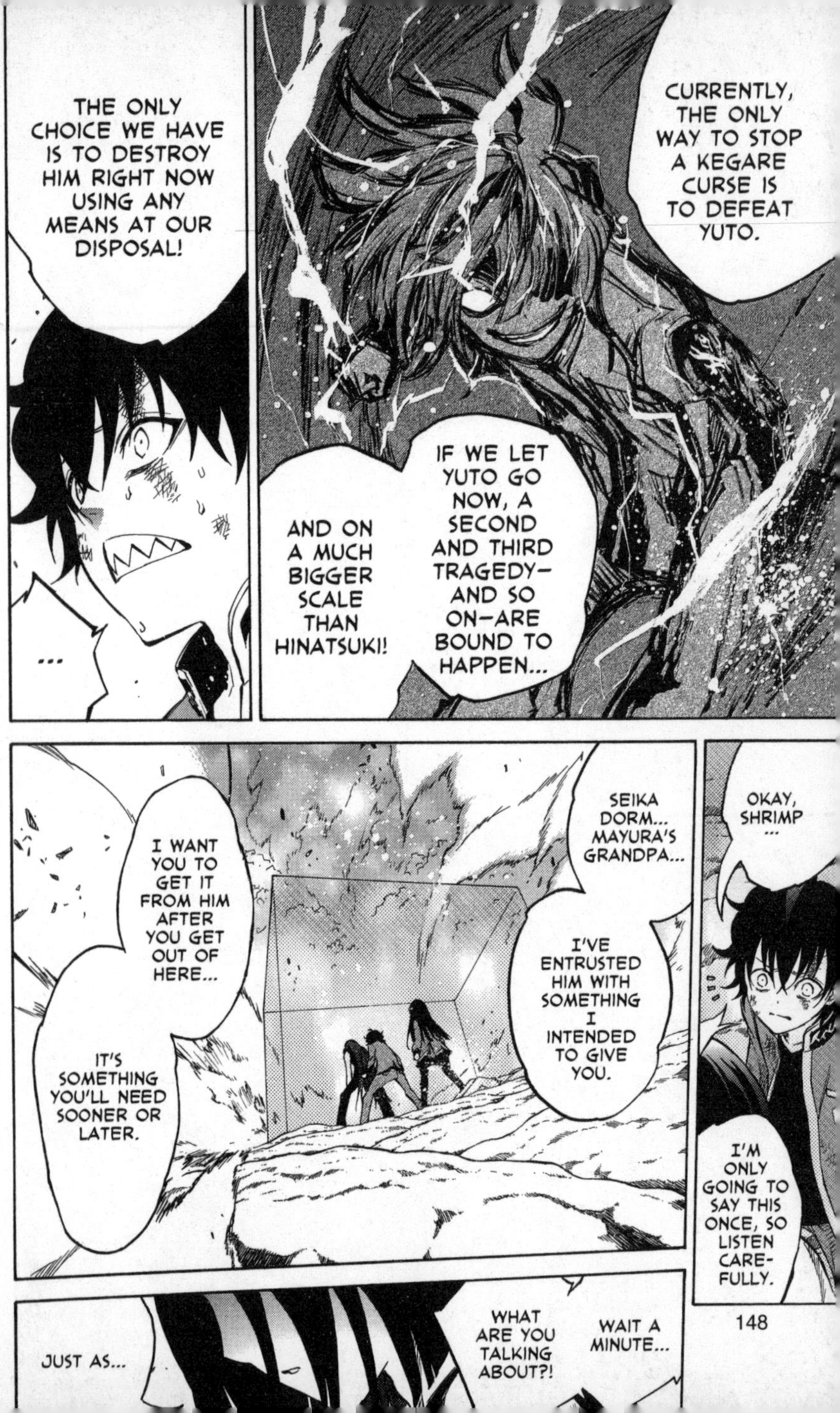
CURRENTLY, THE ONLY WAY TO STOP A KEGARE CURSE IS TO DEFEAT YUTO.
IF WE LET YUTO GO NOW, A SECOND AND THIRD TRAGEDY—AND SO ON—ARE BOUND TO HAPPEN...
AND ON A MUCH BIGGER SCALE THAN HINATSUKI!
THE ONLY CHOICE WE HAVE IS TO DESTROY HIM RIGHT NOW USING ANY MEANS AT OUR DISPOSAL!
...
OKAY, SHRIMP...
I'M ONLY GOING TO SAY THIS ONCE, SO LISTEN CARE-FULLY.
SEIKA DORM... MAYURA'S GRANDPA...
I'VE ENTRUSTED HIM WITH SOMETHING I INTENDED TO GIVE YOU.
I WANT YOU TO GET IT FROM HIM AFTER YOU GET OUT OF HERE...
IT'S SOMETHING YOU'LL NEED SOONER OR LATER.
WAIT A MINUTE...
WHAT ARE YOU TALKING ABOUT?!
JUST AS...

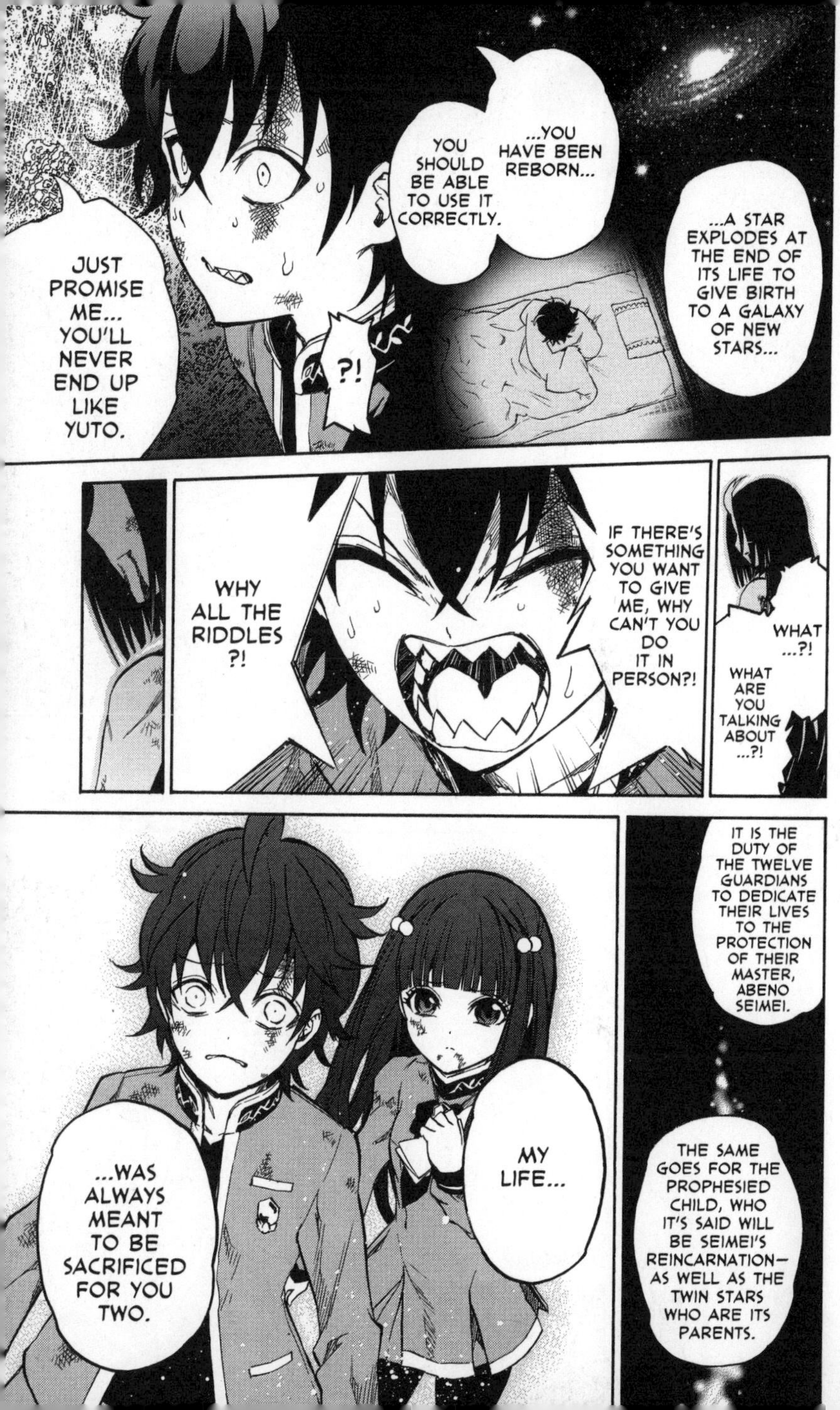
...A STAR EXPLODES AT THE END OF ITS LIFE TO GIVE BIRTH TO A GALAXY OF NEW STARS...
...YOU HAVE BEEN REBORN...
YOU SHOULD BE ABLE TO USE IT CORRECTLY.
?!
JUST PROMISE ME... YOU'LL NEVER END UP LIKE YUTO.
WHAT ...?!
WHAT ARE YOU TALKING ABOUT ...?!
IF THERE'S SOMETHING YOU WANT TO GIVE ME, WHY CAN'T YOU DO IT IN PERSON?!
WHY ALL THE RIDDLES ?!
IT IS THE DUTY OF THE TWELVE GUARDIANS TO DEDICATE THEIR LIVES TO THE PROTECTION OF THEIR MASTER, ABENO SEIMEI.
THE SAME GOES FOR THE PROPHESIED CHILD, WHO IT'S SAID WILL BE SEIMEI'S REINCARNATION—AS WELL AS THE TWIN STARS WHO ARE ITS PARENTS.
MY LIFE...
...WAS ALWAYS MEANT TO BE SACRIFICED FOR YOU TWO.

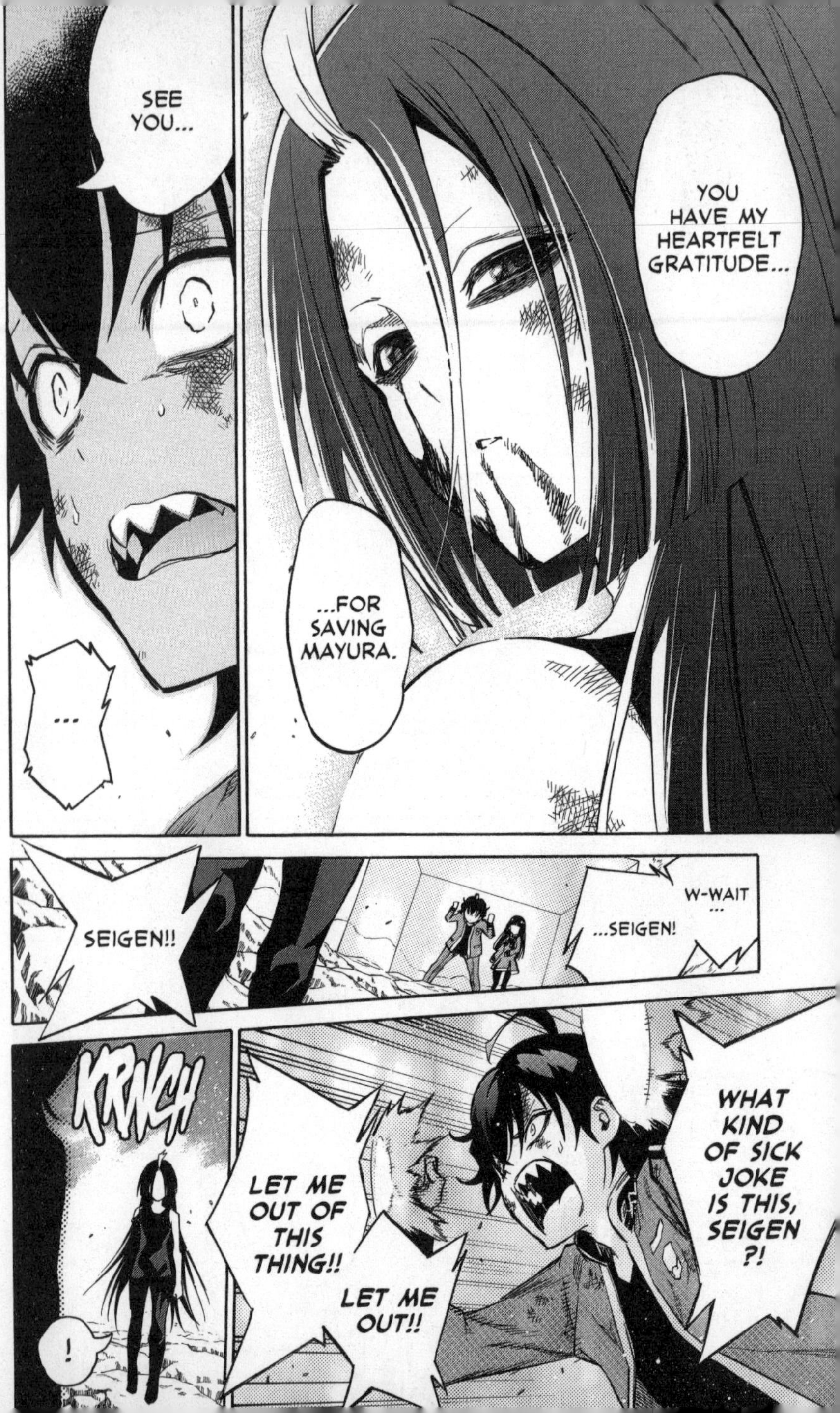
YOU HAVE MY HEARTFELT GRATITUDE...
...FOR SAVING MAYURA.
SEE YOU...
...
W-WAIT...
...SEIGEN!
SEIGEN!!
WHAT KIND OF SICK JOKE IS THIS, SEIGEN?!
LET ME OUT OF THIS THING!!
LET ME OUT!!
KRNCH
!

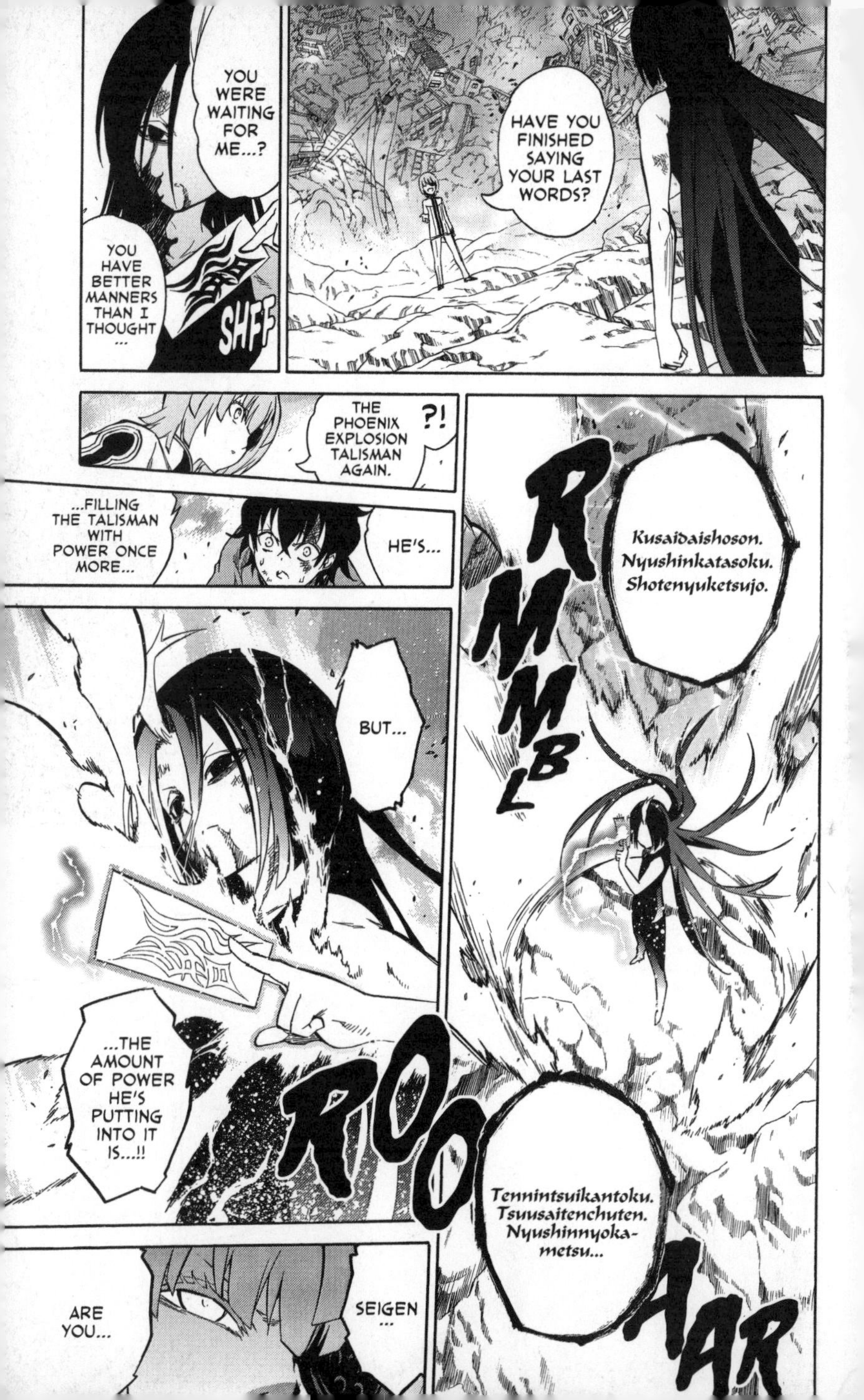
HAVE YOU FINISHED SAYING YOUR LAST WORDS?
YOU WERE WAITING FOR ME...?
YOU HAVE BETTER MANNERS THAN I THOUGHT...
SHFF
RMMBL
Kusaidaishoson. Nyushinkatasoku. Shotenyuketsujo.
ROOOAR
Tennintsuikantoku. Tsuusaitenchuten. Nyushinnyoka-metsu...
?!
THE PHOENIX EXPLOSION TALISMAN AGAIN.
HE'S...
...FILLING THE TALISMAN WITH POWER ONCE MORE...
BUT...
...THE AMOUNT OF POWER HE'S PUTTING INTO IT IS...!!
SEIGEN...
ARE YOU...

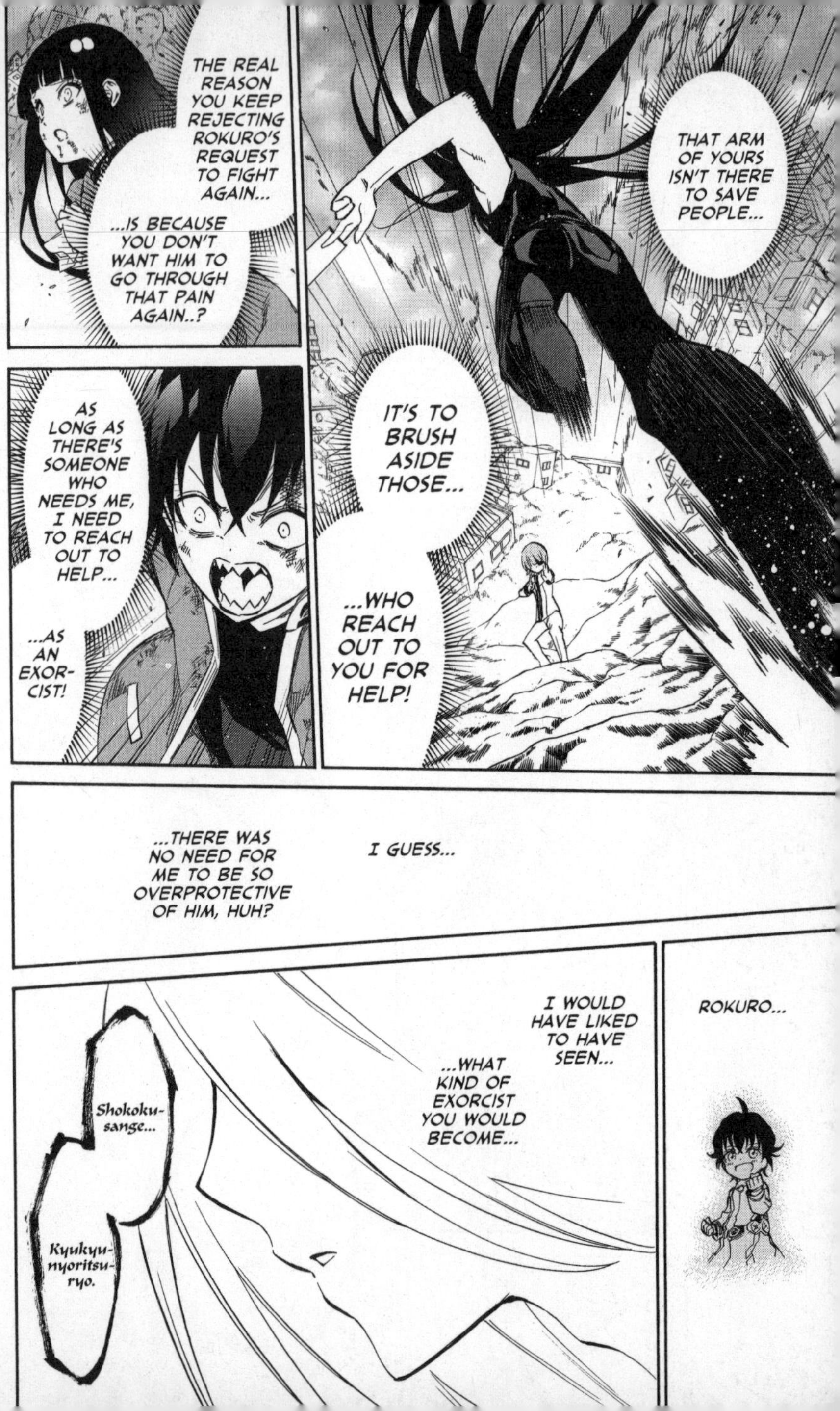
THAT ARM OF YOURS ISN'T THERE TO SAVE PEOPLE...
IT'S TO BRUSH ASIDE THOSE...
...WHO REACH OUT TO YOU FOR HELP!
THE REAL REASON YOU KEEP REJECTING ROKURO'S REQUEST TO FIGHT AGAIN...
...IS BECAUSE YOU DON'T WANT HIM TO GO THROUGH THAT PAIN AGAIN..?
AS LONG AS THERE'S SOMEONE WHO NEEDS ME, I NEED TO REACH OUT TO HELP...
...AS AN EXORCIST!
I GUESS...
...THERE WAS NO NEED FOR ME TO BE SO OVERPROTECTIVE OF HIM, HUH?
ROKURO...
I WOULD HAVE LIKED TO HAVE SEEN...
...WHAT KIND OF EXORCIST YOU WOULD BECOME...
Shokoku-sange...
Kyukyu-nyoritsu-ryo.

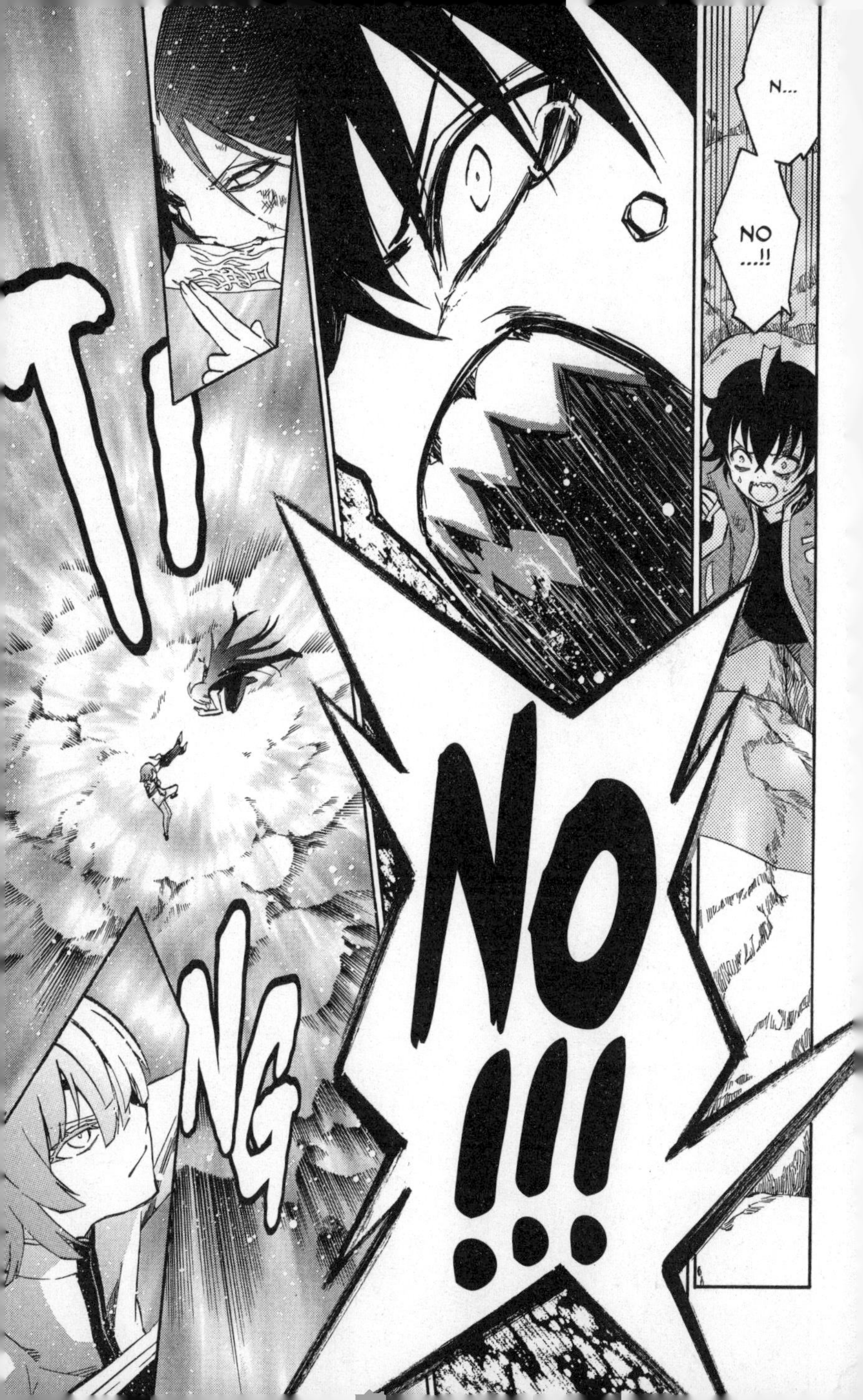
N...
NO ...!!
NO!!!
TI
NG

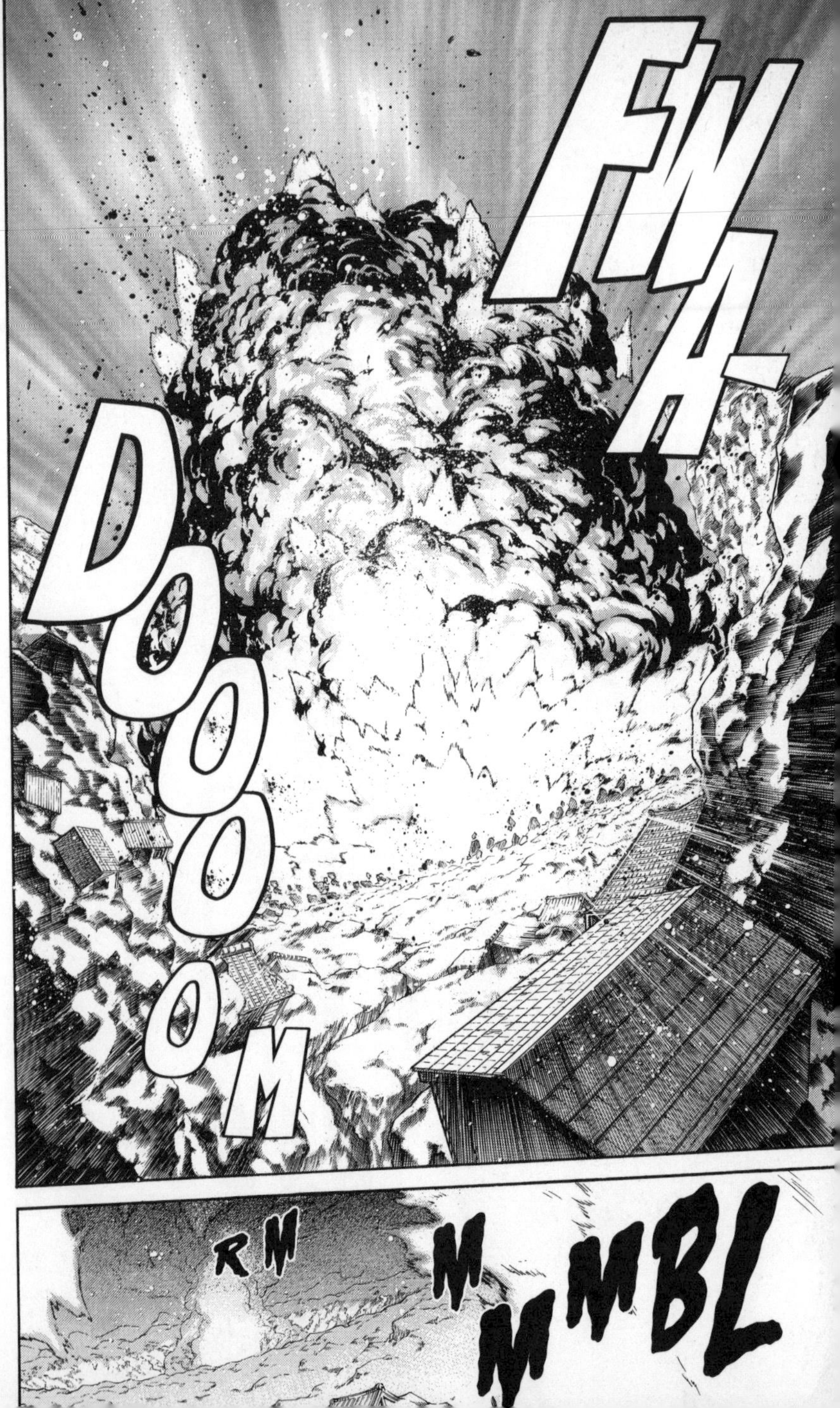
FWA-
DOOOOOM
RM
MMMBL

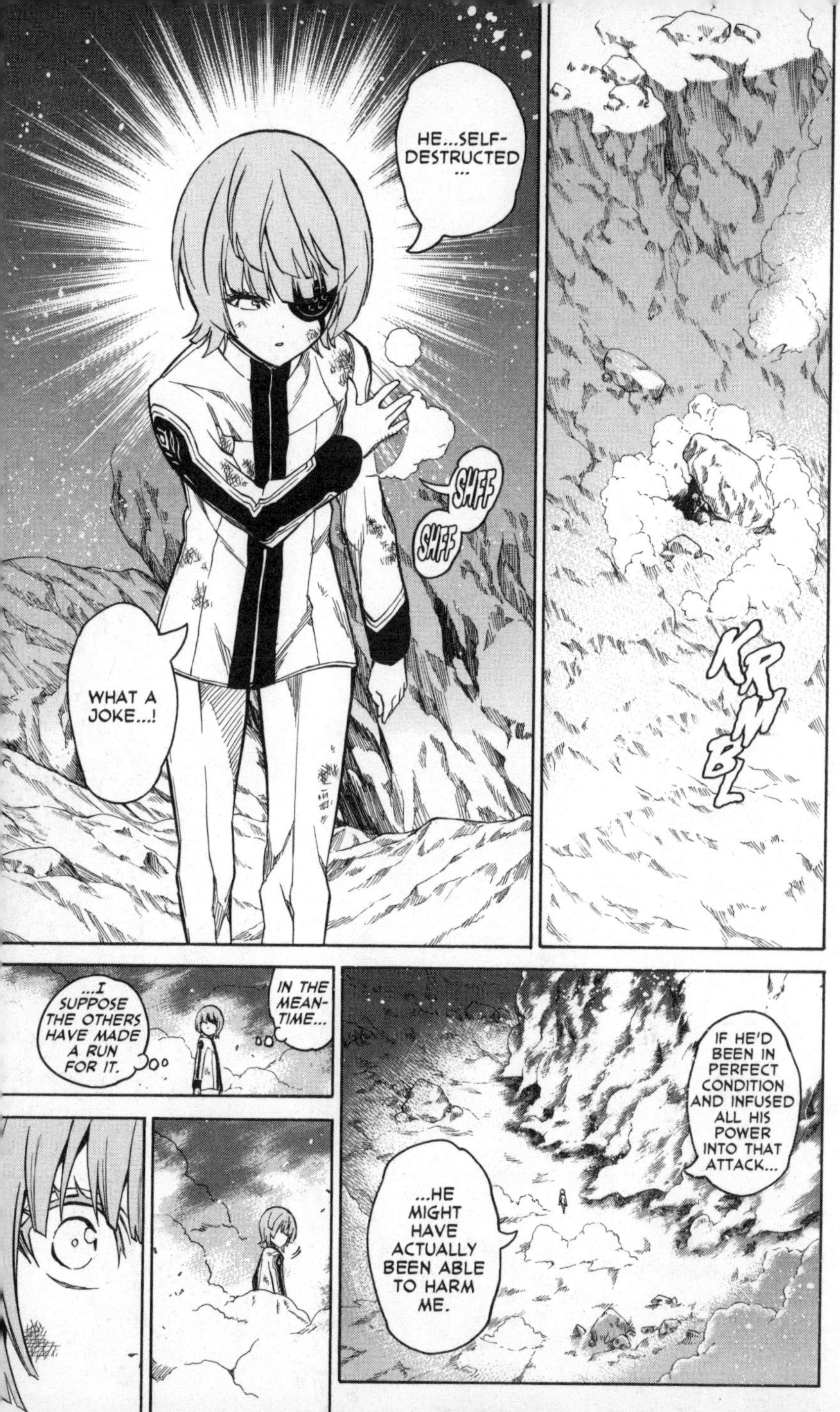
KRMBL
HE...SELF-DESTRUCTED...
SHFF
SHFF
WHAT A JOKE...!
IF HE'D BEEN IN PERFECT CONDITION AND INFUSED ALL HIS POWER INTO THAT ATTACK...
...HE MIGHT HAVE ACTUALLY BEEN ABLE TO HARM ME.
IN THE MEAN-TIME...
...I SUPPOSE THE OTHERS HAVE MADE A RUN FOR IT.

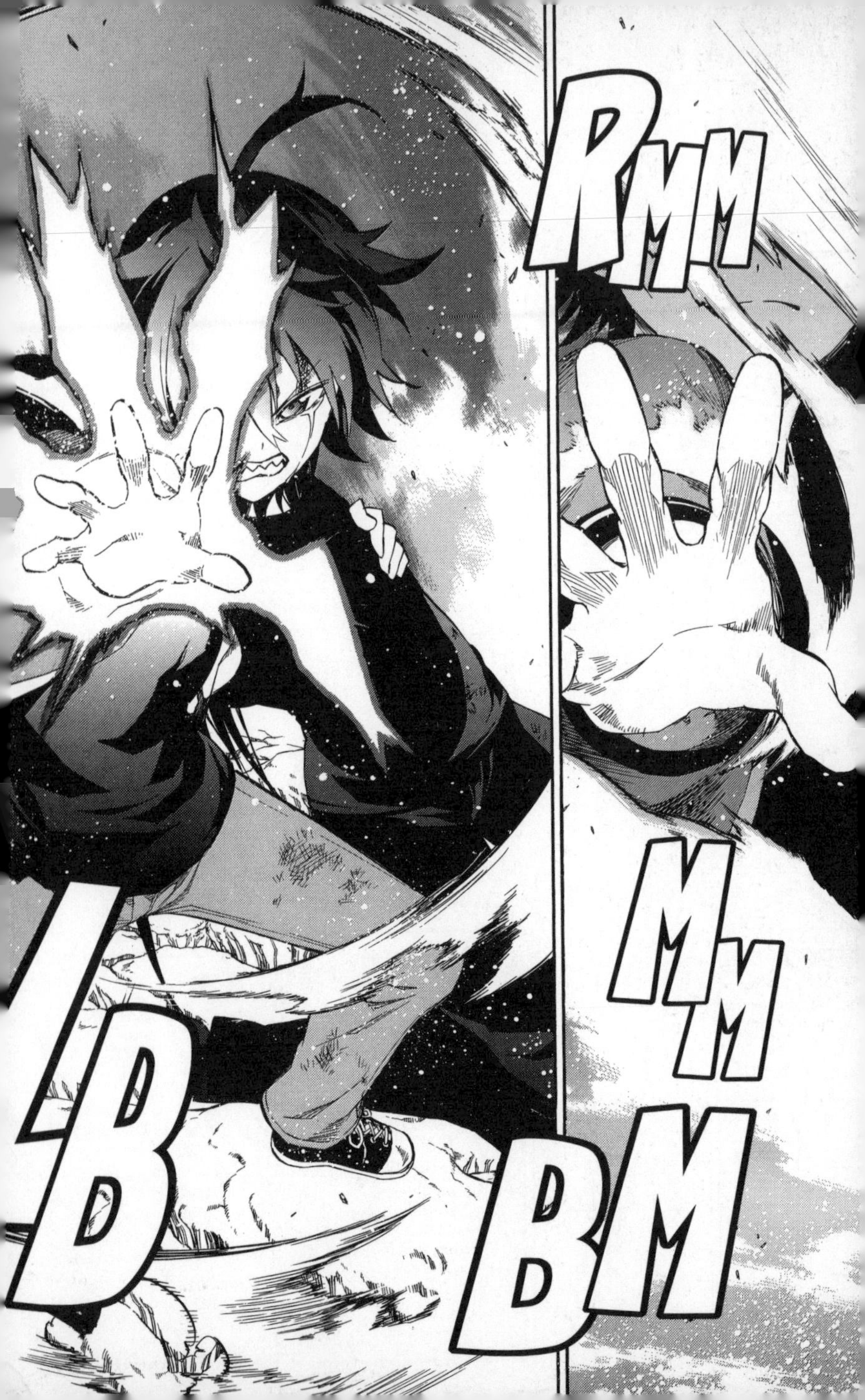
RMM
MMM
BM
B
D

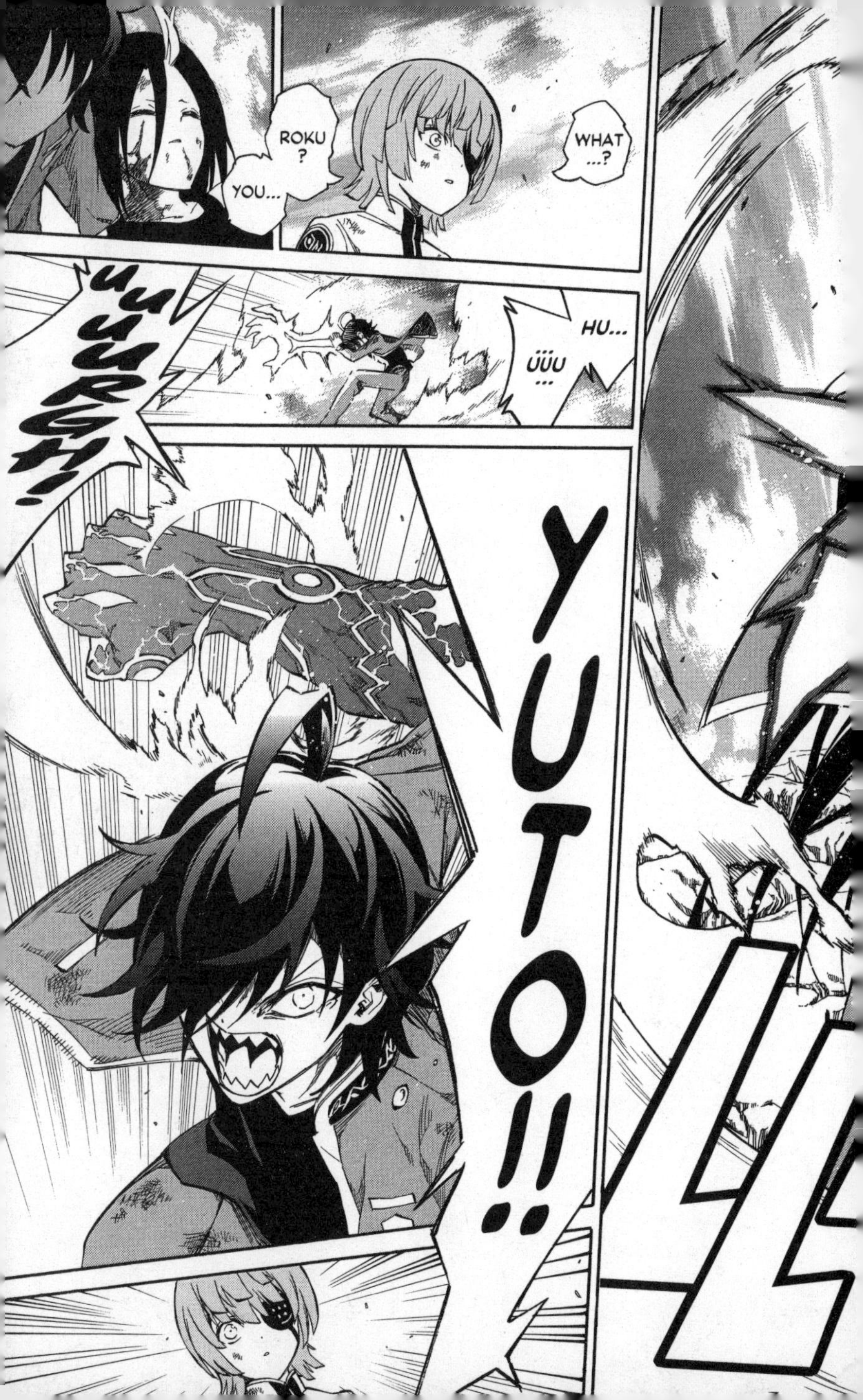
WHAT ...?
ROKU ?
YOU...
HU... ...ÜÜU...
UUUURGH!!
YUTO!!!

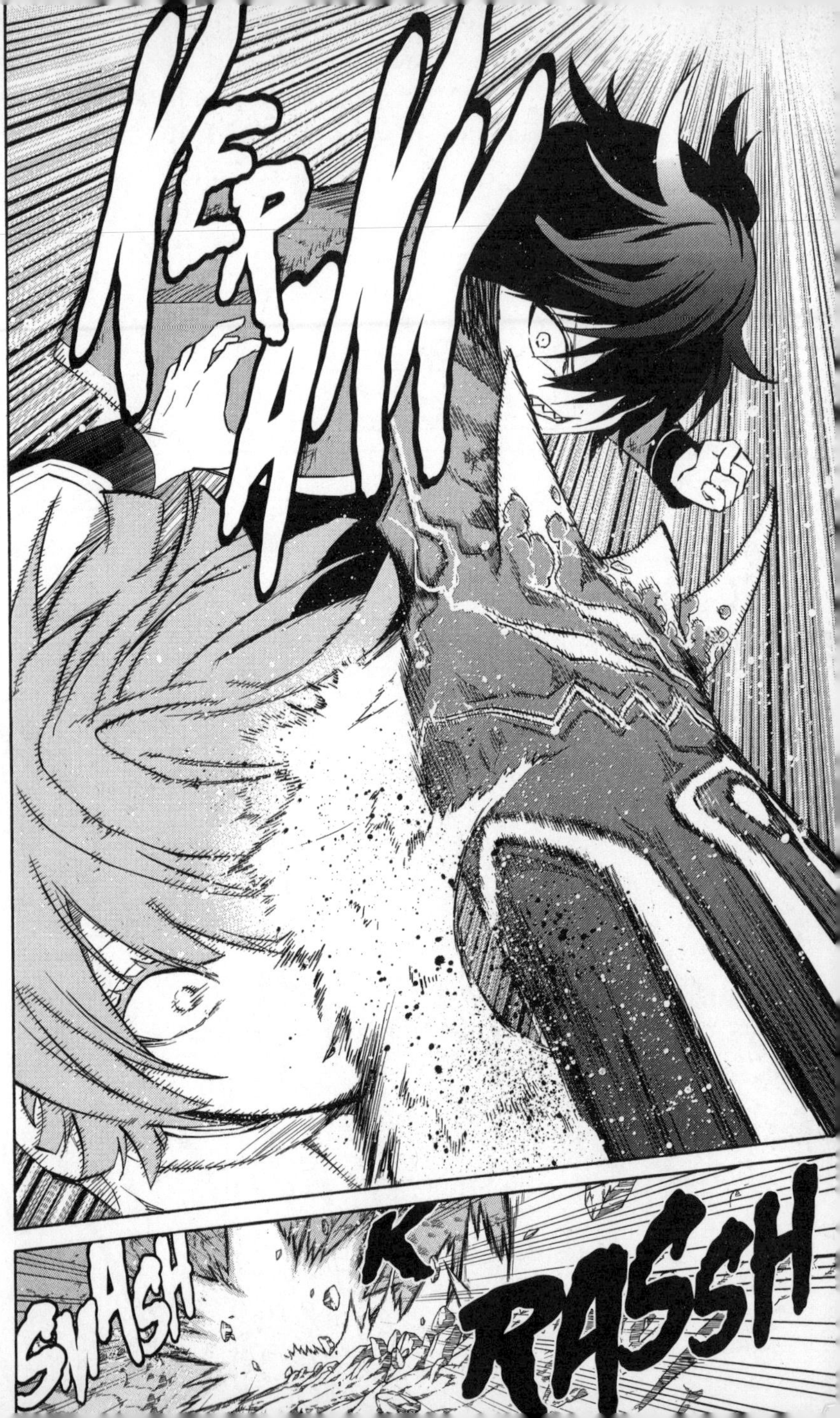
KRASSH
SMASH

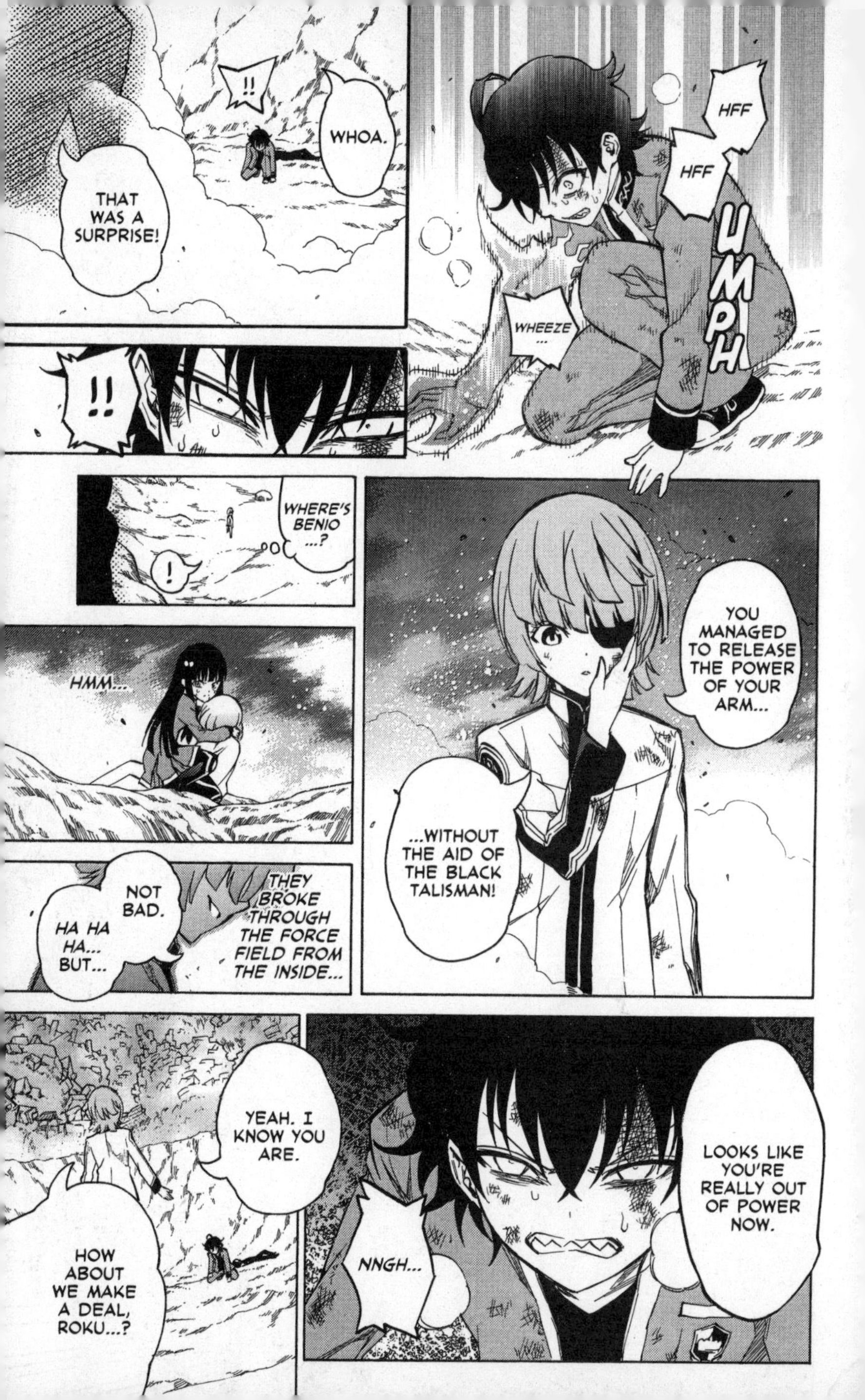
HFF
HFF
UMPH
WHEEZE ...
!!
WHOA.
THAT WAS A SURPRISE!
!!
YOU MANAGED TO RELEASE THE POWER OF YOUR ARM...
...WITHOUT THE AID OF THE BLACK TALISMAN!
WHERE'S BENIO ...?
!
HMM...
THEY BROKE THROUGH THE FORCE FIELD FROM THE INSIDE...
NOT BAD.
HA HA HA... BUT...
LOOKS LIKE YOU'RE REALLY OUT OF POWER NOW.
NNGH...
YEAH. I KNOW YOU ARE.
HOW ABOUT WE MAKE A DEAL, ROKU...?

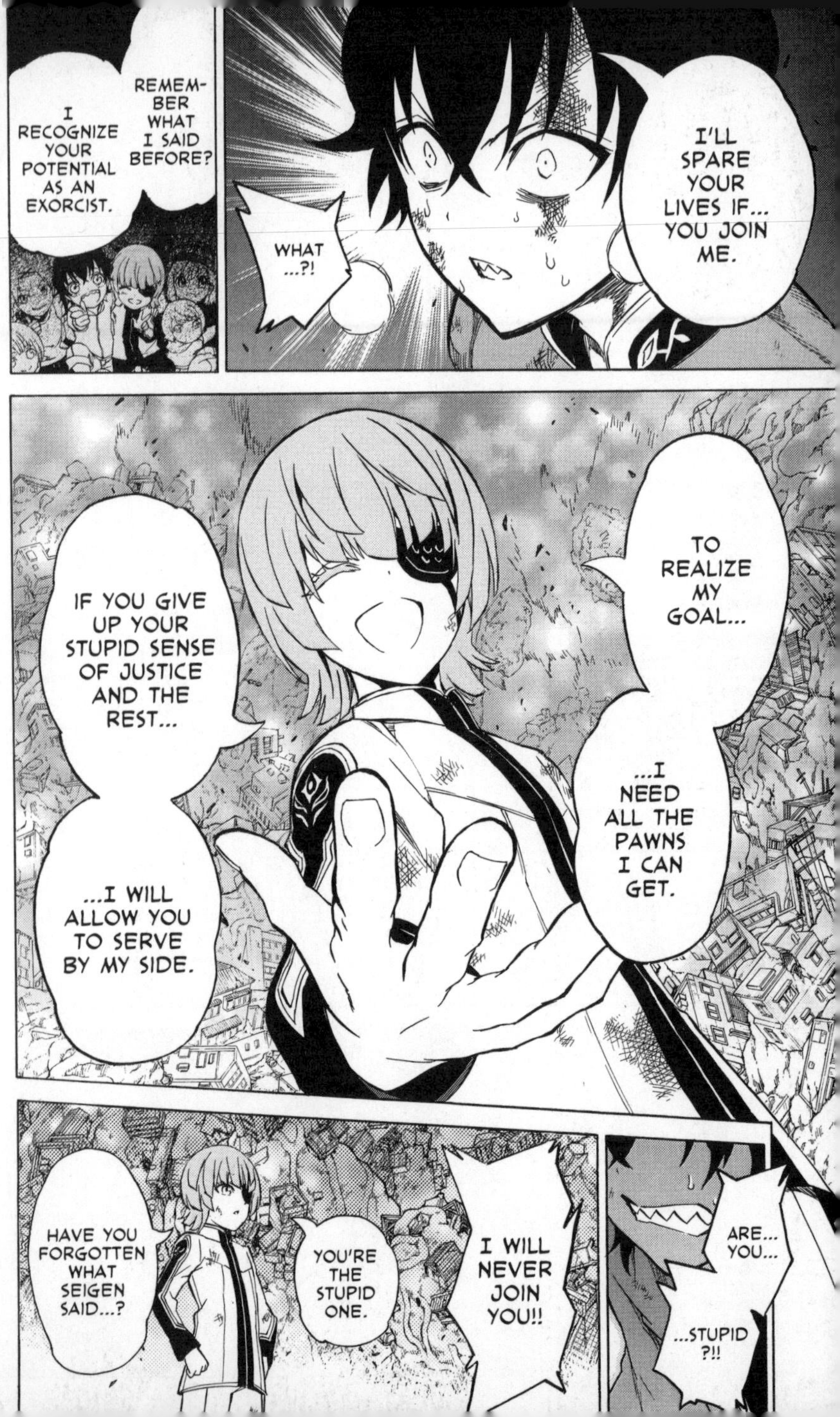
I'LL SPARE YOUR LIVES IF... YOU JOIN ME.
WHAT ...?!
REMEMBER WHAT I SAID BEFORE?
I RECOGNIZE YOUR POTENTIAL AS AN EXORCIST.
TO REALIZE MY GOAL...
...I NEED ALL THE PAWNS I CAN GET.
IF YOU GIVE UP YOUR STUPID SENSE OF JUSTICE AND THE REST...
...I WILL ALLOW YOU TO SERVE BY MY SIDE.
ARE... YOU...
...STUPID ?!!
I WILL NEVER JOIN YOU!!
YOU'RE THE STUPID ONE.
HAVE YOU FORGOTTEN WHAT SEIGEN SAID...?

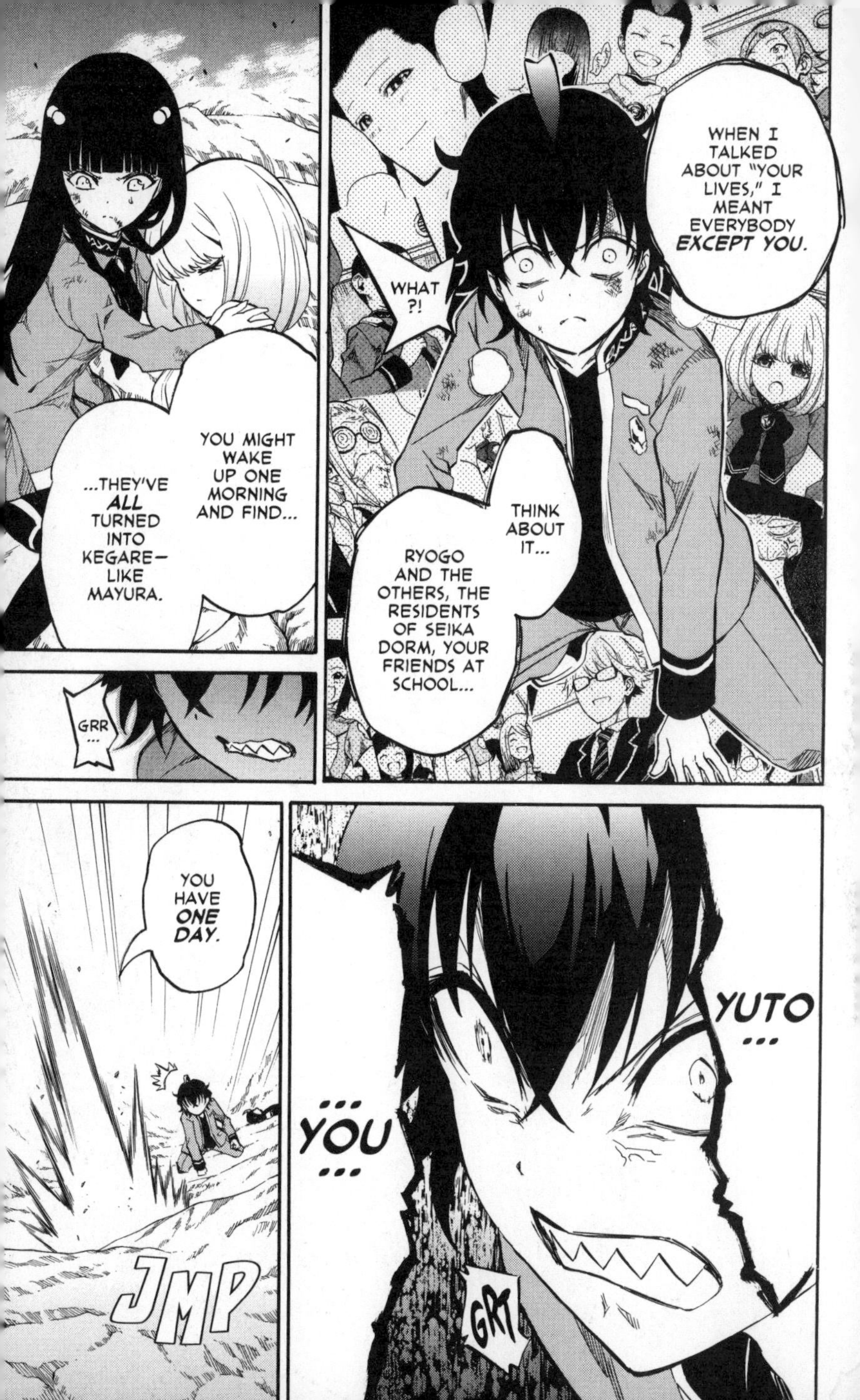

WHEN I TALKED ABOUT "YOUR LIVES," I MEANT EVERYBODY EXCEPT YOU.
WHAT ?!
THINK ABOUT IT...
RYOGO AND THE OTHERS, THE RESIDENTS OF SEIKA DORM, YOUR FRIENDS AT SCHOOL...
YOU MIGHT WAKE UP ONE MORNING AND FIND...
...THEY'VE ALL TURNED INTO KEGARE—LIKE MAYURA.
GRR...
YUTO...
...YOU...
GRT
YOU HAVE ONE DAY.
JMP

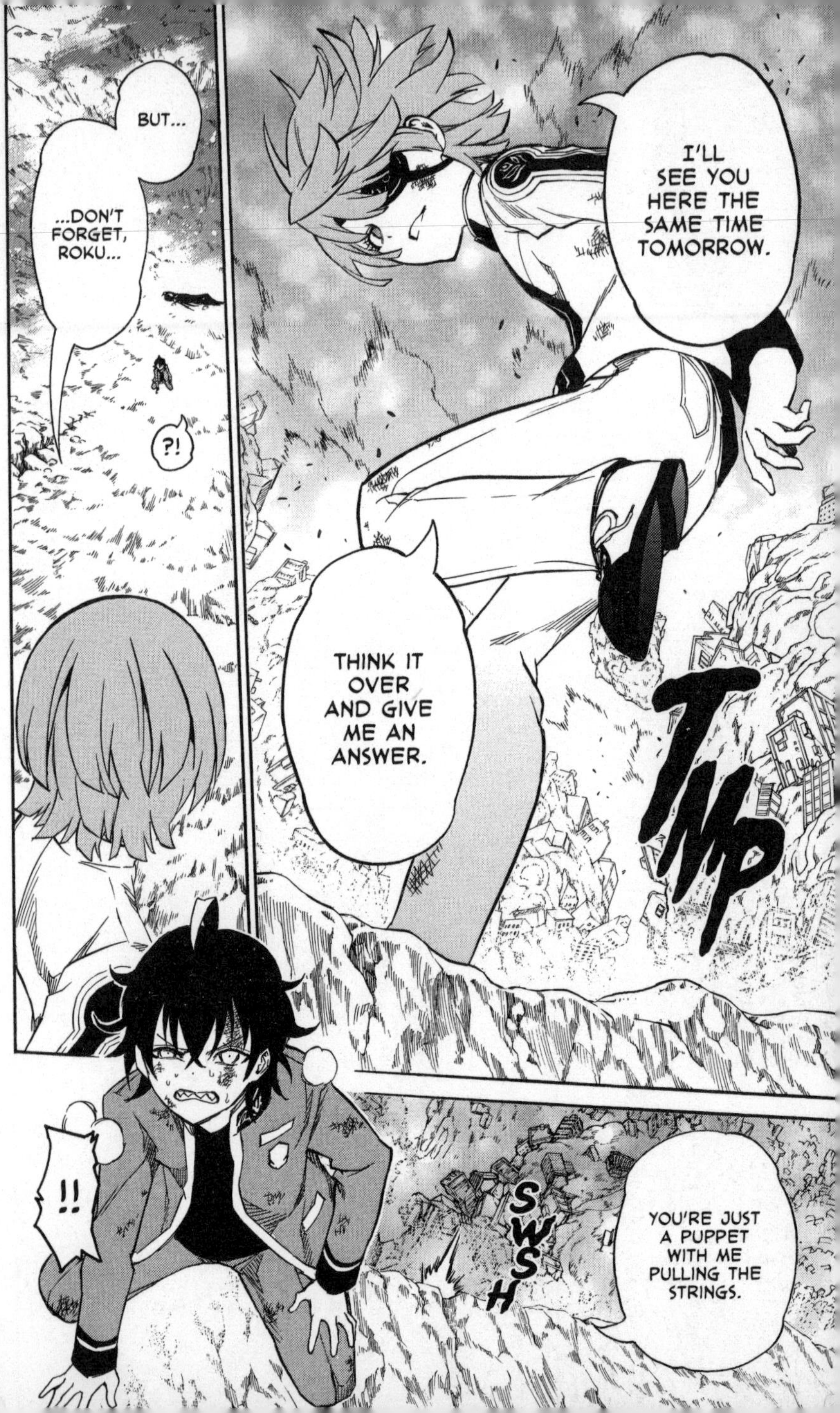
I'LL SEE YOU HERE THE SAME TIME TOMORROW.
THINK IT OVER AND GIVE ME AN ANSWER.
TMP
BUT...
...DON'T FORGET, ROKU...
?!
YOU'RE JUST A PUPPET WITH ME PULLING THE STRINGS.
SWSH
!!

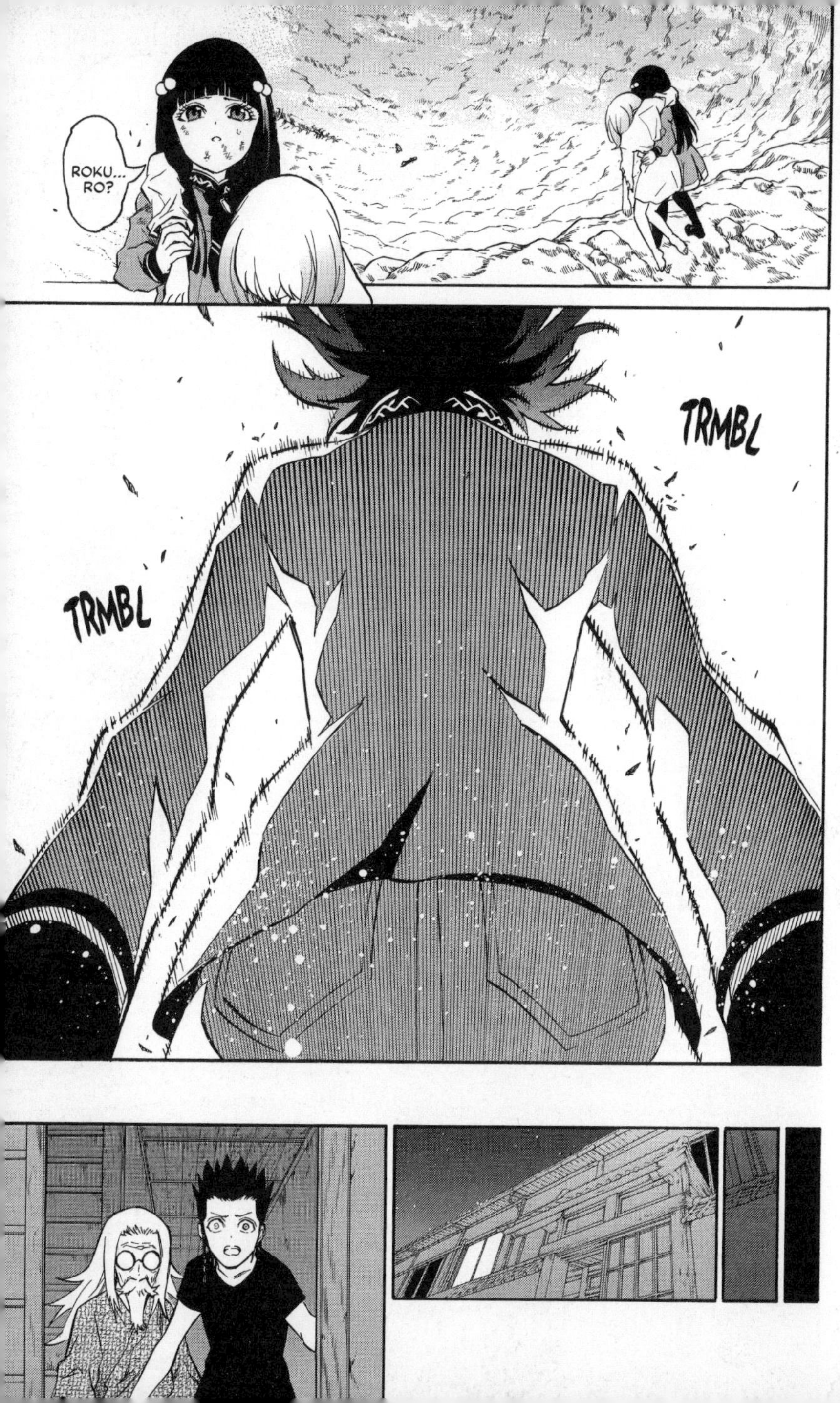
ROKU... RO?
TRMBL
TRMBL

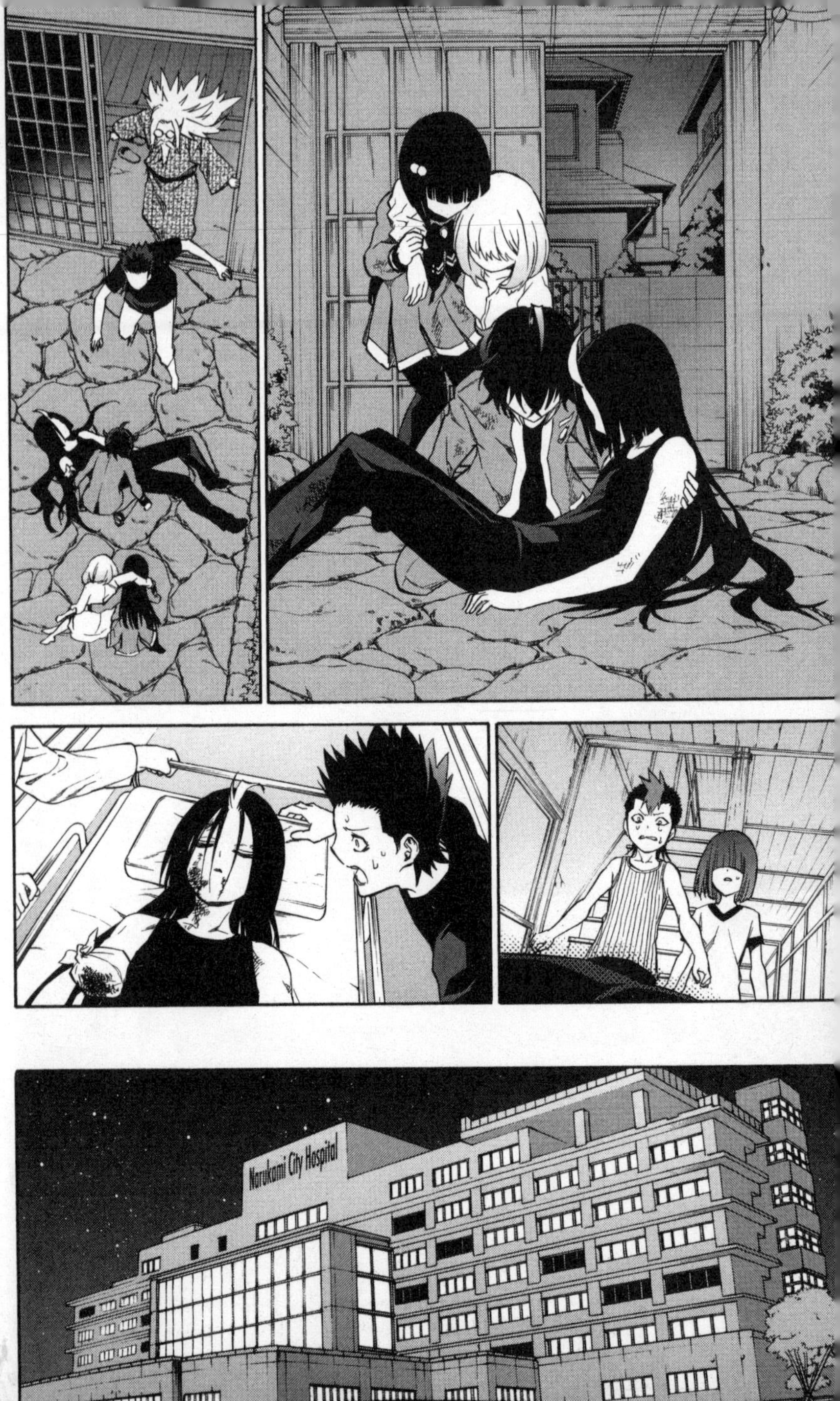
Narukami City Hospital

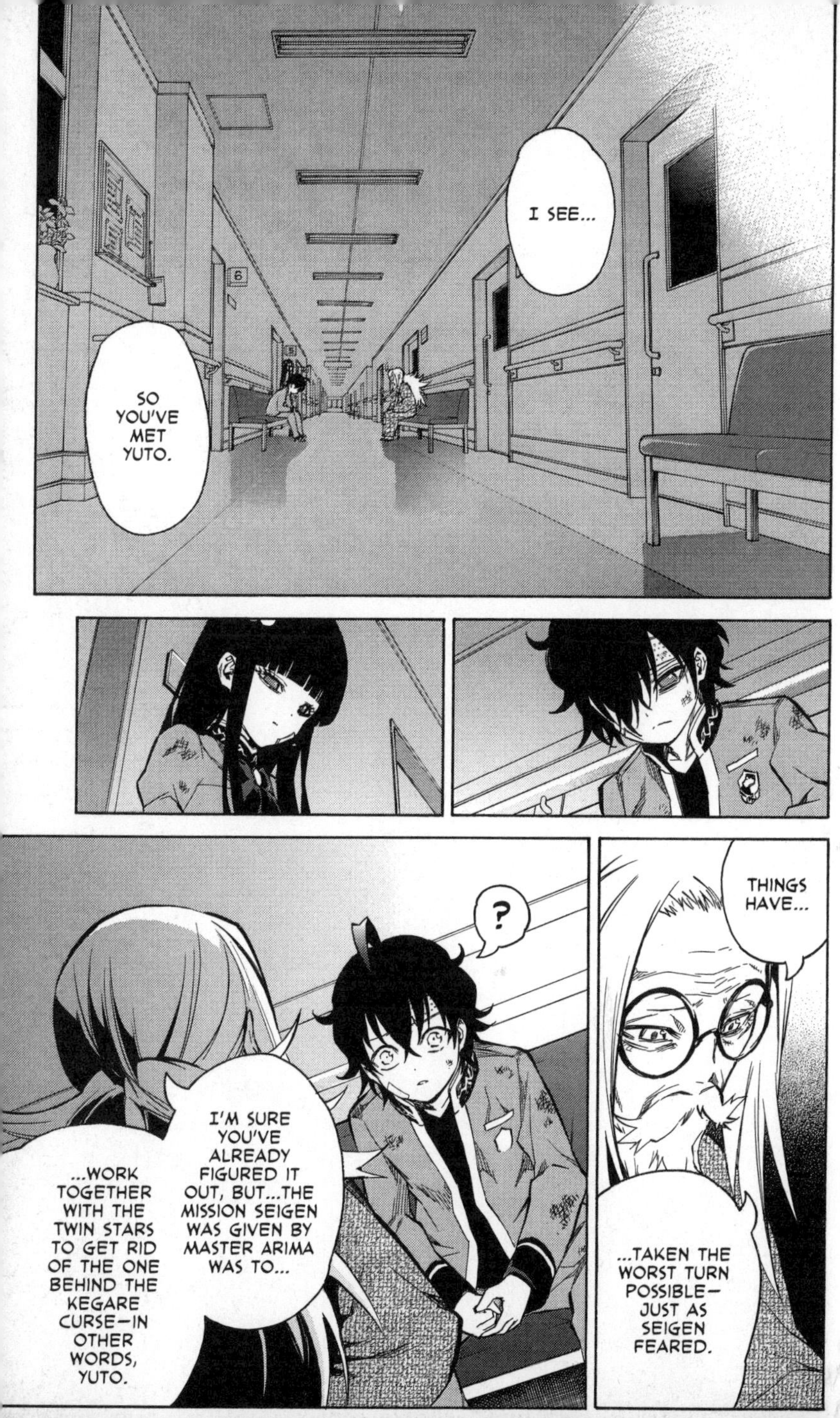
I SEE...
SO YOU'VE MET YUTO.
THINGS HAVE...
...TAKEN THE WORST TURN POSSIBLE—JUST AS SEIGEN FEARED.
?
I'M SURE YOU'VE ALREADY FIGURED IT OUT, BUT...THE MISSION SEIGEN WAS GIVEN BY MASTER ARIMA WAS TO...
...WORK TOGETHER WITH THE TWIN STARS TO GET RID OF THE ONE BEHIND THE KEGARE CURSE—IN OTHER WORDS, YUTO.

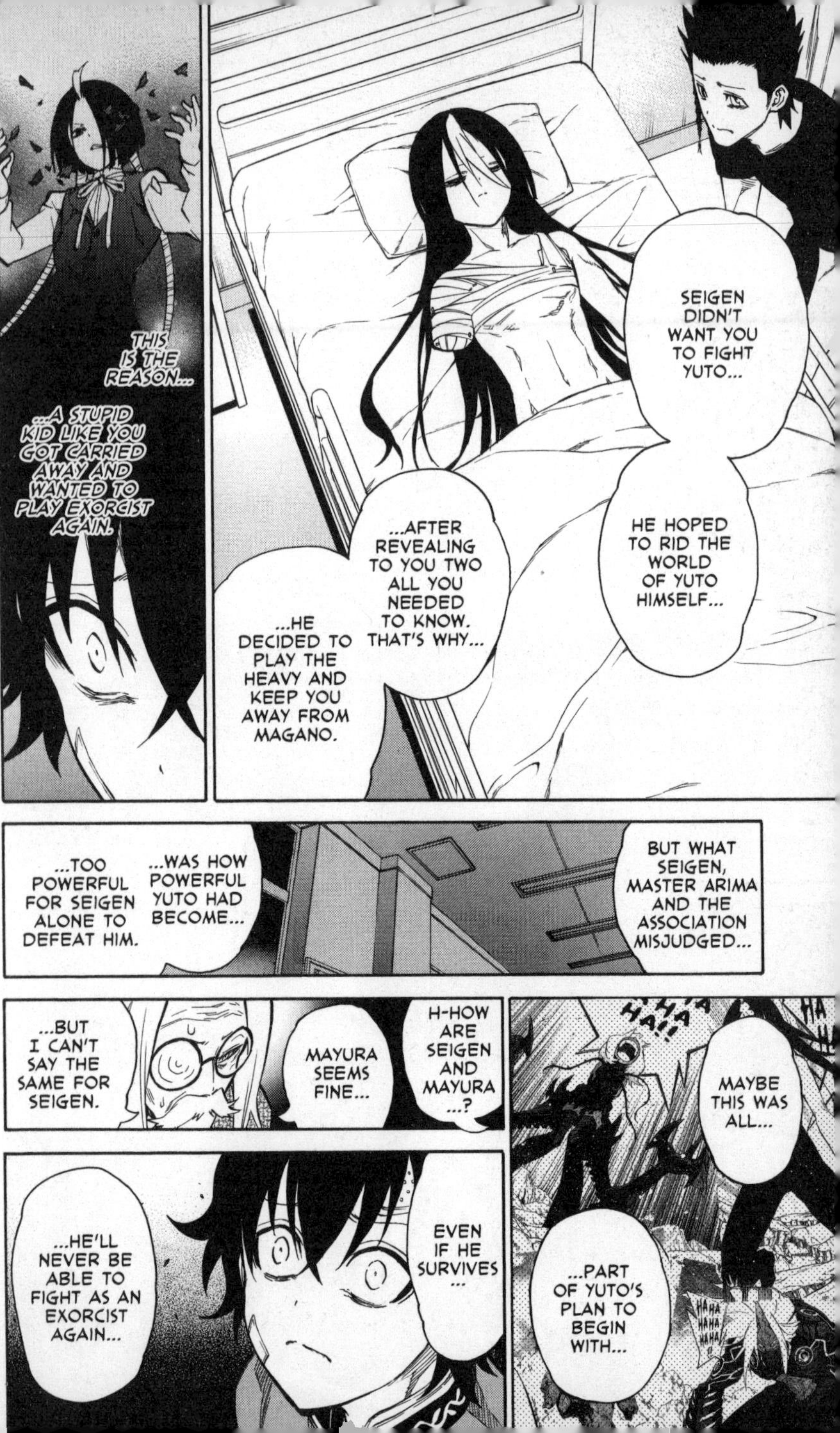
SEIGEN DIDN'T WANT YOU TO FIGHT YUTO...
HE HOPED TO RID THE WORLD OF YUTO HIMSELF...
...AFTER REVEALING TO YOU TWO ALL YOU NEEDED TO KNOW. THAT'S WHY...
...HE DECIDED TO PLAY THE HEAVY AND KEEP YOU AWAY FROM MAGANO.
THIS IS THE REASON...
...A STUPID KID LIKE YOU GOT CARRIED AWAY AND WANTED TO PLAY EXORCIST AGAIN.
BUT WHAT SEIGEN, MASTER ARIMA AND THE ASSOCIATION MISJUDGED...
...WAS HOW POWERFUL YUTO HAD BECOME...
...TOO POWERFUL FOR SEIGEN ALONE TO DEFEAT HIM.
MAYBE THIS WAS ALL...
...PART OF YUTO'S PLAN TO BEGIN WITH...
HAHA HAHA HAHA!
H-HOW ARE SEIGEN AND MAYURA ...?
MAYURA SEEMS FINE...
...BUT I CAN'T SAY THE SAME FOR SEIGEN.
EVEN IF HE SURVIVES ...
...HE'LL NEVER BE ABLE TO FIGHT AS AN EXORCIST AGAIN...

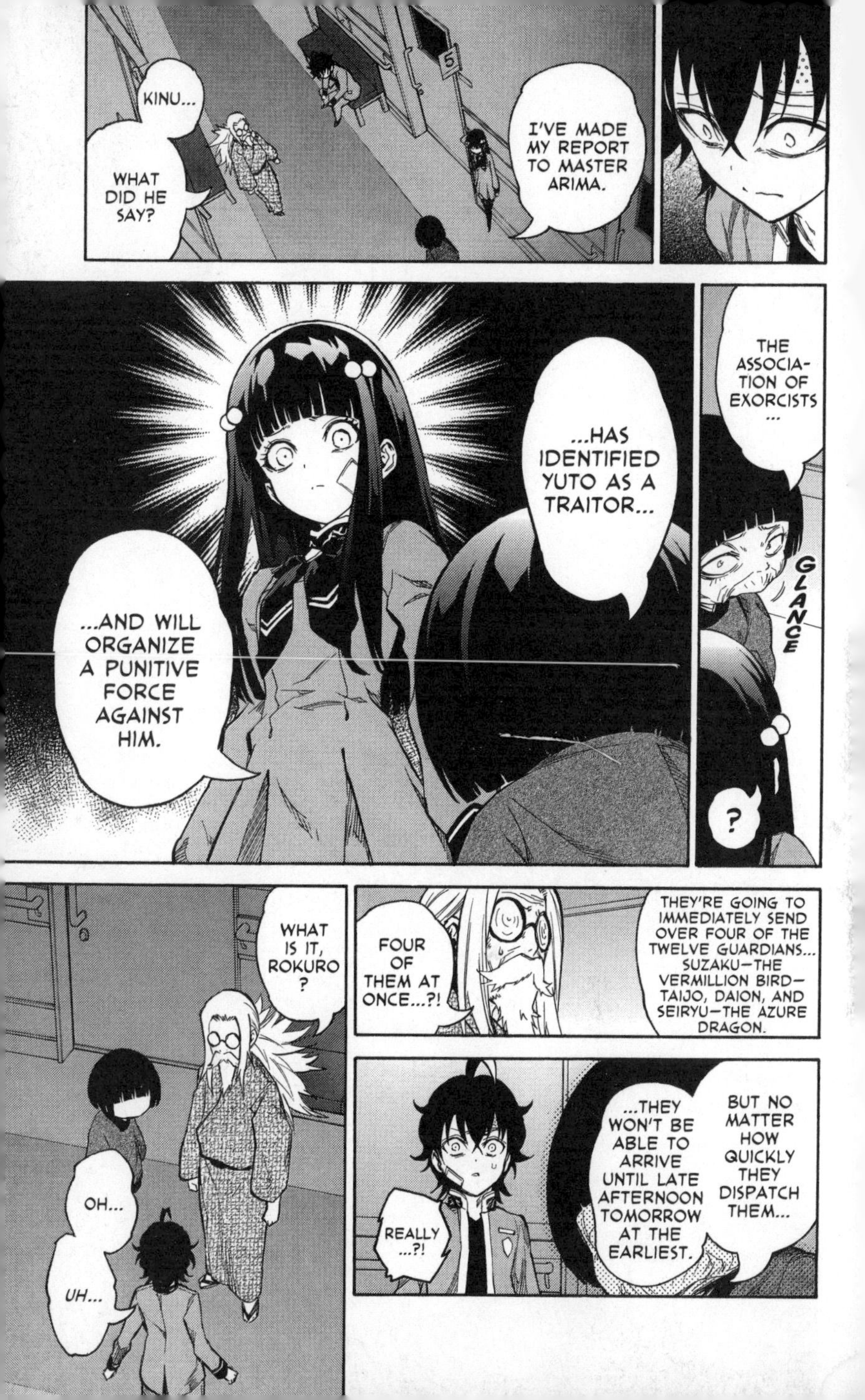
I'VE MADE MY REPORT TO MASTER ARIMA.
KINU...
WHAT DID HE SAY?
THE ASSOCIATION OF EXORCISTS...
GLANCE
?
...HAS IDENTIFIED YUTO AS A TRAITOR...
...AND WILL ORGANIZE A PUNITIVE FORCE AGAINST HIM.
THEY'RE GOING TO IMMEDIATELY SEND OVER FOUR OF THE TWELVE GUARDIANS... SUZAKU—THE VERMILLION BIRD—TAIJO, DAION, AND SEIRYU—THE AZURE DRAGON.
FOUR OF THEM AT ONCE...?!
BUT NO MATTER HOW QUICKLY THEY DISPATCH THEM...
...THEY WON'T BE ABLE TO ARRIVE UNTIL LATE AFTERNOON TOMORROW AT THE EARLIEST.
REALLY...?!
WHAT IS IT, ROKURO?
OH...
UH...

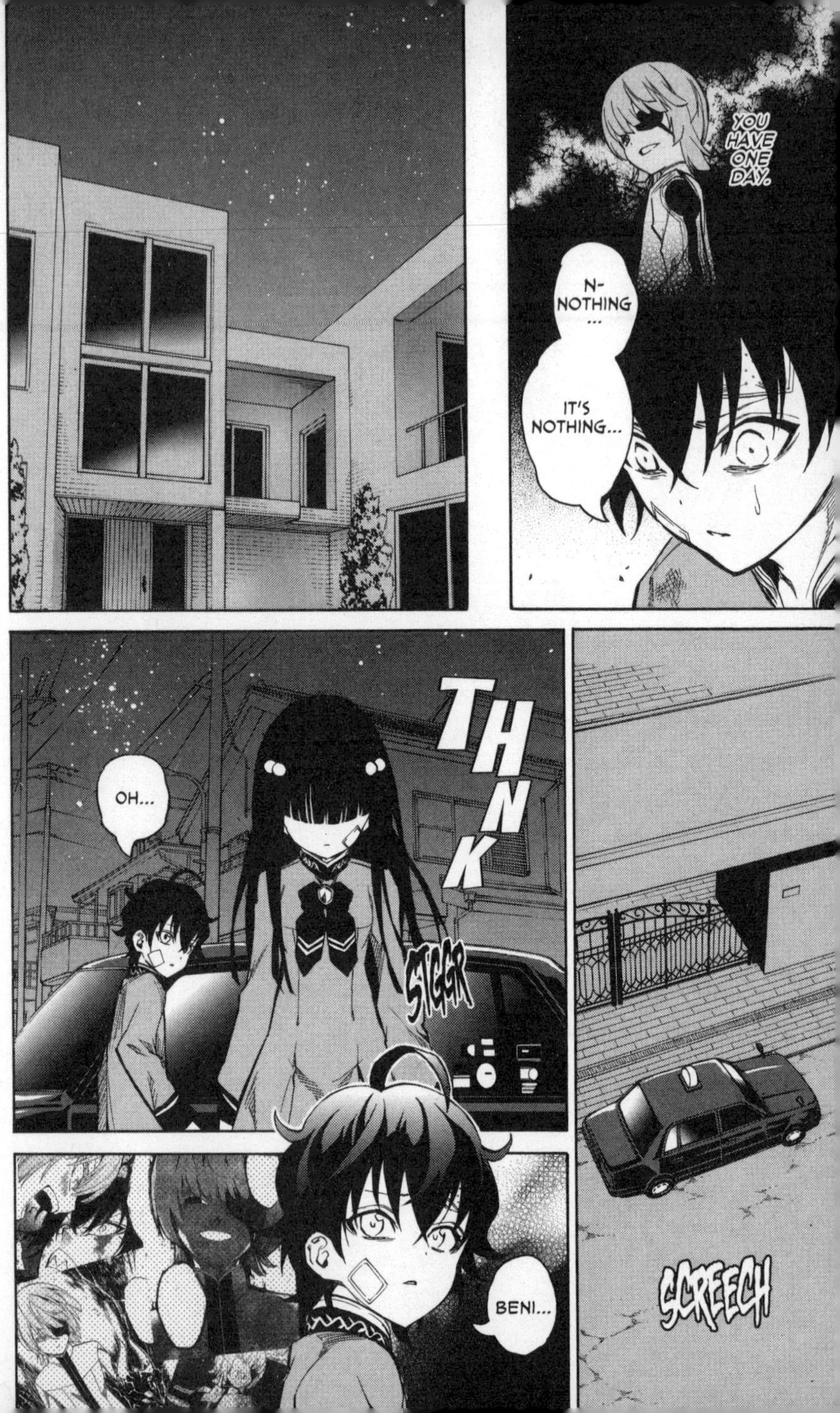
YOU HAVE ONE DAY.
N-NOTHING...
IT'S NOTHING...
SCREECH
THNK
STGGR
OH...
BENI...

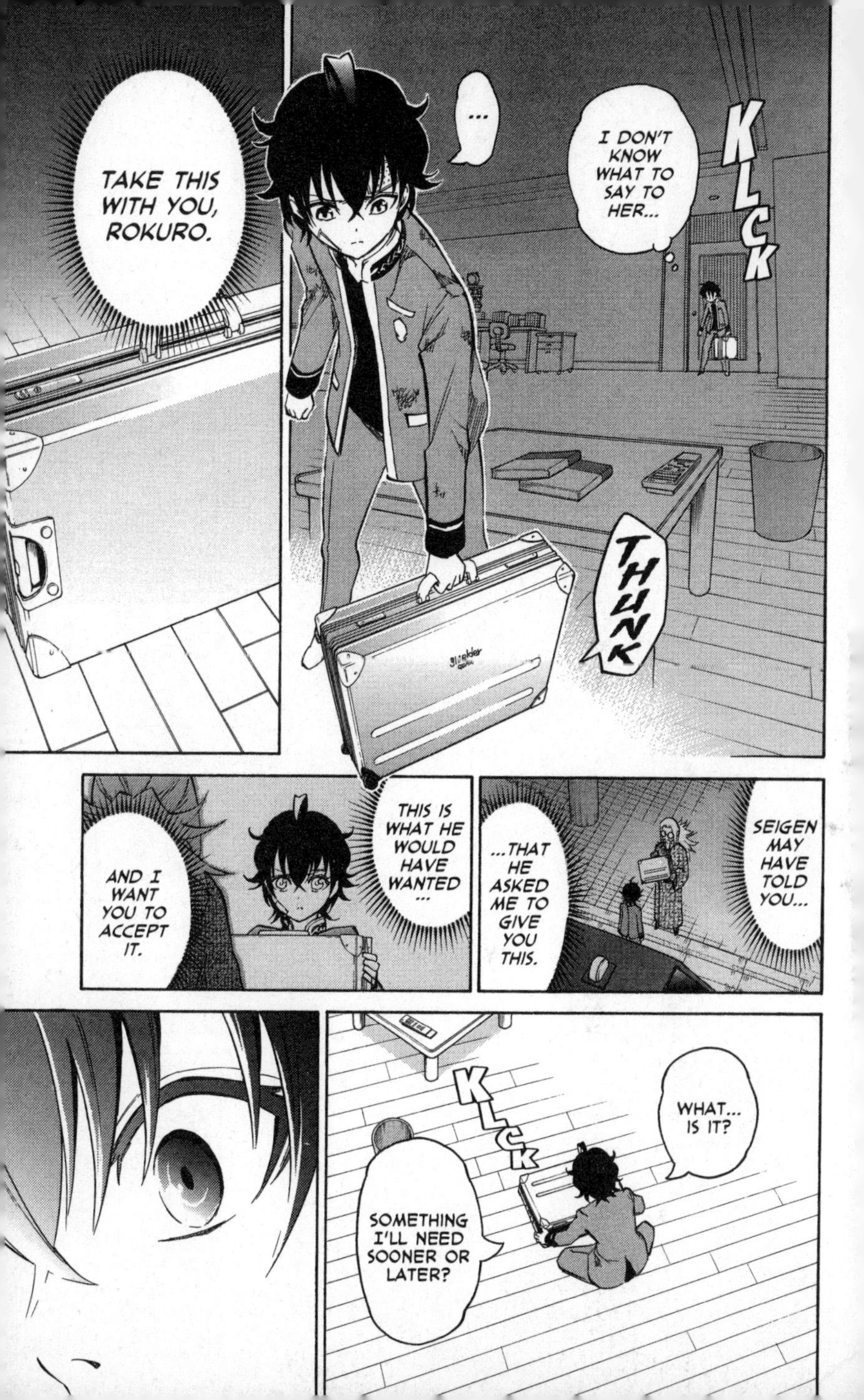
KLCK
I DON'T KNOW WHAT TO SAY TO HER...
...
THUNK
TAKE THIS WITH YOU, ROKURO.
SEIGEN MAY HAVE TOLD YOU...
...THAT HE ASKED ME TO GIVE YOU THIS.
THIS IS WHAT HE WOULD HAVE WANTED...
AND I WANT YOU TO ACCEPT IT.
WHAT... IS IT?
KLCK
SOMETHING I'LL NEED SOONER OR LATER?

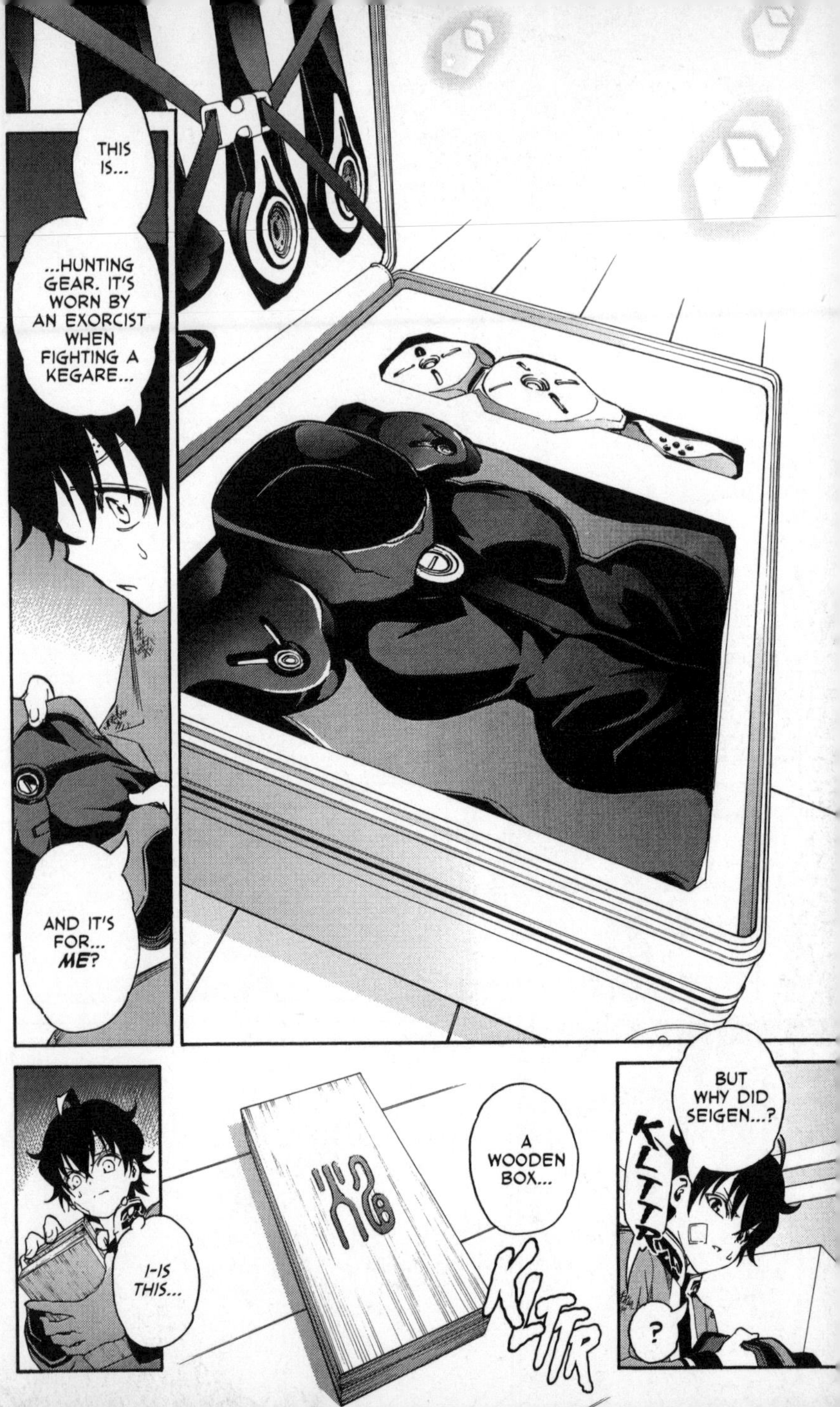
THIS IS...
...HUNTING GEAR. IT'S WORN BY AN EXORCIST WHEN FIGHTING A KEGARE...
AND IT'S FOR... *ME*?
BUT WHY DID SEIGEN...?
KLTTR
?
A WOODEN BOX...
KLTTR
I-IS THIS...

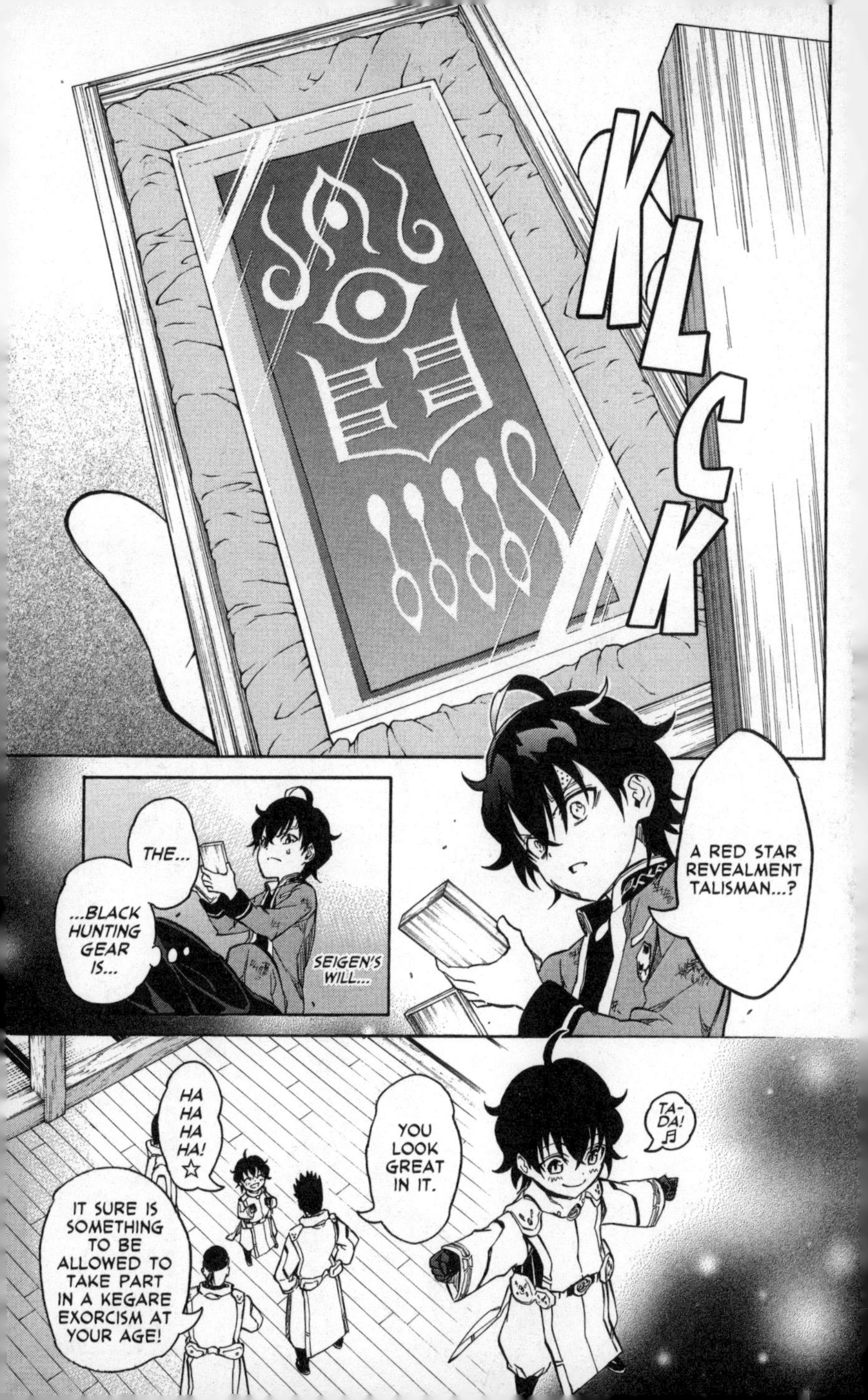
KLICK
A RED STAR REVEALMENT TALISMAN...?
THE...
...BLACK HUNTING GEAR IS...
SEIGEN'S WILL...
TA-DA! ♬
YOU LOOK GREAT IN IT.
HA HA HA HA! ☆
IT SURE IS SOMETHING TO BE ALLOWED TO TAKE PART IN A KEGARE EXORCISM AT YOUR AGE!

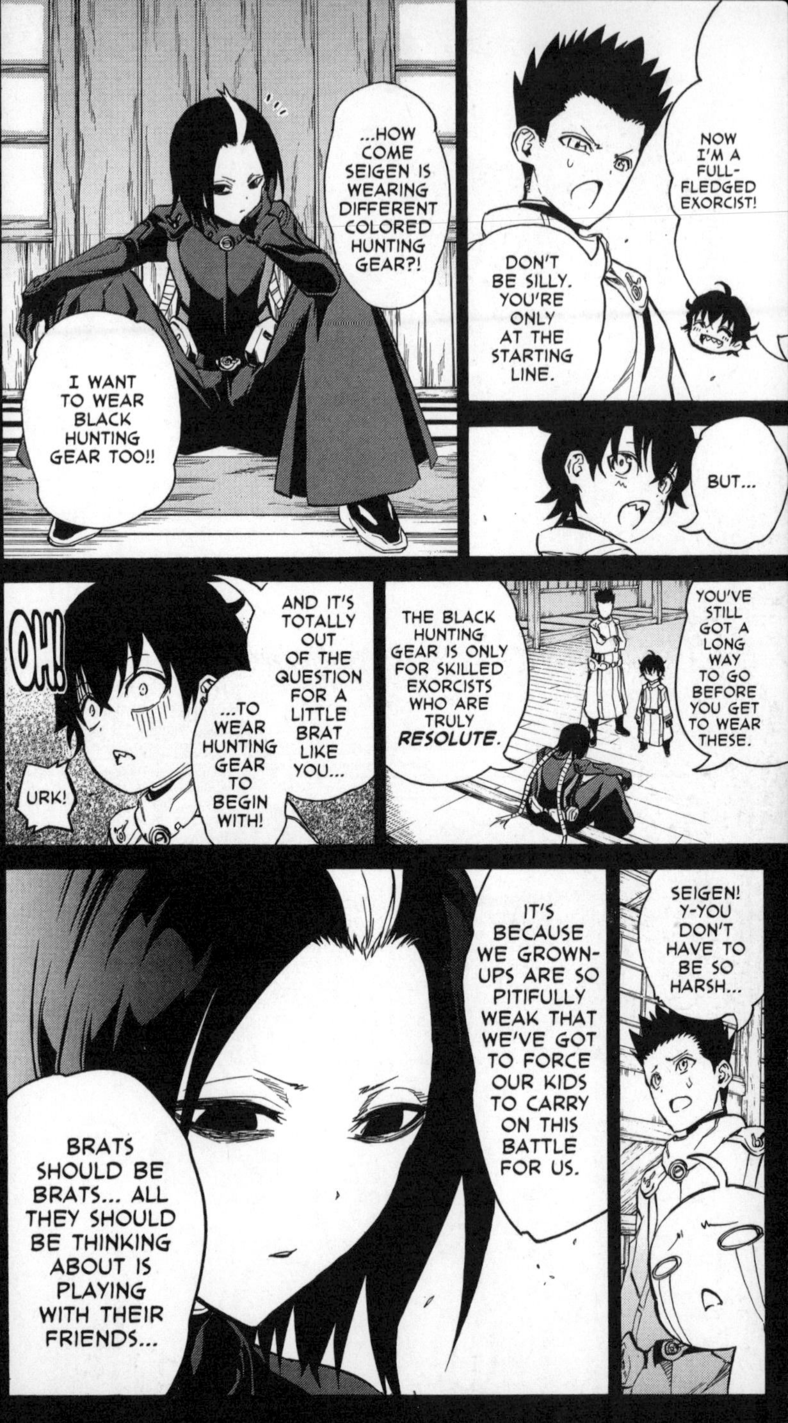
NOW I'M A FULL-FLEDGED EXORCIST!
DON'T BE SILLY. YOU'RE ONLY AT THE STARTING LINE.
BUT...
...HOW COME SEIGEN IS WEARING DIFFERENT COLORED HUNTING GEAR?!
I WANT TO WEAR BLACK HUNTING GEAR TOO!!
YOU'VE STILL GOT A LONG WAY TO GO BEFORE YOU GET TO WEAR THESE.
THE BLACK HUNTING GEAR IS ONLY FOR SKILLED EXORCISTS WHO ARE TRULY ***RESOLUTE***.
AND IT'S TOTALLY OUT OF THE QUESTION FOR A LITTLE BRAT LIKE YOU...
...TO WEAR HUNTING GEAR TO BEGIN WITH!
OH!
URK!
SEIGEN! Y-YOU DON'T HAVE TO BE SO HARSH...
IT'S BECAUSE WE GROWN-UPS ARE SO PITIFULLY WEAK THAT WE'VE GOT TO FORCE OUR KIDS TO CARRY ON THIS BATTLE FOR US.
BRATS SHOULD BE BRATS... ALL THEY SHOULD BE THINKING ABOUT IS PLAYING WITH THEIR FRIENDS...

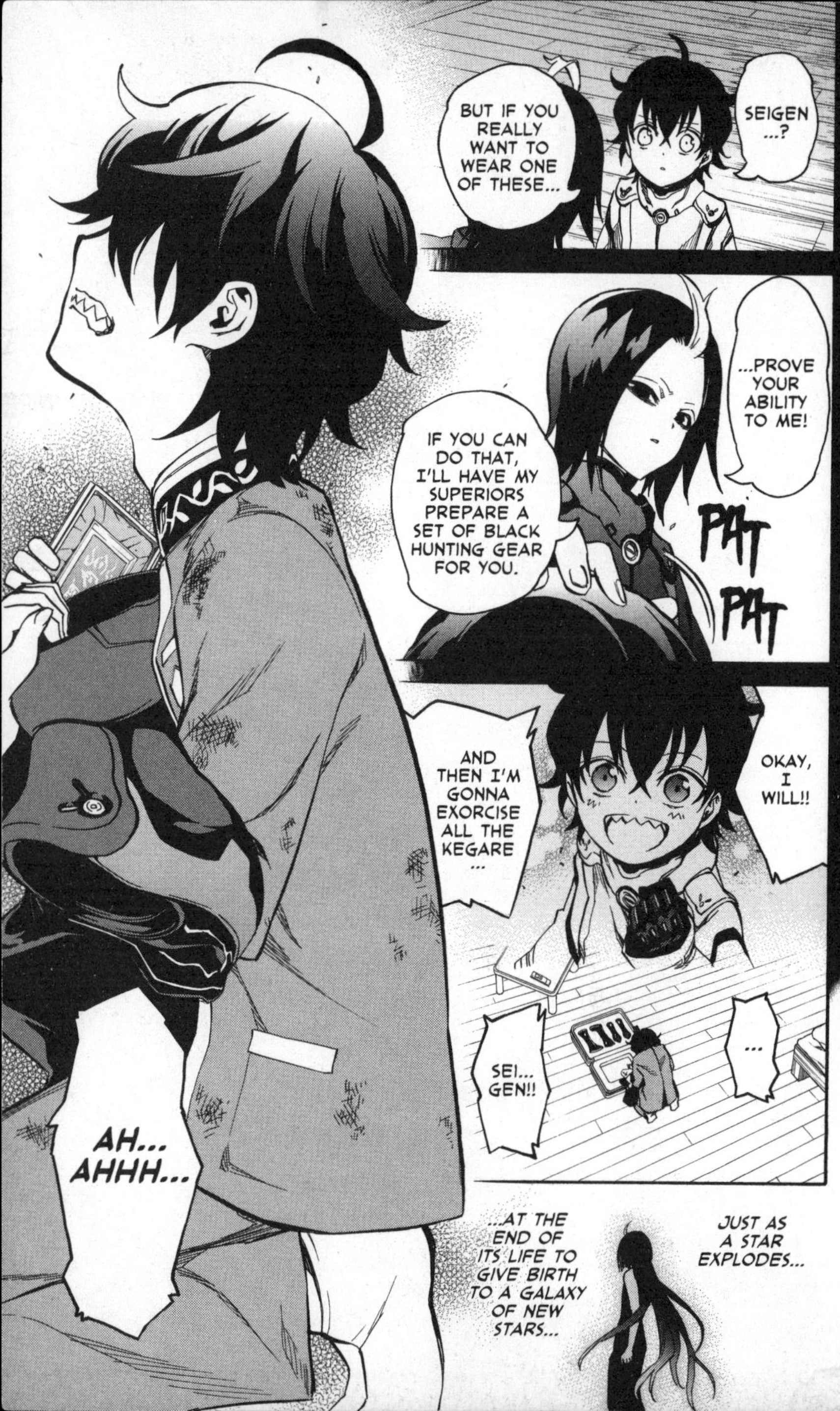
SEIGEN ...?
BUT IF YOU REALLY WANT TO WEAR ONE OF THESE...
...PROVE YOUR ABILITY TO ME!
IF YOU CAN DO THAT, I'LL HAVE MY SUPERIORS PREPARE A SET OF BLACK HUNTING GEAR FOR YOU.
PAT PAT
OKAY, I WILL!!
AND THEN I'M GONNA EXORCISE ALL THE KEGARE ...
...
SEI... GEN!!
JUST AS A STAR EXPLODES...
...AT THE END OF ITS LIFE TO GIVE BIRTH TO A GALAXY OF NEW STARS...
AH... AHHH...

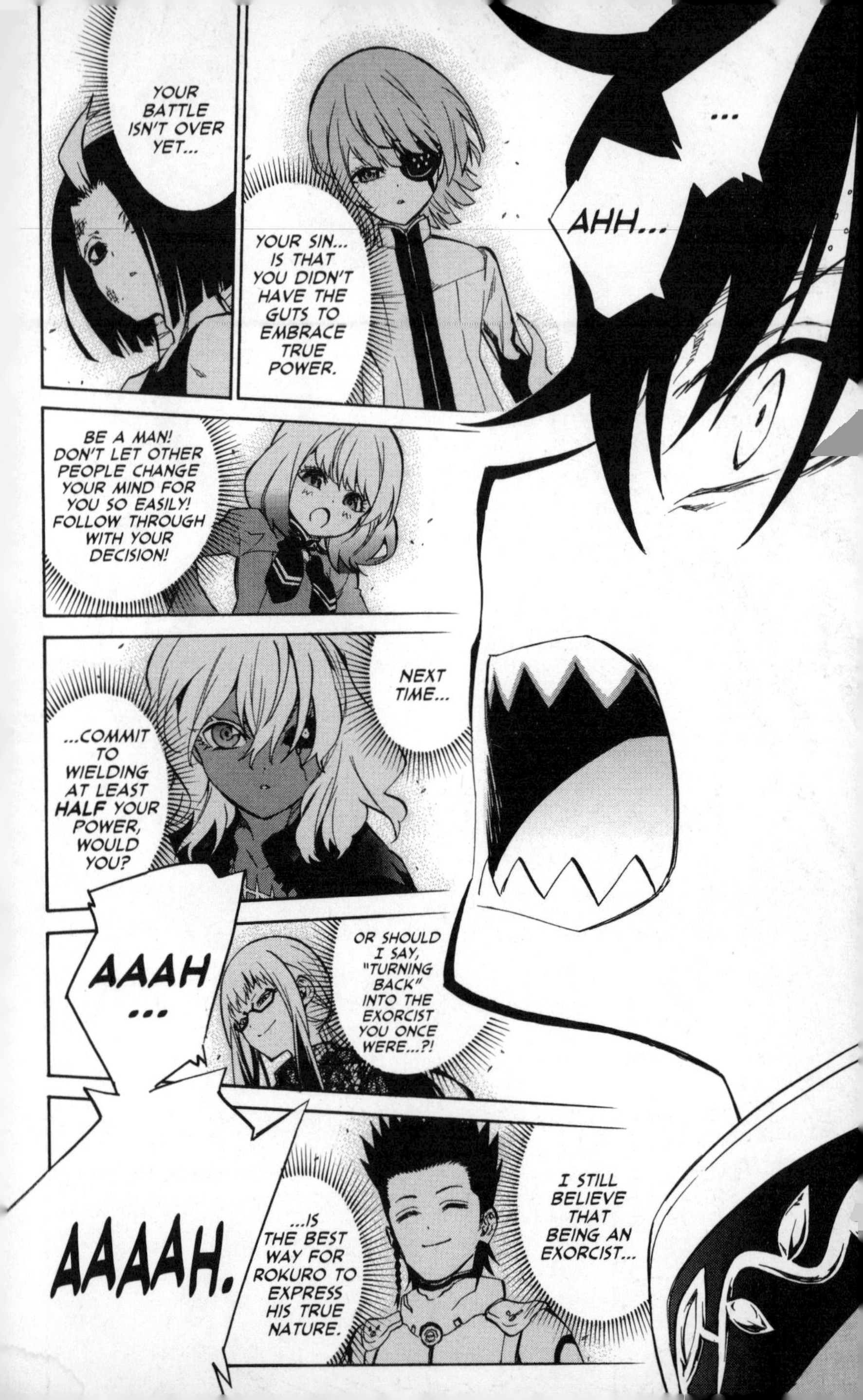
...
AHH...
AAAH ...
AAAAH.
YOUR SIN... IS THAT YOU DIDN'T HAVE THE GUTS TO EMBRACE TRUE POWER.
YOUR BATTLE ISN'T OVER YET...
BE A MAN! DON'T LET OTHER PEOPLE CHANGE YOUR MIND FOR YOU SO EASILY! FOLLOW THROUGH WITH YOUR DECISION!
NEXT TIME...
...COMMIT TO WIELDING AT LEAST HALF YOUR POWER, WOULD YOU?
OR SHOULD I SAY, "TURNING BACK" INTO THE EXORCIST YOU ONCE WERE...?!
I STILL BELIEVE THAT BEING AN EXORCIST...
...IS THE BEST WAY FOR ROKURO TO EXPRESS HIS TRUE NATURE.

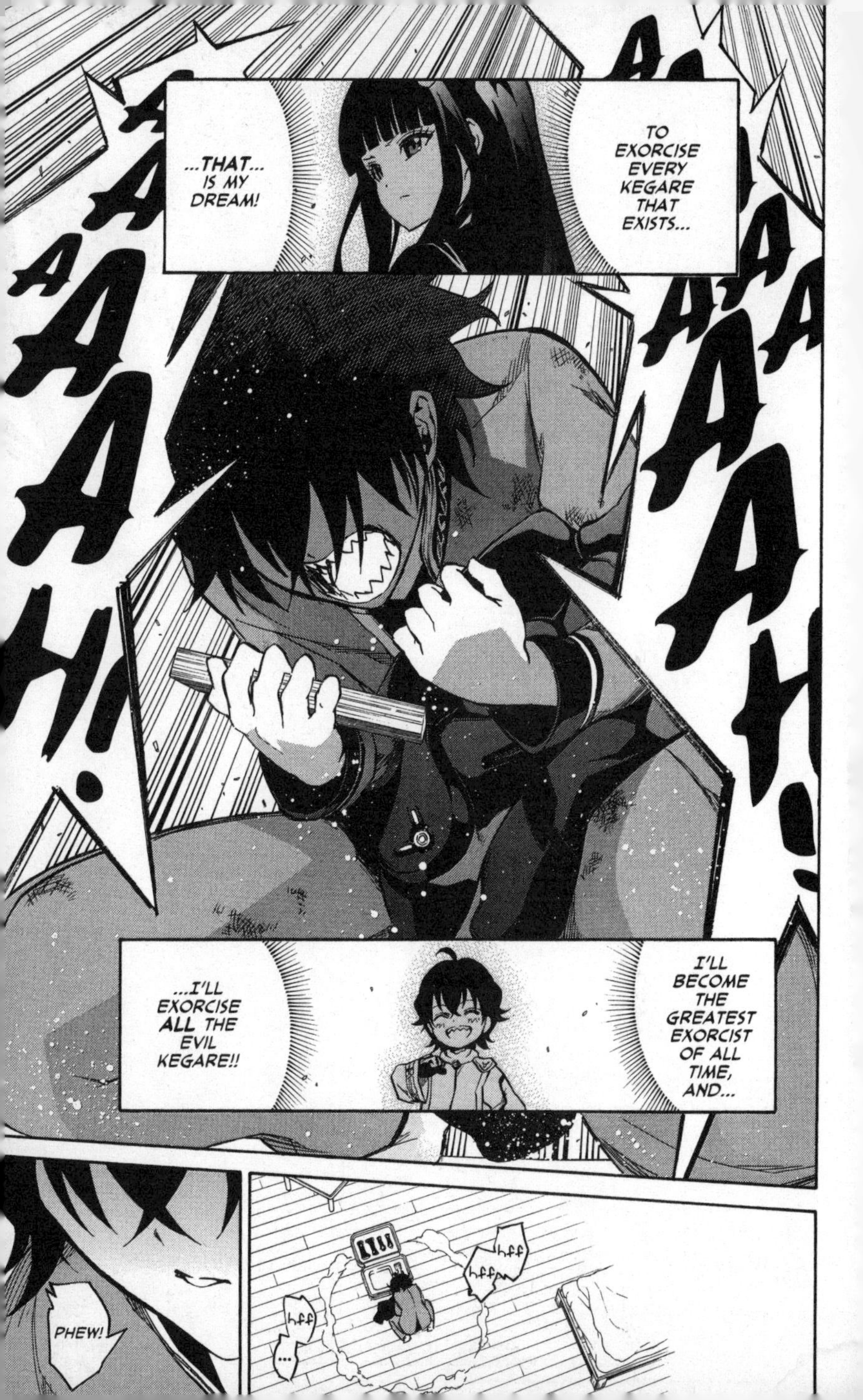

TO EXORCISE EVERY KEGARE THAT EXISTS...
...THAT... IS MY DREAM!
AAAAAAAH!!
AAAAAAAH!!
I'LL BECOME THE GREATEST EXORCIST OF ALL TIME, AND...
...I'LL EXORCISE ALL THE EVIL KEGARE!!
hff
hff
hff
...
PHEW!

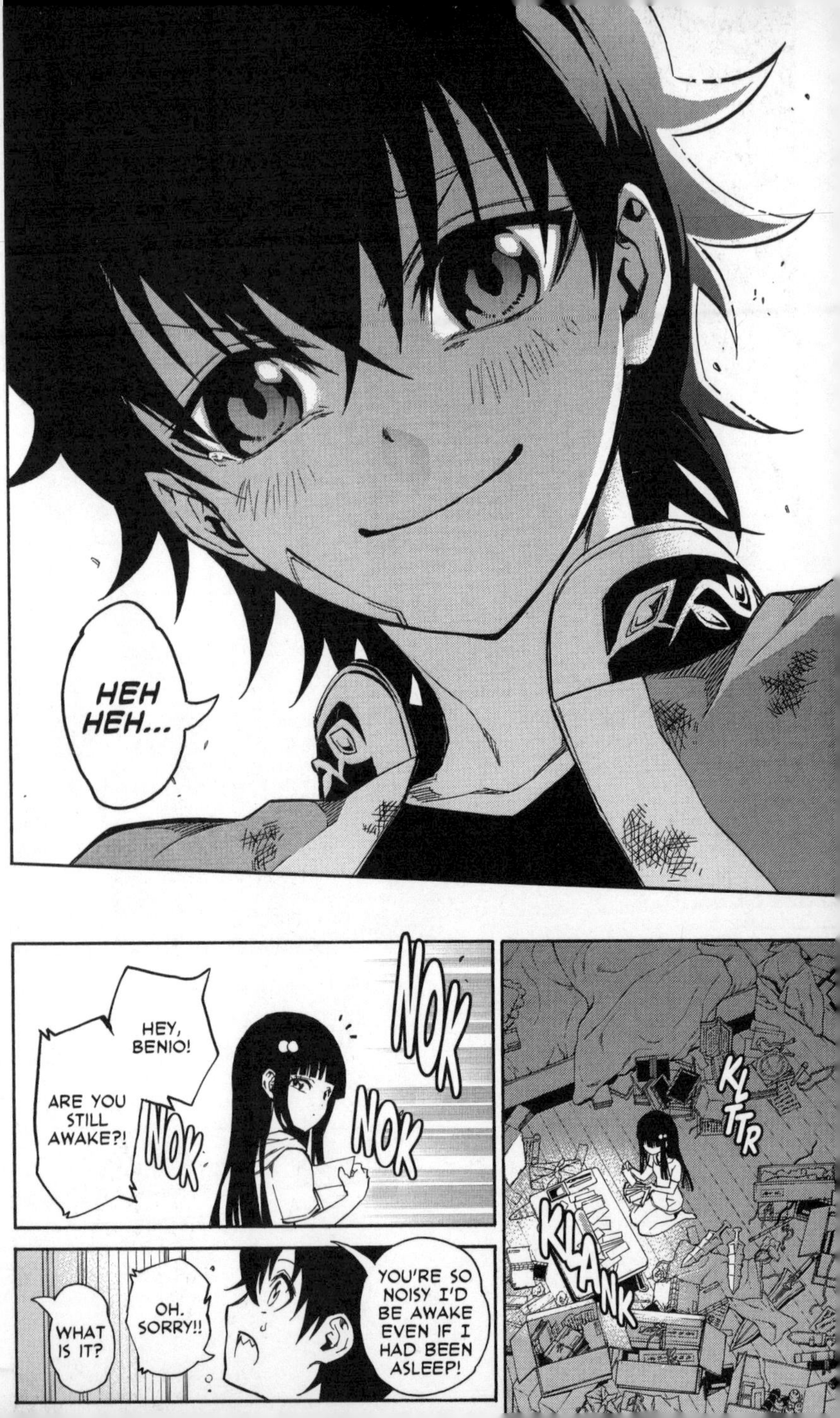
HEH HEH...
KLTTR
KLANK
NOK
NOK
NOK
HEY, BENIO!
ARE YOU STILL AWAKE?!
YOU'RE SO NOISY I'D BE AWAKE EVEN IF I HAD BEEN ASLEEP!
OH. SORRY!!
WHAT IS IT?

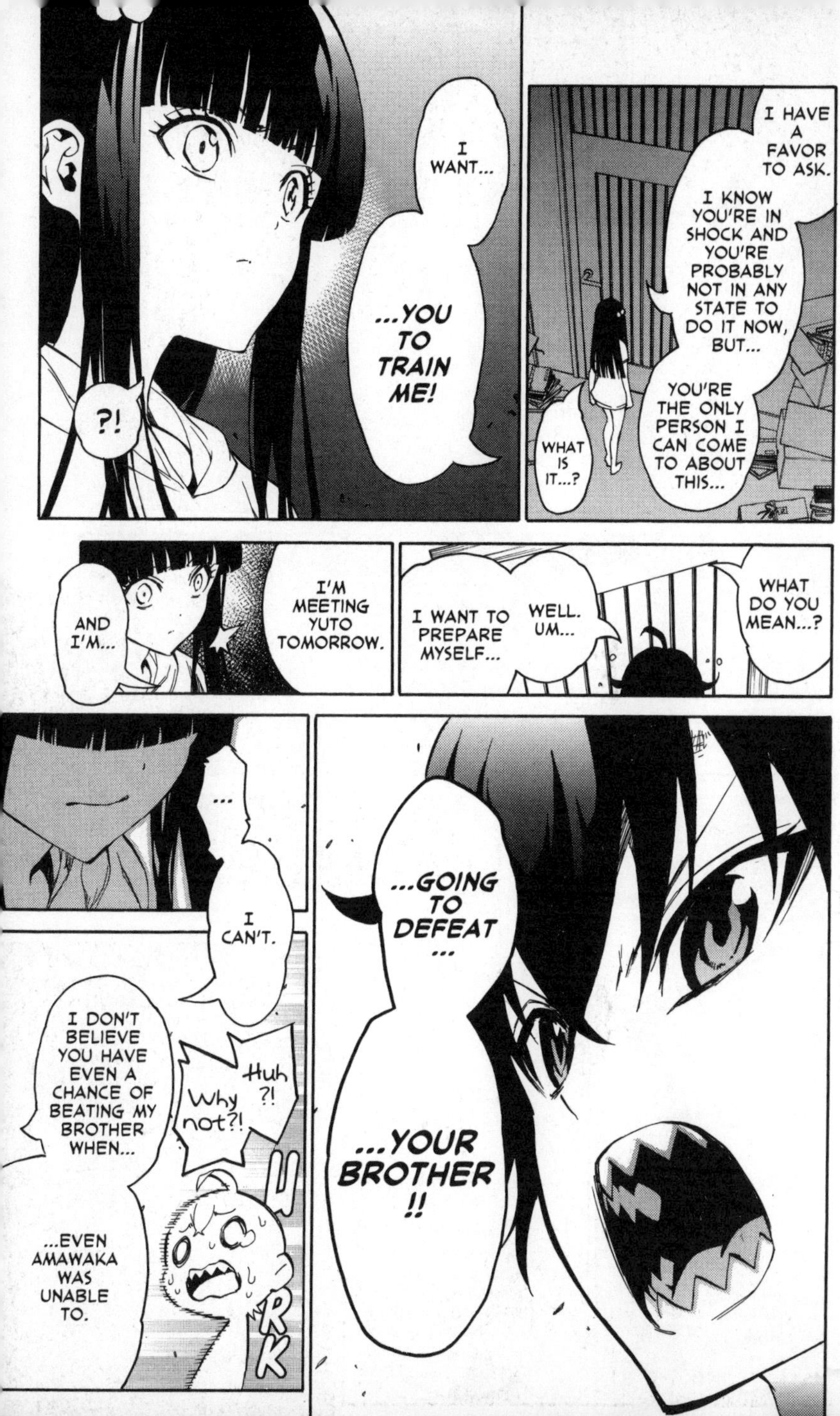
I HAVE A FAVOR TO ASK.
I KNOW YOU'RE IN SHOCK AND YOU'RE PROBABLY NOT IN ANY STATE TO DO IT NOW, BUT...
YOU'RE THE ONLY PERSON I CAN COME TO ABOUT THIS...
WHAT IS IT...?
I WANT...
...YOU TO TRAIN ME!
?!
WHAT DO YOU MEAN...?
WELL. UM...
I WANT TO PREPARE MYSELF...
I'M MEETING YUTO TOMORROW.
AND I'M...
...GOING TO DEFEAT ...
...YOUR BROTHER !!
...
I CAN'T.
Huh ?!
Why not?!
I DON'T BELIEVE YOU HAVE EVEN A CHANCE OF BEATING MY BROTHER WHEN...
URK
...EVEN AMAWAKA WAS UNABLE TO.

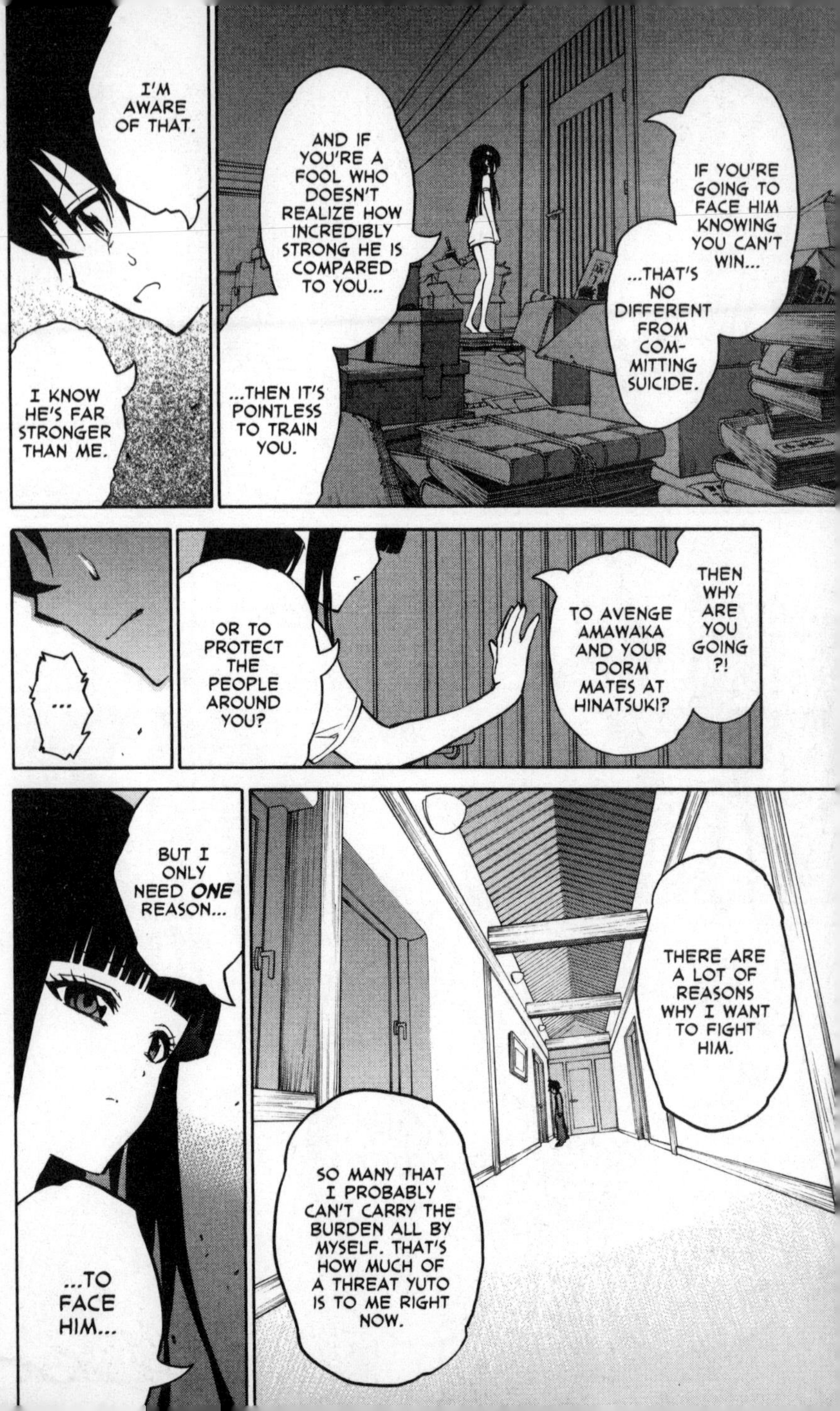
IF YOU'RE GOING TO FACE HIM KNOWING YOU CAN'T WIN...
...THAT'S NO DIFFERENT FROM COM-MITTING SUICIDE.
AND IF YOU'RE A FOOL WHO DOESN'T REALIZE HOW INCREDIBLY STRONG HE IS COMPARED TO YOU...
...THEN IT'S POINTLESS TO TRAIN YOU.
I'M AWARE OF THAT.
I KNOW HE'S FAR STRONGER THAN ME.
THEN WHY ARE YOU GOING?!
TO AVENGE AMAWAKA AND YOUR DORM MATES AT HINATSUKI?
OR TO PROTECT THE PEOPLE AROUND YOU?
...
THERE ARE A LOT OF REASONS WHY I WANT TO FIGHT HIM.
SO MANY THAT I PROBABLY CAN'T CARRY THE BURDEN ALL BY MYSELF. THAT'S HOW MUCH OF A THREAT YUTO IS TO ME RIGHT NOW.
BUT I ONLY NEED *ONE* REASON...
...TO FACE HIM...

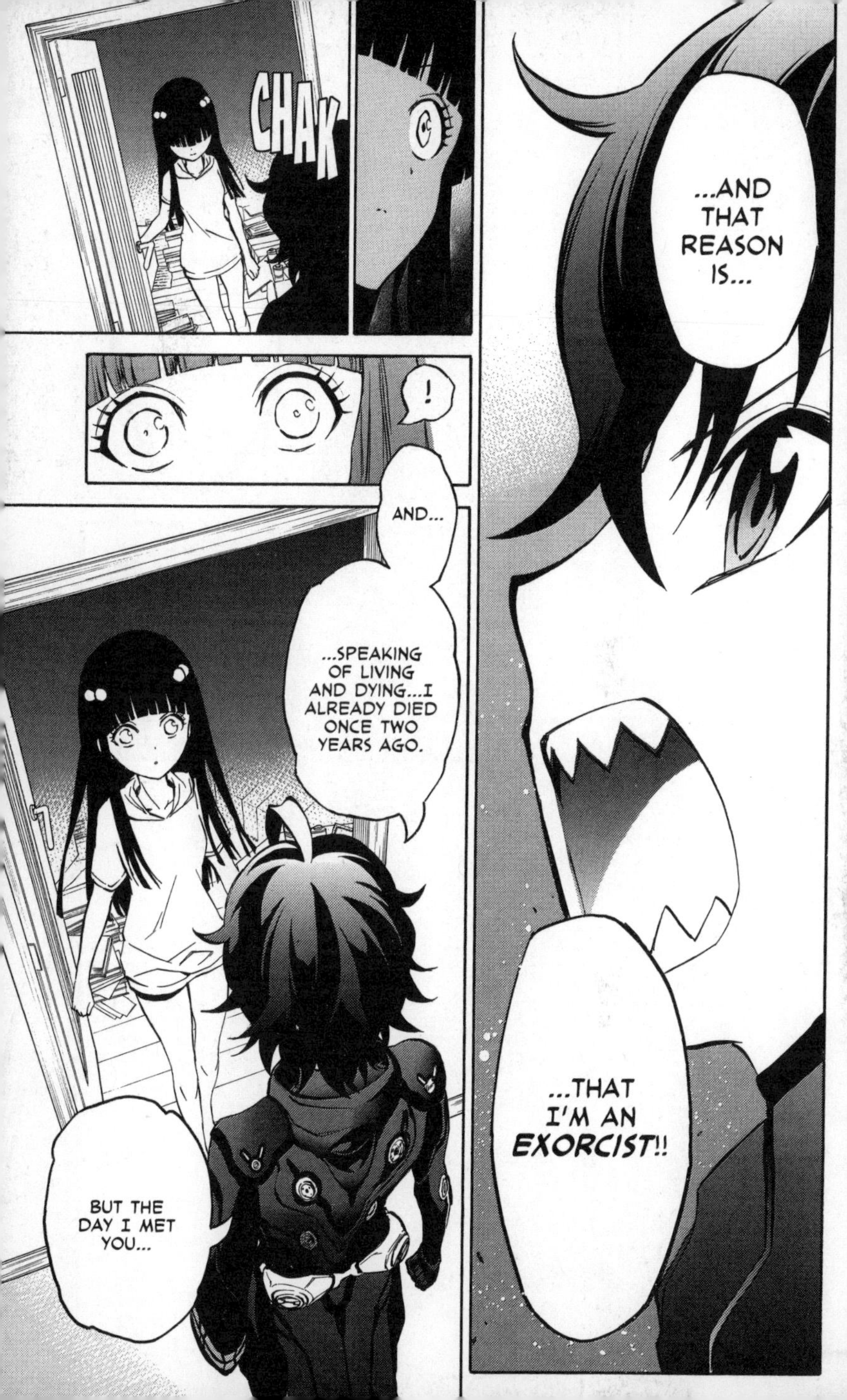
...AND THAT REASON IS...
...THAT I'M AN EXORCIST!!
CHAK
!
AND...
...SPEAKING OF LIVING AND DYING...I ALREADY DIED ONCE TWO YEARS AGO.
BUT THE DAY I MET YOU...

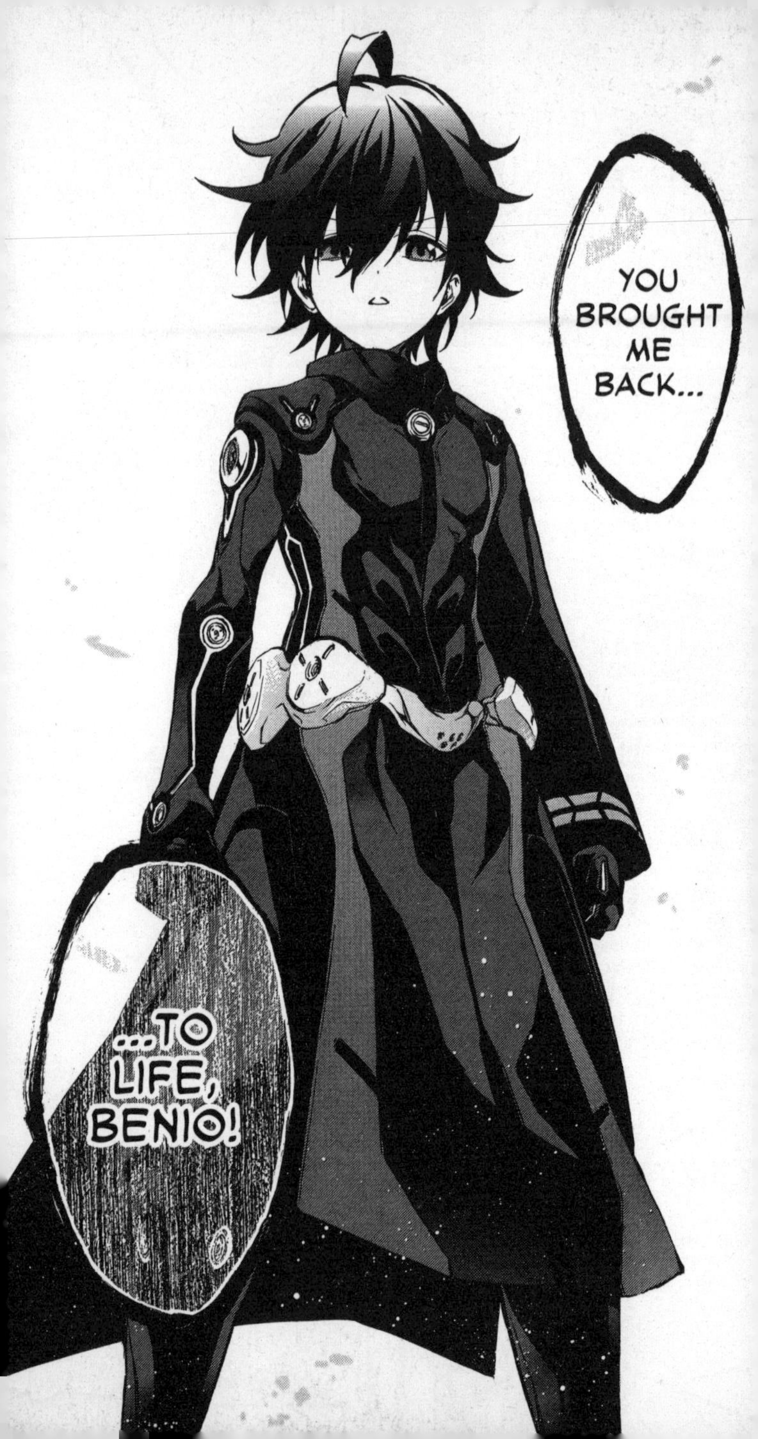
YOU BROUGHT ME BACK...
...TO LIFE, BENIO!

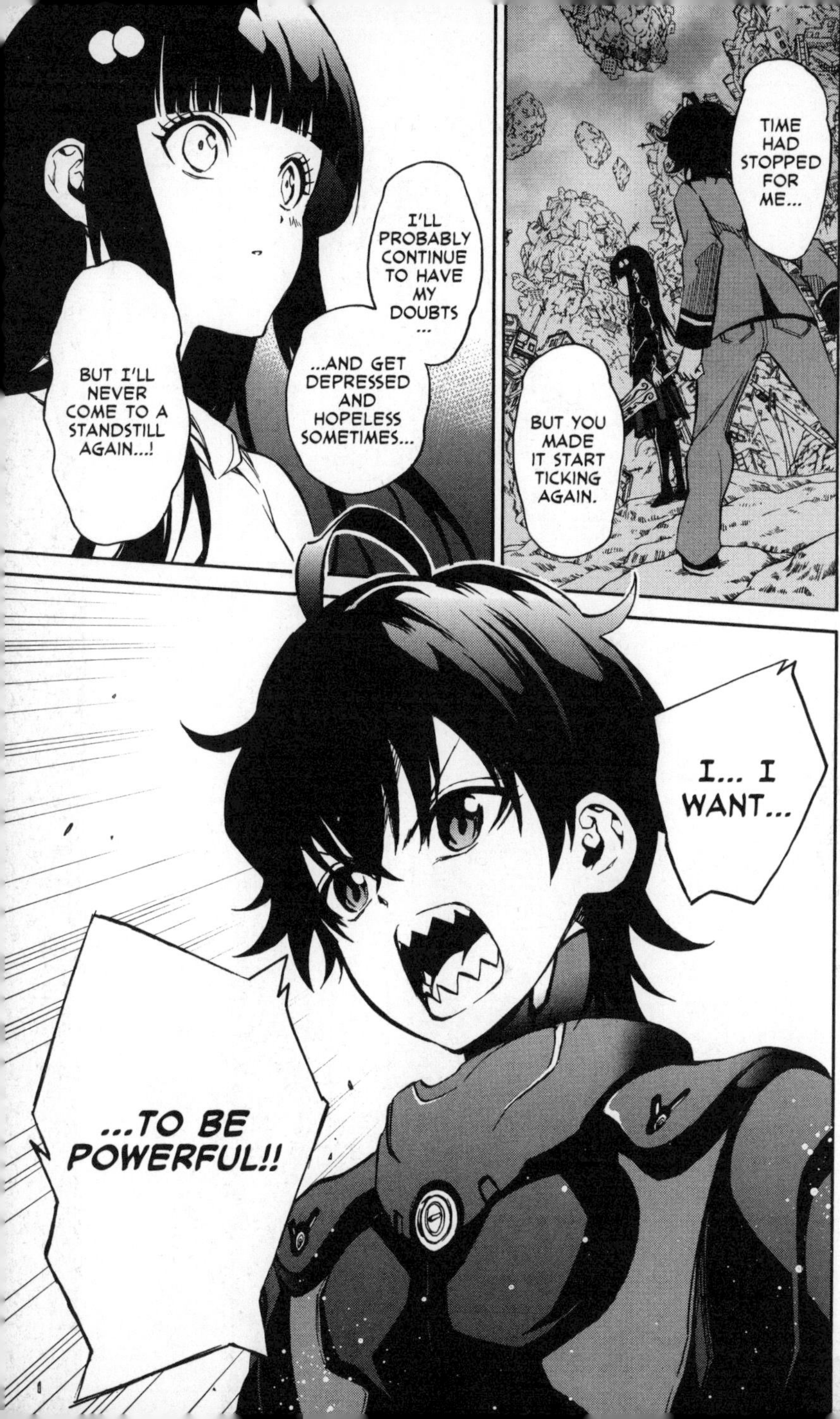
TIME HAD STOPPED FOR ME...
BUT YOU MADE IT START TICKING AGAIN.
I'LL PROBABLY CONTINUE TO HAVE MY DOUBTS...
...AND GET DEPRESSED AND HOPELESS SOMETIMES...
BUT I'LL NEVER COME TO A STANDSTILL AGAIN...!
I... I WANT...
...TO BE POWERFUL!!

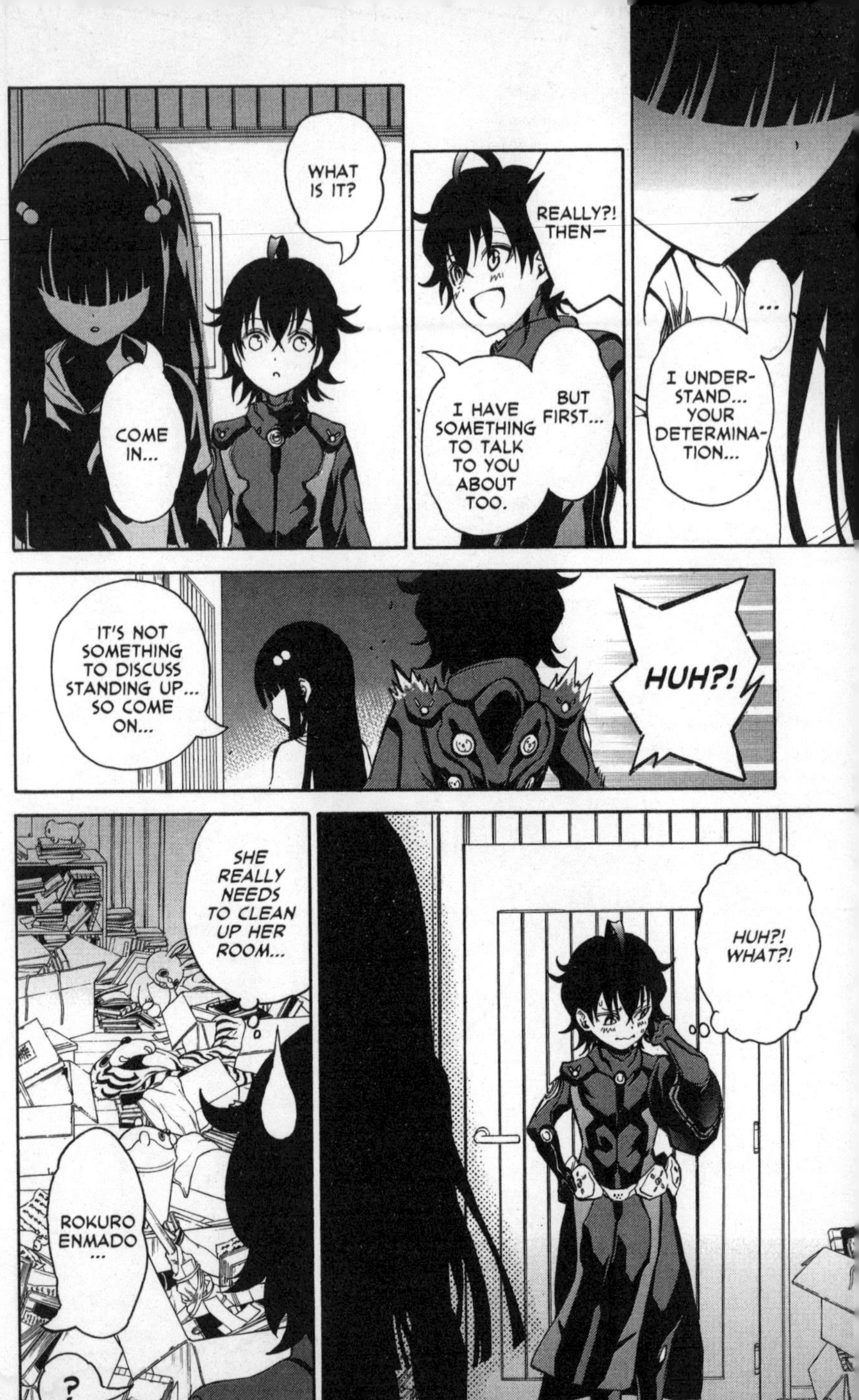
...
I UNDER-STAND... YOUR DETERMINA-TION...
REALLY?! THEN—
BUT FIRST...
I HAVE SOMETHING TO TALK TO YOU ABOUT TOO.
WHAT IS IT?
COME IN...
HUH?!
IT'S NOT SOMETHING TO DISCUSS STANDING UP... SO COME ON...
HUH?! WHAT?!
SHE REALLY NEEDS TO CLEAN UP HER ROOM...
ROKURO ENMADO ...
?

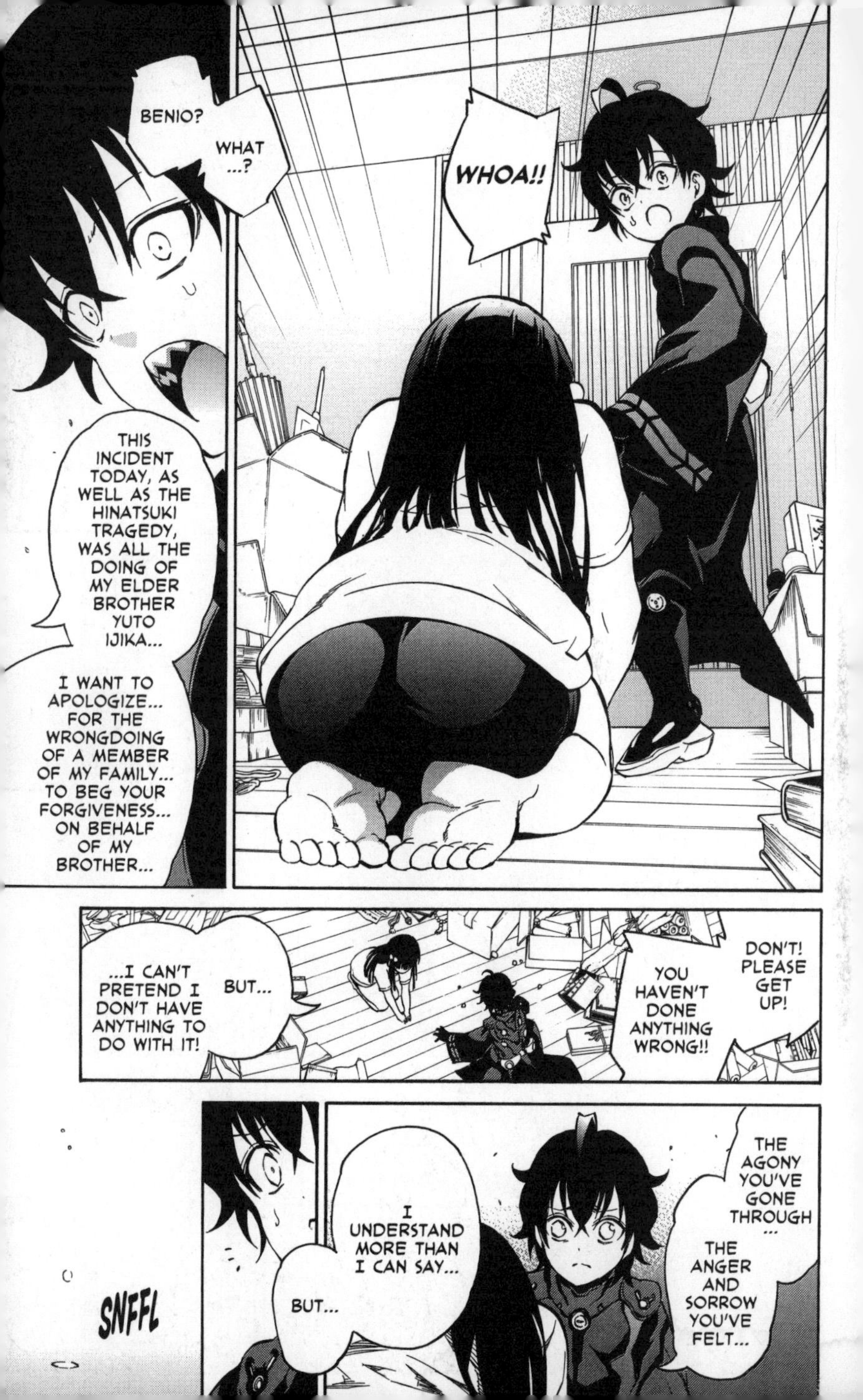
WHOA!!
BENIO?
WHAT ...?
THIS INCIDENT TODAY, AS WELL AS THE HINATSUKI TRAGEDY, WAS ALL THE DOING OF MY ELDER BROTHER YUTO IJIKA...
I WANT TO APOLOGIZE... FOR THE WRONGDOING OF A MEMBER OF MY FAMILY... TO BEG YOUR FORGIVENESS... ON BEHALF OF MY BROTHER...
DON'T! PLEASE GET UP!
YOU HAVEN'T DONE ANYTHING WRONG!!
BUT...
...I CAN'T PRETEND I DON'T HAVE ANYTHING TO DO WITH IT!
THE AGONY YOU'VE GONE THROUGH...
THE ANGER AND SORROW YOU'VE FELT...
I UNDERSTAND MORE THAN I CAN SAY...
BUT...
SNFFL

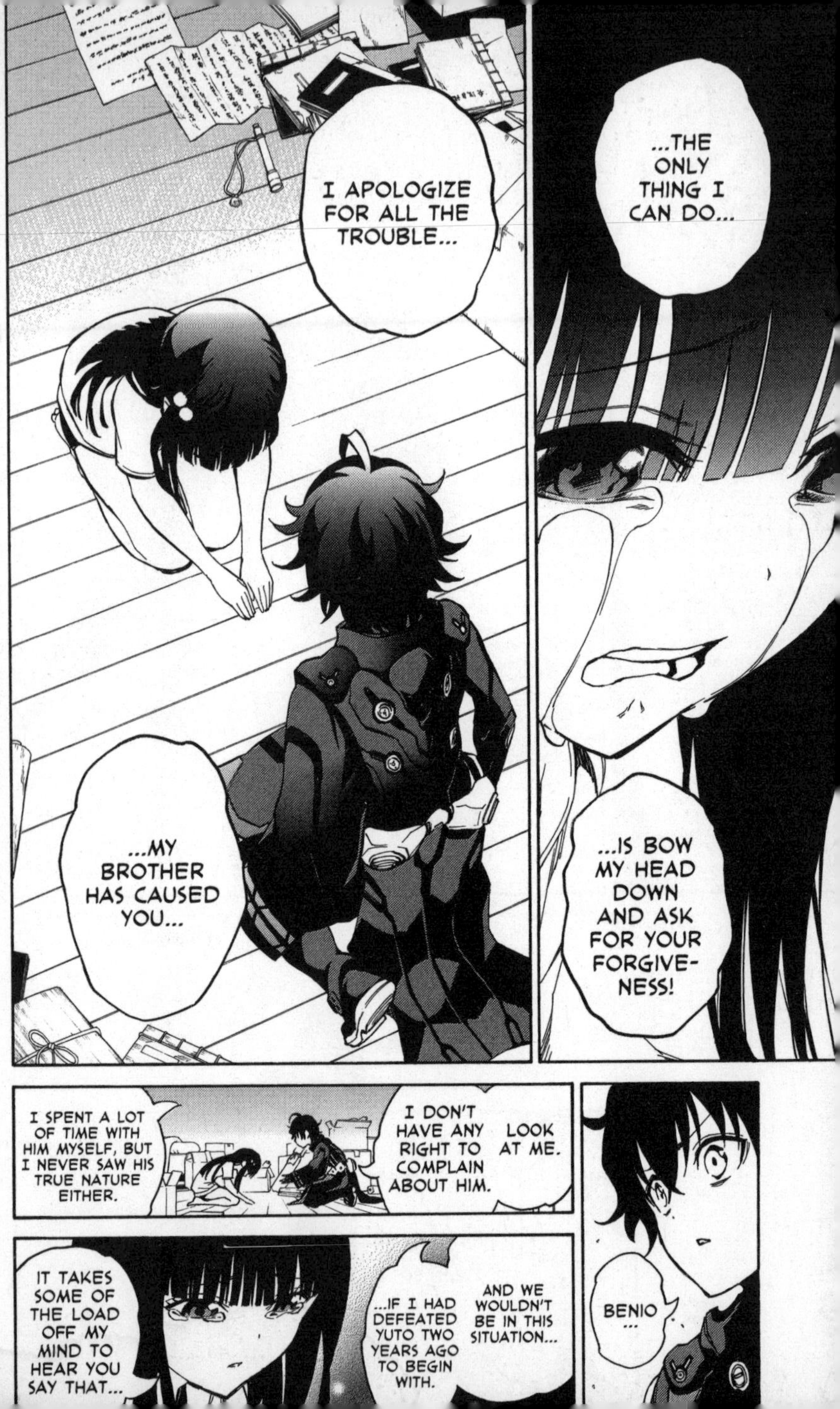

...THE ONLY THING I CAN DO...
...IS BOW MY HEAD DOWN AND ASK FOR YOUR FORGIVE-NESS!
I APOLOGIZE FOR ALL THE TROUBLE...
...MY BROTHER HAS CAUSED YOU...
BENIO ...
LOOK AT ME.
I DON'T HAVE ANY RIGHT TO COMPLAIN ABOUT HIM.
I SPENT A LOT OF TIME WITH HIM MYSELF, BUT I NEVER SAW HIS TRUE NATURE EITHER.
AND WE WOULDN'T BE IN THIS SITUATION...
...IF I HAD DEFEATED YUTO TWO YEARS AGO TO BEGIN WITH.
IT TAKES SOME OF THE LOAD OFF MY MIND TO HEAR YOU SAY THAT...

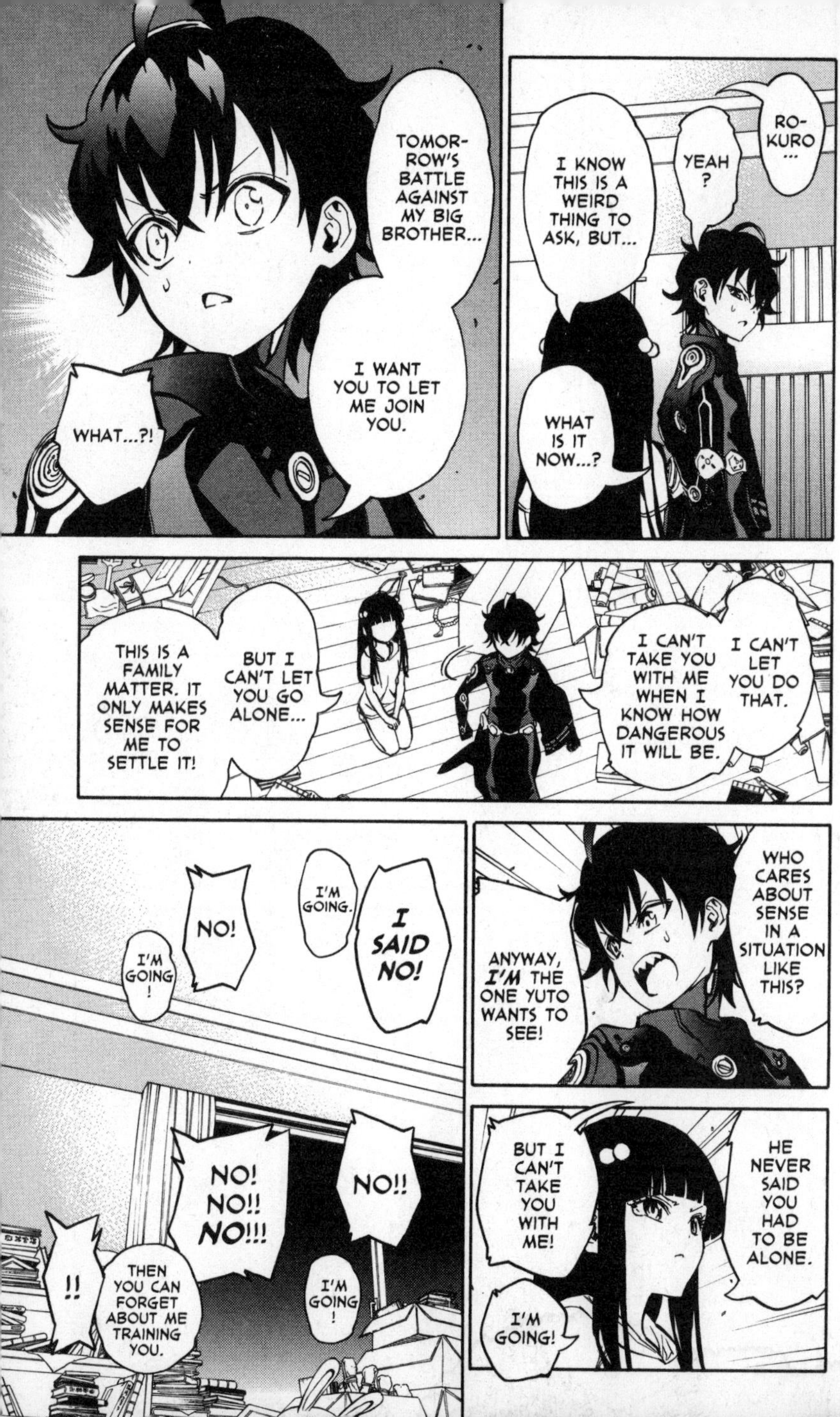
RO-KURO...
YEAH?
I KNOW THIS IS A WEIRD THING TO ASK, BUT...
WHAT IS IT NOW...?
TOMORROW'S BATTLE AGAINST MY BIG BROTHER...
I WANT YOU TO LET ME JOIN YOU.
WHAT...?!
I CAN'T LET YOU DO THAT.
I CAN'T TAKE YOU WITH ME WHEN I KNOW HOW DANGEROUS IT WILL BE.
BUT I CAN'T LET YOU GO ALONE...
THIS IS A FAMILY MATTER. IT ONLY MAKES SENSE FOR ME TO SETTLE IT!
WHO CARES ABOUT SENSE IN A SITUATION LIKE THIS?
ANYWAY, *I'M* THE ONE YUTO WANTS TO SEE!
HE NEVER SAID YOU HAD TO BE ALONE.
BUT I CAN'T TAKE YOU WITH ME!
I'M GOING!
I'M GOING.
I SAID NO!
NO!
I'M GOING!
NO!!
NO! NO!! *NO*!!!
I'M GOING!
THEN YOU CAN FORGET ABOUT ME TRAINING YOU.
!!

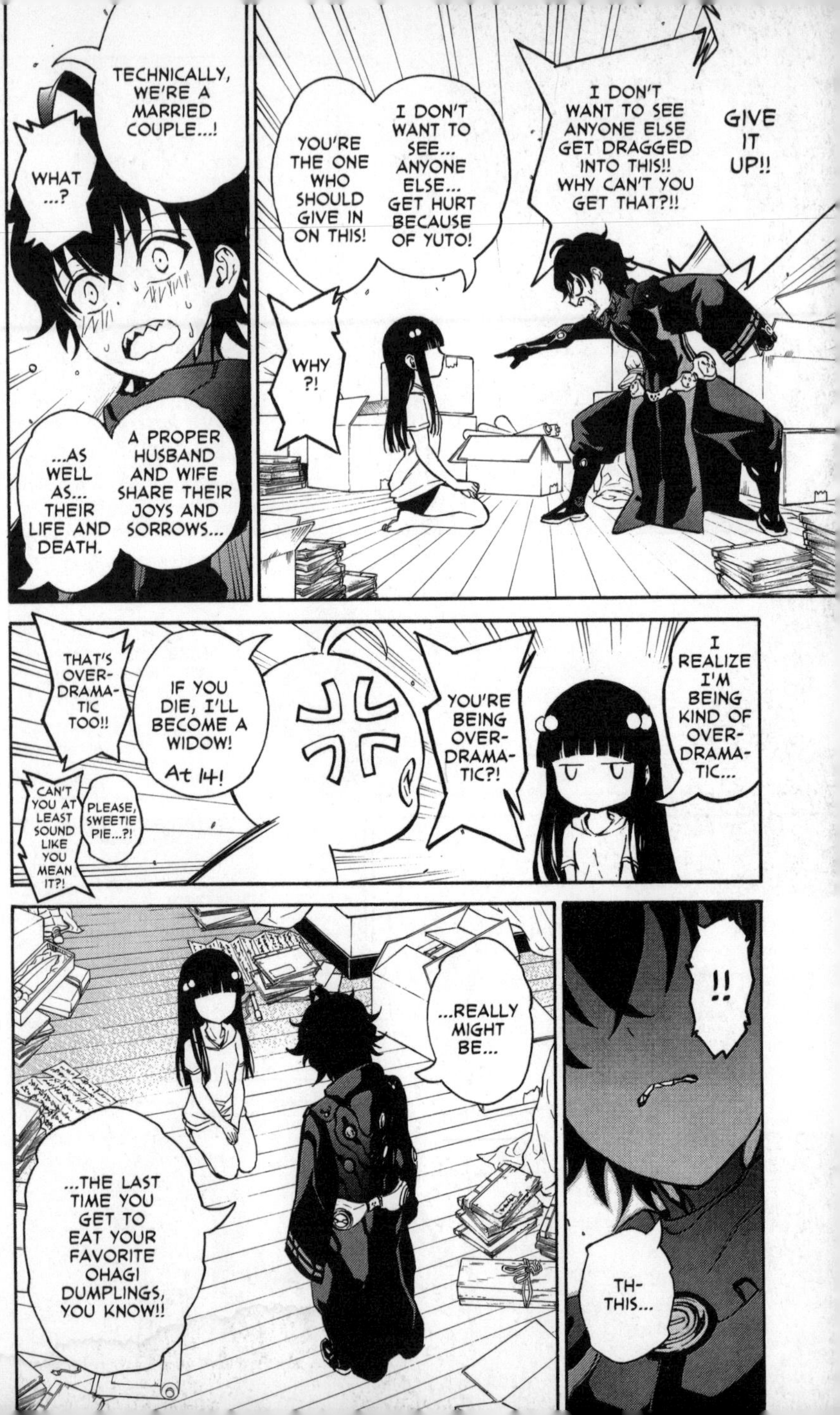
GIVE IT UP!!
I DON'T WANT TO SEE ANYONE ELSE GET DRAGGED INTO THIS!! WHY CAN'T YOU GET THAT?!!
I DON'T WANT TO SEE... ANYONE ELSE... GET HURT BECAUSE OF YUTO!
YOU'RE THE ONE WHO SHOULD GIVE IN ON THIS!
WHY?!
TECHNICALLY, WE'RE A MARRIED COUPLE...!
WHAT...?
A PROPER HUSBAND AND WIFE SHARE THEIR JOYS AND SORROWS...
...AS WELL AS... THEIR LIFE AND DEATH.
I REALIZE I'M BEING KIND OF OVER-DRAMATIC...
YOU'RE BEING OVER-DRAMATIC?!
IF YOU DIE, I'LL BECOME A WIDOW!
At 14!
THAT'S OVER-DRAMATIC TOO!!
PLEASE, SWEETIE PIE...?!
CAN'T YOU AT LEAST SOUND LIKE YOU MEAN IT?!
!!
TH-THIS...
...REALLY MIGHT BE...
...THE LAST TIME YOU GET TO EAT YOUR FAVORITE OHAGI DUMPLINGS, YOU KNOW!!

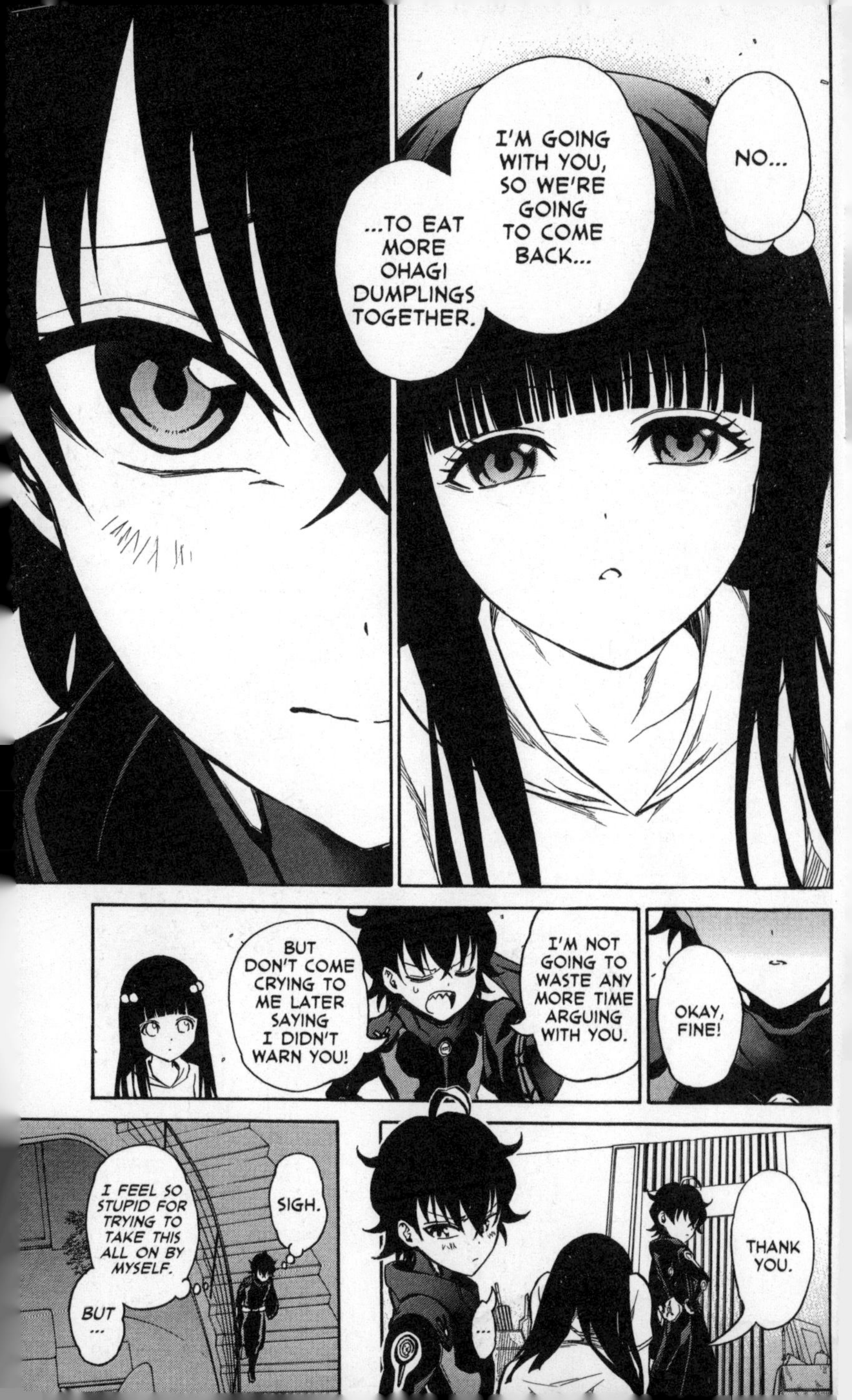
NO...
I'M GOING WITH YOU, SO WE'RE GOING TO COME BACK...
...TO EAT MORE OHAGI DUMPLINGS TOGETHER.
OKAY, FINE!
I'M NOT GOING TO WASTE ANY MORE TIME ARGUING WITH YOU.
BUT DON'T COME CRYING TO ME LATER SAYING I DIDN'T WARN YOU!
THANK YOU.
...
SIGH.
I FEEL SO STUPID FOR TRYING TO TAKE THIS ALL ON BY MYSELF.
BUT ...

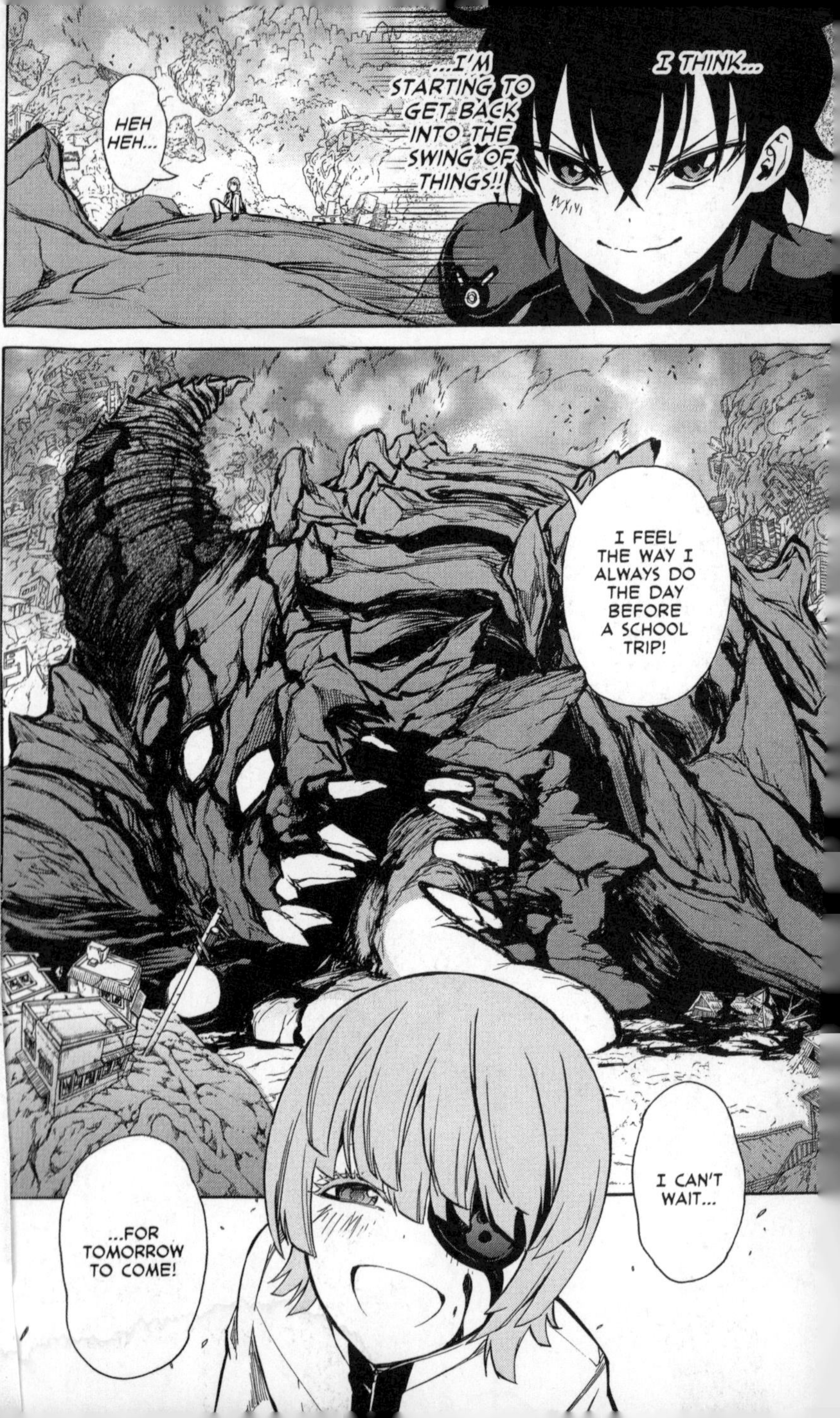
I THINK...
...I'M STARTING TO GET BACK INTO THE SWING OF THINGS!!
HEH HEH...
I FEEL THE WAY I ALWAYS DO THE DAY BEFORE A SCHOOL TRIP!
I CAN'T WAIT...
...FOR TOMORROW TO COME!

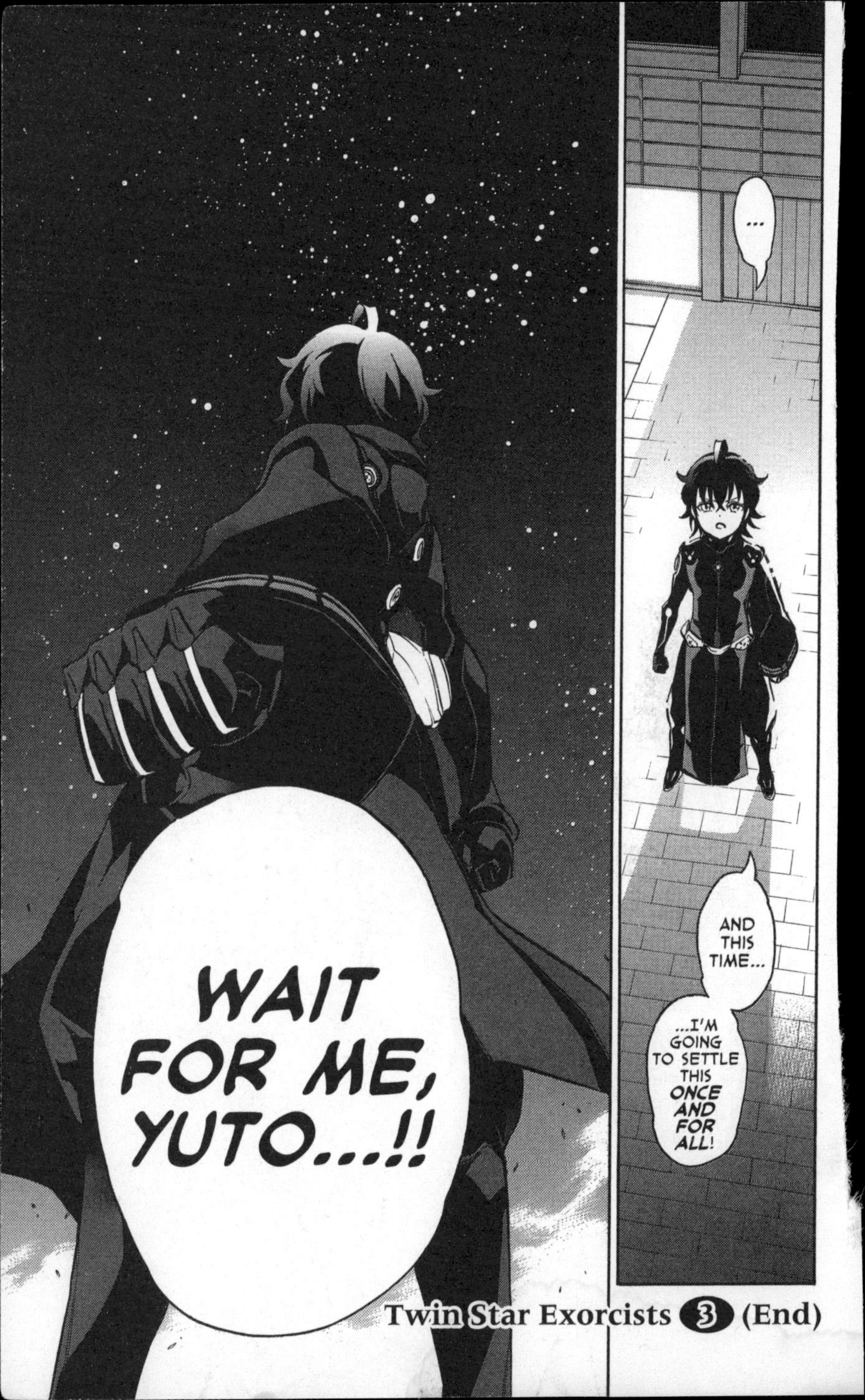
...
AND THIS TIME...
...I'M GOING TO SETTLE THIS ONCE AND FOR ALL!
WAIT FOR ME, YUTO...!!

Twin Star Exorcists 3 (End)

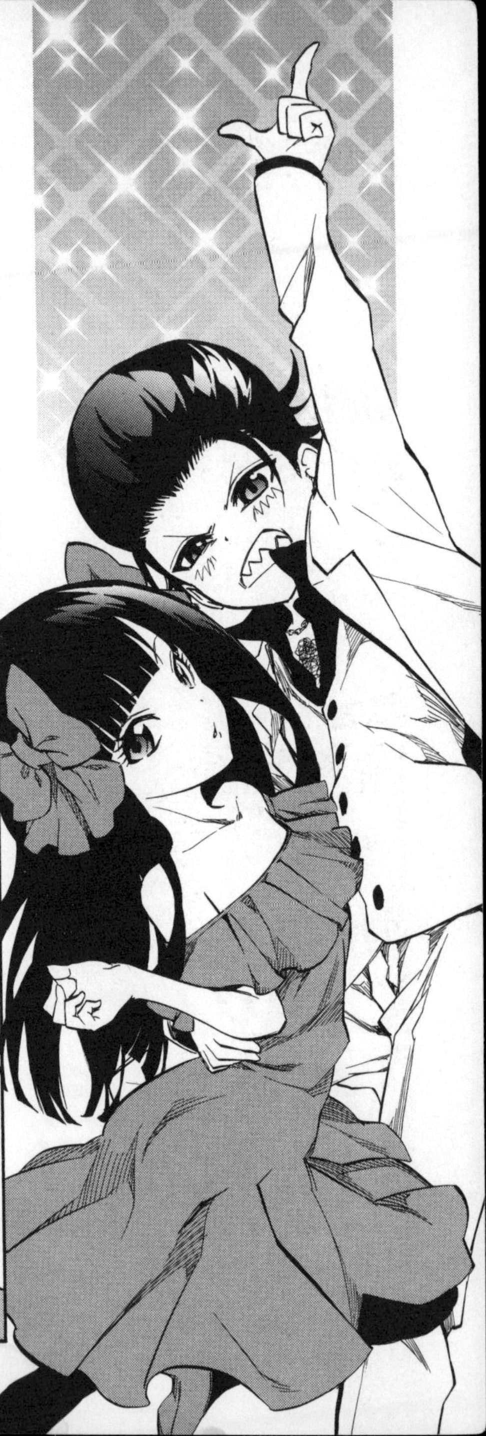

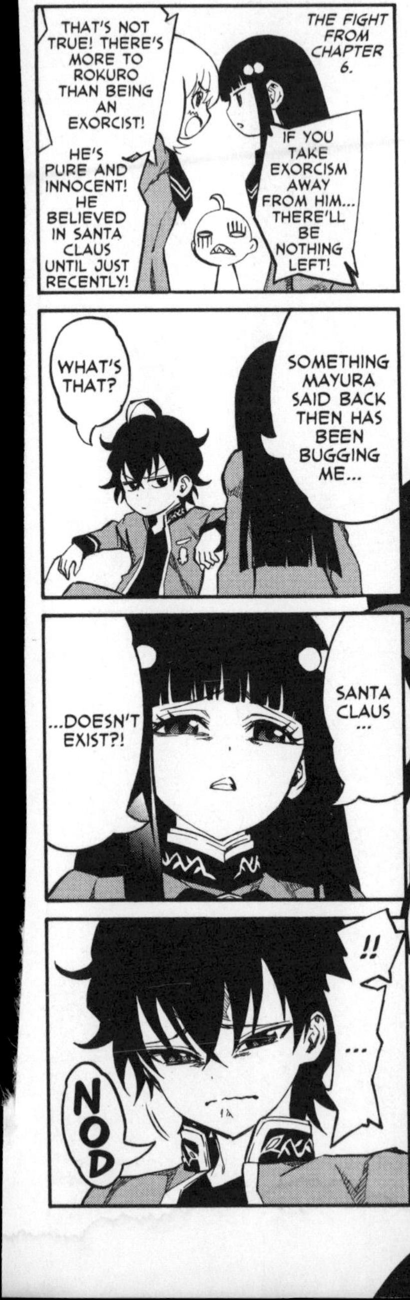
THE FIGHT FROM CHAPTER 6.
IF YOU TAKE EXORCISM AWAY FROM HIM... THERE'LL BE NOTHING LEFT!
THAT'S NOT TRUE! THERE'S MORE TO ROKURO THAN BEING AN EXORCIST!
HE'S PURE AND INNOCENT! HE BELIEVED IN SANTA CLAUS UNTIL JUST RECENTLY!
SOMETHING MAYURA SAID BACK THEN HAS BEEN BUGGING ME...
WHAT'S THAT?
SANTA CLAUS ...
...DOESN'T EXIST?!
!!
...
NOD

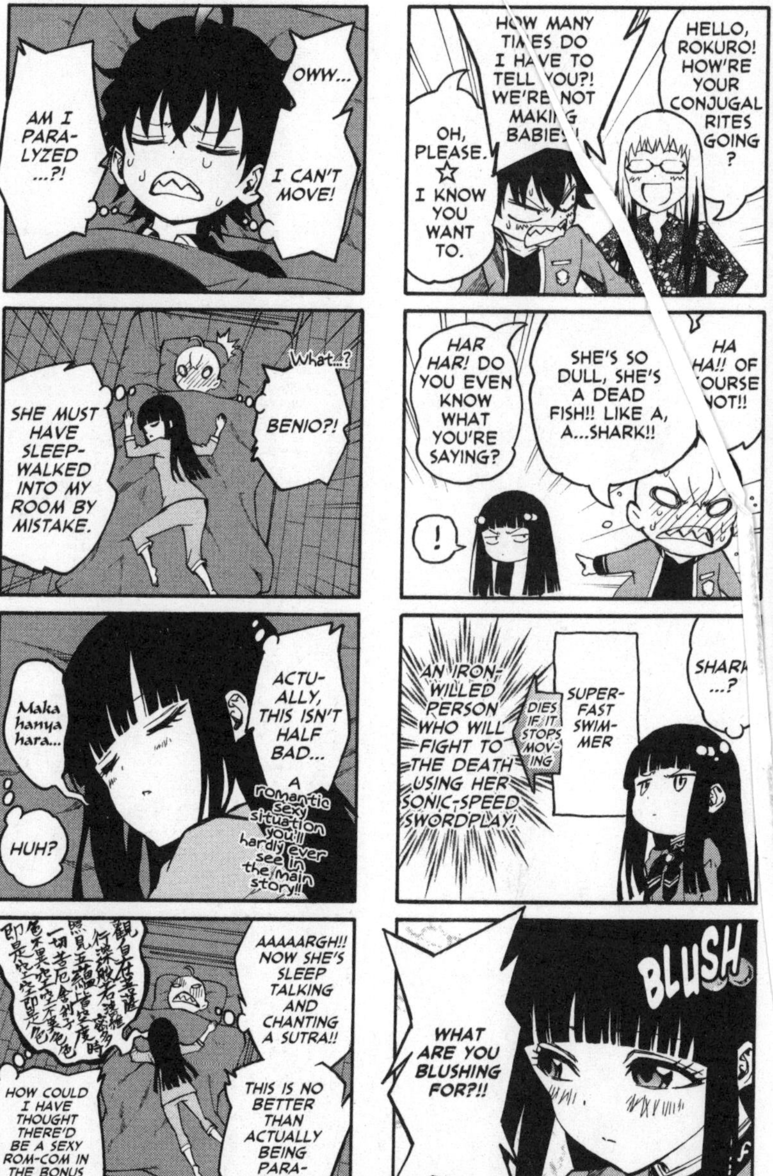
HELLO, ROKURO! HOW'RE YOUR CONJUGAL RITES GOING?
HOW MANY TIMES DO I HAVE TO TELL YOU?! WE'RE NOT MAKING BABIES!!
OH, PLEASE. ☆ I KNOW YOU WANT TO.
HA HA!! OF COURSE NOT!!
SHE'S SO DULL, SHE'S A DEAD FISH!! LIKE A, A...SHARK!!
HAR HAR! DO YOU EVEN KNOW WHAT YOU'RE SAYING?
!
SHARK ...?
SUPER-FAST SWIMMER
DIES IF IT STOPS MOVING
AN IRON-WILLED PERSON WHO WILL FIGHT TO THE DEATH USING HER SONIC-SPEED SWORDPLAY!
BLUSH
WHAT ARE YOU BLUSHING FOR?!!
OWW...
I CAN'T MOVE!
AM I PARALYZED ...?!
What...?
BENIO?!
SHE MUST HAVE SLEEPWALKED INTO MY ROOM BY MISTAKE.
ACTUALLY, THIS ISN'T HALF BAD...
A romantic sexy situation you'll hardly ever see in the main story!!
Maka hanya hara...
HUH?
観自在菩薩行深般若波羅蜜多時照見五蘊皆空度一切苦厄舎利子色不異空空不異色色即是空空即是色
AAAAARGH!! NOW SHE'S SLEEP TALKING AND CHANTING A SUTRA!!
THIS IS NO BETTER THAN ACTUALLY BEING PARALYZED!!
HOW COULD I HAVE THOUGHT THERE'D BE A SEXY ROM-COM IN THE BONUS FUNNIES?!

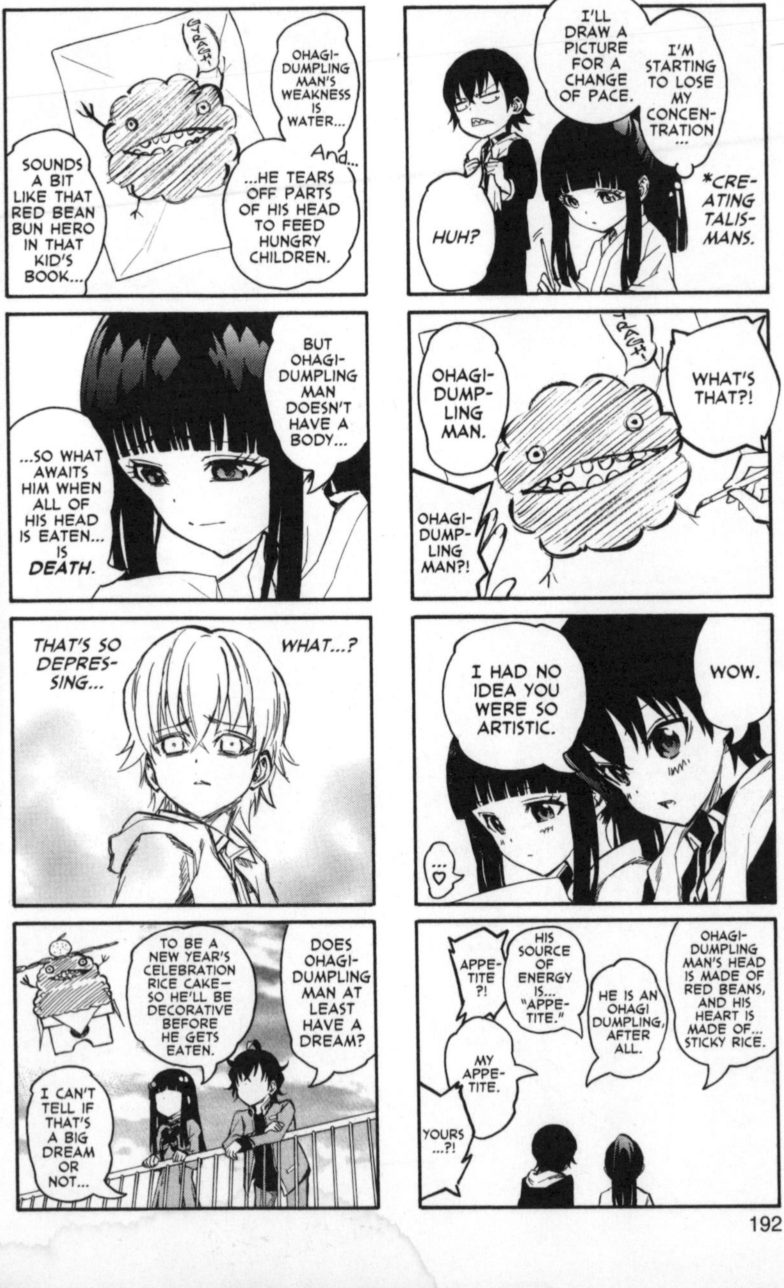
I'M STARTING TO LOSE MY CONCENTRATION...
I'LL DRAW A PICTURE FOR A CHANGE OF PACE.
*CREATING TALISMANS.
HUH?
WHAT'S THAT?!
OHAGI-DUMPLING MAN.
OHAGI-DUMPLING MAN?!
WOW.
I HAD NO IDEA YOU WERE SO ARTISTIC.
...♡
OHAGI-DUMPLING MAN'S HEAD IS MADE OF RED BEANS, AND HIS HEART IS MADE OF... STICKY RICE.
HE IS AN OHAGI DUMPLING, AFTER ALL.
HIS SOURCE OF ENERGY IS... "APPETITE."
APPETITE?!
MY APPETITE.
YOURS...?!
OHAGI-DUMPLING MAN'S WEAKNESS IS WATER...
And...
...HE TEARS OFF PARTS OF HIS HEAD TO FEED HUNGRY CHILDREN.
SOUNDS A BIT LIKE THAT RED BEAN BUN HERO IN THAT KID'S BOOK...
BUT OHAGI-DUMPLING MAN DOESN'T HAVE A BODY...
...SO WHAT AWAITS HIM WHEN ALL OF HIS HEAD IS EATEN... IS *DEATH*.
WHAT...?
THAT'S SO DEPRESSING...
DOES OHAGI-DUMPLING MAN AT LEAST HAVE A DREAM?
TO BE A NEW YEAR'S CELEBRATION RICE CAKE—SO HE'LL BE DECORATIVE BEFORE HE GETS EATEN.
I CAN'T TELL IF THAT'S A BIG DREAM OR NOT...

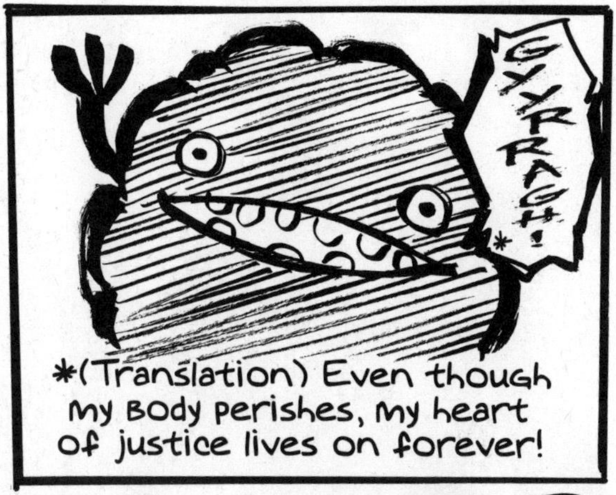
GYYRAGH!*
*(Translation) Even though my body perishes, my heart of justice lives on forever!

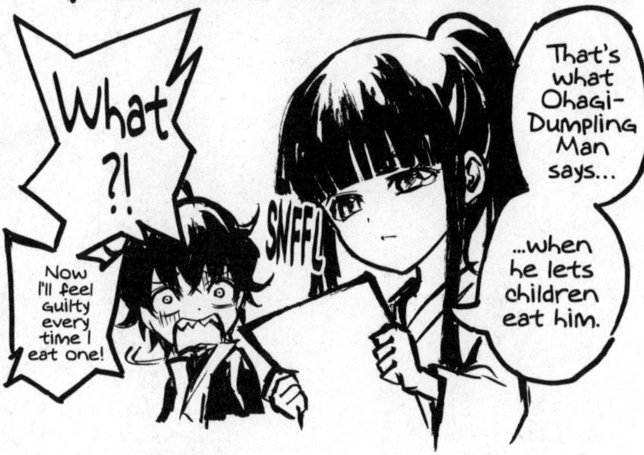
That's what Ohagi-Dumpling Man says...
...when he lets children eat him.
SNFFL
What?!
Now I'll feel guilty every time I eat one!

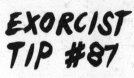

EXORCIST TIP #87

Growing Boys shouldn't order clothes in their current size...

EXCUSE ME...

I'D LIKE THIS IN A LARGER SIZE, PLEASE...

—SHONEN JUMP Manga Edition—

STORY & ART Yoshiaki Sukeno

TRANSLATION **Tetsuichiro Miyaki**
ENGLISH ADAPTATION **Bryant Turnage**
TOUCH-UP ART & LETTERING **Stephen Dutro**
DESIGN **Shawn Carrico**
EDITOR **Annette Roman**

SOUSEI NO ONMYOJI © 2013 by Yoshiaki Sukeno
All rights reserved.
First published in Japan in 2013 by SHUEISHA Inc., Tokyo.
English translation rights arranged by SHUEISHA Inc.

The stories, characters and incidents mentioned in this
publication are entirely fictional.

Printed in the U.S.A.

Published by VIZ Media, LLC
P.O. Box 77010
San Francisco, CA 94107

10 9 8 7 6 5 4 3 2 1
First printing, January 2016

www.viz.com

PARENTAL ADVISORY
TWIN STAR EXORCISTS is rated T for Teen
and is recommended for ages 13 and up.
This volume contains fantasy violence.
ratings.viz.com

www.shonenjump.com

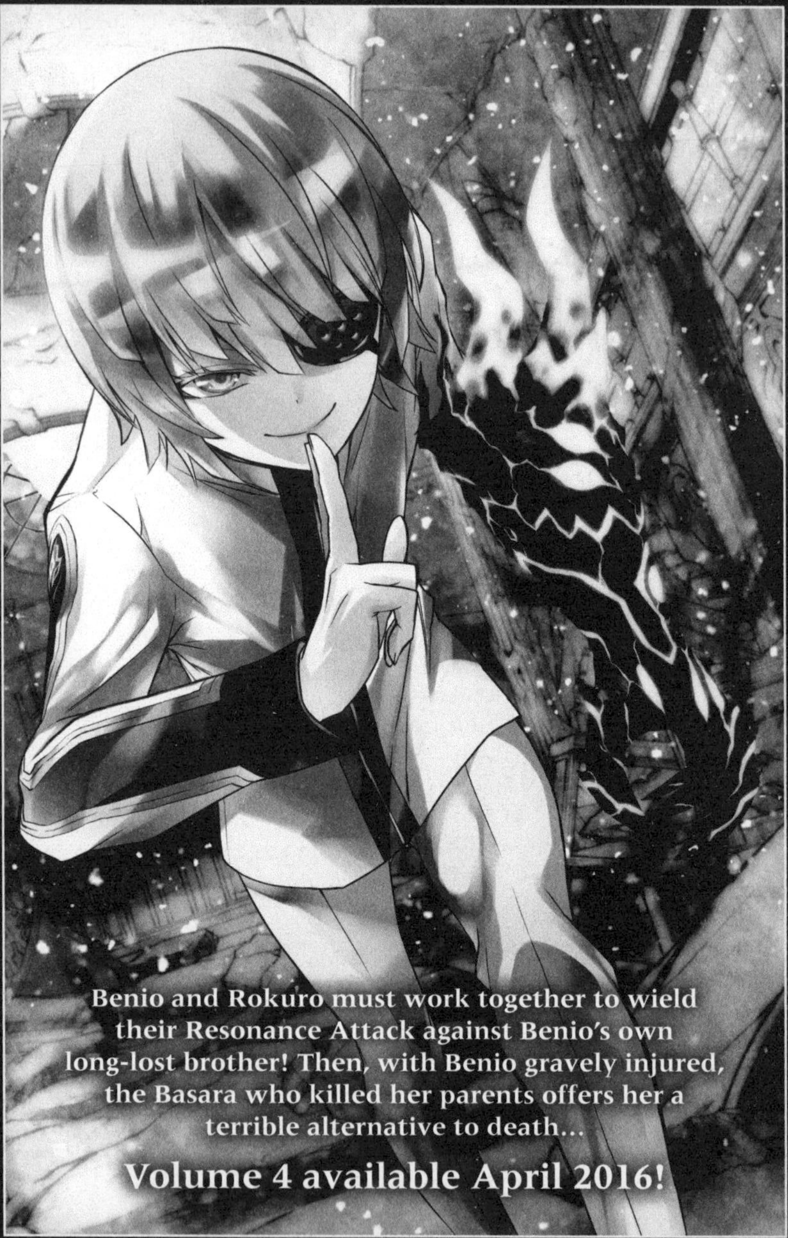
Benio and Rokuro must work together to wield their Resonance Attack against Benio's own long-lost brother! Then, with Benio gravely injured, the Basara who killed her parents offers her a terrible alternative to death...
Volume 4 available April 2016!

Twin Star Exorcists

ONMYOJI

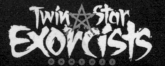

YOU'RE
READING
THE
WRONG WAY!

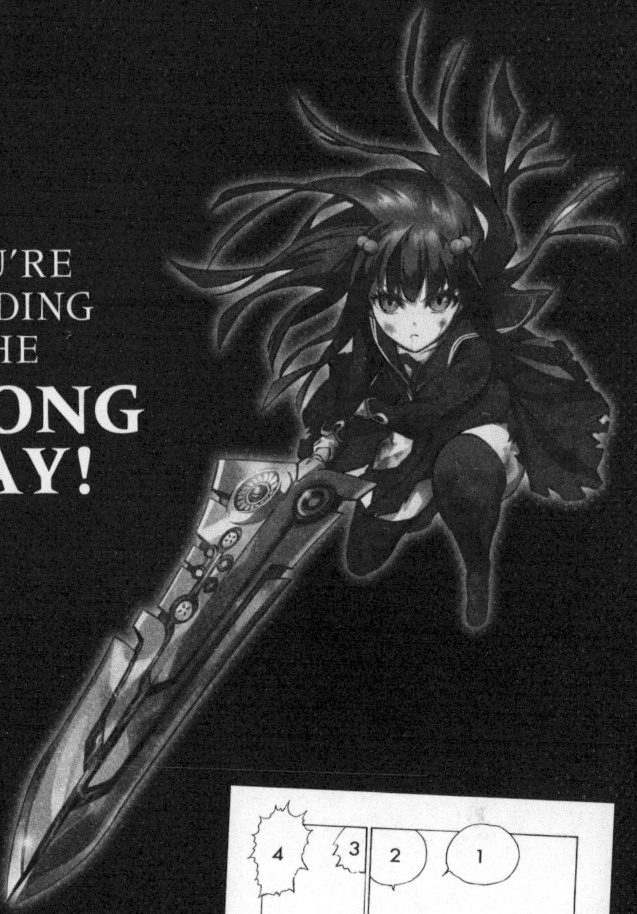

Twin Star Exorcists reads from right to left, starting in the upper-right corner. Japanese is read from right to left, meaning that action, sound effects and word-balloon order are completely reversed from English order.

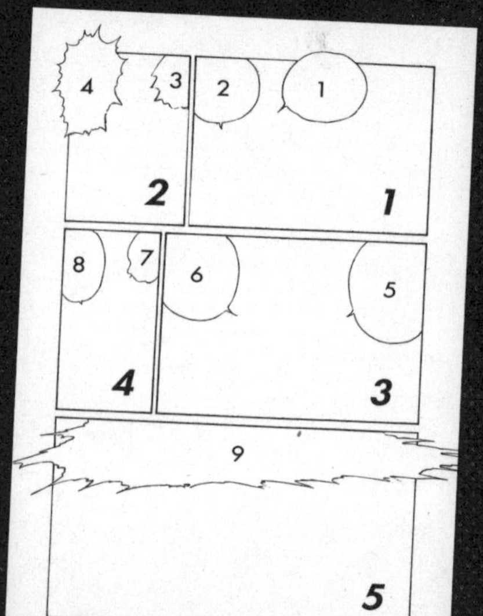

1
2
3
4
1
2
5
6
7
8
3
4
9
5
142